BEYOND BOUNDARIES

BEYOND BOUNDARIES: SEEING ART HISTORY FROM THE CARIBBEAN

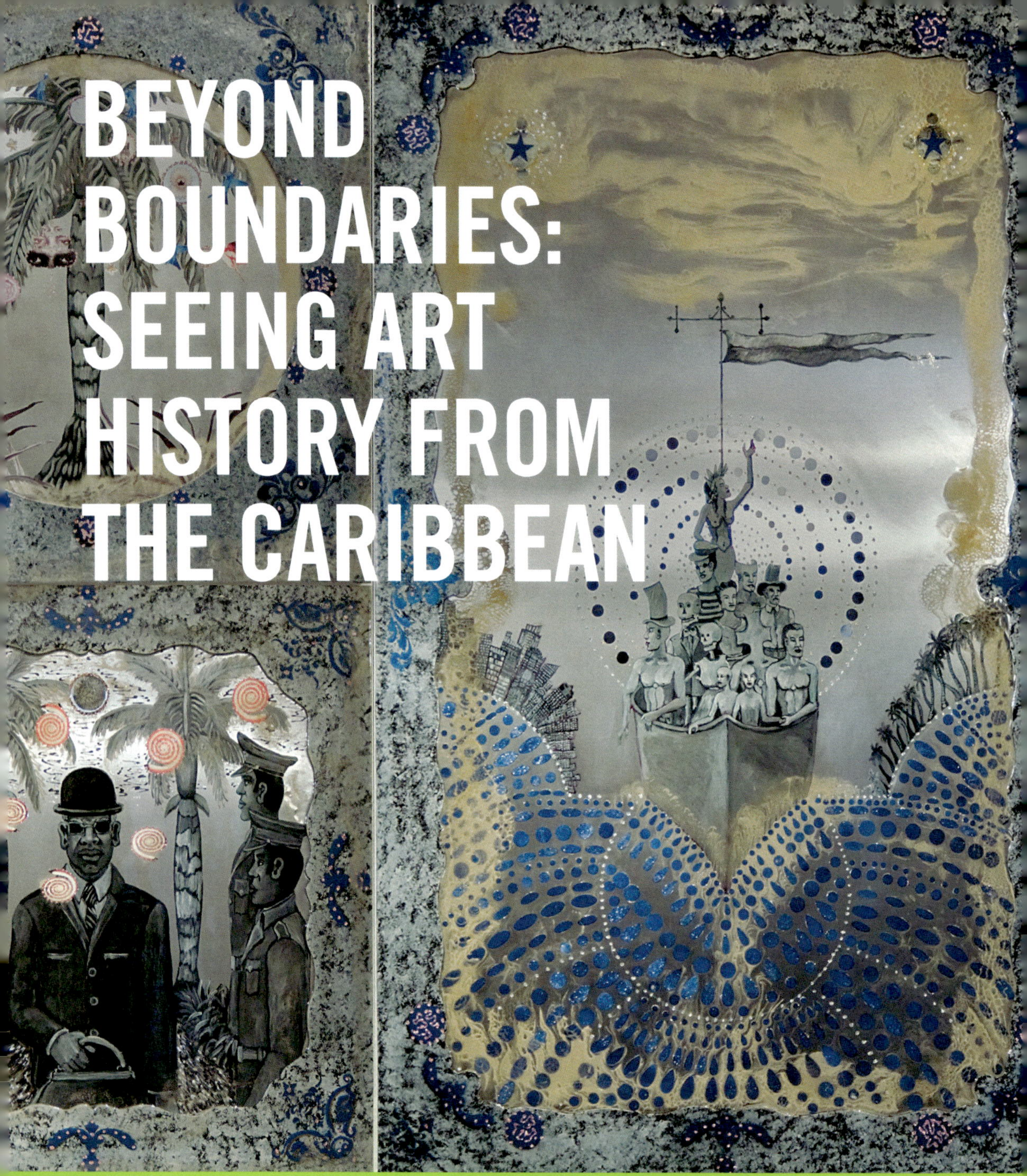

Clark Studies in the Visual Arts

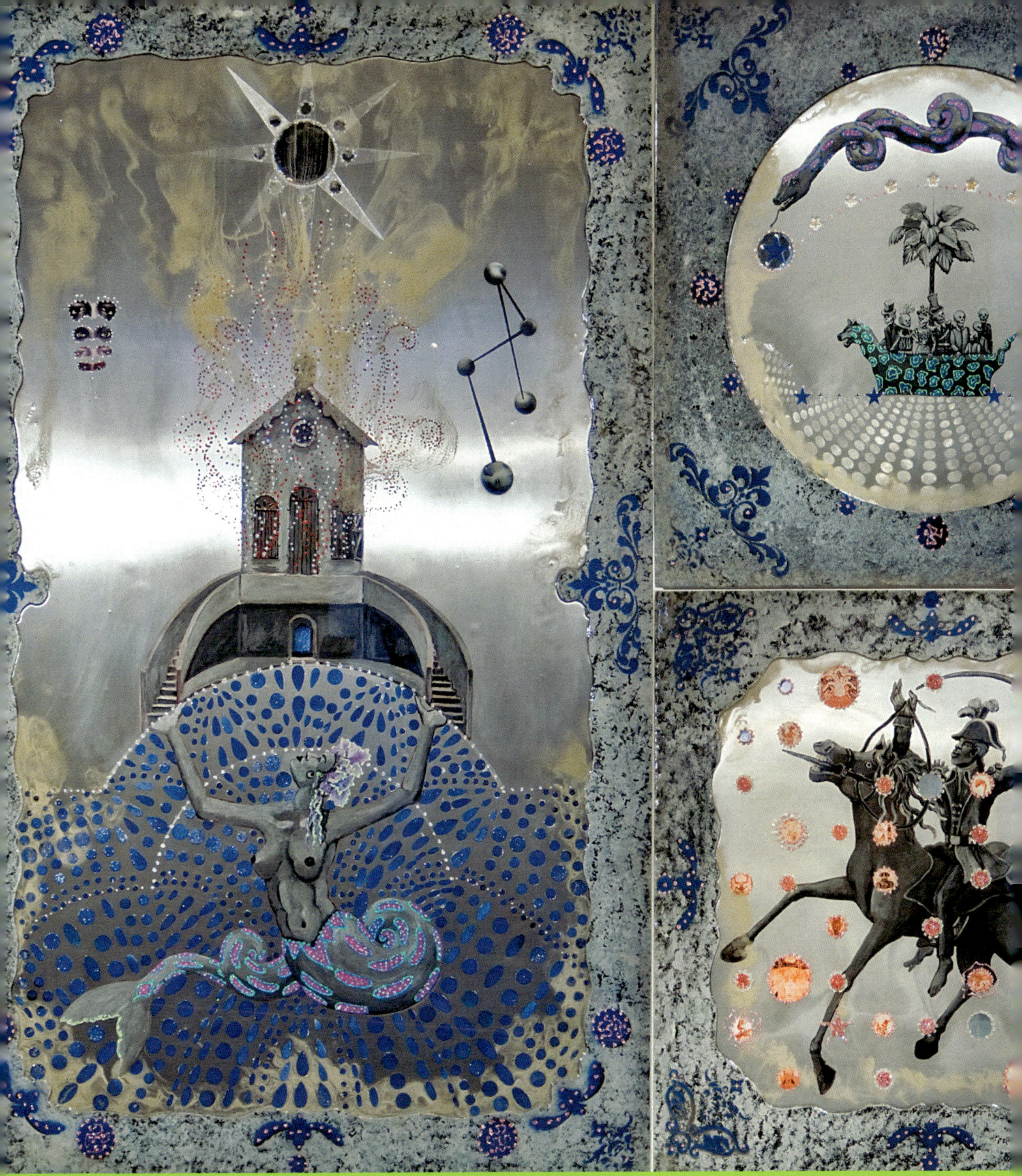

Edited by
Anna Arabindan-Kesson
and Wayne Modest

Clark Art Institute
Williamstown, Massachusetts

Distributed by Yale University Press
New Haven and London

CONTENTS

INTRODUCTION 6
Anna Arabindan-Kesson and Wayne Modest

PART I
RETHINKING RACE

CHAPTER 1 28
COOLIE CRÉOLE
Andil Gosine

CHAPTER 2 44
WHO DISAPPEARED THE TALLAWAHSAURUS
THE VISUAL AFTERLIFE OF CARIBBEAN HEROIC HISTORY
Petrina Dacres

CHAPTER 3 70
DREAMING IN THE FACE OF THE IMPOSSIBLE
AN INTERVIEW WITH ANDREA CHUNG
Anna Arabindan-Kesson and Wayne Modest

CHAPTER 4 82
MICHAEL RICHARDS AND THE POLITICAL WORK OF BLACK ECSTASY
Erica Moiah James

PART II
RETHINKING MODERNISM

CHAPTER 5 102
BEYOND THE ARCHIVES AND VODOU ICONOGRAPHY
LUCE TURNIER, A FEMINIST HAITIAN MODERNIST
Jerry Philogene

CHAPTER 6 118
CARIBBEAN THOUGHT AND HAITIAN ART
THE CATEGORY OF THE MARVELOUS
Anthony Bogues

CHAPTER 7 130
JOHN DUNKLEY'S PHOTOGRAPHIC EYE
A CLOSE LOOK AT *BANANA PLANTATION*
Nicole Smythe-Johnson

PART III
RETHINKING CARIBBEAN ART HISTORIES

CHAPTER 8 146
RETHINKING CARIBBEAN ART HISTORIES
LESSONS FROM DAVID BOXER'S *JAMAICAN ART, 1922–1982*
Veerle Poupeye

CHAPTER 9 168
"WHAT LOVELINESS ESCAPES THE SCHOOLS"
CARIFESTA'S EPISTEMOLOGICAL CRITIQUE
Adrienne Rooney

PART IV
RETHINKING INSTITUTIONS

CHAPTER 10 192
THE CARIBBEAN AND US
María Elena Ortiz

CHAPTER 11 202
THE ARCHIPELAGIC METHOD
A MODEL AND POETIC TOOL FOR COMPLEXIFYING THE HISTORY OF LATINX ART AND PHOTOGRAPHY
Aldeide Delgado

CHAPTER 12 220
OTHER ART WORLDS ARE POSSIBLE
INTRODUCING THE KIBII FOUNDATION, A CONVERSATION WITH MARCEL PINAS
Anna Arabindan-Kesson and Wayne Modest

CHAPTER 13 224
TRANSFORMATIVE JUSTICE
AN INTERVIEW WITH patricia kaersenhout
Anna Arabindan-Kesson and Wayne Modest

CHAPTER 14 236
ATLANTIC TRANSFORMERZ AND ARTS INFRASTRUCTURE
AN INTERVIEW WITH CHARL LANDVREUGD
Wayne Modest

PART V
CODA

CHAPTER 15 252
REORIENTATIONS
Faith Smith

CONTRIBUTORS 258

PHOTOGRAPHY CREDITS 263

INTRODUCTION

Anna Arabindan-Kesson and Wayne Modest

The Haitian artist Tessa Mars's 2020 painting series *A Vision of Peace, Harmony and Good Intelligence* (see p. 256, fig. 15.4) focuses on an elderly woman as she moves, searchingly, across different landscapes with lush ground cover, through bodies of water, and beneath drooping fronds, journeying through layers of time and space. The recurring figures and colors – deep reds, blues, and purples contrasted with a pale apricot background – connect the series, so that the scenes appear to unfold in a realm of magic and memory. In the second painting, *A Vision of Peace, Harmony and Good Intelligence II* (see p. 256, fig. 15.3), the elderly woman stands next to a statuesque, indigo-skinned woman with horns. This is Tessalines, Mars's fictional alter ego and a reimagining of the Haitian revolutionary and political leader Jean-Jacques Dessalines, who in 1804 declared Haiti to be the first free, Black-led republic and independent Caribbean nation. For Mars, this figure also stands in for the countless female revolutionaries and freedom fighters whose stories remain silenced in public discourse. While evoking a kind of magical realism, this series depicts a reality familiar to the artist, where past and present commingle, where spiritual practices such as Vodou resonate in the everyday, and where individual and collective identities continue to be reimagined in the wake of colonial histories of power.

Mars incorporates conventional tropical imagery, and her canvases resonate with a vibrant materiality – akin to the Martinican cultural theorist and activist Suzanne Césaire's notion of a vegetal vitality – through which histories unfold into the present via the central role of women in Caribbean communities. They direct viewers to renewed relationships with land, with belonging, and with movement, conjuring ecologies of human and more-than-human interdependence. In Mars's depiction, the Caribbean does not come into view solely in the wake of its violent pasts; rather, it is a place where resistance, insurgency, and possibility converge in practices of the everyday and the extraordinary.

Articulating this alternative reality—this elsewhere—and alternative conception of modernity, Mars's work both makes use of and gestures to the limits of certain art historical narratives, which have often relied on the Caribbean for forms of visual innovation while visualizing it as somehow antecedent to modernity. The figures she paints, and the alternative histories they propose, offer a reflective gaze back onto these frameworks, asking us to consider what might follow when we look at art historical scholarship from the Caribbean. In this moment of mounting calls to decolonize disciplines and institutions, what yield might there be if art historians engage rigorously with a region that has remained peripheral to the field, yet has always seemed to extend beyond academic disciplinary boundaries? Thinking from the Caribbean requires an engagement with aspects of concepts such as race, migration, diaspora, and the global.[1] Among other concerns, this volume asks what these terms compel the discipline of art history to do differently. The essays that follow explore the temporal and material implications of patterns and processes of migration, along with the global contexts of circulation and (mis)translation. We are focused not on expanding the field, per se, but on assembling a range of conceptual responses that address the frictions of movement, the flows between local and global modes of production, the asymmetries of power, and differences of practice that emerge from a critical engagement with these mobile conditions.

This volume is also a response to the times we inhabit, arriving at a moment of growing unrest, felt in many places across the world, in the context of rising xenophobic nationalism. Images of the murder of George Floyd by a Minnesota police officer, which circulated through social media, inflamed widespread alarm over rampant, blatant state and police violence against some racialized individuals around the globe. As the second decade of the twenty-first century came to a close in 2020, the global COVID-19 pandemic made clear our shared vulnerability as humans; it also made clear that such precarity was not equally distributed but was likewise racialized. Important for our concerns in this volume are the violent afterlives of colonialism, the many ways that—as Saidiya Hartman has poignantly argued—the "racial calculus and a political arithmetic that were entrenched centuries ago" under colonial rule continue to imperil and devalue Black lives, as well as those of many other formerly colonized and racialized people, today.[2] In response to these afterlives, many took to the streets of former imperial and settler-colonial states across the world demanding change during the past decade. They protested for the removal of monuments erected to celebrate colonialism and fought for the renaming of streets, buildings, public institutions, and infrastructure such as bridges named to honor colonists. Such were the demands of movements from Decolonize This Place in the United States—which staged protests across several museums in New York, for example—to #decolonisethemuseum in the Netherlands, Berlin Decolonial in Germany, and #RhodesMustFall and #FeesMustFall in South Africa.

These movements demanded change, including change in the infrastructure of the arts and education. The essays and interviews in this volume developed from a conference at the Clark Art Institute, held during this period of global tensions and extreme unrest, that focused on the possibilities of seeing art history from the vantage point of the Caribbean, of rethinking the discipline and its futures.[3]

Importantly, this unrest was not restricted to public protest. Even as activists working outside museums, universities, and other heritage and educational institutions were advocating for accountability in the wake of the death of George Floyd—and at the same time as the global pandemic—similar demands were being made within these institutions. Students at universities across Europe and North America, for example, were also pressing for change. Such demands were not new. Already in 2016, students at the University of Amsterdam staged large-scale protests calling for the decolonization of the university and its curriculum. For more than two months, they took over the university's senate building and challenged the university administration on multiple issues: its neoliberal approach to education, the lack of diversity of its staff, the lack of transparency in its decision making, its complicity in gentrification, and the growing planetary precarity. These protests would lead to the resignation of the university's president. To push forward the curriculum change they wanted, the students organized lectures by scholars from both inside and outside the university who included decolonized perspectives in their teaching. And they coordinated lectures on the works of thinkers such as Audre Lorde, Frantz Fanon, Stuart Hall, and Aimé Césaire, who offered other critical approaches to colonialism. Notably, several of the student activists involved in these movements were also part of the #decolonizethemuseum project at the Tropenmuseum, one of the three museums that form part of the Netherlands' ethnographic museum group, now called the Wereldmuseum.[4]

Parallel protests were happening in other places across the world. In the United Kingdom, for example, activists at Oxford University involved in the #RhodesMustFall movement sought similar curriculum changes. Students across the United States were also organizing, pushing for universities to be accountable for their role in slavery and colonialism, while asking for a more diverse curriculum. What does a survey course in art history look like today? Which theorists should students be asked to read? What histories or artists' work should be explored?

This is also the context of this publication. Focused on the Caribbean, many of the authors in this volume have long been involved in attempts to rethink the field of art history and the arts infrastructure more broadly. The essays here do not constitute a comprehensive art history "of" the Caribbean. Instead, they offer a range of responses—by artists, curators, and academics—to the implications of studying art through the lens of the Caribbean. Some essays are personal reflections, while others offer critical models that, in engaging with the intellectual foundations or everyday conditions of life in the Caribbean, demand rethinking the configurations and contradictions that form art history. In our conversation with Andrea Chung, the Caribbean, through its formation, emerges as a set of questions that trouble the foundations on which many of the disciplines we inhabit are based. It is for this reason that we chose the title *Beyond Boundaries* for this volume, paraphrased from the Trinidadian historian C. L. R. James's now-seminal book *Beyond a Boundary* (1963). Part memoir, it is celebrated as both one of the best accounts of the game of cricket and a Marxist analysis of cultural life under colonialism.[5] The "Beyond" in our own title is not meant to foreclose what art history can or cannot do but instead to offer what we hope is an invitation. What and how does the Caribbean help us think differently? And what does this different way of thinking require?

In her reflection on the 2022 convening at the Clark, Faith Smith described our framework as an invitation to unsettle what has already been, at least conventionally, settled upon. If our questioning suggests that the Caribbean stands outside of art history, this is not to relegate it as undeserving of art historical scholarship but to emphasize how it, as a region, has "troubled" conventional disciplinary framings. Thinking in relation to the discipline of anthropology, for example, the Jamaican scholar and curator David Scott, quoting from the historical anthropologist Sidney Mintz, wrote in 2004:

> Neither properly "primitive" nor "civilized," neither "non-Western" on the conventional criteria nor unambiguously "Western" (in short, neither fish nor fowl), the Caribbean has never quite fit securely within any anthropological agenda. "Whereas New Guinea, Africa, Amazonia offered kinship systems, costumes, coiffures, cuisines, languages, beliefs, and customs of dizzying variety and allure," . . . "[w]hether it was kinship or religion or language or anything else, Caribbean people all seemed culturally midway between there and here—everything was alloyed, mixed, ground down, pasted on, the least common denominator."[6]

Indeed, writing from the vantage point of material anthropology, Wayne Modest notes elsewhere that while art and ethnographic museums in the North Atlantic, with their early interest in "primitive" art, were busy collecting objects from across the world—objects now contested in growing global discussions around restitution—the arts of the Caribbean remain underrepresented in many major museum collections.[7] Where they do exist, they are largely understood as objects of archeological interest—associated with a people long presumed dead—or as objects of natural history or botanical interest, rather than as objects of anthropological, historical, or art historical interest. This may be seen by some as a blessing, an escape from the reductive ethnographic gaze or, with growing questions about restitution, from the increasingly contested practices of colonial looting. And yet, this absence evidences one way that the region exists as "beyond" conventional fields, and it speaks to why seeing with and from the Caribbean may require moving beyond boundaries as they currently stand.

We contend that the Caribbean's status is similar within the discipline of art history. Scott's article was an invitation for us to think about the "Caribbean as a precociously modern formation"[8] that emerged from the specifically modern character of the colonial plantation. As Scott notes, the scholar Sidney Mintz described this as a modernity that predates the modern, a "social form" or "societal area"—a space of multiplicity—as opposed to a singular "culture area."[9] What does this mean for the discipline of art history? To be a "Caribbeanist" in a scholarly sense requires an attunement to a place formed of multiplicity, with multilingual and polyphonic histories. While the essays that follow are written in English, the subject matter makes this a uniquely pan-Caribbean volume that spans the English-, Spanish-, French-, Dutch-, and Creole-speaking Caribbean, where Patois, Papiamento, Sranan Tongo, and Kreyòl are the everyday languages spoken by the majority of the population. Many of these would not have been regarded as worthy second languages for art history graduate students. In choosing this configuration of subjects, then, we also wanted this volume to demonstrate the disciplinary challenges facing art historians who study Caribbean-focused material.

Our title was not chosen by coincidence. While the region today is constituted as a set of nation-states, most of which gained their independence from European imperial powers in the mid-twentieth century, these national boundaries have a kind of porosity: What happens inside is impacted by the outside and vice versa, often in tense friction. At the end of the 1950s—at least in the English-speaking Caribbean—the idea of a federation emerged as a regional option for postcolonial sovereignty, only to falter in the face of nationalist pressures. Similarly, whether under an earlier imperial political system characterized by struggles between the imperial center and periphery, or in the struggles of small regional economies within a global economic system in the immediate postcolonial period, when some countries in the region were trapped within structural adjustment arrangements by the International Monetary Fund, the situation inside the boundary was always shaped by the world beyond it. James attunes us to these arrangements of relation between inside and outside, which we wanted to address in this publication as well. Cricket was never just cricket. The boundary was never fixed—just as the West Indies, like India, Pakistan, and other formerly colonized regions, were never simply playing a game.

As a geographical region composed of multiple states, the Caribbean immediately sits outside the associations between art and the nation-state that have shaped art history. Essays by María Elena Ortiz, Aldeide Delgado, Andil Gosine, Nicole Smythe-Johnson, and Adrienne Rooney take this up in different ways, foregrounding regional networks and patterns of circulations beyond national boundaries. But all the essays also rethink the Caribbean's relationship to the Global North, looking beyond periphery-metropole models, or at least addressing their limitations for understanding Caribbean artistic formations in the context of what Erica Moiah James describes as the "global Caribbean." Art history's tendency to categorize artistic production geographically cannot account for the legacies of serial colonialism — a term Delgado works through in this volume — in the Caribbean, the resulting genocide of Indigenous communities, the longue durée of the trans-Atlantic slave trade, the forced migration of indentured, unfree Asian laborers, and the shifting geopolitics affecting Caribbean communities today. For example, to be grounded in the terrain of post-revolution Haitian visual culture (a subject that is not specifically examined here) also requires moving among the art histories of early nineteenth-century Britain, France, and the United States, tracking printed matter across the globe, and grappling with theorizations of political formations across the early nineteenth-century Americas. A growing number of scholars are engaged in this work, albeit often from very national or single-imperial perspectives — British or French, Spanish or Dutch.[10] These historical processes require scholars to engage with the histories of multiple — sometimes converging — European empires, to work across different languages, and to hold multiple visual and political formations in dialogue. The artists, curators, and academics we brought together for this project are all invested in this multivocal, multi-temporal, and multi-spatial approach to the region.

Taking the trans- or global Caribbean seriously, we can see how one aspect of the region's challenge to art history is a challenge to the temporal and spatial categories that structure the academy more broadly, and that are inevitably reproduced through pedagogy.[11] On the other hand, the conception of the Caribbean as a site of convergence, as a crossroads already shaped by transnational networks, offers a model to the field of art history for attending to the global and the transnational, to combat the limitations of its own formations.[12] Across the field, deeper attention is now being paid to the networks that connect different geographical regions and visual forms, and sometimes to the ways these movements also create disjuncture.[13] These strategies are also geared toward deconstructing the cohesiveness of the nation-state as a category, often emphasizing how such unified constructions are themselves mediated through the movement of art itself. However, it is less clear whether, in making this turn toward the transnational and global, art history as a discipline can adequately grapple with the colonial formations at its center: In other words, to think about the global or the transnational requires first engaging with the processes of extraction and commodification that underpin Western modernity.[14]

Asking where the Caribbean might bring art history required our essay writers to think about both space and time. The authors acknowledge what seeing (art history) from the Caribbean reveals about both the past and the future of scholarly practice. In this sense, while our question might seem amorphous—Where is this elsewhere / somewhere else? What is beyond?—it also resonates with a more general recognition within (but surely not limited to) the discipline of art history that the field is not where it should be. While addressing the state of the field was not a primary concern, the essays in this volume do track the events that bring us to this point of questioning. They do so both to imagine what *would have had to have happened*, and to speculate on what *would have to happen* (now), to bring art history to this other place, this somewhere else, to this otherwise.

We might seem to be walking toward slippery ground here. The otherness of the Caribbean is a "repeating" visual construction.[15] It is a place that has often been imagined and disciplined through the conventions of, and as the subject for, art histories, as it has been for anthropology. The Caribbean has, in the process, become recognizable on some level while remaining an imagined elsewhere.[16] But for us, the idea of somewhere else emerges from other frameworks, approaches that foreground the Caribbean as a space from which new imaginaries and the visualizing of new (art historical) futures have always been taking place. We are not describing a utopian investment in the region but instead identifying starting points. We know that with its colonial, material, and visual histories, the Caribbean is a prerequisite for, and sustained the formation of, European modernity. As a discipline, art history emerged alongside these networks of racial capitalism and coheres around the transmission, materiality, production, and consumption of form.[17] What does it mean that, and in what ways might it be that, the Caribbean is antecedent to the field of art history itself?[18]

Anti-imperial in its outlook, James's *Beyond a Boundary* also explores the constitutive relations between culture, politics, and society before and amid the tumultuous shifts of decolonization. As such, it is a text—like the author's earlier book *The Black Jacobins: Toussaint L'Ouverture and the San Domingo Revolution* (1938)—that engages deeply with the conjunctures of its (present) moment to explore the possibilities of a yet-to-emerge future.[19] Anticipation is also central to the theoretical poetics of the Martinique-born poet, critic, and philosopher Édouard Glissant, whose writings on relationality and the poetics of form are widely taken up among the authors gathered in this volume. Glissant's corpus of work has, in the words of Alvan A. Ikoku, "establish[ed] the groundwork for a future conception of the global South, for a practice of reading its artistic production that presumes a yet-to-come acceptance of the region as emerging from the polyvalent histories of the Caribbean."[20] We wanted to foreground these two temporal registers, to reinforce how the Caribbean is central to the development of art history and art from the African diaspora as academic disciplines—intellectually, economically, and discursively. The Caribbean is also a theoretical space where terms like the poetics of form, the right to opacity, and modes of relationality align with art history's own methodological commitments. Returning to that earlier invocation to "unsettle," looking at Caribbean artistic production not only defamiliarizes the disciplinary conditions of art history but also questions the limits of Black and Caribbean studies. It is in these academic fields that such theoretical formulations are often foregrounded, although often without close attention to their unfolding in Caribbean visual production.

The essays in this volume are less concerned with an analysis of the structural challenges the Caribbean poses to art history's pedagogy, organization, and canon formations. Instead, they lean toward methods for unsettling established frameworks and intellectual formations. They do this by working from the Caribbean, attending to the "differently configured conjunctions"[21] of its complex terrain, and in the process put critical pressure on constructions of race, conceptions of modernity, and the role of the institution—concepts that are central to the development of art history as a discipline, and whose meanings are also constituted through the colonial histories that shape the Caribbean. These histories emerge in different ways throughout the essays—whether as the conditions against which new artistic collaborations, and histories, take form in Caribbean nations, or as the conditions through which new kinds of solidarity and alliance are constructed. The legacies of these histories are also apparent in the contemporary moment within which artists are reaching toward and creating new political imaginaries. In addressing these legacies, however, this is also an invitation to look beyond them, not to leave them behind but to forge something outside their limits.

In the first section of this volume, "Rethinking Race," Erica James raises the question of legacies and limits vis-à-vis the Jamaican writer Sylvia Wynter, who asked in a 2000 interview, "How do you [as an artist] deal with the stereotyped view of yourself [cultivated in colonialism] that you yourself have been socialized to accept?"[22] For James, this interrogation "haunts postcolonial creative practices," where it is the *how* that matters: How do artists push back? How do they affirm and continually re-create? How do they claim and enact freedom? And how do they do so as a form of justice? These questions also emerge in our conversation with Andrea Chung, an artist whose practice explores her own familial histories of indentureship and slavery in the Caribbean. For Chung, indentureship offers another kind of relational praxis for imagining space, for holding in conversation multiple constructions of race and experiences of fugitivity. Tracing the routes of indentureship between Jamaica and Mauritius for example, Chung considers how these colonial histories shaped connected experiences and thus provide the grounds for contemporary forms of affiliation. Through a deep engagement with materiality, Chung teases out a "conceptual togetherness" that tracks across the Indian and Atlantic Oceans.

For the artist and scholar Andil Gosine, a descendent of Indo-Trinidadian indentured laborers, the creolized history of Indo-Trinidadians offers a starting point for rethinking visual formations of race and addresses the legacy of colonial trauma without seeing it as a totalizing framework. He describes how "a truthful telling of my traumas and joys, my anxieties and anguish" requires "iconographies of indentureship." Gosine also asks that in visualizing indentureship we think beyond popular constructions of indentureship that situate it as "not slavery," thereby dismissing its generational consequences, and he explains that his work's "principal objective is to truthfully represent the human condition and to consider the indentured worker and their descendants as like any human, layered and flawed." His varied multimedia work has always foregrounded indentureship's relationship to the economics and legacy of slavery in the Caribbean and emphasized the Creole identity of Indo-Caribbean communities, revealing the ways that Indo-Caribbean culture has been co-constituted with African, European, and Indigenous cultures of the Americas.

Gosine's iconography of indentureship draws on the relationality embedded in the term *Creole*. This term encapsulates the political-economic conditions he works from—as an artist and curator who straddles the professional bounds of academia and art making—and the historical and cultural relations that continue to shape the diverse experiences of Indo-Caribbean communities in the Caribbean and the diaspora. He also describes how the term *Creole*, while a signifier of the cataclysmic forced movements that shaped the Caribbean, holds the capacity for both violence and pleasure, a nexus he explores throughout his work. Gosine's attention to these layers of meaning insists on "recognition of the complex humanity of the post-indenture subject: neither reducible to the historical experience nor detached from it."

In Petrina Dacres's essay, she examines how Caribbean artists participate in ongoing conversations on history and representation by creatively reimagining the commemorative and heroic form. Dacres offers a brief history of these practices and their role in constructing changing meanings of Blackness before drawing our attention to another conjuncture in the contemporary (Anglophone) Caribbean: the absence of state investment in the heroic figure. She attributes this to the shifting relationships of state formation and sovereignty in the region and considers their implications for experiences of citizenship. This "retreat from history" by state actors has opened up new aesthetic possibilities in non-sculptural or nonfigurative sculptural forms to create space for new conversations about history—and about Black historicity, in particular.

James also addresses the importance of the popular, and the public, in the artistic formation and discursive production of constructions of race, focusing on the intersections of art and popular music as cultural spaces for the experience of the "Black ecstatic." As with Chung and Gosine, James puts pressure on the relationship between artistic expression and "colonial form," moving us beyond the often dialectical frameworks that are used in art history to address forms of resistance, subversion, or mimicry in processes of transnational or cross-cultural artistic exchange.[23] Drawing on the work of the Cuban poet and essayist José Lezama Lima, she argues, "To view language and other forms of creative expression as colonial possessions creates an artificial ideological barrier between language and the colonized. It implies that colonized people have no right to those 'other people's things.'" This framing returns us to the artistic form itself and the idea of criticism as creation: "The thing that will be archived, exhibited, and exist in the world becomes the eternal critique of colonialism." James proposes a history of the Black ecstatic to inform her reading of the work of the US-born, Kingston-raised sculptor Michael Richards, Jamaican popular music, and theories of modernism. Her interdisciplinary methodology (in the lineage of Caribbean cultural theorists and art historians) is grounded in the analysis of popular cultural expression and advances the art historical methods of close reading and interpretation. The essay weaves together relations of materiality and erasure, art and music, forms of self-recognition, and the limits of the nation-state in order to consider how freedom can look in "the wake of intimate devastation that too often repeats in Black life." Looking for freedom, in this way, James also rethinks how a Caribbean modernism could look. She models how we can shift from time-bound definitions (and their art historical implications for the often time-bound dismissal of Caribbean art) to methods that look toward the unfinished and unfurling nature of the modern self and its subjectivity, and that look for, in this Caribbean context, the restitutive imperative within modernism's forms.

James's essay raises questions that become more focused in our second section, "Rethinking Modernism." Here, Jerry Philogene addresses the "conspicuous invisibility" of the artist Luce Turnier, a feminist Haitian modernist, asking, "What would it mean to study an existent yet under-recognized transnational, Haitian modernist painter active within the mid- to late twentieth-century arts of the African diaspora?" Philogene's essay is an important historical intervention in the field, offering one of the few close analyses of Turnier's "contradictory absence and presence in the historiography of modern Haitian art specifically and in mid-twentieth-century art of the African diaspora more generally." Her essay offers a much-needed Black feminist critique that begins with the lack of intersectionality in the practice of both art history and the subfield of African diaspora art, and the subsequent elisions of key women artists from Haiti (and the broader Caribbean) from art historical texts. Beginning with a photograph that visualizes Turnier's centrality to narratives of twentieth-century modern Haitian art, Philogene tracks the gaps between what is in the archive (evidence of these women's contributions) and what has been written about them. Thus, the essay offers a close reading of Turnier's work while also reflecting on the structures of art historical narration (or perhaps historiography) that have maintained her invisibility. Philogene theorizes—and indeed demonstrates—a method of "strategic looking," which is "a deep, thoughtful looking that recognizes, acknowledges, and allows for different modalities of seeing (and writing) in order to comprehend what is not supposed to be seen." In the case of Turnier—and certainly other unrecognized female Caribbean artists—Philogene's essay offers a nuanced model of the transformative implications of seeing from the Caribbean. To do so means expanding the material contours of twentieth-century modernism as we know it, as well as expanding the role of the visual in the creation of Haitian (and perhaps more broadly Caribbean) modernity, materializing what otherwise goes unwritten.

Also concerned with Haitian art and modernity, Anthony Bogues's essay offers a reflection on the framing and categorization of Haitian art within the language of art history, and especially the ways in which categories such as *primitivism* have come to define how we see Haitian art. Using a method that recalls Tessa Mars's exploration of Haitian history and spirituality as modes of contemporary aesthetic, Bogues describes what he calls "living history"—tied to the lived experience of politics and history—as an essential aspect of Haitian art that relies on the "marvelous real," an aesthetic category that requires an entirely new kind of (art historical) descriptive grammar. The essays of both Philogene and Bogues implicitly critique the stubborn persistence of too-limited representations of Haiti and of Haitian art through a particular kind of anthropological lens, overwhelmed by inaccurate representations of Vodou and of the country as a land of zombies.[24]

Nicole Smythe-Johnson's essay also takes up the challenges of "alternate modernisms," as conceptualized within the dominant Eurocentric perspectives of art historical scholarship. She explains, "Generally, the story is that modernists visited Europe . . . and returned home to develop their own homegrown, often nativist modernisms to counter the hegemony of European modernism. In short, alternate modernisms remain essentially belated, the outcome of a developed Europe's influence on the backward rest." The essay examines a painting from around 1945 by the Jamaican artist John Dunkley, *Banana Plantation* (see p. 132, fig. 7.1), teasing out how its "attentiveness to and criticality of photography . . . nourishes Dunkley's modernist formal innovation." Like Philogene, Smythe-Johnson also unearths new sources in her examination of Dunkley's practice and consequently formulates important new readings of his work. In particular, she foregrounds Dunkley's cosmopolitan subjectivity—against the more traditional framework of self-taught artist—by tracing his interventions in, and responses to, the interlocking histories of photography, labor migration, and imperialism in the first half of the twentieth century. Smythe-Johnson contends that Dunkley's paintings "begin" where photography ends, exposing the "very limits of a photograph." She follows the routes of his cosmopolitanism within a circum-Caribbean movement shaped by labor movements and a circulating-print economy. These moves lead to a new definition of, and location for, Dunkley's own modernism, one the author calls a "subaltern modernism" that, while drawing on cultural forms and mobilities usually associated with the (artistic) elite, offers a very different narrative of modernism from the art historical status quo. "Instead," Smythe-Johnson writes, Dunkley's work "recasts modernity from the perspective of the laboring classes of the Americas."

In both Philogene's and Smythe-Johnson's contributions to this volume, the Caribbean offers a place from which to attend to the discursive possibilities of modernism and to see how "certain positions continually get constructed and reconstructed."[25] In their acknowledgement of art's capacity to exceed any given interpretative structure, these essays also demonstrate the generative possibilities of art history's own recursive priorities of attentive return and description as method. In a different way, the two essays in this volume's third section, "Rethinking Caribbean Art Histories," examine the production of Caribbean art histories during two crucial moments in the region's political formation. Focusing on the local and expanding to the regional, these texts pay close attention to the writing—the emplotment—into "being" of Caribbean artistic production, looking closely at the pedagogical implications of such narratives for constructions of Caribbean identity and at how these narratives have been taken up by the field of art history itself.

Veerle Poupeye's essay focuses on a foundational text in the development of Jamaican art history, David Boxer's *Jamaican Art, 1922–1982*, published in 1983. Through a close examination of Boxer's essay and its historical contexts, Poupeye offers a reading of its tensions, affiliations, and "challenge to the cultural impact of colonization." Looking back at earlier field-defining historiographies requires an empathetic criticality. Acknowledging this, Poupeye addresses the significant impact Boxer's publication had on the field and also highlights its limitations. Poupeye's essay is a genealogy of sorts that traces further developments in Jamaican art history and suggests new directions for scholarship that can, as she says, both fill the gaps in Boxer's account and do so in ways that ensure these histories are circulated beyond the academy. Importantly, Poupeye addresses the structures of academic and artistic education that have facilitated the production and circulation of art historical writing, and she acknowledges the asymmetrical power relations that continue to structure art historical research and scholarship today. Drawing on the work of the French political theorist and curator Françoise Vergès, she argues for a reimagination of art histories of the Caribbean that, rather than being merely additive, can be transformative in their engagement with the creativity of artistic form and with the institutional structures that mediate, or impede, its production.

Adrienne Rooney's essay is located in the early 1980s, at the fourth edition of the Caribbean Festival of Arts (Carifesta) held in Barbados. Drawing on an interdisciplinary array of archival materials, the essay explores two of the festival's epistemological critiques during a revolutionary Caribbean moment. Rooney examines how Carifesta '81 countered "representations of the region as a space of extractive economic production or touristic pleasure." The essay traces how organizers claimed "the Caribbean as a space of vibrant and intertwined cultural production—cultural production rooted in traditions that evolved on, despite, and in relation to the plantation system that recanted their possibility." Secondly, the essay describes how Carifesta made palpable the region's cultural and linguistic plurality. Rooney argues that these two frameworks of critique challenge (then and now) how an enduring Eurocentric art historical canon posited its universality within colonized spaces. In its place, Rooney argues that the organizers gathered artists, intellectuals, and residents to help materialize or witness the development of locally rooted and defined criteria for art, aesthetics, music, dance, literature, and more. In the production of new narratives of creative formation—that were also creative critiques—and the production of pedagogical resources, Rooney demonstrates how this fourth Carifesta amassed the (imperfect) makings of an anticolonial story of art, one (like Carifesta as a whole) interrogating the very boundaries of the region and necessarily grounded in plurality.

For the most part, all the essays here are anticipatory, imagining directions for new kinds of art historical formations drawn from the social and political imaginaries of Caribbean artists and actors. Rooney and Poupeye more specifically address the challenges of writing the Caribbean's polyphonic and polyvalent creative formations, not only in the context of disciplinary conditions but also in the context of art history's circulation through pedagogy and public-facing scholarship. This is a challenge also taken up in the final section of the book, "Rethinking Institutions," and addressed through an emphasis on the relational possibilities of working between the Caribbean and its diaspora communities. María Elena Ortiz provides a personal reflection on the challenges and joys that are part of working within, and working to change, museological institutions to centralize, and to value, Caribbean artistic production. For Ortiz, positionality is everything. Her essay charts the potential of diasporic networks in building and sustaining institutional change to center Caribbean communities in their curatorial and public programming. This centering also involves addressing the politics of location, acknowledging the power dynamics between Caribbean and US-based institutions, and establishing networks that meaningfully center the cultures and histories of Caribbean art making. (Fellow-contributor Erica Moiah James similarly invokes this broader spatialization of the Caribbean with her theorization of the "global Caribbean" in her recent book *After Caliban: Caribbean Art in a Global Imaginary*.[26]) As a curator and scholar, Ortiz moves between the academy and the museum, so her essay provides a generous description of the kinds of collaborative practices that can be formed between these spaces to cultivate local and sustainable infrastructure that centers Caribbean artistic production within the region.

Centering the Caribbean as a framework and method for building new kinds of cultural connections between institutions and artists is also a concern for Aldeide Delgado. Her essay considers the intersections of feminist, Latinx, Caribbean, and photographic histories, canonical formations that have long been siloed, with implications for the creation of supportive and sustainable cultural networks for promoting and preserving the work of women-identifying photographers from the region. Delgado understands these siloed histories as one component of a coloniality that has shaped the formation of art historical modernism. Instead, she proposes what she describes as an "archipelagic method" that remaps the boundaries between Latin America and the Caribbean. Drawing from Caribbean intellectual frameworks, her essay charts the archipelagic through the work of contemporary Caribbean artists whose practices exceed the limitations of national disciplinary bounds. Through them, Delgado addresses the entangled networks connecting Black women photographers across the geographies of the Caribbean. This, Delgado argues, becomes a method through which to build and grow a radical collaborative network of women photographers whose intellectual labor might be marshaled in pursing institutional change.

In an interview that closes this section, the Surinamese artist Marcel Pinas discusses the Kibii Foundation, an arts initiative established in 2009 in the town of Moengo, in the district Marowijne, Suriname, a South American nation that, like Guyana, is socially, culturally, and historically identified as part of the Caribbean. The Kibii Foundation was established to foster the preservation and development of the cultural heritage of the Maroons in Suriname, the descendants of Africans who liberated themselves from enslavement on plantations and established their own communities inland. Pinas describes the devastating history of colonial and capitalist extraction in Moengo, leaving its economy precarious after the departure of the companies that had long exploited the region's bauxite. This too is a story of the Caribbean, a region that has for centuries been a site for resource extraction, a destructive history that has harmed both the people and the land. The story of Pinas and the Kibii Foundation reminds us of the long history of the arts in the service of national or community development: Dance, drama, museums, festivals, and the visual artists have been an essential part of the growing (cultural) nationalist movements across the region at least since the end of the 1920s, through the mid-twentieth-century independence movements, and still today.[27]

In our interview with patricia kaersenhout, a Dutch artist and activist of Surinamese descent, questions about institutional change and the possibilities of the relational were central. kaersenhout reckons with the inheritances of both colonial histories and art histories—and their entanglements—noting, "I think it's important that we keep in mind that art institutions and the art world in general are, at their core, capitalist and racist systems." Foregrounding these institutions' centrality to the project of colonial modernity, kaersenhout describes how they navigate this system while also seeking its transformation. As she explains, "I need to use my work to create a form of justice and to disrupt spaces—but always with the thought of bringing people together. It's not only disrupting. It's also looking for ways to connect those different groups and make them have different conversations about painful topics." This relationality also extends across time; as the artist remarks, "I feel that I need to make things right or just for my ancestors who were involuntarily displaced." Disrupting institutions, and their histories, is a means for transformation in kaersenhout's practice. Transformation in this sense is both a deconstructive practice and one that reaches toward justice, toward renewal, toward pleasure, toward joy, that reaches toward the grounds from which we began: an otherwise.

Rethinking institutions and the question of transformation are also important aspects of the practice of Charl Landvreugd, a Suriname-born Dutch artist and the last artist we interviewed for this publication. With his focus "on the Caribbean from a European perspective . . . the Caribbean in the European," Landvreugd takes as self-evident that "the Caribbean is like a blueprint for the world we live in today. It is the blueprint for a changing Europe . . . a model for thinking about art created from a different space, from another 'original' that isn't just a derivative of what we already know." Both in his work as an artist and as part of the senior management team of a major European contemporary art museum, thinking with and from the Caribbean, specifically the Dutch Caribbean, Landvreugd helps to transform the museum into a place that can account for the multiplicity of Blackness, the multiplicity of being, in a world that too often reduces the Black person to singularities. He explains how doing this more broadly would require new kinds of research and collections policies for museums that would make the works of Caribbean artists integral to the telling of the history of art. This is the kind of institutional transformation to which he is committed.

While none of these essays or interviews might categorically describe what that otherwise world "is," each of them models or demonstrates, in generative and hope-full ways, how it can look to move in that direction. As Faith Smith writes in her coda, seeing from the Caribbean is also a reaching toward—an anticipation—that is grounded both in a willingness to have one's orientations rescripted and in the possibilities of being disoriented. In writing from the Caribbean, the essays in this volume demonstrate how the field of art history can be thought of as a "problem space" whose discursive conditions remain in formation. There is something generous about this position, which moves beyond hand-wringing or mere criticism. Through their methods and interpretations, the authors here suggest that seeing art history from the Caribbean holds an ethical imperative both to deconstruct and to actively build practices of creative interpretation. They offer new methodologies that sustain the promise and possibilities of freedom and alternative forms of value that emerge from the unique space of the Caribbean. This has been the work for decades of Caribbean scholars, including C. L. R. James, Derek Walcott, Stuart Hall, Sylvia Wynter, Édouard Glissant, Aimé Césaire, Frantz Fanon, Anton de Kom, Otto and Hermine Huiswoud, Alejo Carpentier, Gloria Wekker, and many others who have given shape to what we now know as the Caribbean intellectual tradition. The essays in this publication build on their work as we try to formulate answers to the question: What can the Caribbean mean for the fashioning of a different kind of art history?

NOTES

1. See, for example, Saloni Mathur, ed., *The Migrant's Time: Rethinking Art History and Diaspora* (Clark Art Institute, 2011); and Aruna D'Souza and Jill H. Casid, eds., *Art History in the Wake of the Global Turn* (Clark Art Institute, 2014).

2. Saidiya Hartman, *Lose Your Mother: A Journey Along the Atlantic Slave Route* (Macmillan, 2008).

3. The conference, also titled "Beyond Boundaries: Seeing Art History from the Caribbean," was held at the Clark Art Institute in Williamstown, Massachusetts, October 20–21, 2022. Event details, including participant biographies, conference paper abstracts, and videos of prerecorded conversations with artists, are available at https://www.clarkart.edu/research-academic/rap-events/clark-conference-2022.

4. Vittoria Caradonna, "'All the Things Happening Outside of the Museum Push Me Back In': Thinking Through Memory and Belonging in Amsterdam's Tropenmuseum," *International Journal of Heritage Studies* 28, no. 1 (January 2, 2022): 59–73, https://doi.org/10.1080/13527258.2021.1910064; and Nataša Petrešin-Bachelez, ed., *Decolonising Museums* (L'Internationale Online, 2015), https://framerframed.nl/wp-content/uploads/2015/11/Decolonising-Museums.pdf.

5. C. L. R James, *Beyond a Boundary*, 1st American ed. (1963; Pantheon, 1983).

6. David Scott, "Modernity That Predated the Modern: Sidney Mintz's Caribbean," *History Workshop Journal* 58, no. 1, Oxford University Press (2004): 192, quoting from Sidney W. Mintz, foreword to Jean Besson, *Martha Brae's Two Histories: European Expansion and Caribbean Culture-Building in Jamaica* (Chapel Hill, 2002), xv–xvi.

7. See Wayne Modest, "We Have Always Been Modern: Museums, Collections, and Modernity in the Caribbean," *Museum Anthropology* 35, no. 1 (2012): 85–96.

8. Scott, "Modernity That Predated the Modern," 199.

9. Scott, "Modernity That Predated the Modern," 199, quoting from Sidney W. Mintz, "The Caribbean as a Socio-Cultural Area," *Journal of World History* 9, no. 4 (1966): 914–15.

10. See, for example, Erica Moiah James, "Decolonizing Time: Nineteenth-Century Haitian Portraiture and the Critique of Anachronism in Caribbean Art," *Nka: Journal of Contemporary African Art* 44, no. 1 (2019): 8–23; and Esther Chadwick, "The Aesthetics of Postrevolutionary Haiti: Currency, Kingship, and Circum-Atlantic Numismatics," *Art History* 46, no. 5 (2023): 1014–45, https://doi.org/10.1111/1467-8365.12758.

11. For scholarship that explicitly addresses nonbinary thinking in transhistorical approaches, see, for example, Tom Boellstorff et al., "Decolonizing Transgender: A Roundtable Discussion," *TSQ: Transgender Studies Quarterly* 1, no. 3 (August 1, 2014): 419–39, https://doi.org/10.1215/23289252-2685669.

12. Maja Horn, "José E. Muñoz's Critical Caribbean Crossroads," *Small Axe* 19, no. 2 (2015): 77–84; Annie Paul, Nicolette Ramirez, and Brooklyn Museum, *Infinite Island: Contemporary Caribbean Art* (Bloomsbury USA, 2007); Deborah Cullen and Elvis Fuentes Rodríguez, *Caribbean: Art at the Crossroads of the World* (Yale University Press, 2012); and Lisa Blackmore and Liliana Gómez, eds., *Liquid Ecologies in Latin American and Caribbean Art* (Routledge, 2020), https://doi.org/10.4324/9780367199005.

13. Maggie Cao, "What Is the Place of Empire in the History of American Art?," *Panorama* 6, no. 1 (Spring 2020), https://journalpanorama.org/article/what-is-the-place-of-empire/; Joan Kee, *The Geometries of Afro Asia: Art Beyond Solidarity* (University of California Press, 2023); Thomas DaCosta Kaufmann, Catherine Dossin, and Béatrice Joyeux-Prunel, *Circulations in the Global History of Art* (Routledge, 2016); and Elizabeth Harney and Ruth B. Phillips, *Mapping Modernisms: Art, Indigeneity, Colonialism* (Duke University Press, 2018).

14. Catherine Grant and Dorothy Price, eds., "Decolonizing Art History," *Art History* 43, no. 1 (February 1, 2020): 8–66, https://doi.org/10.1111/1467-8365.12490.

15. Antonio Benítez Rojo, *The Repeating Island: The Caribbean and the Postmodern Perspective*, 2nd ed., Post-Contemporary Interventions (Duke University Press, 1996), 1–10, https://doi.org/10.1215/9780822382058.

16. Krista A. Thompson, *An Eye for the Tropics: Tourism, Photography, and Framing the Caribbean Picturesque* (Duke University Press, 2006); Kay Dian Kriz, *Slavery, Sugar, and the Culture of Refinement: Picturing the British West Indies, 1700–1840* (Yale University Press, 2008); Mia L. Bagneris, *Coloring the Caribbean: Race and the Art of Agostino Brunias* (Manchester University Press, 2018); and Mimi Sheller, *Consuming the Caribbean: From Arawaks to Zombies* (Routledge, 2003).

17. Simon Gikandi, *Slavery and the Culture of Taste* (Princeton University Press, 2011); Kriz, *Slavery, Sugar, and the Culture of Refinement*; and Anne Lafont, "How Skin Color Became a Racial Marker: Art Historical Perspectives on Race," *Eighteenth-Century Studies* 51, no. 1 (October 19, 2017): 89–113, https://doi.org/10.1353/ecs.2017.0048.

18. For a discussion of the question of temporality, of notions of priority, in relation to the Caribbean, see Deborah A. Thomas, "Time and the Otherwise: Plantations, Garrisons and Being Human in the Caribbean," *Anthropological Theory* 16, nos. 2–3 (2016): 177–200.

19. C. L. R. James, *The Black Jacobins: Toussaint L'Ouverture and the San Domingo Revolution* (1938; Knopf Doubleday, 1989).
20. Alvan A. Ikoku, "Forêts del Sur and the Pretexts of Glissant's Tout-Monde," *Small Axe* 19, no. 2 (2015): 4.
21. Roshini Kempadoo, "Timings, Canon, and Art History," *Small Axe* 19, no. 2 (47) (July 1, 2015): 172, https://doi.org/10.1215/07990537-3139298.
22. David Scott, "The Re-Enchantment of Humanism: An Interview with Sylvia Wynter," *Small Axe* 8 (September 2000): 119–20.
23. It is not for nothing that we describe the pressure point between artistic expressions and colonial form. Pressure was the theme of Kingston Biennial 2022, curated by David Scott, together with Nicole Smythe-Johnson, Wayne Modest, and O'Neil Lawrence. For these curators, *pressure* or *pressha* is a capacious concept, a set of feelings that describes a Caribbean region and its people struggling under, and in the wake of, colonial oppression, that seems unabated in the present. In his catalogue essay for the Biennial, Modest, as James does in her essay here, thinks through the entanglements of music and art as he explores what he describes as an aesthetics of social suffering that emerges as people in the Caribbean attempt to narrate lives elided, to survive, to fashion livable presents and futures. See Wayne Modest, "Weh yuh know 'bout presha?: On the Popular Aesthetics of Pressure," in *Pressure: The Kingston Biennial*, ed. David Scott (National Gallery of Jamaica, 2022).
24. See, for example, the 2024–25 exhibition *Zombis: Death Is Not the End?* at the Museé du quai Branly–Jacques Chirac, the French national museum of Indigenous arts and cultures, in Paris, https://www.quaibranly.fr/en/exhibitions-and-events/at-the-museum/exhibitions/event-details/e/zombis.
25. Deborah A. Thomas, *Modern Blackness: Nationalism, Globalization, and the Politics of Culture in Jamaica*, Latin America Otherwise (Duke University Press, 2004), 15.
26. Erica Moiah James, *After Caliban: Caribbean Art in a Global Imaginary* (Duke University Press, 2025).
27. Rex M. Nettleford, *Caribbean Cultural Identity: The Case of Jamaica, an Essay in Cultural Dynamics* (Ian Randle and Markus Wiener, 2003).

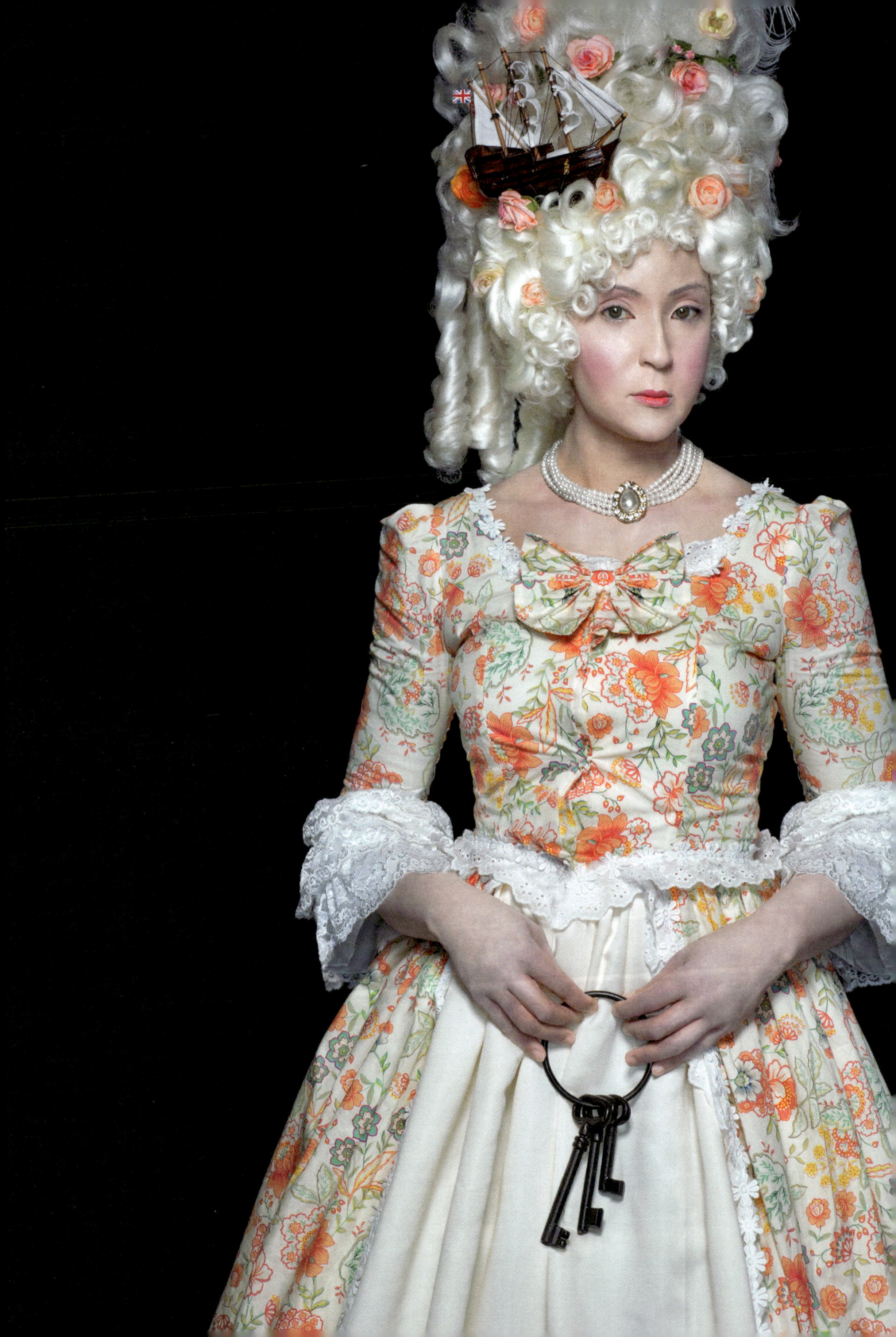

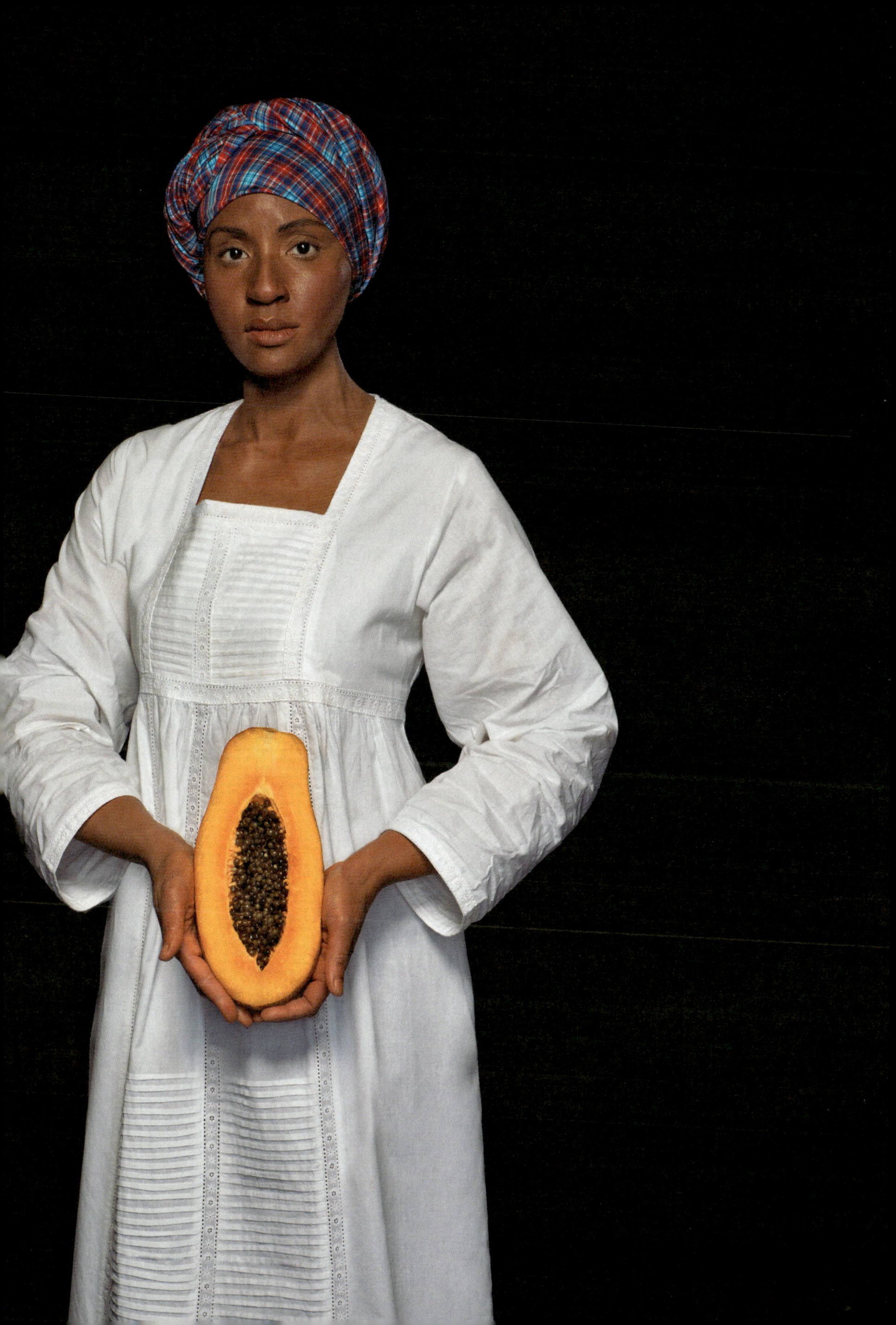

PART I
RETHINKING RACE

CHAPTER 1

COOLIE CRÉOLE

Andil Gosine

Two news stories published by Dutch outlets in 2023 laid out the limited territory of ideas that continues to plague reflections about the afterlife of indentureship, the system of contracted labor that brought Indians—by force, deceit, and/or choice—to work Caribbean plantations following the abolition of slavery and continuing until 1917. Both articles offered reflections on the 150th anniversary of the first landing of indentured workers in Suriname on June 5, 1873. The established, corporate Dutch daily *Trouw* framed the occasion as a celebration. Titled "Hindustani Dutch Celebrate 150 Years of Migration: 'The Positive Sides Often Remain Underexposed,'" *Trouw*'s article featured a photograph of four middle-age Indian women in traditional saris.[1] In response to this article, *One World*, which touts itself as "the only Dutch Black-owned opinion magazine," published "Hindustani Dutch: 'Our History Is Being Distorted.'"[2] Notably, it too featured photographs of four women, although theirs were individual portraits, and the women were younger in appearance. Of the four, three of the portraits signaled the "Indianness" of the women, either through wardrobe and jewelry or through framing and positioning that employed familiar ethnicizing tropes. The *One World* article challenged *Trouw*'s trivializing angle on indentureship: "The 'positive sides' of the Hindustani colonial past? On the occasion of 150 years of *pravasi*, the newspaper *Trouw* wanted to highlight the migration of Hindustanis, first as 'contract workers' to Surinam, later to the Netherlands. 'In a sense, their journey to a better future has been successful: We now drink latte macchiatos on the terrace.'"

The dissenting voices of the four Indo-Surinamese women based in Holland followed. "It's nonsense," the artist Anima Jhagroe-Ruissen said of the perspective offered in *Trouw*. She went on:

> The Surinamese-Hindustani history of pain and violence has been deliberately underexposed, ignored, and distorted for years. Colonial perspectives have also been internalized from the

Surinamese-Hindustani diaspora. A romanticized picture of our history has been painted, which leaves no room for marginalized stories. They also form that history. For me, there are no positive sides to colonialism, of which forced indentured labor is a part.

Jhagroe-Ruissen additionally pointed to the enduring model of labor it established as evidence of its legacy. "Latte macchiatos are not innocent either," she noted. They are "an example of international trade routes exploiting the Global South for the benefit of the Global North. There are still people who work in appalling conditions on plantations, just like our ancestors. And now we benefit from it."

Santoecha Rangai rejected the longstanding characterization of indentureship as an entirely separate process from slavery. That position has been adopted both by Indo-Caribbean people invested in a racialized hierarchy that situates them as mythologically apart from servitude and by Afro-Caribbean folks like the Amsterdam radio host Iwan Leeuwin, who incorrectly stated, "With all due respect, . . . contract workers were transferred to Suriname on luxury steamers." As Rangai pointed out, "Oppression didn't stop at slavery. Contract labor took place all over the world, and the Dutch State has a responsibility in this painful and violent history." Jhagroe-Ruissen similarly explained that "the contract labor system was an international distribution system of underpaid workers—if they were paid at all," and the artist Sarojini Lewis added that Indian contract laborers en route to Suriname "died on board from diseases, but also from suicide." Addressing Leeuwin's comments in particular, Lewis countered, "The Afro-Surinamese and Hindustanis share a colonial history and are victims of the same system. History teaches us, for example, that Afro-Surinamese women were an example for emancipation for Hindustani women in colonial times. This is in contrast to the polarization that you now see in [Leeuwin's] quote." The historical entwinements of Indians and Africans go further; as part of the accord to transport laborers from India to Suriname, the Dutch turned over control of a few West African ports to the British.

An exchange recorded in a third Dutch media publication, *NRC*, on June 2, 2023, also conveyed this disagreement among descendants about how to view indentureship.[3] As Moen Nehal begins to share the journey of her indentured ancestors with the interviewer, a fellow Indo-Surinamese community member interrupts:

Nehal: . . . my grandmother did say that [my grandfather] was lured to Suriname under false pretenses. He had been lied to. They said he was going to paradise. But they were treated like slaves—just a little more modern, maybe.
Gafar Imamdi: No, not as slaves. Our ancestors were indentured servants. At least they got paid something.

Nehal: A few dimes.

Imamdi: On weekends they were allowed to work for themselves. They were given a machete to grow their own food.

Nehal: But the treatment was bad.

Imamdi: Yes, the treatment was not good.

As observed by the reporters Juliet Boogaard and Jamila Meischke, "Their one-two punch shows the split in the Hindustani community: what one sees as a traumatic past of oppression is, for the other, an opportunity that the ancestors seized to escape abject poverty in India. Many feel both; pride and sadness for the past are intertwined."

These tensions are not new and have been pervasive across every space where indentureship succeeded slavery. Ideological battles waged among descendants of indentured workers in Guyana and Trinidad and Tobago, for example, have similarly set Indo- and Afro-Caribbean people in opposition to each other, despite mostly shared economic interests—one effect of which is the undermining of cross-ethnic alliances among working-class people. In some folks' view, situating indentureship as "not slavery" obviates its function as a successor to slavery; for others, it facilitates claims to a kind of exceptionalism. Importantly, these tensions register in varied ways and are also framed by relations of class and urban-rural divides, despite their ostensible grounding in race and ethnicity. While violence has been historically ethnicized in Guyana, for example, that has not been so in Trinidad. The larger populations of indenture-descended people means greater visibility in those countries, as in Suriname, but throughout the rest of the Caribbean and in its diasporic communities, indentureship and Indo-Caribbean culture are more often rendered invisible, despite indentureship and Asian migration to the region having foundationally shaped its contemporary social, cultural, and economic organization. The ongoing debate within the Indo-Caribbean community over how to characterize indentureship is epitomized by objections to the celebratory marking of its *beginning* rather than its end.[4]

While the perspectives reported in the *Trouw*, *One World*, and *NRC* articles differ, they all respond to the historical under-consideration of indentureship and of Indo-Caribbean people.[5] Even as these Dutch media stories address how Indo-Surinamese people are made invisible, they also reproduce flattened tropes. On the one hand is the neoliberal framing of indentured workers and their descendants as hardworking, "successful" migrants ("not slaves") who "now sip lattes on patios," alongside accounts of entrepreneurial initiatives like the Indo-Caribbean Canadian Association. On the other is their framing as long-suffering laborers ("nearly slaves"), as in the *One World* article and most other representations of indentureship in literature and the arts, as well as initiatives like the effort to rename Indian Arrival

Day as Indian Survival Day.[6] Either way, the Indo-Caribbean migrant registers as an uncomplicated subject.

Common to both approaches, for example, is the reverential representation of "ancestors," which deifies indentured workers such that they become beyond human—and simultaneously *not* human. Rituals and speeches "honoring Indian indentured ancestors" rarely stray from their valorized representation as virtuous and flawless. The formulaic focus on Indo-Caribbean women as "doubly oppressed" is, while not incorrect, similarly effective in flattening their experiences. Artistic and literary representations have tended to render Indo-Caribbean women as pious and powerless against the brutality of heteropatriarchal, emasculated Indo-Caribbean men, rather than speak to the nuances, fullness, and complications of all lived human experience. A simplified telling of the coolie's story is appealing to the market both because it provides an easy way to report a lesser-known history and because it offers the colonial imaginary what it wants.

I entered into artistic and curatorial practice following a principal education in Black British cultural studies, particularly through Stuart Hall's theorizations of culture and representation[7] and Kobena Mercer's critiques of contemporary art practices,[8] and in the company of the African American artist Lorraine O'Grady, whose works were focused on a refusal of cultural essentialism in Black contemporary art.[9] As an artist and scholar, I pursued creative endeavors with a determined commitment to counter the kind of identity reification described above. I am the descendant of indentured workers, and I grew up around former sugarcane plantations following the decline of the industry in the 1970s. There were sugarcane fields across from my childhood home, and most of the villagers with whom I lived in Tableland, Trinidad and Tobago, were themselves descendants of indentured workers. Indentureship and its legacies structured my experience of growing into a person and of understanding the world and my place in it. My artistic practice, which always stems from personal interrogation, would be dishonest if that process were made invisible or left unacknowledged. A totalizing framing of my experience through indentureship would be equally problematic, especially a framing of indentureship as specifically tied to Indianness and Indian culture. Just as indentureship's primary economic relationships are to slavery and colonization, so too is Indo-Caribbean identity fundamentally *Creole*: There is no Indo-Caribbean culture in which African, European, or Indigenous cultures of the Americas are not formative elements.

Iconographies of indentureship populate my art simply because a truthful telling of my traumas and joys, my anxieties and anguish, requires that I register them. But my work is not pitched in the polemical tradition of most discursive production on indentureship; rather, its principal objective is to truthfully represent the human condition and to consider the indentured worker and their descendants as like any human, layered and flawed. Like anyone, the coolie is complex.

I started to make things as many—possibly most—artists do: because *I had to* in order to survive, to live through a traumatic experience. My project *Wardrobes: A Preview*, completed in 2011, was the result of a yearlong research fellowship at the Fashion Institute of Technology (FIT) in New York. It comprised four components that foregrounded iconographies of indentureship: *Cutlass* (fig. 1.1), a white gold brooch in the form of the machete used by enslaved and indentured people to cut sugarcane; *Ohrni*, a headscarf that was reimagined by Indian women following migration to the Caribbean; *Rum and Roti*, a satchel; and *Scrubs (Made in Love)*, a set of medical scrubs made from fabric printed with an image of my parents. Each piece was subsequently reinterpreted through a series of performances, beginning with the 2013 staging of *(Made in Love)* at the inaugural gala of the Indo-Caribbean Alliance in Queens, New York (discussed below).

Because the iconography of indentureship was so visibly foregrounded in these objects, critics and curators read the project as being principally about Indo-Caribbean people. But it was not about indentureship, per se. Rather, these objects and this iconography emerged in an organic, unplanned, and unresearched manner, an expression of vulnerability stemming from the experience of heartbreak that underpinned them. Signs and symbols of indentureship emerged in this process as important, informing the historical context of this transoceanic, multi-century story. A framing short text attempted to make clear the principal catalyst for the project:

> In 1845 Savitri leaves Calcutta for Trinidad. She boards the *Fath Al Razack*, and is ordered to change into the stockings, woolen trousers, shoes and a petticoat provided. In 2009 Jimmy leaves Paris with a broken heart and four suitcases of couture. Jimmy meets Savitri in Trinidad, New York, and Toronto in 2017, on the 100th anniversary of the end of the British system of indentureship that had brought Savitri and others to Trinidad and elsewhere in the Caribbean. *WARDROBES* is one story of Indentureship and After and everything in-between.

I arrived at FIT with a plan to focus on Yoko Ono's fashion sensibilities and influence, but the recent and sudden end of my decade-plus-long relationship with my first love was overwhelming. In the midst of this grief, I was struck by how much the images that floated into my subconsciousness took me back to my childhood. This trajectory perplexed me, given that most of the relationship had taken place in France, with a Frenchman, and I was in New York. Strange, I thought, to be pulled into a place that appeared to be far removed from the context of the

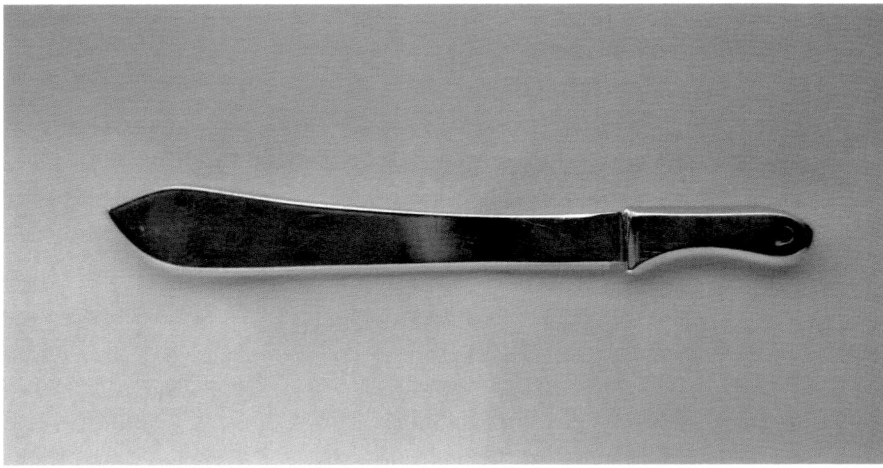

Fig. 1.1. Andil Gosine (Canadian, b. 1973, Trinidad and Tobago), *Cutlass*, from *Wardrobes: A Preview*, 2012. 18K white gold, ¾ × 2 ½ in. (1.75 × 6.5 cm). Courtesy of the artist

relationship or the environment to which I fled following its demise. With time and psychoanalytical treatment, the connections between Jimmy and Savitri became clear. The loss of a partner, following movement back and forth between many spaces (Trinidad, Canada, the United Kingdom, France, the United States, St. Lucia), had felt akin to the loss of home. The result was the skittishness of a lost animal suddenly without its tribe.

This yearning for home was echoed in the performance of *(Made in Love)*, later developed into the continuing series *Cane Portraiture* (fig. 1.2). I constructed a photo studio and invited the elegantly dressed participants—first at the 2013 Indo-Caribbean Alliance gala in Jamaica, New York, and subsequently at museum and gallery spaces like the Art Gallery of Ontario and, most recently, the Esker Foundation in Calgary, Alberta, in 2023—to pose for a portrait against a backdrop of sugarcane. This tropical image replaced the backdrops of European scenes (London's Big Ben, Paris's Eiffel Tower, or the Swiss Alps) that were most common in Caribbean photo studios in the early and mid-twentieth century. Consciously, I was constructing an experience through which participants, mostly diasporic Caribbean residents in New York, could consider and confront their own nostalgia for their imagined Caribbean, as well as the historical idealization of Europe in the region. But unconsciously, I realized later, I had created a piece that was fundamentally about feelings of exile and displacement, a performance in which I was inviting connection in a moment of feeling alone. Through the performance and its invitation to the cane field, I was reaching back to my childhood home.

Each piece in the *Wardrobes* collection—*Cutlass*, *Ohrni*, *Rum and Roti*, and *Scrubs (Made in Love)*—echoed a detailed personal circumstance or anxiety. In the performance of *Cutlass*, I emphasized, following O'Grady's practice with her diptychs, the entwinement of pleasure with violence. Three memories were wrapped together: my maternal grandmother, Ramadai, using her cutlass to clean the bark off sugarcane and slice the inside into treats for me; her own mother being brutally murdered by the cutlass; and my uncle using a cutlass to kill a boa constrictor that almost killed me. The performance also included elements of identifiably African and American culture, advancing the position that Indo-Caribbean culture is always formatively Creole. The Haitian-Canadian singer-songwriter Mélissa Laveaux performed a concert of music tied to our shared Créolité, ending her set with a cover I commissioned of Tina Turner's "Private Dancer," the first song whose lyrics I ever memorized. When I performed Turner's song as a child, I had no idea the song was told from the position of a sex worker. When I learned about the likelihood that many indentured women were sex workers, I wondered whether there was a subconscious connection between that history and the resonance this young boy felt with "Private Dancer."

Ohrni, in turn, referenced my relationship to my paternal grandmother, translating the tattoo of the anchor on her arm into gold embroidery on the headscarf. In *Rum and Roti*, as I further explained in the Richard Fung documentary *Dal Puri Diaspora* (2012), I emphasized the ambivalence of these two dominant heritages of indentureship, at once beloved and destructive, as experienced in my own childhood, where rum was the most common form of alcohol addiction and carbohydrate-heavy roti was the center of the poor diets that exacerbated diabetes and heart disease. Rum and roti are powerful emblems of the simultaneity of pleasure and violence as the legacy of indentureship.

Following *Wardrobes*, I staged *Our Holy Waters, and Mine* in two parts. Part one was presented at the Queens Museum in March 2014.[10] During this performance, an audio track repeated the phrase "Our holy waters are not the Ganges" 108 times, interspersed with the names of twelve waterways: six crossed by indentured workers on their way to the Caribbean (Bay of Bengal, Indian Ocean, Atlantic Ocean, Gulf of Paria, Berbice River, and Caribbean Sea) and six from cities that had shaped my own life (the Seine, the Thames, Rio Manzanares, Lake Ontario, the Potomac River, and the Hudson River). The track concluded with a looped recording, voiced by O'Grady, repeating "Our holy waters are not the Ganges." While the audio played, the Black Canadian surrealist Sur Rodney (Sur) appeared on stage holding a silver bucket covered with white hydrangeas, which were also a specific, whimsical reference to my former partner.[11] Sur was dressed in white, as was I. I then entered from stage left carrying a white cotton bindle resembling those carried by indentured workers on their journeys from India. I unpacked my bindle to reveal twelve

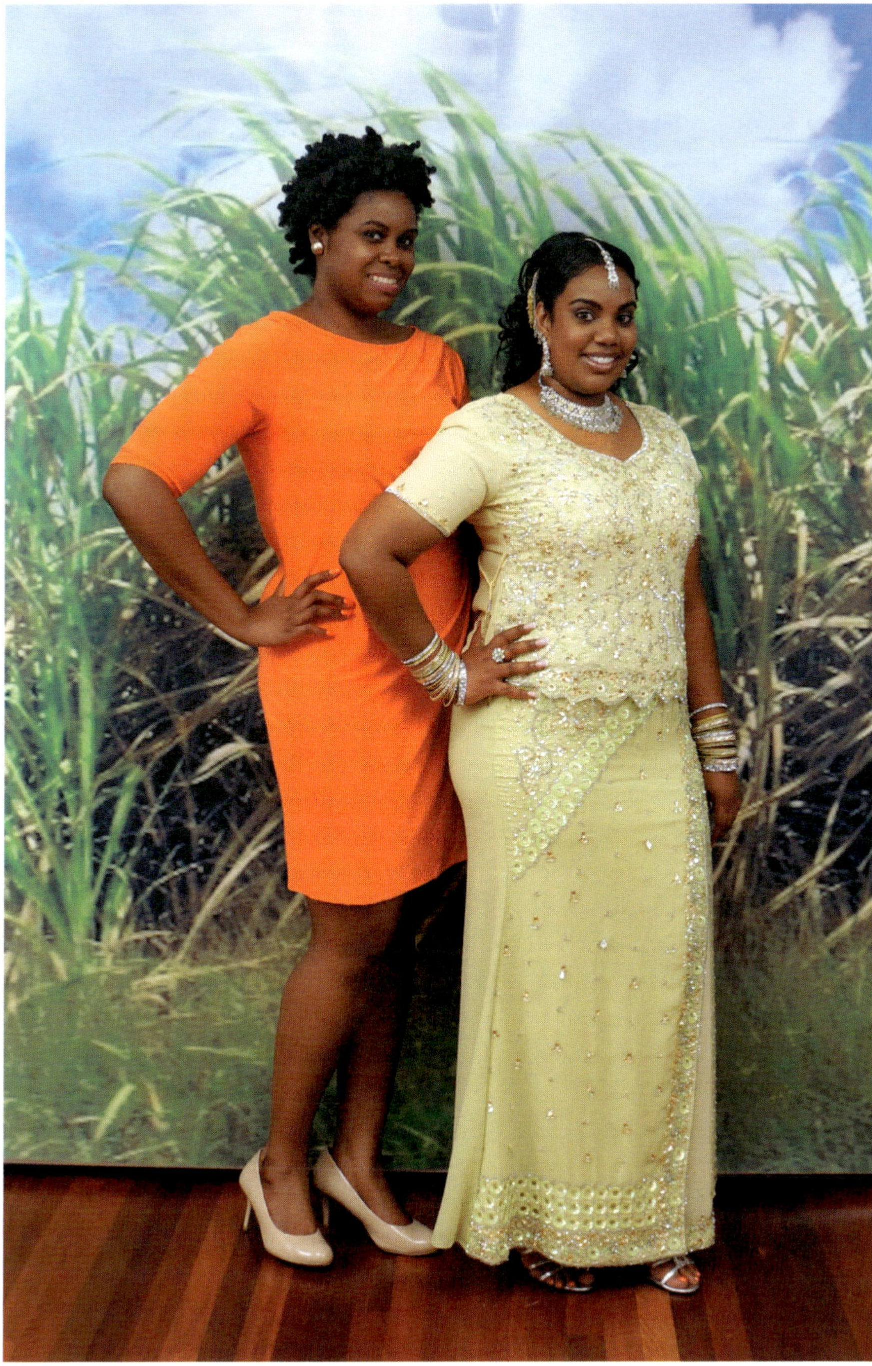

Fig. 1.2. Andil Gosine, *Cane Portraiture (Made in Love)*, 2013, digital print, various sizes

jars, each etched with one of the names of the waterways from the audio. After lining up the jars in two groups of six, I turned to Sur and poured water from his bucket to fill the jars. Flowers were placed in the one marked "Hudson River." I read this text to situate the performance:

> I do not remember my grandfather especially fondly. He was a cantankerous, noisy old man who fancied himself a kind of Lord-King, who ranted harsh judgments and wailed callous insults against his sons and daughters, and he was ever demanding of my grandmother, though she was equipped with strategies of her own to thwart his fantasies of control.
>
> One fond and recurring childhood memory I have is of having to keep watch as one of my aunts tried to dodge his gaze and escape to evening plans. Escape often involved having to climb over locked gates trimmed with barb-wire fence, which many an aunt achieved gracefully, mascara intact or high heels unscratched.
>
> My grandfather, like members of a few other Hindu families in Trinidad and Guyana, kept a jar of water from the Ganges River at home. It would be brought out for special ceremonies, like Divali Puja. The priest performing the puja would pour some into a round brass vessel (a lotha) and use the flicker of a mango tree leaf to sprinkle blessings on the offerings to gods, on the food, and on our bodies.
>
> But Our Holy Waters are not the Ganges—our Holy Waters are the ones that birthed us: the Kala Pani.
>
> Our Holy Waters were the ones crossed by Hindus and Muslims, agnostics and atheists, from India to Trinidad and Guyana: the Bay of Bengal, the Indian Ocean, the Atlantic, the Caribbean Sea, the Gulf of Paria, the Berbice River—the waters that carry the truths of our history and experiences, all of it.
>
> In Trinidad and Guyana, the official record keepers still mostly pour from the Ganges, resuscitating and reinscribing fictitious narratives of "real" India and "real Indians" reverentially held over and against the truths of our actual history and, also, our creativity. It's Arrival Day that's celebrated, our ancestors' entrapment into a reinvented form of slavery, not emancipation from it.
>
> You hear people describe themselves as exceptional: "Our family were not indentures," they'll say, or "We were high caste," even as everything else about their history remains a blur. "Indentureship was not slavery," insist those who work hard to maintain racial tensions in our communities, as if indentureship was not simply the most efficient way in which to execute slavery in its time. . . .

> Our Holy Waters are the dark waters of the Kala Pani, in the comradeship and creativity that grew in and with and from the misery of this journey, to give us Chutney music and doubles and the lovely lilts of our speech, and the punishing gaze we deliver to ourselves, and also our interventions into those we lived with, to remake calypso and language and simply the way we live with each other and remake each other; it is all of it, the pleasure and the violence, the pain and the possibility. As the poet Khal Torabully reminds us, we are linked forever not by some benign essential connection to some space once called India, to some bodies that look Indian, but by our shared heritage in that treacherous journey across the dark waters, and all that unfolded after. But we are also not contained by it.
>
> Our Holy Waters are also in the experiences that dispersed us further, to London and Toronto, Miami and Montreal, and here in Queens. For me, that meant too the incursions of Lake Ontario after my family moved to Canada, and the Thames and Seine, where love was won and lost, and the healing banks of the Hudson River.
>
> These, I would say to my cantankerous old grandfather, whom I loved anyway, are Our Holy Waters and Mine.

This text emphasizes rejection of Indo-nationalism and cultural essentialism and outlines the general veneer of my art practice—to always simultaneously invoke and attend to the social-historical with the contours of the personal-intimate, to insist that they are entwined always, but that neither is entirely productive of the other. Refusing the overarching symbolic significance of a point of origin ("not the Ganges"), it relocates the "holy" aspect of indentureship in the journey, represented by the waters. Including both the historical waterways passed by indentured workers and the ones that were part of my own life, *Our Holy Waters, and Mine* further insists on recognizing the complex humanity of the post-indenture subject: neither reducible to the historical experience nor detached from it.[12]

My subsequent creative efforts, including the solo exhibitions *All the Flowers* (2017) and *Coolie Coolie Viens* (2017–19), continued this trajectory. Yet my experience of the contemporary art world has been that it tends to work more readily with cultural reification as a principal mode in which to include and engage the histories and experiences of non-white Others—particularly of those, like indentured workers and their descendants, whose stories are not well known to general audiences. In both of those solo exhibitions, the first host institutions refused to grant much space for works operating outside the dominant modes of representation with which they were most familiar. The specificities and contours of the pieces in both exhibitions were constantly collapsed and reoriented around whiteness. For the first staging of *Coolie Coolie Viens* at the Glenhyrst Gallery in Ontario, I was asked to make a video tour of the works because the sugarcane portraits would be "too confusing" for the gallery's audiences—despite the fact that no such demand would be made of white artists producing abstract work. Similarly, despite *All the Flowers* being focused on the specific experience of my migration to Canada as a teenager and its shaping of my adolescence, the gallery's promotional text emphasized my "Other" identities and framed the project as entirely representational of queer migrants. These outcomes were not, I think, the consequences of personal failings or bad intentions by the host institutions. Rather, they reflect the default, normative operating modes of exhibiting and curating in the contemporary art world, where reified "identity" and simpler narratives serve as an easier shorthand, particularly for communicating to the public and the marketplace.

Institutions can and sometimes will do things differently. Dissatisfaction with the framing of my own works by these galleries in Canada led to my withdrawal from exhibiting my creative work, particularly since I create very little for the market, and instead taking a more active interest in research and curation. Between 2014 and 2019, I led the research project Visual Arts After Indenture,[13] through which I began to identify and gather works by artists who had descended from indentured workers. There were numerous results of this work, including special editions of the journals *Wasafiri* and *Small Axe*, and the project was ultimately important in the making of the field.[14] Its most significant culmination thus far was the exhibition *everything slackens in a wreck*, which I curated for the Ford Foundation Gallery in New York in 2022 (fig. 1.3).

The Ford Foundation supported me as a curator and granted me the freedom and resources to make decisions that resisted dominant modes of cultural representation in museum practice. Comprising work by Caribbean artists who were descendants of indentured workers and whose practices cite the experience indentureship, the exhibition was about the operation of the human condition in the situation of crisis. It suggested that examining the experiences of indentured workers arriving in the Caribbean could help us understand how we might contend with contemporary crises such as the COVID-19 pandemic and climate change. I chose existing works by artists Wendy Nanan (Trinidad and Tobago) and Margaret Chen (Jamaica), who connected their personal experiences to the social history of indentureship. I also invited the artists Andrea Chung and Kelly Sinnapah Mary to create works they felt were connected to the theme of the exhibition, giving them broad leeway to produce however abstract an interpretation they wanted. An ecological aesthetic strongly connected their works as they progressed, and the exhibition space brought together the natural elements of land, air, and sea.

The Ford Foundation also accorded me space to veer away from their usual exhibition practices. For example, the gallery's shows typically include many artists, while for *everything slackens in a wreck* I was allowed to program just four in the space—a strategic choice on my part, to draw closer attention to and more elaborate engagement with each work. This decision was a deliberate move against a grand representative narrative, forcing the visitor to contend with the individuality of each piece. I was also permitted to not include descriptive labels on the gallery walls, a choice that went against the traditional practices of many public institutions, which see them as a key component of the educational work of an exhibition. By omitting wall labels, I wanted audiences to find their own connections to the works without being oriented by instructions that tend to rely on culturally reifying modes of discourse. That did not deny visitors educational opportunities; a laminated sheet detailing the list of works was available at the gallery sitter's desk, and a resource center featuring videos of two of the artists and a library of books was tucked into the gallery space. Likewise, the supporting public program included talks on related themes.

Additionally, the Ford Foundation published and distributed three thousand copies of an accompanying catalogue featuring scholarly essays on each artist.[15] Community participation was also a main feature of the exhibition, and I recruited members of the Jahajee Sisters—a group comprising women working on issues of domestic violence in the community—to create an accompanying soundscape in the Ford Foundation's large indoor garden.

Buoyed by the experience of *everything slackens in a wreck*, I intend to bring a similar spirit to the production of *Nature's Wild*, which will debut at the Art Museum of the Americas in Washington, DC, in 2025.[16] A companion to my 2021 monograph, this exhibition will foreground its key findings about the historical animalization of non-white people as a strategy of racialization—a key component of the genocide of Indigenous people and enslavement of African people, and a foundational element of the colonization of the Americas—as well as my argument for embracing humans' animality. As in the book, the experiences of indentured workers and their descendants are taken up as Caribbean stories, and the Créolité of Indo-Caribbean peoples is claimed. The exhibition emphasizes a collaborative spirit, and each newly presented work is a co-creation I developed with another artist from the Americas, including Llanor Alleyne (Barbados), Bev Koski (Canada), Kelly Sinnapah Mary (Guadeloupe), Natalie Wood (Trinidad and Tobago), and Zachari Logan (Trinidad and Tobago). I am also working with the Cross Atlantic Chocolate Collective toward the creation of one work.

The fluidity of my practices as an artist, critic, and curator is a challenge to the field's dominant Euro-American professional disciplinary tradition, but it does offer a Caribbean way of working. I would perhaps go so far as to call it a working-class Creole Caribbean sensibility. By this characterization, I do not mean to recklessly invoke a kind of essentialism or to claim a kind of Caribbean

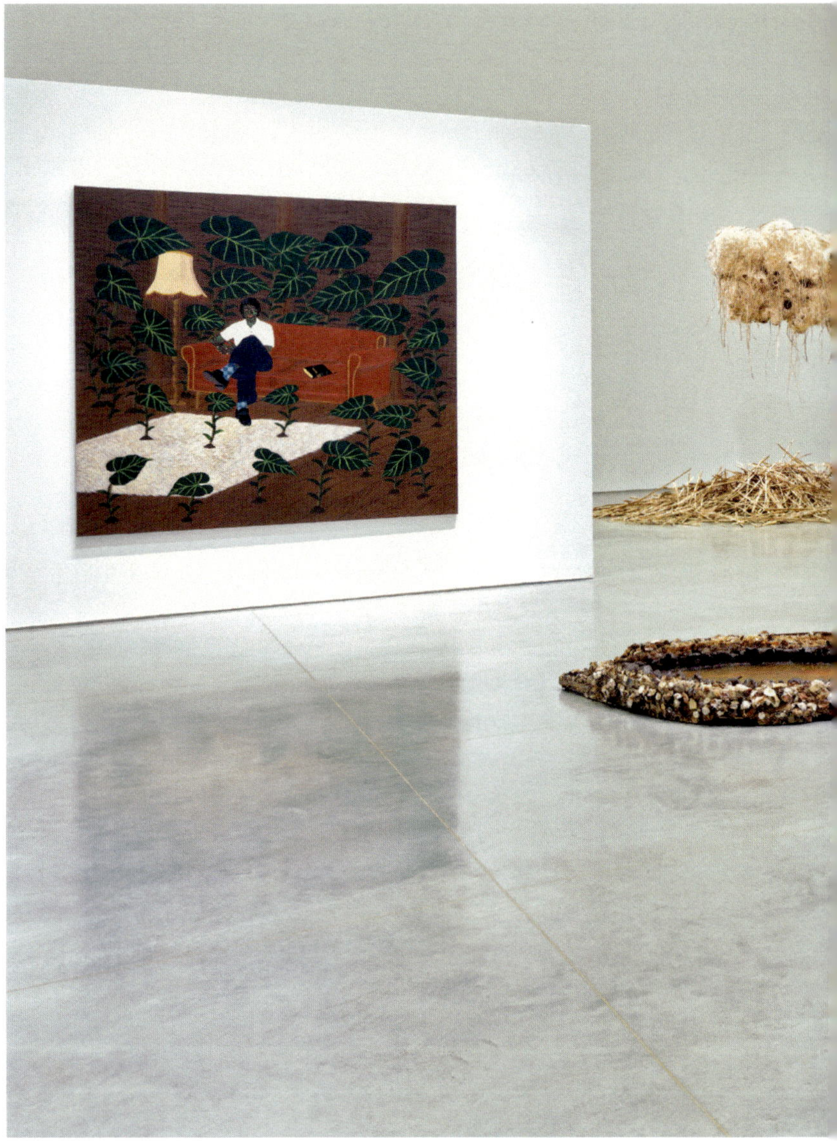

Fig. 1.3. Exhibition installation view, *everything slackens in a wreck*, Ford Foundation Gallery, New York, 2022

exceptionalism. Instead, I wish to recognize how both the social history and the political-economic conditions that produce me and my understanding of myself as a Caribbean person have resulted in this particular way of working. I can look to other Caribbean thinkers and artists as examples of this kind of approach, including Roshini Kempadoo, who similarly straddles various professional roles as artist and critic, along with the two Caribbean artists who have been my primary influences, each of whom, in their own way, challenged and transgressed the

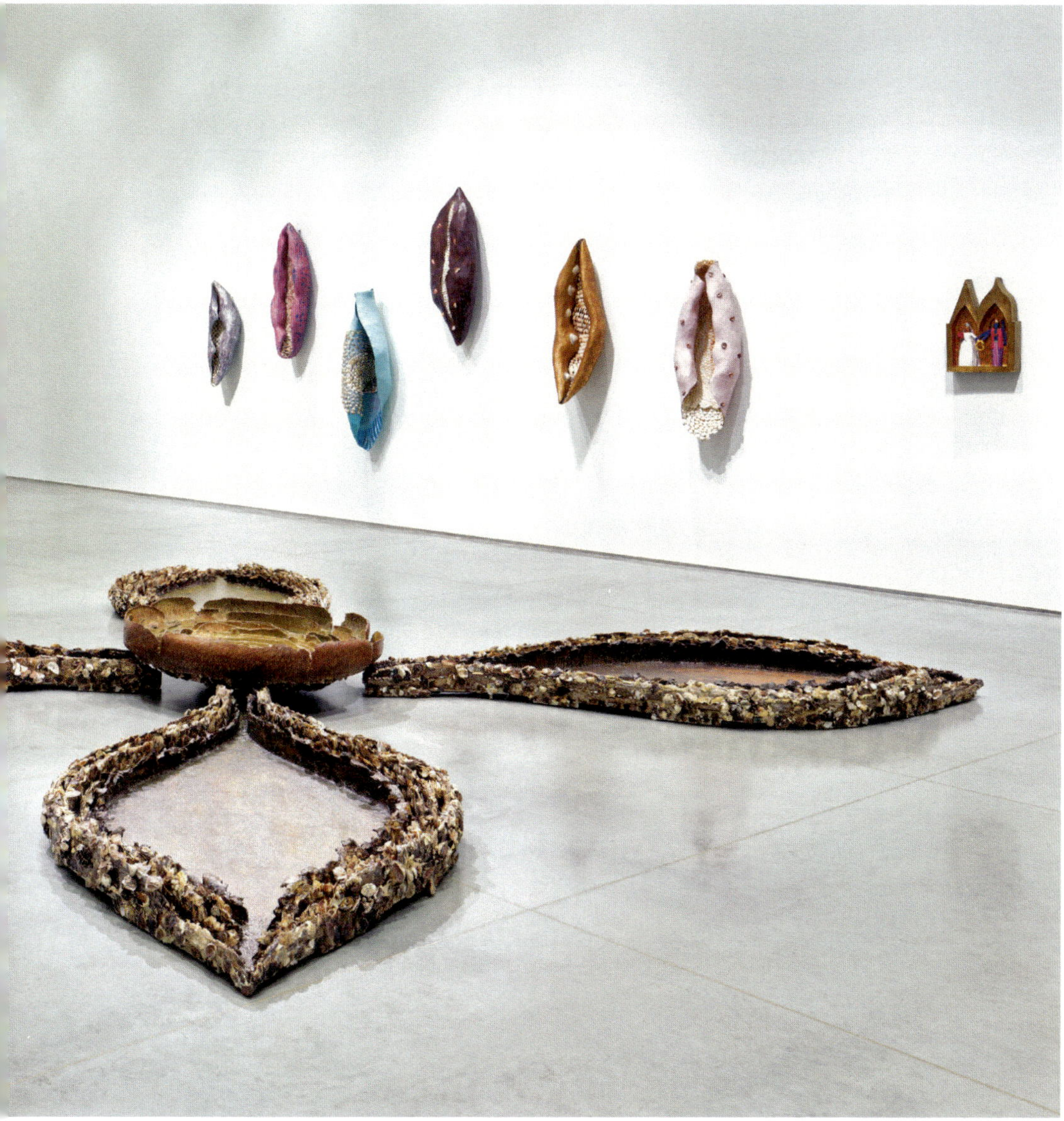

boundaries of contemporary art practice. In O'Grady, I found an intellectual mentor whose career offers some important parallels, particularly in coming to art practice after an entirely different professional life (she was an economist who worked for the US State Department, and I was a specialist in international development whose policy work included a stint at the World Bank). She was for years also her own best critic, and she always felt underserved by art critics who found the complexity of her work challenging. And in Felix Gonzalez-Torres, I found a deeply resonant aesthetic and methodological lineage, including through his membership in Group Material.[17]

Over the past decade, O'Grady and Gonzalez-Torres have been the primary guides in the development of my practice. As for many artists, contending with love, desire, and heartbreak instigated my creative production. I was intrigued by how the loss of an enduring first love who was not Caribbean had sent me to Caribbean history. I found myself, for reasons then unknown to me, returning to iconographies of my childhood in rural Trinidad and infusing them with the understanding of pleasure and violence as being simultaneous. In my creative practice, more than trying to say anything about indentureship or the Caribbean, I am using this heritage to try and work through an understanding of my own humanity. This approach might register as messy, or illegible, or perhaps just not seriously committed enough to any one practice. But in many ways, I am simply continuing along paths set by O'Grady and Gonzalez-Torres, among others.

NOTES

1. Chiel de Groot, "Hindoestaanse Nederlanders vieren 150 jaar migratie: 'De positieve kanten blijven vaak onderbelicht,'" *Trouw*, April 25, 2023, https://www.trouw.nl/religie-filosofie/hindoestaanse-nederlanders-vieren-150-jaar-migratie-de-positieve-kanten-blijven-vaak-onderbelicht~bf2a36be/.

2. Tamara Hartman, "Hindostaanse Nederlanders: 'Opvallend weinig aandacht voor onze geschiedenis,'" *One World*, June 2, 2023 (reposted June 3, 2025), https://www.oneworld.nl/mensenrechten/hindostaanse-nederlanders-contractarbeiders-geschiedenis-misverstanden/.

3. Juliët Boogaard and Jamila Meischke, "Elke groep Surinamers heeft z'n eigen koloniale pijn," *NRC*, June 23, 2023, https://www.nrc.nl/nieuws/2023/06/02/elke-groep-surinamers-heeft-zn-eigen-koloniale-pijn-a4165989.

4. Rajiv Mohabir, "Why I Will Never Celebrate Indian Arrival Day," Asian American Writers' Workshop, June 2, 2016, https://aaww.org/indian-arrival-day/.

5. One important exception to this pattern is the Mauritian poet Khal Torabully's theorization of "coolitude," which explicitly addresses the erasure of South Asian culture in formulations of Créolité, or Creole identity. Torabully's term emphasizes the experience of the indentured worker, reformulating the derogatory term "coolie" (meaning "money" in Tamil) used for laborers of Chinese or Indian descent, to underline the formative influence of Asian culture in the making of the Caribbean. Torabully's "coolitude" follows from the French Martinican poet Aimé Césaire's concept of "Négritude," which was instrumental in the founding of a Francophone literary movement of the same name, whereby writers found solidarity in Black identity as a rejection of French colonial racism. Importantly, coolitude is at once a poetics, an appeal for research, and a theoretical framework through which to consider cultural production. Coolitude also emerges from and echoes the notion of Caribbean culture as hybrid and perpetually in flux, as advanced by the Martinique-born poet, critic, and philosopher Édouard Glissant's "Créolité" and in the work of other Caribbean thinkers. Coined by Torabully in his text *Cale d'Etoiles*, and further elaborated with Marina Carter, coolitude constructs itself on two pillars: "firstly, the reconstitution of a memory, which veers between an imagination drawn back to the atavistic homeland, and secondly, the contribution of a poetics based on the Indian element and shaped by the fact that the coolie was chronologically the last to contribute to the making of diversified societies." As Torabully suggests, the shared "heritage" comes from the experience of the journey. For more on this progression, see Marina Carter and Khal Tourabully, *Coolitude: An Anthology of the Indian Labour Diaspora* (Anthem, 2002).

6. The Cutlass Magazine, "Having said 'Indian Survival Day' for some time in my family, I adopted it as an alternative to 'Indian Arrival Day' in a commemoration post from last year . . .," Facebook, April 29, 2022, https://www.facebook.com/127658582488455/posts/having-said-indian-survival-day-for-some-time-in-my-family-i-adopted-it-as-an-al/492456312675345/.

7. See Stuart Hall, "Un-Settling 'the heritage,' Re-Imagining the Post-Nation: Whose Heritage?," *Third Text* 13, no. 49 (1999–2000): 3–13, https://doi.org/10.1080/09528829908576818; and Stuart Hall, "Black Diaspora Artists in Britain: Three 'Moments' in Post-War History," *History Workshop Journal* 61, no. 1 (2006): 1–24, https://doi.org/10.1093/hwj/dbi074.

8. See Kobena Mercer, "Black Art and the Burden of Representation," *Third Text* 4, no. 10 (1990): 61–78, https://doi.org/10.1080/09528829008576253; and Kobena Mercer, "Ethnicity and Internationally," *Third Text* 13, no. 49 (1999–2000): 51–62, https://doi.org/10.1080/09528829908576822.

9. Lorraine O'Grady, "Olympia's Maid: Reclaiming Black Female Subjectivity," *Afterimage* 20, no. 1 (1992): 14–15, https://doi.org/10.1525/aft.1992.20.1.14; and Lorraine O'Grady, *Writing in Space, 1973–2019*, ed. Aruna D'Souza (Duke University Press, 2020).

10. An earlier, frequently cited article erroneously listed the performance date as 2013, but the performance took place in March 2014.

11. He was a devoted fan of the pop singer Madonna, and she notoriously hated the flower. See "Madonna Hates Hydrangeas," September 6, 2011, posted by CNN, YouTube, https://www.youtube.com/watch?v=wTiZz_Poc74.

12. For a detailed analysis of part one, see Nalini Mohabir, "*Kala Pani*: Deathscapes and the Flow of Water After Indenture," *Asian Diasporic Visual Cultures and the Americas*, December 5, 2019, https://brill.com/view/journals/adva/5/3/article-p293_293.xml; and Ramabai Espinet, "Andil Gosine: Coolie, Coolie Veins," *Pree*, November 15, 2018, https://preelit.com/2018/11/15/andil-gosine-coolie-coolie-viens/. Subhalakshmi Gooptu discusses part two, which was staged at the Museum of Latin American Art in Long Beach, California, in 2018, in "Watery Archives: Transcoeanic Narratives in Andil Gosine's *Our Holy Waters, and Mine*," *Feminist Review* 130, no. 1 (2022), https://journals.sagepub.com/doi/full/10.1177/01417789211073294.

13. Visual Arts After Indenture website, launched 2017, www.afterindenture.com.

14. Andil Gosine and Nailini Mohabir, eds., "Afterlives of Indenture," special issue, *Wasafiri* 110 (Summer 2022); and Andil Gosine, ed., "After Indenture," special issue, *Small Axe* 21, no. 2 (53) (2017).

15. Andil Gosine, ed., *everything slackens in a wreck: Wendy Hanan, Margaret Chen, Andrea Chung, Kelly Sinnapah Mary* (Ford Foundation Gallery, 2022). Contributors to the catalogue included Kafia Abdulkader, Elena Chou, Richard Fung, Lisa Kim, Shivanee Ramlochan, Aitak Sorahitalab, Darren Walker, and Amber Williams-King.

16. Following the writing of this essay, the Art Museum of the Americas canceled the planned *Nature's Wild* exhibition in early 2025, just five weeks before it was due to open in Washington—as extensively covered by the international media. See "*Nature's Wild with Andil Gosine* CANCELLED by the Organization of American States, Art Museum of the Americas, March 21–June 29, 2025," https://andilgosine.persona.co/Cancellation. Paul Petro Contemporary Art in Toronto subsequently staged *Nature's Wild with Andil Gosine (RETURNS)* in late 2025. For details, see Paul Petro's exhibition web page, https://www.paulpetro.com/exhibitions/674-nature-s-wild-with-andil-gosine.

17. Importantly, there are questions about reading both artists as Caribbean: O'Grady has long described herself as West Indian, and her experiences of growing up as part of Boston's "Black Brahmin" community of socially mobile Jamaican migrants in the 1930s and '40s are foundational to her work. But she never visited the Caribbean, and the extensive attention her work has enjoyed—near the end of her life, she sat for over one hundred interviews with art and media publications in a single year—has tended to represent her as African American rather than Caribbean. Similarly, the emphasis on Felix Gonzalez-Torres's queerness and his practice during the HIV/AIDS era displaced attention from his Cuban heritage for a long time.

CHAPTER 2

WHO DISAPPEARED THE TALLAWAHSAURUS

THE VISUAL AFTERLIFE OF CARIBBEAN HEROIC HISTORY

Petrina Dacres

Throughout the twentieth century, artists in the Caribbean utilized specific heroic icons in their work to affirm their cultural experiences, reexamine and activate aspects of historical memory, and challenge social and aesthetic conventions. In the Caribbean context, the use and proliferation of select iconic images in art occurred in tandem with nationalist projects and policies that sought to create a new (art) history that could sustain a contemporary, postcolonial cultural and political imaginary and to position an anti-imperialist and anticolonial stance. New official heroes such as José Martí and Marcus Garvey were immortalized in public sculptures, and their likenesses became a common iconography in twentieth-century Caribbean art. Simultaneously, the status of older colonial heroes, such as Queen Victoria, became the subject of public debate, resulting in their statues being attacked or shifted to new locations in the landscape. In addition, artists have reimagined these older heroic figures in other artistic forms to meditate on the Caribbean's complex and ongoing relationship to imperial power, culture, and authority.

Analysis of Caribbean art can show us how artists participate uniquely in ongoing conversations on history and representation. Indeed, heroic Caribbean art intersects with the deeply political, and sometimes violently iconoclastic, ongoing global discourse on colonial monuments and American Civil War statues, as well as initiatives to publicly commemorate Black subjects in the Caribbean, North America, Europe, and Latin America. Within the last fifteen years, the subject of the heroic colonial statue has been directly addressed by contemporary Caribbean artists in various ways. The Guyanese British artist Hew Locke is well known for his series of photographs of colonial statues in which he creatively reimagines their histories and imagery. Acrylic paint, marker drawings, and mass-produced decorative items enliven the surfaces of his large photographs; effusively laden with colorful materials and symbolic imagery, they intervene against or "attack" the statues,

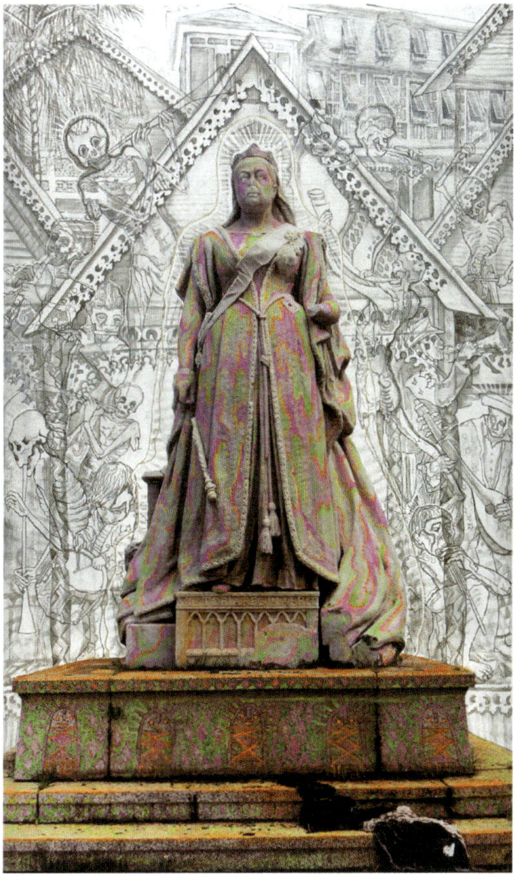

Fig. 2.1. Hew Locke (Guyanese British, b. 1959), *Victoria (Law Courts)*, 2013. Acrylic, ink, and pen on chromogenic print, approx. 78 × 50 in. (198.1 × 127 cm)

making visible the power and iconicity of colonial heroic figures and, by extension, the complex and violent colonial project.

In Locke's *Victoria* (2013), the artist manipulates an image of Queen Victoria's statue in front of the High Court in Georgetown, Guyana (fig. 2.1). The 1894 statue was damaged in a bombing during anticolonial protests in 1953;[1] it was restored but later moved to the city's Botanical Garden after independence in 1966, until another restoration in 1990 when it was again placed at the court.[2] Locke's photograph of Victoria's statue overlaid with paint and ink drawings of skeletal musicians and deteriorating local Creole architecture is a meditation on the sublime Caribbean colonial experience, which is marked by the production of new cultures under violence. The work reveals how histories of domination haunt the present. They can guide cultural policy that determines whether particular artifacts of the built environment are preserved or allowed to fall into disrepair.[3] As Locke has noted, "History is both now and in the past."[4] The artist's painted photographs, or what he calls his "impossible proposals," have also sought to challenge the status of materials such as marble and bronze in statuary conventions. Locke has suggested other materials and colors to "reinvigorate" how we commemorate.[5]

One of Locke's recent artworks, *Foreign Exchange* (2022), directly engaged with Sir Thomas Brock's statue of Queen Victoria in Birmingham. Locke's work was created in the wake of the toppling of the slave trader Edward Colston's statue in England during the Black Lives Matter movement in 2020.[6] Locke encased the original Victoria statue, unveiled in 1901 in Victoria Square, in a golden crate and built a large boat around the statue's base, atop its plinth. Accompanying the statue on its journey were five reduced-scale reproductions of Brock's Victoria, in cast resin that was made to look like patinated bronze. The figural group, all decorated with Locke's golden Britannia-like helmet masks, were meant to remind us of the practice of statuary reproduction that was central to Victoria's iconicity in the British empire.[7] Victoria statues were created by a handful of British artists who then reproduced their work throughout Britain and the world.[8] *Thomas Brock: Forgotten Sculptor of the Victoria Memorial* catalogued fourteen statues of Queen Victoria by Brock in England, India, Ireland, and South Africa, as well as other Victoria-related sculptural works.[9] Locke's *Foreign Exchange* draws our attention to the role of statues in the constitution of British monarchical power and in the service of colonial administration. The creative reimaging of the monumental form and heroes of the past draws our attention to the processes of icon shaping and history making, as well as to historical omissions in public sculptural practices.

Elsewhere, the artists La Vaughn Belle, who is from the US Virgin Islands, and Jeannette Ehlers, who is Danish Trinidadian, have staked their claim in public sculpture through their work *I Am Queen Mary* (2018). This sculpture was unveiled in Copenhagen in recognition of Denmark's often unacknowledged role in slavery—the country was formerly the colonial ruler of the Virgin Islands—and to honor women such as Mary Thomas, who led the 1878 labor revolt on the island of Saint Thomas.[10] Similarly, the US-based Jamaican architect and artist Nina Cooke-John recently created a public monument in honor of Harriet Tubman that replaced the Christopher Columbus statue in Newark, New Jersey. These sculptures represent a historical reckoning, and they intentionally center Black individuals and the Black experience in public discourse and spaces, particularly in the Global North. It is significant, for instance, that Cooke-John's monument, *Shadow of a Face* (2023), included not only portrait sculptures of Tubman but also a timeline of Newark's civil rights movement and audio narratives and artworks by members of the city's contemporary Black community. As much as these artworks by Caribbean artists demonstrate aesthetic and social investment in the convention of public statues and monuments, they also remind us of the instability of (heroic) sculpture today in maintaining a single narrative and memory.

The Jamaican experience of late twentieth-century, post-independence heroic statues and memorials offers us another opportunity to explore how Caribbean artists have engaged with the heroic convention from a different perspective. I am interested in how visual artists today have responded to the corpus of heroic nationalist, postcolonial imagery in twentieth-century Jamaican art. Two years after gaining independence in 1962, the Jamaican government created a formal pantheon of National Heroes, supported by political monuments. This endeavor established a discourse and iconography that recognized the importance of Jamaica's heroic history to the development of the nation's freedom, citizenship, and governance. By discussing the work of contemporary artists as afterimages[11] of Jamaica's mid-century pantheonization project, the essay highlights the postcolonial investment in heroic public sculpture and allows us to reflect on how artists in the twenty-first century reconsider the inherited meanings and conventions of the heroic and national ideals such as sovereignty, leadership, citizenship, and memory. These afterimages—or, perhaps, antiheroic images—by Caribbean artists utilize the impression of the postcolonial hero to challenge received narratives of the state and the idea of the redeemed Black body. I want to argue that, since independence, successive governments have abandoned state investment in the (sculpted) Black historical hero (though not the athlete), and that this retreat from history has opened up the possibility for nonsculptural or nonfigurative sculptural forms to foster new conversations about history and Black historicity.

ENTANGLED HISTORIES

Between 2009 and 2012, the graphic artist Michael Thompson created two poster series. The first set of prints features portraits of five of Jamaica's National Heroes: Paul Bogle, the leader of the 1865 Morant Bay peasant rebellion; George William Gordon, a nineteenth-century politician; Marcus Garvey, a twentieth-century Pan Africanist leader; Sam Sharpe, the leader of the 1831 Christmas Rebellion, the last major slave rebellion before emancipation; and the seventeenth-century Maroon leader Nanny, who led a community of formerly enslaved people in a guerrilla war against the British plantocracy. Notably absent from Thompson's series are two National Heroes, the political leaders Norman Manley and Alexander Bustamante, who led Jamaica to independence. Thompson's second poster series refers to police brutality and the lack of accountability during the Tivoli incursion of May 24, 2010, when members of the police force and army engaged in an armed conflict with gang members in Tivoli Gardens, a working-class community in Kingston, Jamaica. As police officers and soldiers attempted to apprehend Christopher "Dudus" Coke, the reputed don of the West Kingston area,[12] to extradite him to the United States, over seventy civilians were killed.[13] Past and present are linked in these two sets of images, as they both tell histories of violence in Jamaica.

In *Exceptional Violence*, Deborah Thomas argues that plantation and colonial violence continue to shape Jamaica's contemporary economic and political contexts.[14] Thompson's posters, like other types of commemorative art such as public monuments and statues, are evidence of the myriad ways that violence and narratives of violence reassert themselves in present-day Jamaica. One set of his images (with the iconography of Jamaican National Heroes) tells of the violent attempts to thwart the slave regime in the eighteenth and nineteenth centuries and of the judicial and economic violence of colonial governing powers. Thompson's first poster series calls back to the mid-twentieth-century articulation of Jamaica's heroic history through a specific iconography. The other set asks us to consider the significance of these concepts in relation to instances of spectacular public violence by successive postcolonial Jamaican governments.

Given Jamaica's historical context, I have been thinking about how artists have engaged ideas of governance, violence, and the heroic. Can a different typology of artworks tell us something about the unfinished process, which began in the 1960s, of nation building and statehood in the region? I am interested in the generation of artists who draw from a nationalist heroic iconography or the militarized hero in general, but also artists who ask new questions about the state project developed around this iconography, particularly around the meaning of power and violence in our own time. I am interested in how their images and experiences reveal the ways that we think of creating heroic monuments today.

POST-INDEPENDENCE POLITICAL FIGURATION AND THE HEROIC-IMAGE COMPLEX

Michael Thompson's portraits of the National Heroes are a legacy of the state's heroizing process that began in the 1960s. Jamaica's pantheon of National Heroes and their political monuments were intended to create a new history and culture for the newly independent nation. The activities of the heroes against colonial authorities, racism, and classism were narrated as important steps toward a national freedom. Drawing from the practices, folklore, and experiences of the African Jamaican population, this public history and imagery aimed to support an emerging government by giving citizens confidence in an updated image of political authority and leadership—a Black, Brown, and Jamaican image.

The governments of the 1960s and '70s commissioned figurative statues of Jamaica's National Heroes and placed most of them in the heroes' birth parishes (fig. 2.2). Most of the statues were created by the sculptor Alvin Marriott, one of the best-known artists in twentieth-century Jamaican art. The beginning of the pantheonization project can be traced back to Marriott's 1956 portrait bust of Marcus Garvey, whose supporters had repeatedly called for a public statue to memorialize him following his death in 1940. But it was only after Jamaica achieved universal

Fig. 2.2. Unveiling ceremony for the National Hero statue of Alexander Bustamante by Alvin Marriott (Jamaican, 1902–1992), Kingston, Jamaica, May 24, 1970

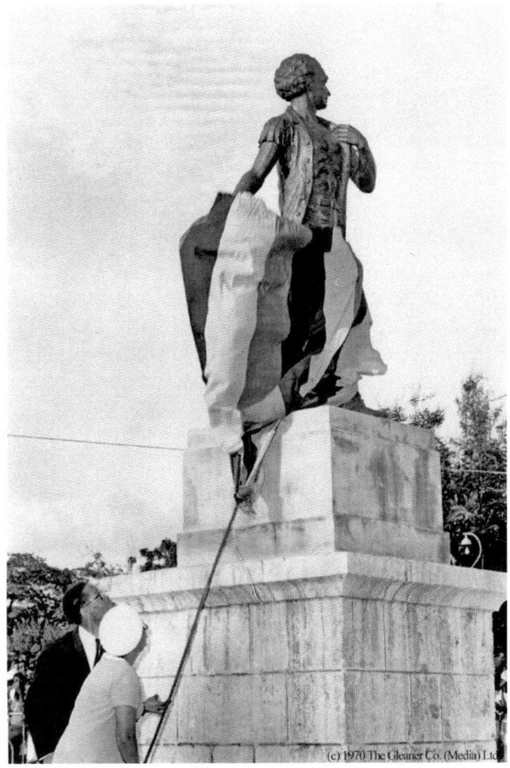

adult suffrage in 1944 and restarted the self-government process in 1953 that the funds were finally raised for a public bust. Marriott's Garvey bust shifted the regime of public sculpture in Jamaica by inserting a Black face into a landscape that had hitherto been dominated by statues of British personalities like Admiral George Rodney and Queen Victoria. As I have argued elsewhere, these colonial statues worked alongside other sites of knowledge and display to orient Jamaican historical subjectivity toward Britain and to shape the ways in which Jamaicans saw themselves as disciplined subjects of empire.[15] Marriott's bust was part of the process that propelled the self-government movement—nearly a hundred years after the Morant Bay Rebellion of 1865 and the British government's subsequent abolishment of Jamaica's colonial House of Assembly—which eventually took Jamaica into independence. During that time, definitions of art, culture, history, and leadership were being reimagined.[16]

Marriott's bust of Garvey was displayed in King George VI Memorial Park in the capital city of Kingston. The freestanding sculpture was eventually incorporated into the Monument to the Right Excellent Marcus Garvey, which included his mausoleum, designed in the shape of a black-bordered star by the town planner G. C. Hodges in 1964 (fig. 2.3). This monument officially initiated the National Heroes

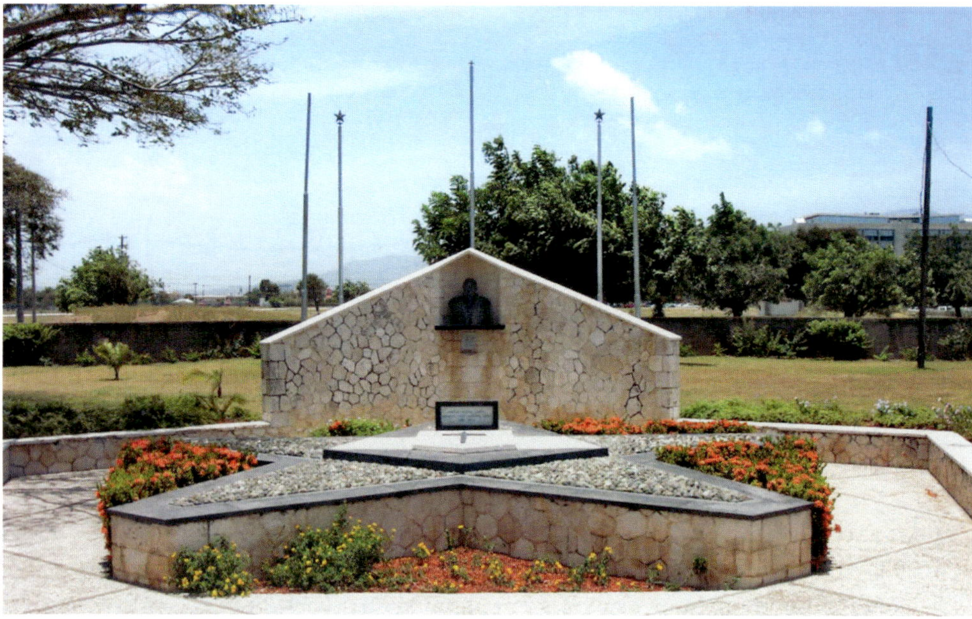

Fig. 2.3. Monument to the Right Excellent Marcus Garvey, designed by Graham C. Hodges (Jamaican), with a 1956 portrait bust by Alvin Marriott, National Heroes Park, Kingston, 1964

pantheon project. Its unveiling was the culmination of a series of lavish, state-planned commemorative events that involved the retrieval of Garvey's embalmed body from England, where he had died during World War II; an official public day of viewing his coffin; and his reburial in the public monument. Thereafter, other National Heroes were inducted into the pantheon. Although this cultural program was only formally voted on as parliamentary policy in 1968, the creation of the National Heroes pantheon and its subsequent annual commemoration in Heroes Week is one of the most significant and lasting cultural initiatives of the 1960s.

As the new, state-sponsored commemorative culture became more defined, figurative statues and other heroic images were created and positioned throughout Jamaica. Marriott would eventually create a full-length statue of Garvey in the mid-1970s, and King George VI Memorial Park was renamed National Heroes Park in 1973. The Shrine, a designated sacred area of National Heroes Park, was created to house memorials to the heroes. Monuments in The Shrine were developed with design features established by the Garvey monument. These included open, modernist architectural forms made from concrete as well as other locally harvested materials through which viewers could move and interact; the inclusion of portrait busts or abstract figurative imagery as reliefs; and centrally placed mausoleums of the heroes, who were born in the late-nineteenth and twentieth centuries. The monuments to the last two heroes to join the pantheon in the 1970s, Nanny of the Maroons and Sam Sharpe, were unveiled in The Shrine over twenty years later, in 1999.

These statues and memorials encouraged the reconstruction of new historical, political, and racial subjects and in a mode of representation that was in some measure different from that of colonial statues. The heroes were meant to serve the newly revised governing structure and encourage citizens to identify with these images of power.[17] The use of early sepulchral monument aesthetics, along with the well-orchestrated retrieval and reinterment of Garvey's body, indicated how the managing of death was to become an important aspect of governance.[18] Of course, Jamaica's pantheon project was vexed for various reasons. And, as some of the heroes were involved in violent conflict with the slave regime and plantocracy, anxieties surfaced over the role and acceptability of violence in processes of social transformation. On the occasion of the unveiling of a monument, speeches and newspaper articles would make a distinction between the necessary violence of the past and the unacceptable violence in the new nation.[19] This anxiety must also be contextualized amid the contemporaneous radicalization of Black people both within and outside of Jamaica around issues of Black civil rights and decolonization, along with fears provoked by the rebellious image of Rastafari.

The monument-building impulse of the governments of the 1960s and '70s grew in tandem with and supported a new heroic iconography in Jamaican art. While sculptors such as Edna Manley, Christopher González, and Alvin Marriott received government commissions to create public statues and sculptures in honor of the National Heroes, other artists such as Mallica "Kapo" Reynolds and Barrington Watson painted and sculpted portraits and episodes in Jamaica's history that centered on the heroes. Watson, for instance, would return to the subject of the 1865 Morant Bay Rebellion in a number of his history paintings.[20] His 1964 interpretation, *The Morant Bay Rebellion*, emphasizes the frenzied violence of the peasant rebellion with bloodied and slain bodies overlapping each other as weapons are poised for attack (fig. 2.4). Similarly, *The Hanging of George William Gordon* (1968, private collection) — a subject Watson had also painted in 1964 — is a sentimental representation of mourning and sacrifice. The body of Gordon, a politician, still hanging from the gallows where he has just been executed by the colonial army, is supported by his faithful followers, who must remove him for a proper burial. Watson's *Hanging of George William Gordon* captures this postcolonial process of establishing national reverence and loyalty as central to the formation of our communal "ancestral" heroes. The *Morant Bay Rebellion* painting, on the other hand, visualizes the violence upon which their heroism was based, a violence whose meaning and value in the present was being publicly discussed.

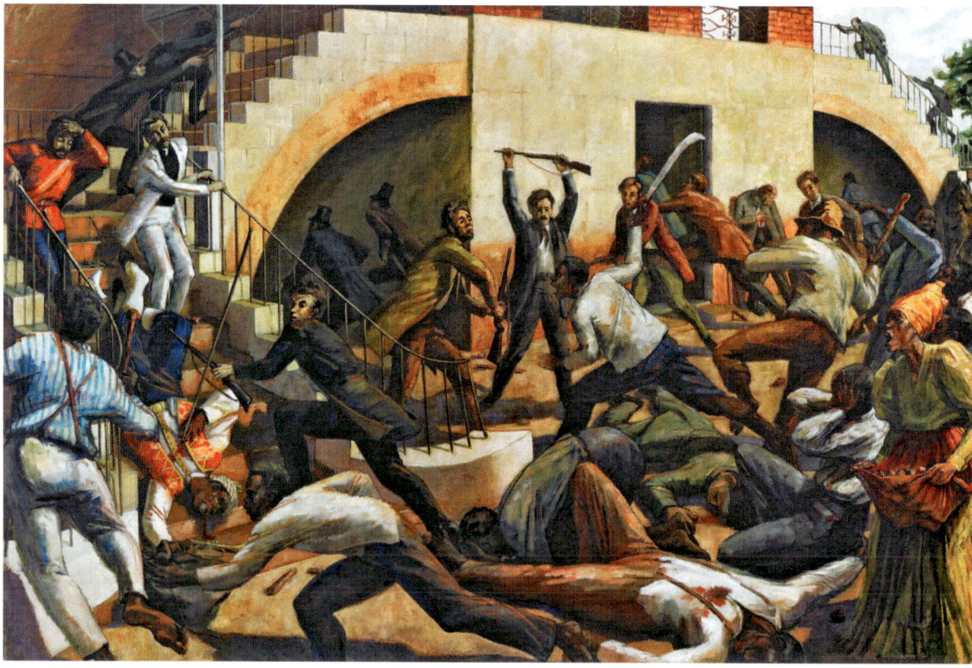

Fig. 2.4. Barrington Watson (Jamaican, 1931–2016), *The Morant Bay Rebellion*, 1964. Oil on canvas, 72 × 96 in. (183 × 244 cm). National Collection, Kingston

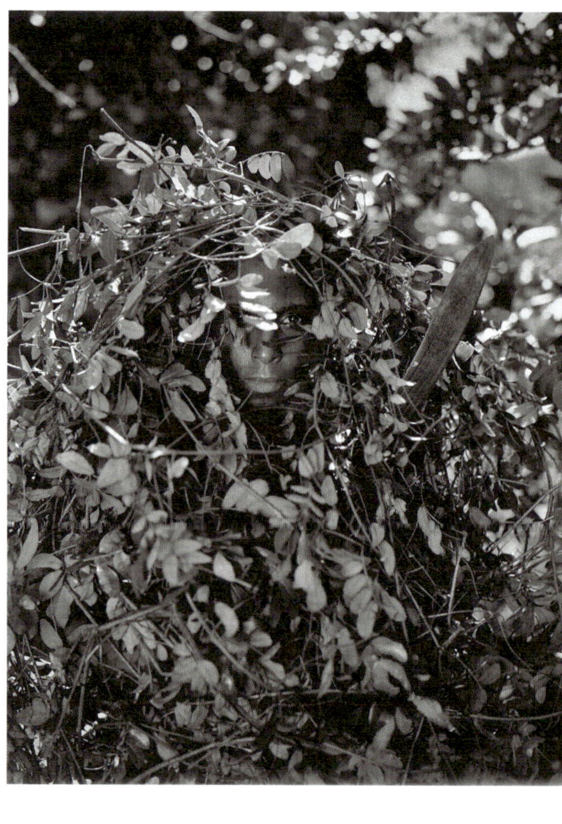

Fig. 2.5. Renee Cox (Jamaican American, b. 1960), *Ambush*, 2004, from the series *Queen Nanny of the Maroons*. Inkjet print, dimensions variable. Collection of the artist

Fig. 2.6. Michael Thompson (Jamaican, 1958–2016), ***Nanny of the Maroons, Jamaican Hero and Freedom Fighter***, 2009. Digital print, dimensions variable. Collection of the artist's estate

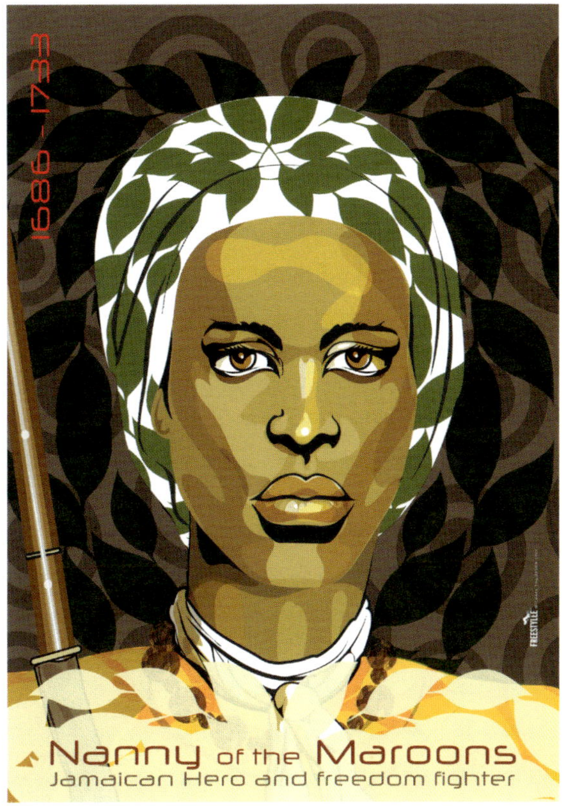

The heroic image complex of public statues, memorials, paintings, and sculptures in the immediate decades after independence would influence later artists such as Renee Cox, who in her *Queen Nanny of the Maroons* series (fig. 2.5) created monumental photographic self-portraits as Nanny in different settings and inhabiting different characters, including a river goddess, a defiant maid, and a guerrilla warrior. This series connects to her earlier series of color photographs in which she represented herself as a superhero, Raje. In *Liberation of Aunt Jemima and Uncle Ben* (1998), Cox-as-Raje appeared poised to rescue African Americans from the history of stereotypical graphic conventions exemplified by the Uncle Ben and Aunt Jemima characters on American package designs and in advertising campaigns. Both series exemplify how the heroic icon, presented in the form of the self-portrait, offers Caribbean artists a mode of exploring personal and historical storytelling and subjectivity—even as it also challenges the status and value of heroizing.

Post-independence heroic imagery also influenced Michael Thompson's vibrant and modern-looking portraits of the heroes. He created two digital posters of Nanny: *Nanny of the Maroons, Jamaican Hero and Freedom Fighter* (fig. 2.6) and *Queen Nanny, African-Jamaican Freedom Fighter*. Thompson features his subject surrounded by foliage to evoke camouflage and remind us of how the Maroons were considered fierce guerrilla fighters. In *Nanny of the Maroons*, the suggestion of a rifle in the foreground emphasizes her warrior or military status. Nanny's feats as a leader are often mythologized, but Thompson modernizes and glamorizes her appearance in these portraits. When Nanny entered the pantheon of heroes in the mid-1970s, there were no recorded images of her; consequently, the government sponsored a competition to create a representational image. A portrait of a head-wrapped Nanny completed in pen and ink by the art student Claude Gayle was chosen for dissemination and, eventually, a modified version would appear on the five-hundred-dollar banknote. Thompson's and Cox's works developed from this process of imaginative reembodiment. A full-length statue of Nanny, the only female hero in the pantheon, was never commissioned. Therefore, Thompson's double emphasis on Nanny in his series, like Cox's *Queen Nanny* series, highlights the role of women in Jamaica's liberation struggles while drawing our attention to the limitations of Jamaica's postcolonial public history project. Their two-dimensional works alert us to how rarely the sculpted female body has served as a site of historical recovery and cultural and political affirmation.[21]

Thompson, who died suddenly a few years after creating his heroes portraits, was an enthusiast of Jamaican popular culture, particularly reggae music; he cofounded the International Reggae Poster Contest. Consequently, his icon images also included portraits of reggae stars and personalities related to Rastafari, such as Haile Selassie. The Rastafari pan-African philosophy of reggae stars in the 1960s and '70s was deemed suspect by some nationalists concerned about Black radicalization. According to Rex Nettleford, there was anxiety around Rastafari's internationalism, particularly its Africa-focused cultural rhetoric and its interest in repatriation, which might curtail believers' involvement in the politics and processes of nation building.[22] Nevertheless, in the body of heroic portraiture in Jamaican art, reggae artists and pan-Africanist imagery exist side-by-side with that of National Heroes.

Like Thompson's work, the street artist Michael Robinson's diverse heroic icon paintings depict both popular and official heroes. He creates portraits of National Heroes in local schools in and near the working-class community of Denham Town in Downtown Kingston and on walls in the neighborhood. His work also features reggae artists and celebrities, such as cricketers and other athletes who have made an impression on the international scene, as well as portraits of dons (fig. 2.7). In Jamaica, dons are community leaders who are often involved in criminal activities ranging from extortion to drug trafficking; historically, dons have also maintained close ties to politicians. The inclusion of dons in Robinson's body of heroic portraits demonstrates the intersection of different types of heroic icon images within Jamaican (public) art and illustrates the complex nature of civic leadership and sovereignty in Jamaica today.

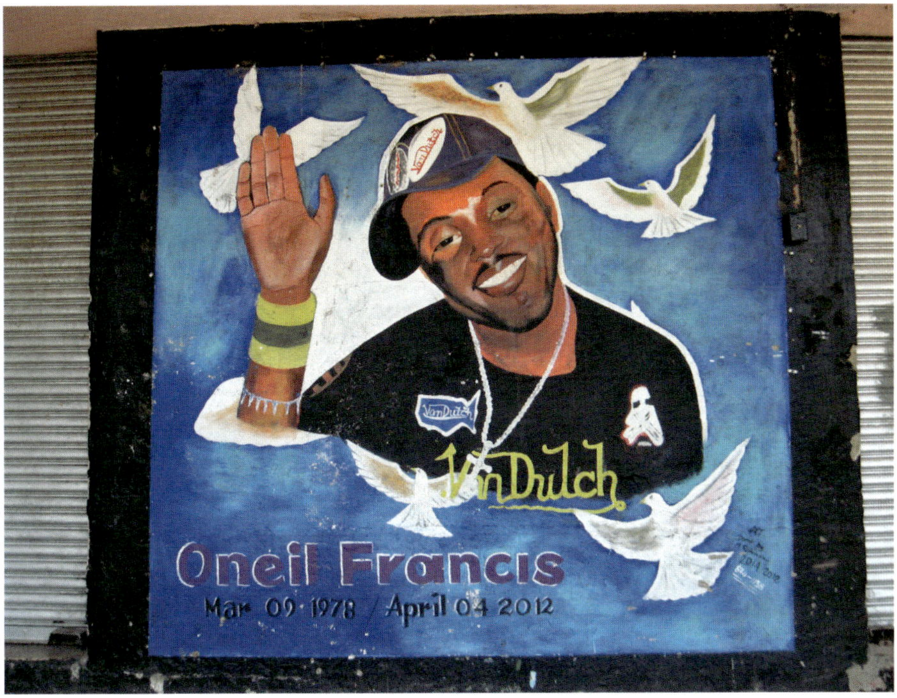

Fig. 2.7. Michael Robinson (Jamaican, b. 1959), *Oneil Francis*, 2012. Wall mural, exterior-grade wall paint. Kingston, Jamaica

Rivke Jaffe argues that dons, like Dudus in Tivoli, take on a range of governmental functions and signal a "hybrid state formation" in Jamaica. Jaffe writes about how "multiple governmental actors – in this case, criminal organizations, politicians, police, and bureaucrats – are entangled in a relationship of collusion and divestment, sharing control over urban spaces and populations."[23] This has an effect on how we understand the dimensions of state authority and the ways in which citizenship is experienced in Jamaica. Indeed, Jaffe notes that dons used strategies of community engagement comparable to those used by political parties, including sponsoring street dances. Before the 2010 state incursion, which I mentioned earlier in this chapter, the community of Tivoli Gardens hosted the popular weekly Passa Passa street dance, which was associated with Coke for several years. This brought income into the community, since middle-class partygoers and foreign tourists understood it to be a safe environment under Coke's organization. Like the National Heroes program, the memorials, and the annual Heroes Day recognition, icon paintings of dons and gang-sponsored events became an important aspect of Jamaica's commemorative universe – sometimes shaping communal values and loyalties away from the state and toward the don and the gang. Interestingly, they also tell us how the development of the Jamaican state was complicated by its connections with the criminal hero. Indeed, since the Tivoli incursion, there have been campaigns to paint over the images of dons on public walls.

ART AFTER HISTORY

Thompson, who considered himself a creative activist and was committed to social design, believed that art could impact how we think about pressing social issues. In his 2010 *Tivoli* poster series, which he designed days after the incursion, he featured anxious and terrified faces with tears running from their eyes, bodies with bullet holes or with guns pointed at them, and texts calling for investigation. As he wrote in an emailed statement to the National Museum, Jamaica:

> It was clear to me that waging a military offensive on a civilian community with hundreds of women and children inside was an absurd and crazy idea. . . . It represents grossly an unconstitutional and immoral act. What kind of democracy would attack its own citizens with a military operation? Were the people of Tivoli Gardens protected by the Jamaican constitution? Why was it necessary to trample their human rights? I was compelled to do something to draw attention to the terrifying injustice and breach of human rights that was clearly taking shape there.[24]

His *I Am Tivoli* poster from the series is a portrait of a frightened little girl who looks up at the viewer anxiously; surrounding her are stylized chrysanthemums, a symbol of adversity, grief, and mourning (fig. 2.8). The text above her head, "I am Tivoli," entreats us to identify with her and her fear. The idea of identification with the subject was important for the series because the artworks were partly inspired by the language of social media. According to Thompson, "It was clear that a terrible wrong had been unleashed and the debate on social media was frighteningly leaning to the side of the state. . . . I wanted to draw attention to the fact that humans lived in Tivoli Gardens, not cockroaches."[25] The text on his poster was therefore a deliberate strategy to humanize the victims of the incursion. He also put a sympathetic face to the name Tivoli. As an early political garrison, the community has a legendary significance in Jamaica's postcolonial history. It is notorious for the power its dons wielded and the collusion of elected officials in securing their authority. Such intimacy ensured that the community consistently voted en masse for the Jamaica Labour Party, despite a lack of economic development and repeated violent conflicts between residents and state security forces.[26] By encouraging viewers in Jamaica to identify with the poster's fearful child, Thompson suggests that the experience of the people in Tivoli could be that of any citizen: You could be the next Tivoli and be violated by the state.

Fig. 2.8. Michael Thompson, *I Am Tivoli*, 2010. Digital print, dimensions variable. Collection of the artist's estate

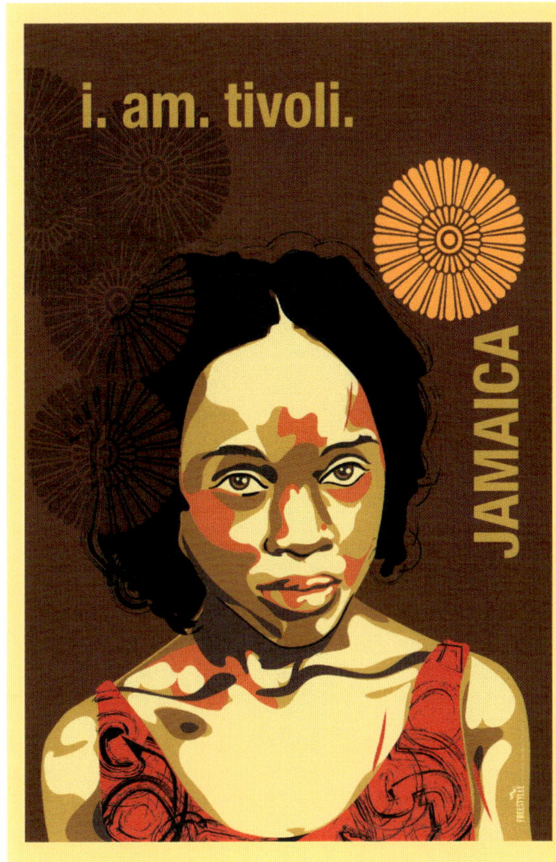

Thompson's *I Am Tivoli* prints developed into explicit images featuring the Jamaican constabulary force. One poster, titled *Stop Police Corruption and Violence in Jamaica* (2010), is a portrait of a rather ominous-looking police officer with his eyes covered by dark sunglasses—a figure likened to the controversial former Senior Superintendent of Police Reneto Adam, who wore gold-framed sunglasses (fig. 2.9). The figure is framed by prison bars in the foreground, and the familiar red stripe in the uniform of the Jamaican police is transformed into thick red bars.

These prints remind us of other artworks that address issues of accountability and police brutality in Jamaica, including Ebony G. Patterson's mixed-media work *The Of 72 Project* (2012). Patterson printed and embellished seventy-two photographs on bandanas, inspired by the families involved in the Tivoli incursion who retrieved the bodies of the disappeared; the artist also intended to give visibility to the youths whose names, images, and circumstances of death are still denied to the public. Another Jamaican contemporary artwork on the topic of state violence is Stanford Watson's painting *Malnourished Dog for an Independent State* (1996, National

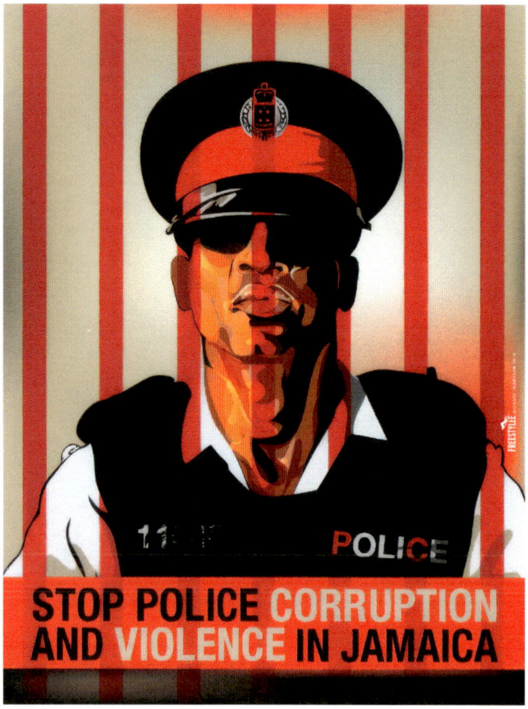

Fig. 2.9. Michael Thompson, *Stop Police Corruption and Violence in Jamaica*, 2010. Digital print, dimensions variable. Collection of the artist's estate

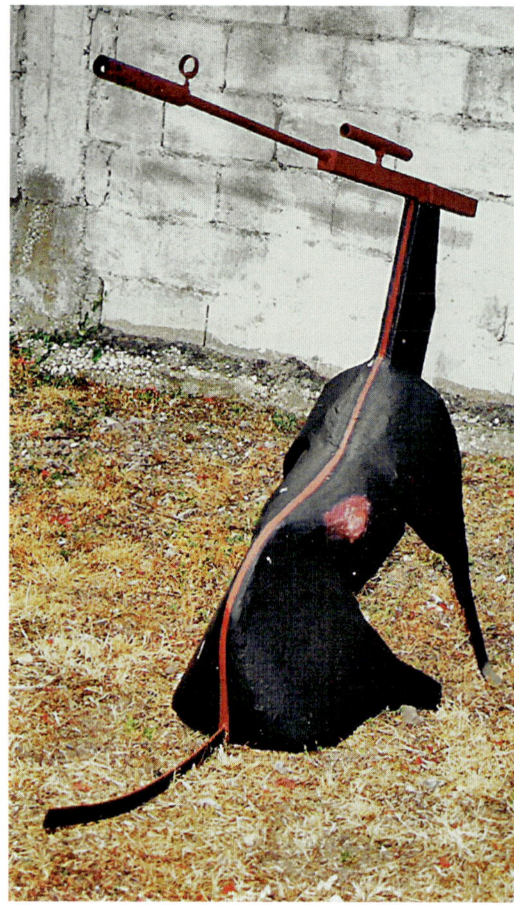

Fig. 2.10. Christopher Irons (Jamaican, b. 1973), *Braeton Brutality*, 2001. Mixed media with metal and wood, dimensions variable. Annie Paul Collection

Gallery of Jamaica)—a triptych of animal-skeleton images inspired by the artist witnessing a police officer shooting a dog that was barking at him. The artist was so profoundly moved by the incident that the dissected dog became a motif in his paintings, sometimes of the same name, to reflect on the "perception of freedom." He wrote, "The image of the dog appeared in my paintings somewhere around 1988 after an incident where a police officer shot a little dog no taller than maybe around 8 inches. Nothing could be done for that dog. . . . Imagine the score of young men and people generally without the means to defend themselves who on a daily basis is gunned down by the police. Unfortunately this is the community we have crafted."[27]

Braeton Brutality (fig. 2.10), Christopher Irons's 2001 sculpture composed of found-metal parts, was inspired by another example of spectacular police violence in postcolonial Jamaica, one that occurred ten years before the Tivoli incursion. In March 2001, the police, led by Reneto Adams, raided a house in the community of Braeton and killed seven young men between the ages of fourteen and twenty under questionable circumstances. Irons's work makes reference to the police force through the red stripe—echoing their uniform—that runs along the spine of a sickly and potentially violent dog whose body appears bruised, while its mouth is shaped into a rifle. According to Amnesty International, 133 people were killed by the Jamaican police in 2002, the year following the Braeton Seven incident. Amnesty alleged that many of the killings appeared to be extrajudicial and, citing the Braeton case and others, noted that such executions—as well as unlawful detentions, arrests, and police mistreatment—often occur with impunity.[28] Irons developed *Braeton Brutality* through reflecting on our collective responsibility to young men and on the need for state accountability. As he noted, "The consequence of an action or behavior is never a done deal."[29] For the artist, the problem with extrajudicial violence by the state, as with the killing of the "Braeton Seven," is that it does not allow for personal or social redemption for its citizens.

Redemption is a powerful metaphor in the Black diasporic experience, but Jamaica's high crime rates have led some people to believe that there can be no redemption for "criminals." The same Amnesty International report noted that another 1,045 people were murdered in Jamaica in 2002, including sixteen police officers who seemed to have been targeted because of their jobs.[30] The anxiety around violence in Jamaica means that some people support the heavy hand of the state. This has resulted in the formation of special crime-fighting units within the police force, such as the one Adams led. Aggressive officers like Adams have even been celebrated as folk heroes. Nonetheless, while the police have occasionally appeared in celebratory neighborhood wall paintings, the heroic status of the police is rarely endorsed in contemporary art—as Irons's and Thompson's artworks suggest.

Like Thompson, Camille Chedda has used portraiture to recognize the many people who have died violently or recklessly at the hands of state authorities,

Fig. 2.11. Camille Chedda (Jamaican, b. 1985), *Wholesale Degradables*, 2014–15. Acrylic on disposable plastic bags, dimensions variable. Collection of the artist

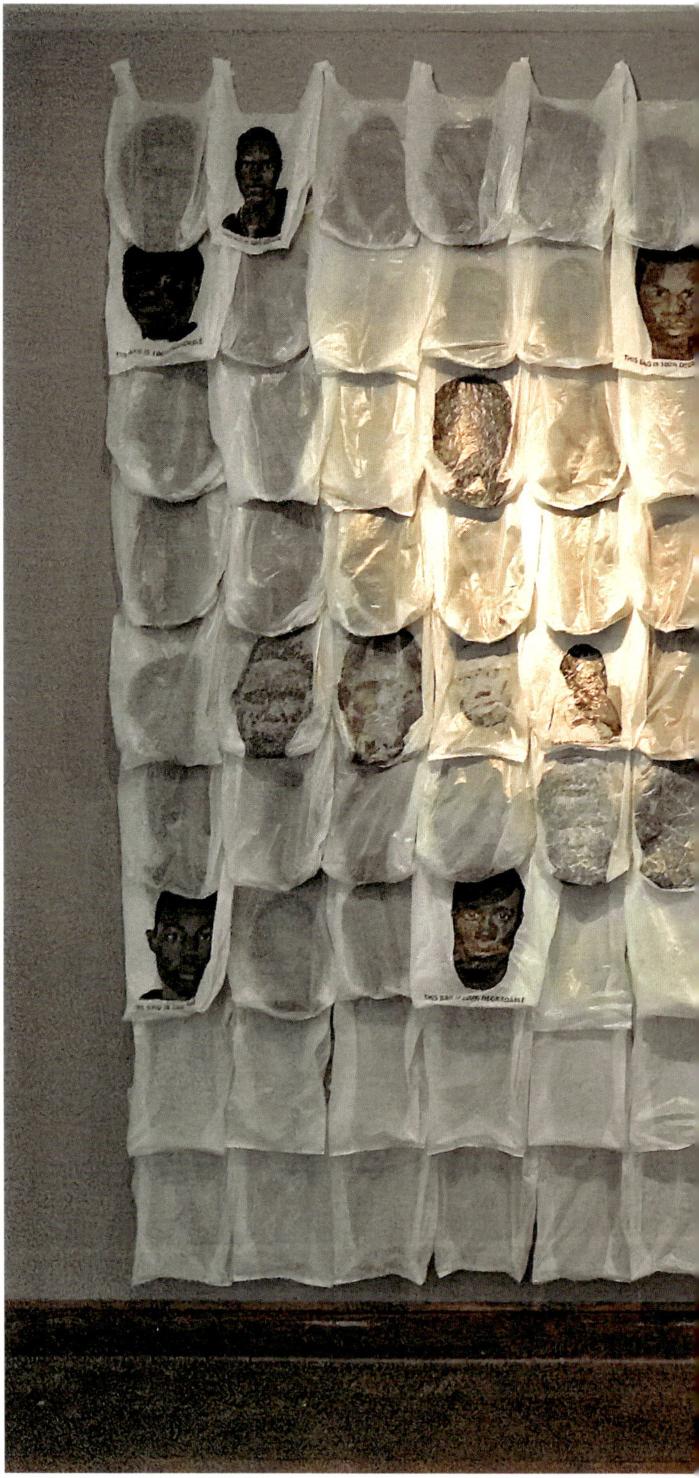

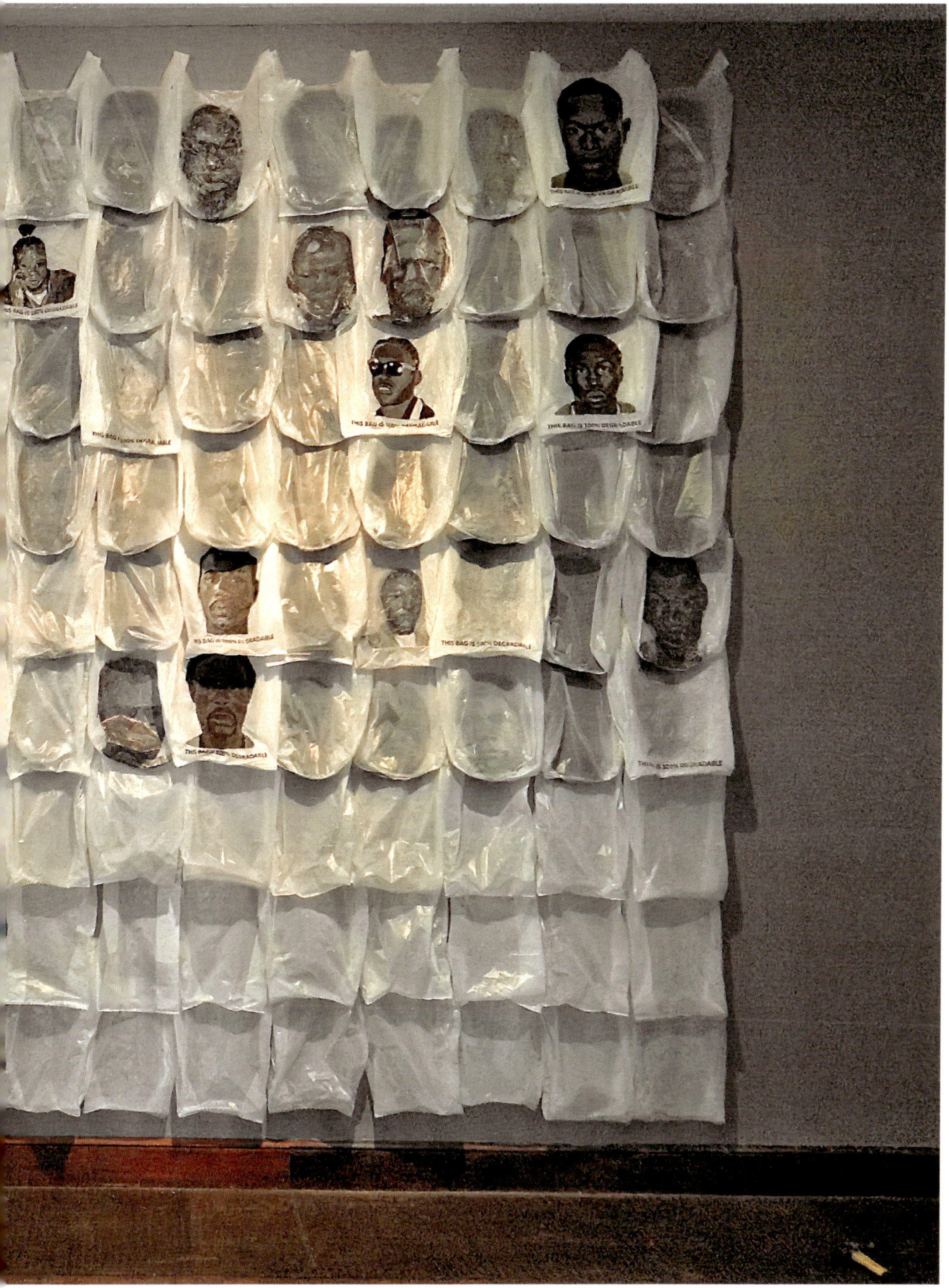

providing a counternarrative to the image of police as folk heroes. In the installations *Wholesale Degradables* (fig. 2.11) and *Sketch for Exchange Value* (2014), the artist considers the vulnerability of Black bodies and the statistics on extrajudicial police killings in Jamaica in relation to a global history of violent policing of Black people. *Wholesale Degradables* is a wall installation of rows of white plastic bags that feature acrylic portraits of men and women who died between 2014 and 2015 in extrajudicial killings in Jamaica. The black-and-white portraits are painted on bags that state this bag is 100% degradable. Chedda also emphasized the precarity and expendability of Black bodies in *Sketch for Exchange Value*, in which the artist presented layers of food crates filled with transparent plastic bags on which she had drawn faces in black marker. Chedda initially filled the bags with air, but over time they would deflate, simulating an experience of vulnerability. Both artworks include a portrait of the National Hero Paul Bogle, who was hanged by the colonial government. When the artist could not find a photograph of an individual killed in Jamaica, she substituted their portrait with one of a historical figure, such as Bogle or a Herero in Namibia killed by German authorities in its Herero-Nama genocidal campaign of 1904–8. In *Wholesale*, these historical portraits were placed inside the bags, which hampered their visibility and lent the installation a muted and solemn mood. Past and present, local and global are linked in Chedda's powerful installations.

Similar to Chedda, Phillip Thomas employed images of National Heroes in a series of paintings and installations that considers the idea of the heroic state leader and includes portraits with figures in military uniform. The subjects of his 2015 diptych *General Bustamante* and *General Manley* (figs. 2.12, 2.13) are decorated with military pins, ribbons, and medals, while repeating stars form the background of each work. The artist has also given both heroes a military title, General, that they did not hold in real life, but which in Jamaican colloquial expression refers to their importance and their status as fighters. Given the history of violence between the political parties these men founded, Thomas seems to be linking contemporary experiences of Jamaica's state militarization and state-sponsored violence to the mid-twentieth-century partisan political activities of these National Heroes.[31]

On closer inspection, however, the metal pins affixed to the canvas on the so-called generals' uniforms, such as the image of Aunt Jemima and a "Smile Jamaica" tourist pin featuring a dancing Rasta figure, undercut the power suggested by the paintings' heraldry. The history of a global discourse that undermines Black leadership and heroism through the comic and exaggerated stereotypical icons that feed the advertising and tourism industries literally weighs on the figures. The stereotypical pins in Thomas's artworks are also symbols of Black masquerade—smiling happily while serving the tourist, or the madam or sir of the house. These paintings of Jamaican leaders ask: What does Black leadership mean in the context of a continued history of state violence? What does Black leadership mean as it continues

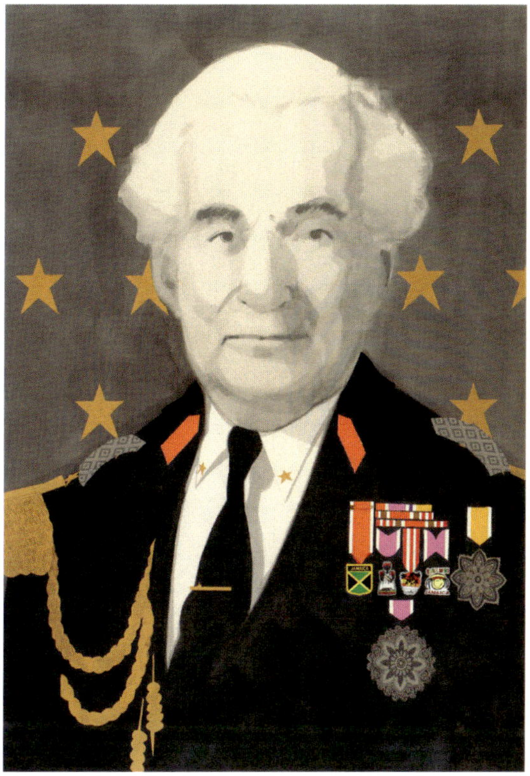

Fig. 2.12. Phillip Thomas (Jamaican, b. 1980), *General Bustamante*, 2015. Oil on canvas, 67 ¾ × 47 ¼ in. (172.1 × 120 cm). Collection of the artist

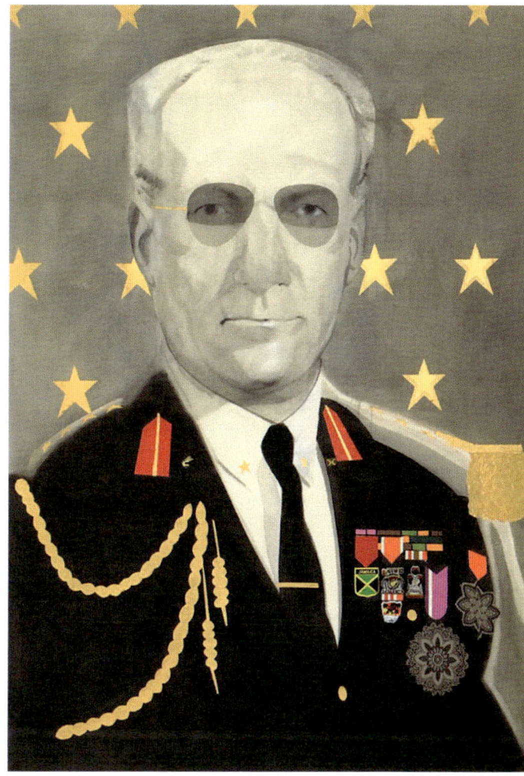

Fig. 2.13. Phillip Thomas, *General Manley*, 2015. Oil and mixed media on canvas, 69 × 47 ½ in. (175.3 × 120.7 cm). Collection of the artist

to face visual and discursive racialized violence? How do we articulate Black leadership in what Samir Puri describes as "the shadows of empire"?[32]

The themes of power and sovereignty are evident in many of Thomas's stylized self-portraits or digitally collaged figures in militaristic dress. Although he has said that he related to certain aspects of Jamaican militarism (he was in the cadets as a child and later spent time with soldiers),[33] his paintings reflect on the bizarre and dangerous aspects of power and on the limits of sovereignty in Caribbean nations. His approach to the bodies of his subjects varies, not least through the formal strategy of darkening the skin so that his mysterious figures at times appear as black silhouettes. This strategy illustrates the influence of the American artist Kerry James Marshall's epic insistence on Blackness in painting, combined with the Cuban artist Belkis Ayón's otherworldly Blackness. In other figure paintings by Thomas, which revel in the carnivalesque dimensions of leadership, certain bodily features (heads, arms) are missing altogether, and the artist's collages contain clear nods to the grotesque.

By the end of the twentieth century, as the scholar Deborah Thomas notes, politicians and other cultural actors in Jamaica were bemoaning the loss of history and calling for its revitalization.[34] In some respects, Chedda's and Phillip Thomas's works can be considered afterimages of the period of pantheonization and its contribution to the construction of ideals of national belonging, national history, and the celebration of heroic Black and Brown leadership. These artists came to prominence in the twenty-first century, witnessed episodes of spectacular state violence in Jamaica and elsewhere, and experienced the vulnerability of Jamaica's sovereignty vis-à-vis other states such as the United States and China. As much as Chedda's and Thomas's artworks are deeply critical of Jamaican state authority and violence, they also draw connections to global issues of racialized violations. Their layered artworks allow us to meditate on Deborah Thomas's characterization of violence in Jamaican society as both historical and transnational, while opening the conversation about claiming and asserting Black (heroic) authority in social interactions, global politics, and artistic practice.

BLACK HEROISM AND THE NEW MONUMENTAL IMPULSE

Both Chedda and Thomas were trained by the artist Omari Ra, who throughout his career has painted what he calls "self-referential" portraits. These large-scale, stylized self-portraits on textiles and other materials, such as tarps, merge his image with that of his male or female sitters, creating a universal heroic figure that is unambiguously Black. The portraits reference specific Caribbean historical heroes, such as the seventeenth-century Jamaican folk figures of Tacky and Jack Mansong, or more generally suggest a rebellious male leader. Ra's tendency toward monumental scale (some of his paintings cannot fit in normal-size rooms) and his preference for materials such as brightly hued, fluorescent fabrics are self-conscious visual strategies to, as he asserts, "give history to public notice . . . [to] expand and project onto the world a collective racial identity."[35] In a series of interviews I conducted with the artist, he argued that such images are important because they "feed into the way we see ourselves." The insistent or demanding presence of the hero brings me back to Ehlers and Belle's sculpture of Mary Thomas in Denmark, Cooke-John's sculpture of Harriet Tubman in the United States, the pantheonization of National Heroes in Jamaica in the 1960s and '70s, and to the convention of the heroic statue more broadly. But it is important to note that Ra's images reflect his own political project to remind us of the history of Black (political) betrayal and the legacy of and continued need for Black resistance.

To return to the topic of sculpture, one of Omari Ra's recent series, exhibited amid the global conversation on colonial and US Civil War monuments, includes humorous references to the tradition of the monumental statue. His sculptures feature two or three layers of single wooden blocks that form plinths for plastic dinosaurs. As in some African nkisi statuettes, nails protrude from some of the blocks. In *Who Disappeared the Tallawahsaurus 2* (figs. 2.14, 2.15), the painted plinths feature landscape vistas inspired by the style of eighteenth- and early nineteenth-century picturesque images of Jamaican plantation landscapes, an image of the current prime minister's controversial multimillion-dollar private house, and a variation of the Jamaican coat of arms, parts of which the artist obscures. Drawing from multiple iconographies and artistic traditions, these sculptures represent our complex historical formation—including acts of manipulation and expressions of power—and critique the ways the colonial past continues to affect how we think of ourselves and interact in the world. According to Ra, the potency of the past in the present challenges our ability "to ensure our survival." He states that "if we don't reevaluate our criteria for living, we will walk the way of the dinosaur."

In the *Tallawahsaurus* series, Ra replaced the native Taíno figures on Jamaica's coat of arms with Black subjects whose ankles display broken shackles (fig. 2.14). The female figure holds a baby in her arm instead of a basket brimming with local food, and the artist has replaced the male figure's bow and arrow with a machete. This fearsome blade has become a significant emblem in twentieth-century Caribbean art and one essential to a number of statues of rebel figures throughout the region, including Edna Manley's 1965 statue of the National Hero Paul Bogle. However, in *Who Disappeared the Tallawahsaurus 2*, the harried application of a wash of gray paint over the image hides his weapon. For Ra, it was important to show the figure appearing vulnerable and unable to defend himself or hunt for food. The work draws our attention to the precarity of African Jamaican political subjectivity. Moreover, in Ra's version of the coat of arms, the Jamaican motto "Out of Many, One People" is rewritten as "Out of One, Many People." His textual play

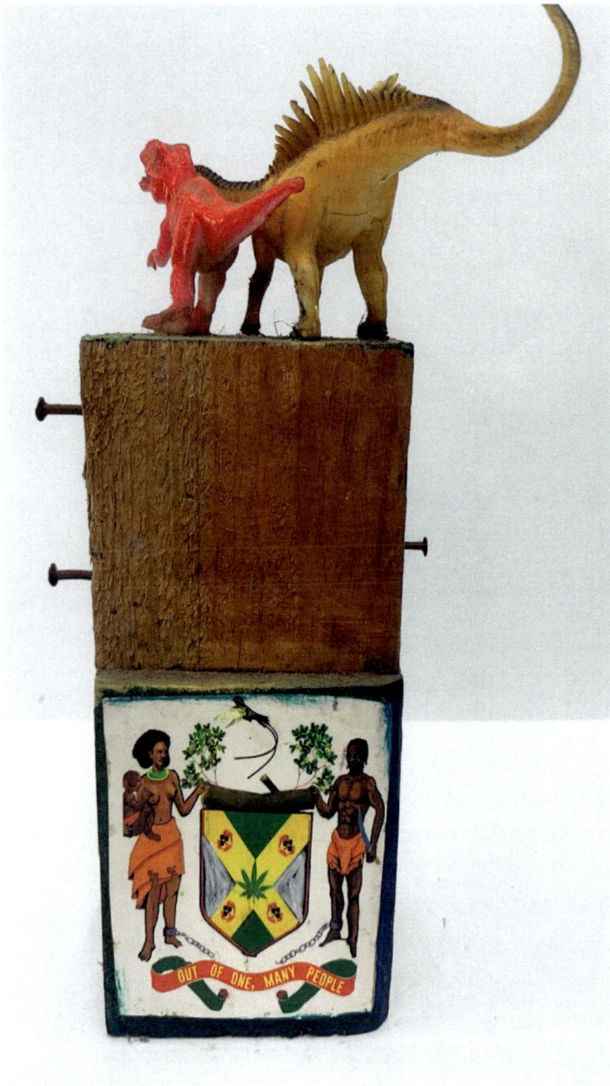

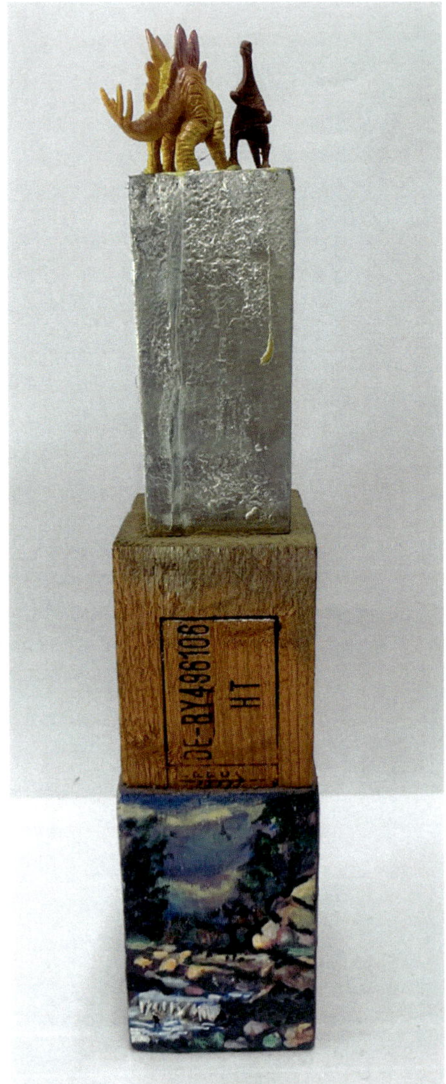

Figs. 2.14, 2.15. Omari Ra (Jamaican, b. 1960), *Who Disappeared the Tallawahsaurus 2*, 2021. Mixed media, dimensions variable. Collection of the artist

challenges the multicultural ethos of the 1960s governing elite exemplified by the national motto — an ethos that, while laudable in its symbolic recognition of various cultures, races, and ethnicities in Jamaica, has come under scrutiny for obfuscating social disparities.

The title *Who Disappeared the Tallawahsaurus 2* refers to the Jamaican phrase "likkle but wi tallawah," or "little but we are also strong." For Ra, dinosaurs are a metaphor for the Jamaican construction of identity, or the "myth," he calls it, of its strength. They also create a tension between the "preservation of human dignity" and the possibility of collective ruin or loss. According to the artist, our existence in Jamaica is so precarious that it would be easy to slip into ruin. I want to think about the idea of anticipation in these sculptures. If monuments are spectacles of presence — of being there — I want to think about what it means to use this Mesozoic symbol of awesome presence and power and, paradoxically, also of loss, extinction, and vulnerability. Ra describes his series as "a monument done in anticipation of our destruction"; it offers a critique of, or a cautionary note about, certain ways of monumentalizing. The use of plastic dinosaurs acts as a counterbalance — in size, weight, material, and subject — to works like Ehlers and Belle's bronze sculpture *I Am Queen Mary*. But Ra has not completely shunned the heroic statue. Instead, his formal strategy of assemblage, his collage aesthetic, and his humor offer ways to reconsider and develop the monumental form in the Caribbean.

I want to end here by emphasizing the entangled histories of Jamaican visual practice around the subject of heroism, leadership, and violence, and to open up a conversation on what this may mean in terms of the monumental impulse in Caribbean contemporary sculptural practice. The postcolonial Jamaican experience has taught us that monumental forms are important modes of psychosocial redress and that they expand notions of historicity and history while also being deeply implicated in the process of governing and reordering social and political power and violence. What Ra and other contemporary Jamaican artists suggest, in this moment of global conversation on the recovery and reconstitution of the Black heroic body in monumental form, is that recovery must also be accompanied by a critical and sustained reflection on Black power and accountability. As monumental public sculpture is mobilized to instantiate new social and political imaginings, Jamaican and Caribbean art beckons us to contemplate the nature of our investment in this tradition. Monuments, Ra argues, "are ideas of knowing and preserving — glorifying a big worldview." His recent sculptures challenge us — the Black diaspora — to consider that worldview, to ask what we want to project onto the world, and to be mindful of how our ideas, values, aspirations, and practices may have been formed.

NOTES

1. For more on the mid-century politics of Guyana, see Stephen Rabe, *U.S. Intervention in British Guiana: A Cold War Story* (University of North Carolina Press, 2005).

2. "Restoration," *Daily Gleaner*, September 24, 1990. For recent reports on the vandalism of the statue, see "Statue of Queen Victoria Defaced," *NewsRoom*, June 4, 2018, https://newsroom.gy/2018/06/04/statue-of-queen-victoria-defaced/; and "Queen Victoria Statue Vandal Faces 12 Months Jail," *Guyana Times Online*, June 6, 2018, https://guyanatimesgy.com/queen-victoria-statue-vandal-faces-12-months-jail/.

3. For a discussion of Guyana's colonial architecture in Locke's series *Beyond the Sea Wall*, see Sasha Dees, "Hew Locke: 'We Are Only a Part of a Great Nameless Procession,'" *arcthemagazine*, November 18, 2014, online publication, no longer available. See also Martina Droth and Allie Biswas, eds., *Hew Locke: Passages* (Yale Center for British Art / Yale University Press, 2025).

4. Tim Adams, "Hew Locke: 'If I Wasn't an Artist, I'd Be a Historian,'" *Guardian* (UK), November 22, 2015, https://www.theguardian.com/artanddesign/2015/nov/22/hew-locke-artist-interview-artist-and-empire-tate-britain.

5. Jon Wood, "Photography, Painting, and Impossible Sculpture: Hew Locke's Natives and Colonials: Jon Woods in Conversation with Hew Locke," *Sculpture Journal* 15, no. 2 (December 2006): 282–86.

6. The statue of Edward Colston (1636–1721) in the city of Bristol had previously been the subject of one of Locke's "impossible proposals." His *Restoration* series of 2006 featured embellished photographs of statues of figures involved in the imperial project, including Colston. In the seventeenth and eighteenth centuries, Bristol was a major maritime center in the transatlantic slave trade, and Colston, a local businessman and politician, derived his wealth and power from slave trading. He was a member and deputy governor of the Royal African Company, the English trading company that held a monopoly along the west coast of Africa. Colston was commemorated for his philanthropic work in Bristol with the 1895 bronze statue in the city center, and his name became attached to many public buildings, institutions, social and sports clubs, and organizations. However, in the twentieth century, he and the statue increasingly became controversial in Britain's public history. By the turn of the twenty-first century, scholars and activists called for the statue's removal or the addition of contextual information to acknowledge Colston's role in the slave trade. Locke's photograph of the statue, affixed with cowrie shells, jewelry, medallions, and replicas of skulls and slave ships, drew attention to Colston's profile and the source of his prestige, Britain's colonial legacy, and the city's history. In the story of the Colston statue and the battle over memory, meaning, and heritage in Britain, Locke's photograph was an important rising action leading to demonstrators toppling the statue and dumping it in the city harbor on June 7, 2020.

7. Elizabeth Fullerton, "Mindful Vandalism: A Conversation with Hew Locke," *Sculpture Magazine*, September 29, 2020; and Dan Hicks, "Hew Locke Challenges Empire in Birmingham," *Hyperallergic*, June 17, 2022, https://hyperallergic.com/741417/hew-locke-challenges-empire-in-birmingham/.

8. See Petrina Dacres, "'Keeping Alive Before the People's Eyes This Great Event': Kingston's Queen Victoria Monument," in *Victorian Jamaica*, ed. Tim Barringer and Wayne Modest (Duke University Press, 2018); Jenny Powell, "The Dissemination of Commemorative Statues of Queen Victoria," in *Modern British Sculpture*, ed. Penelope Curtis and Keith Williams (Royal Academy of Arts, 2011); and Geoff Archer, *Public Sculpture in Britain: A History* (Frontier, 2013), 25–56.

9. Frederick Brock, *Thomas Brock: Forgotten Sculptor of the Victoria Memorial*, ed. John Sankey (Ian Thompson / Author House, 2012).

10. In 2020, the Danish government granted permission for the permanent installation of the *I Am Queen Mary* sculpture in Copenhagen. At the time of this writing, the international fundraising effort for this endeavor is still ongoing. For more on the statue and the fundraising effort, see the public art project's website, https://www.iamqueenmary.com/.

11. Afterimages are lingering visual impressions that remain in our vision after the images have been removed. Our eyes' light-detecting cells keep responding briefly even after we have looked away or the image is gone. Metaphorically, they represent traces or sensations of past experiences that persist in the mind shaping how we perceive and understand the present. See, for instance, Kelann Currie-Williams, "Afterimages and the Synaesthesia of Photography," *Philosophy of Photography* 12, nos. 1–2 (October 2021): 111–27; Andreas Huyssen, *Present Pasts: Urban Palimpsests and the Politics of Memory* (Stanford University Press, 2003); and Jacques Derrida, *Specters of Marx: The State of the Debt, the Work of Mourning and the New International* (Routledge, 1994).

12. Don is a title typically used in Jamaica for community leaders who are involved in criminal activities. See Rivke Jaffe, *The Rule of Dons: Criminal Leaders and Political Authority in Urban Jamaica* (Duke University Press, 2024).

13. Emil George, Anthony Irons, and D. Scharshmidt, *Report of the Commission of Enquiry into the Extradition Request for Christopher Coke* (Jamaica Information Service, 2011). See also Stephen Cordner et al., "The West Kingston / Tivoli Gardens Incursion in Kingston, Jamaica," *Academic Forensic Pathology* 7, no. 3 (2017): 390–414; Livern Barrett, "Were Civilians Killed After Tivoli Secured?," *The Gleaner (Kingston)*, October 23, 2015; Mattathias Schwartz, "A Massacre in Jamaica," *New Yorker*, December 4, 2011, https://www.newyorker.com/magazine/2011/12/12/a-massacre-in-jamaica; and Annie Paul, "73 Civilians Killed in Jamaica. Big Deal! So What?," *Active Voice*, December 13, 2011 (republished by the author online, https://anniepaul.net/tag/civilian-deaths/).

14. Deborah A. Thomas, *Exceptional Violence: Embodied Citizenship in Transnational Jamaica* (Duke University Press, 2011).

15. Dacres, "'Keeping Alive Before the People's Eyes,'" 495–500.

16. Krista Thompson, "'Black Skin Blue Eyes': Visualizing Blackness in Jamaican Art, 1922–1944," *Small Axe* 8, no. 16 (2) (September 2004): 1–31.

17. Petrina Dacres, "'But Bogle Was a Bold Man': Vision, History, and Power for a New Jamaica," *Small Axe* 13, no. 28 (1) (March 2009): 112–34.

18. Achille Mbembe, *Necropolitics* (Duke University Press, 2019); see also Katherine Verdery, *The Political Lives of Dead Bodies: Reburial and Postsocialist Change* (Columbia University Press, 1999).

19. Petrina Dacres, "Modern Monuments: Fashioning History and Identity in Post-Colonial Jamaica" (PhD diss., Emory University, 2008).

20. For a longer discussion of Watson's history paintings and his National Hero portraits, see Claudia Hucke, *Picturing the Postcolonial Nation: (Inter) Nationalism in the Art of Jamaica, 1962–1975* (Ian Randle, 2013); see also Claudia Hucke, "Barrington as History Painter," in *Barrington: A Retrospective*, by David Boxer, Claudia Hucke, and Veerle Poupeye (National Gallery of Jamaica, 2012).

21. In recent years, the sculptor Basil Watson was commissioned by the government to create full-length statues of the athlete Shelly-Ann Fraser-Pryce and the dramatist and folklorist Louise Bennett. In 2018, he was also commissioned to create Heroes Walk, a corridor of bronze busts of the National Heroes, including one of Nanny in Emancipation Park.

22. See Rex Nettleford, *Mirror, Mirror: Identity, Race, and Protest in Jamaica* (Collins, 1970).

23. Rivke Jaffe, "The Hybrid State: Crime and Citizenship in Urban Jamaica," *American Ethnologist* 40, no. 4 (2013): 734.

24. Michael Thompson, quoted in an exhibition label for *Uprising: Morant Bay, 1865, and Its Afterlives*, co-curated by the author for the National Museum, Jamaica, 2015.

25. Thompson, exhibition label, *Uprising*.

26. See Beverley Mullings, "Garrison Communities," in *Keywords in Radical Geography: Antipode at 50*, ed. Antipode Editorial Collective (John Wiley, 2019); Mark Figueroa and Amanda Sives, "Garrison Politics and Criminality in Jamaica: Does the 1997 Election Represent a Turning Point?," in *Understanding Crime in Jamaica, New Challenges for Public Policy*, ed. Anthony Harriott (University of the West Indies Press, 2003); and Carl Stone, *Class, State and Democracy* (Praeger, 1986).

27. Stanford Watson, quoted in an exhibition label for *Uprising: Morant Bay, 1865 and Its Afterlives*, co-curated by the author for the National Museum, Jamaica, 2015.

28. Amnesty International, "Amnesty International Report 2003—Jamaica," May 28, 2003, https://www.refworld.org/reference/annualreport/amnesty/2003/en/92298.

29. Christopher Irons, quoted in an exhibition label for *Uprising: Morant Bay, 1865 and Its Afterlives*, co-curated by the author for the National Museum, Jamaica, 2015.

30. Amnesty International, "Report 2003—Jamaica."

31. See Amanda Sives, *Elections, Violence, and the Democratic Process in Jamaica, 1944–2007* (Ian Randle, 2010); Obika Gray, *Radicalism and Social Change in Jamaica, 1960–1972* (University of Tennessee Press, 1991); and Carl Stone, *Democracy and Clientelism in Jamaica* (Transaction, 1980).

32. See Samir Puri, *The Shadows of Empire: How Imperial History Shapes Our World* (Pegasus, 2021).

33. Phillip Thomas, interview by the author, 2017.

34. Deborah Thomas, *Modern Blackness: Nationalism, Globalization, and the Politics of Blackness in Jamaica* (Duke University Press, 2004).

35. Omari Ra, interview by the author, 2022. All subsequent quotes in the chapter are taken from interviews I conducted with the artist on September 9 and 16, 2022.

CHAPTER 3
DREAMING IN THE FACE OF THE IMPOSSIBLE
AN INTERVIEW WITH ANDREA CHUNG

Anna Arabindan-Kesson and Wayne Modest

Anna Arabindan-Kesson: Some would describe this moment in time as one of growing calls for decolonization. Can you reflect with us on the questions that prompted the "Beyond Boundaries" conference?[1] What does this moment mean for rethinking the discipline of art history, arts institutions, museums, and universities? And what role do you see for artists in this moment of rethinking and of reckoning?

Andrea Chung: I'm skeptical of institutions, quite honestly. I'm particularly skeptical of academic institutions due to the profit-oriented model here in the United States. The horror stories I hear of overworked professors make me not want to teach. As far as museums go, I'm also very skeptical. After the George Floyd murder [in 2020], there was constant institutional messaging in support of the Black Lives Matter movement, but no support for staff or artists of color, for paying people fairly, or for better benefits. Curators of color are continually overworked. I try to stay away from museums unless I have a very personal relationship with the curators, and unless those curators feel that their museums are undertaking real institutional change. I recently had an issue with an institution that tried to whitewash my work by hiding the fact that I was Black and changing the dynamic of the work. They completely changed the narrative. I see how easily that can happen.

I believe that artists have a lot of power, but I think we need to stop thinking institutionally and think about—I don't want to say guerrilla-style—but other means of making work outside of institutions that were not built for us. The whole construct of the museum was basically the colonizer's trophy case, so how can you really expect change from museums when that archaic structure still stands? All these institutions are still acquiring work from other cultures that don't belong to them. The reluctance of museums to repatriate looted artworks, especially in countries like Belgium, is interesting. They contend that the Congo didn't have the resources to take care of its own history. It's a bold thing to say, "You're not capable of caring for your own history." I don't know exactly what I can do as an artist other than bring that to light.

Wayne Modest: If we see this current moment, then, as a moment of anxiety, as a moment of concern, and as a moment when a certain kind of criticality has emerged, then might it also be conceived as a moment when the fallacy of the institution has become most evident? There has always been critique of museums and universities. However, there might be something different about the current moment, when museums seem to be trying to reorganize themselves to be relevant for a different kind of future.

AC: Which museums are you talking about? Because not American museums! [*Laughs*] I'm very pessimistic, particularly because of the George Floyd situation. Here in the States, museums and universities were intent on hiring curators and professors of color. That was fantastic to see, but then there was no support for those curators or professors. We don't speak openly enough about the emotional labor that curators and professors of color are burdened with. They're left to be the representatives of everything non-white—everything colonized. That is a lot to expect of a person to take on by themselves, with no support system and no funding. I've had conversations with professors and curator friends who feel grateful to be hired at high-profile institutions, but then they are met with insufficient support to do their work. Or they must deal with a very conservative board.

WM: I want to come back to this. But I still want to mark the moment. One of the things that strikes me, in the museum context anyway, is the scramble to try and understand how we can sustain ourselves. This is the first time I've seen it in this way. Recently there was a meeting in Prague where museum professionals were trying to come up with a new definition of what a museum is. And even there the question became "What are we? And what are we for?" Let us have a little bit of joy, Andrea, to imagine together what a museum could become.

AC: I'm a pessimist! [*Laughs*]

WM: I'm neither an optimist nor a pessimist. I don't know what it means to be an optimist. I think it's a useless idea, optimism. But I do believe that one needs to fight to create different futures. And that is what I call hope, that fight.

Let us talk a little bit about your work, Andrea. Let us have a little joy in your artistic practice and learn about what animates you. How would you describe your own practice in relationship to this current moment of undoing and redoing of institutionality?

AC: I take joy in making and understanding how things work. Every project that I take on is about learning something new. I have made quite a few cyanotypes, but I'm not a photographer. I built a darkroom out of a half bathroom in my house. I put paper on my toilet, dried the paper in my shower, then printed photographs on the porch. Really DIY. I like the practicality. This is not something that you need to have a sophisticated lab to do. My chemicals cost a total of twenty-four dollars. Anyone can take up this stuff and do it. I like using materials that are affordable for everyone. I think that was part of my original fascination with working with foodways: investigating the things that we take for granted and exploring the power that they have in our world.

Right now, for example, I'm making sculptures out of paper pulp. I've only done it once before, so it's a whole new challenge to make large three-dimensional objects out of paper. My dog goes and chews them up and destroys them and I have to do it over again. In some sense, I always feel that those things happen for a reason. I kept saying that my dog was my best critic because she forced me to go back and rework the piece. In the process, I found a better way to construct it.

I also have an appreciation for labor. I just got my nails done yesterday, and I watched the nail technicians as they worked. It's a skill set that I don't have, so I appreciate the labor of someone who can do what I can't. I have a real passion for learning the day-to-day of people's lives and the labor that we take for granted.

AA-K: I love that idea of the DIY aesthetic because I think it also chimes quite beautifully with what you were saying earlier about spaces for guerrilla interaction. I wonder whether you try to make space for audiences to engage with materiality, too, so that they're in that space of learning and process with you.

AC: When I installed a piece on Eastern Parkway in Brooklyn for the Labor Day parade in 2008, I repurposed text and tourist images—a lot of images of half-naked women, things like that. I juxtaposed those texts and images with actual images of what was happening on the street. Some friends and I wheat-pasted these collages on walls all over Brooklyn so that they sat in contrast with other advertisements that were on the parkway.

Hearing people's initial responses to my work is always great. My audience is not made up of academics or artists. My audience is people like my parents who don't care about art. They're not interested. But I feel that if I can communicate with them, then the work is successful. I'm not making art for art's sake. I'm making work to tell real stories that are identifiable by people who don't necessarily have an art background. I love what I do, but I also don't take it super seriously in the way that some artists do. In my adulthood, I've only lived in the hood. I would love for my neighbors to be able to enjoy the work as well. I grew up in a middle-class area, but my entire adult life I've lived in one hood or another. For me, it's about being able to communicate with the people I see on a daily basis, the people I live with, and tell their stories. That's why I work with the materials that I do. Anyone can just pick them up and make something with them.

AA-K: For someone who is an academic but struggles in academia, it's affirming to hear you talk about what your work does and who it's for. Something Wayne highlighted earlier is your interest in labor. The way you were talking about your relationship with communities, neighborhoods, and families made me wonder: How does that interest in labor work as a process but also a theme? How does labor intertwine with the familial legacies that you talk about?

AC: I try to honor the labor of others through my own labor. I never mean to do this, but I always end up with laborious and time-consuming projects. I recently made a sculpture of a bird's nest for an exhibition, *everything slackens in a wreck*, at the Ford Foundation. It was a physically intense, four-month-long process of weaving baskets to make a gigantic weaver bird's nest. When I was in Mauritius, I found weaver bird's nests made from sugar cane. I thought that was rather ironic, so I decided to make a larger version of a nest as a way of examining migration onto the island. The idea was to take what you have and create a community with it. But the physical aspect was new for me; it's the largest sculpture I've made to date. My back was killing me. My spine was on fire. It required a village of people to help me complete it. All of that—the physical labor that I put into it—is my way of honoring those who have labored so hard. My labor is nothing compared to what they've done. As an artist, the first thing that people always ask me is, "How long did it take for you to make that?" If you can create a work that will prompt people to ask that question, and then use the work as an opportunity to explain other people's labor, it can help your audience reexamine the cost of labor. I never mean to start that way, but everything that I do becomes tedious, from cutting things out repetitively to beading, which has strained my eyes. I do it because it's a conversation that I'm interested in having about physical labor. Especially because the work ends up being in a white cube, I'm always interested in how I can make it inviting and accessible. I have no desire to create a work specifically for a "high art" institution. That's not my goal or my audience.

WM: Your interest in labor recalls why we wanted to do this conference. We wanted to ask the question: What does the Caribbean do to help us to think differently about the writing of art histories? To think differently about the disciplines in which we are embedded? Today I was talking to somebody of Jamaican descent from England about the Revival religious tradition in Jamaica. Within Revival there is an aspect of practice, of performance, that is regarded as cutting and clearing. As I recall, this practice recalls the labor of clearing the fields on the plantation; it is a movement through struggle, a clearing of space. Can you say a little bit about how the Caribbean informs your work, the way you work, or the interests that you have? What is the Caribbean for you?

AC: It's home for me. My grandmother was part of the Revival.

WM: Oh, nice! [*Laughs*]

AC: It's funny that you brought that up. Initially, I was interested in looking at her labor. She would go to the Coronation Market and start simply with eggs or limes and sell those, then move on to the next thing and sell that. That was how she took care of my father's siblings. They worked at a very young age: I think one of my uncles opened his first shop at fifteen or sixteen. When you immigrate to the United States, work is the focus. There's the belief that work will elevate you to the next level—the "pull yourself up by the bootstraps" idea. I don't really believe that. When you're dealing with institutional racism, you can pull yourself up by the bootstraps as much as you want, but that's not going to change anything. You're going to hit that glass ceiling no matter what. But ultimately, I feel like I'm going home when I'm going to the Caribbean. When I'm on the airplane and it's about to land and I can see the water, it feels like home. I feel like I can be me without having to answer a bunch of questions about my last name. Jamaica has always felt more like home than Trinidad has, just because I've had easier access to Jamaica than Trinidad.

It's also important to me to tell my family's story. I try to understand why my family is the way it is—the dysfunction, the motivations for certain people. I want to better understand myself and pass this down to my own child, so that he has knowledge of who he is and he can easily access this history in a way that I was not able to. A lot of my father's siblings choose not to talk about their upbringing because it's too painful—because of the amount of labor that was required of them to survive. They lived in a tenement yard for some time. Their father did not encourage them to go to school; they were to work. Work and labor have always been a huge storyline within my own family. On my mother's side, my grandmother was a midwife. That's a whole lot of labor! But she was loved for it. I'm also fascinated by her as a caretaker who labored for others out of the goodness of her heart. She was so well loved that when she became ill, people took care of her and paid for her medication.

I don't feel like an American all the time. I feel like an American when I travel to other places. But usually, I don't feel like an American. It's impossible not to have a connection to the Caribbean. It defines me. I used to try to visit every couple of years because I felt like I needed to be there. It's very healing for me to sit by the water there—particularly there, not anywhere else. It's home for me.

WM: I sit here in Amsterdam, and one of the things that excites me about your work is that you are one of the few artists or academics I know who try to connect the Indian Ocean and the Caribbean. And I hope you just noticed that I have just described you as an academic!

AC: I was going to say something about that!

WM: But it is a battle space—an intellectual and museological battle space—for us in the Netherlands to try and understand the questions of slavery, of colonialism, not only in its transatlantic formation but also in connection with what was happening in the Indian Ocean. I was at a conference recently where people spoke about the dominance of the Atlantic in our imagination in relation to questions of the colonial and slavery. How did you come to making that connection with the Indian Ocean, and why? And why did you want to push beyond that Atlantic-Caribbean binary?

AC: This is how much of an academic I am: There is a British show that I really liked called *Globe Trekker*. The host was visiting an island, but I wasn't sure what country it was. There was a Black man with locks, so I assumed it was somewhere in the Caribbean. But then the host said he was in Mauritius, and I was like, "Where the hell is that?" I had to look it up. I said, "Oh my God, they're so similar to us."

At the time, I had been making a lot of work with spices. I was interested in looking at foodways and how the movement of food reveals a larger picture about migration. When I looked at the food in Mauritius, the cuisine was so similar to that of the Caribbean. Dholl puri is what we call "roti skins." Everything was the same but different. The Chinese migrants who came to the Caribbean, the Hakka people, also lived in Mauritius. The cultural similarities motivated my decision to apply for a Fulbright to study in Mauritius.

When I was there, I learned, through the Indo-Mauritius community, that Mauritius functioned as a depot, as the "experiment" before people were spread out through the Caribbean. They came into Mauritius first. There are fantastic records of Indian indentured laborers who came into Mauritius first and then were dispersed throughout the Caribbean. Mauritius was the testing ground for how all this labor could function together. The island had been colonized by so many different countries. The Dutch were the first, but people from the Malay Islands also established villages there. After the Dutch couldn't successfully establish any agriculture—and killed off all the dodos—the French came. They were slightly more successful colonizing the island, which is why the language is predominantly Creole and French. And then the English came. The story is so much like the Caribbean. Mauritians have looked to the Caribbean for inspiration as well, in music, for example. Sega is a Mauritian genre of music, and they've also created seggae, which is a mixture of reggae and sega. Mauritians look at Bob Marley as a hero. They have their own version of Bob Marley, named Kaya, who was tragically killed by the police as well. The concept of coolitude shows the relationship between Mauritius and Trinidad.[2] You cannot deny that there are cultural similarities. I think they look to each other.

When I was there, I stayed with a former Fulbrighter who had married a Mauritian. He was Hakka. He taught me a lot about things that my own Hakka grandfather had never shared with anyone. I got to eat Hakka food, and he took me to different Hakka events. I learned how to cook from him and some of his sisters. It was the best year of my life. It was awesome. I just ate for a year! It was amazing to learn through food and understand the history that it carried. I have such an affinity for Mauritius. I would love to be able to go back there. The relationship between Mauritius and the Caribbean is so strong, and it feels so comfortable being there. I didn't have to answer questions about my ethnicity; we passed as Mauritians. I love telling the story about the relationship between the two regions. Those are stories and connections that can be developed.

AA-K: I felt like that when I went to Jamaica. I remember seeing flowers that grew in my grandmother's front yard in Sri Lanka and talking with Maroon communities there. I even noticed the same spices. It goes back to what Wayne said: This is our colonial condition. It's as if we're constantly somewhere else as well as being where we are. There's a multiplicity of seeing that I think your work really opens up, especially in the way that it brings the Indian and Atlantic Oceans together. I think there's also something about the Caribbean where you can't really ignore the inheritance or effects of colonialism.

AC: It's interesting to see how it has affected each colonized space differently.

AA-K: It's different in settler-colonial countries like Australia, for example, where the connection has always been to Britain. Now, more people are thinking about the Indian Ocean as a site of other connections. I'm thinking about a sort of expanded form of the Caribbean. The way that different ideas and capital and people move from the Caribbean to Australia even, and how they enabled other forms of enslavement to develop in Australia. Looking to the ocean as a conduit allows these other perspectives or other orientations to emerge. It's a powerful way of thinking. When I first saw your work, it was as if you materialized a way of seeing that I couldn't quite articulate.

AC: I can't quite articulate it all the time either.

AA-K: It's that way of seeing two or three spaces at once that I think is powerful. I think works like the *Crowning* series are really powerful.

AC: There were many things in Mauritius that were similar to the Caribbean, including the flora. There's a flowering shrub called Pride of Barbados that grows in Mauritius, but they call it a "fire tree" there. Notably, the plant was used by enslaved midwives to perform abortions in both locations. That knowledge was shared and dispersed in both places. There are even Maroons in both places. In Jamaica, for example, Maroons are a specific group of people who live in Accompong and descend from Africans who freed themselves from enslavement, whereas in Mauritius it's a looser description for descendants of those who escaped enslavement. Some of them were Malagasy, and some were East African from the area around Mozambique. Some of the former built boats to try to go back to Madagascar. Some survived and others didn't.

WM: At the conference I mentioned earlier, the invitation to be part of a conversation around the Indian Ocean came from two curators who I know, and whose work I respect a lot. I remember, however, feeling a little bit impatient as the discussion unfolded, because it felt like a conversation about how we have looked too much at the Atlantic world, and now we should stop and start looking at the Indian Ocean instead. That was certainly not their intention, but it just felt like that.

AC: That's a bad way of having the conversation.

WM: Precisely. And what I see in your work is precisely the opposite. It invites us to ask a different kind of question about what can be gained by looking at these regions together. It gives us tools to think more analytically about questions of race or fugitivity or even transplantation and movement. Your work does that for me more than competitive economies of different spaces. I must say that I'm very excited to see that you're teasing out a conceptual togetherness.

AC: I'm not interested in the suffering Olympic Games—when people say, "Oh, I suffered more than you." No. We all suffered, and we all deal with trauma. I don't see the need to compare that. No one's pain is above anyone else's pain. If we could have a conversation from a place of pain, if we could heal together and deal with our trauma together and really point the finger at the cause of that trauma, then I think that there would be a lot more unity. There could be a lot more building—intellectual building, community building, art building. There can be so much more than just wanting to see who suffered the most. We have all suffered in some fashion.

WM: I want to put you back among the academics. [*Laughs*]

AC: If watching PBS defines me as an academic, that's all good! [*Laughs*]

WM: What are some of the themes that surface in your work on the Atlantic and the Indian Ocean? What specifically emerges from the pressures of those places that you think are urgent for this current moment? We are trying to rewrite the history of anthropology and art history. We're trying to think about what we teach students in that first survey course. We're trying to think about how a curriculum could look like otherwise.

AC: I think it's very interesting that both regions have a service economy that was imposed by various colonizers. Each island provided agricultural needs to affluent Europeans with a sweet tooth. It is really that ridiculous when you think about it. Sugar is a drug at this point. However, after the abolishment of slavery, colonizers pivoted from a sugar economy to tourism, which is very common in formerly colonized islands. Their only "resource" is tourism. Why is that? I think that question should come up. And who forces them to be in that situation?

As far as anthropology, maybe I would start from the unknowable question of what was originally there. What was the landscape like? How did we shape the landscape to suit our needs as opposed to the needs of what was already there? Mauritius had no indigenous people. And why was that? What made it "inhospitable" for human beings? What are the possibilities of what it could have been had people not invaded and abused the land?

Colonizers reshaped the land and brought species to the islands that were not indigenous. I think people sometimes forget that what we attribute to being Caribbean or even to island life isn't necessarily natural to those places either. Mangoes are not natural to Jamaica. Breadfruit is not natural to Jamaica—foods that we associate with going home and eating. But that's not the way it was originally. I'm just curious to know what the land was like. How can you anthropologically do those investigations of the land prior to human contact? What would that look like? You'd probably find some weird dinosaur that lived there at some point.

WM: You raise the question of indigeneity. What is that? How do you define it? It's an ongoing conversation for me, because in the register of national and global scientific and policy practices, we use words like "invasive species" to describe some plants or animals or whatever. And whenever people say that, even when I'm in Jamaica, I always say to them, "But are we not 'invasive' as well."

AC: I think about that all the time. I heard something recently on NPR that I thought was interesting. Do you know what a boll weevil is? It is a pest that invades cotton. It made it very hard for plantation owners to produce cotton. I thought, "All right, yeah, boll weevils!" This invasive species was revolutionary for Black folks. And in some ways, there are situations where creatures have been very helpful to certain populations. What if we had eradicated cotton? What would the face of the United States be if we had destroyed the entire cotton industry? That would be transformative for what this country looks like right now. The language that's used to talk about invasive species is also the same language that's often used when talking about immigrants.

AA-K: I was thinking about what you said, Andrea, about how you're not sure what role your work does in terms of institutions. Just listening to you talk with Wayne, it seems like what you do is to change the position and change the orientation, so that it's about seeing connections. Often institutions, and even art history itself, can't do anything but compare. Just think of an art history lecture, right? Compare and contrast. Things end up being value-driven, they become hierarchical in terms of, as you were saying, the Olympics of suffering. That's an important space that you create to make those connections. Perhaps this is what you were asking about earlier, Wayne. Institutions and academia are still not able to do that yet because of how they're set up and how they're structured around geographies or teleologies.

AC: In academia, everyone is competing for the same funding to do research. How can you find similarities if you're competing for the same little bit of funding that's not even enough to begin with? I think that that's another reason why some of these conversations don't naturally generate between the two. In academia and institutions, all the conversations end up feeling very separate from one another. In reality, we're all talking about the same things. I am a pessimist. But could you imagine if we could focus on the similarities and the connections that we have? As opposed to fighting with one another or boxing everything in? To me, that feels like a very colonial thing to do—to segment everything in categories. Break those categories. They're unnecessary. And think about where that comes from. I think we buy into that tendency at times, as opposed to really questioning it.

AA-K: Yeah, I think that kind of aesthetics of affiliation that you're describing is really beautiful. I don't know what that's like in anthropology, Wayne, but thinking about how art history could be different if that was the model. It would be quite transformative.

I have this interdisciplinary position in art history and African American studies. For me, it comes down to what we were talking about and how we were talking. I think it's important to think about the work that we do as a space of gathering and affiliation. It's also about accessibility—as you said, that DIY aesthetic—and expanding who is speaking and where that knowledge or cultural production can go. That's a start. Institutionally, it's something we talk about, but it's an orientation and a framework that's difficult to implement. It's what you were talking about before, about where we are encouraged to start in terms of our little space.

AC: I wonder what effective action looks like. I think that was one of the issues I had with a lot of museums when the whole George Floyd thing happened. It was a lot of "in solidarity" and "we support you." But I'm like, "Okay, well, what are you *doing*?" I keep wondering what institutions can sincerely do to produce the kind of change that we theorize through many symposia and conferences. We could talk about it ad nauseam, but I wonder what an action list would look like for an institution to make those changes, even slight changes.

WM: It's good that you say this, though. In a certain sense, your last statement is why I wanted to do this conference. To ask this question about the Caribbean in relationship to disciplines, to institutions, and to practice is to ask the question about a place so confounding that it might help us to imagine our disciplinary or institutional work differently. But the other side is that I don't believe in institutions. I think institutions are not trustworthy. I think they are impossible. But the museum isn't going anywhere, and neither are the universities.

AC: Yeah. How do you work within that?

WM: The question, then, is what analytical or practical skills we adopt to be able to make institutions less violent—at the least. And at the most, a space where we can imagine flourishing. So that is why I'm not optimistic. I believe that it's such a useless concept to say, "Oh, if you look at it differently it will be better." No, it won't.

AC: When you asked me that question at the beginning, about how we might rethink our disciplines and institutions, I thought, "I don't know how to answer this question," because I feel like when you are constantly in the face of institutions that refuse to change, or only change incrementally, how do you dream? How can you dream of what it would practically look like to make a change? I don't have the ability to dream in that way. I agree with you about optimism. I don't know how to dream, because I've seen so much shut down, with no effort or with condescension. It's very hard for me to dream. In some ways, that hinders my artmaking.

AA-K: That's powerful, Andrea, because the same thing is happening in art history. Post–George Floyd, every department has a Diversity, Equity, and Inclusion Committee. I'm on my department's. It's all about how we can do art history differently. But, in fact, I don't think that's possible at all, because of what art history is. It's a colonial discipline. As Wayne said, it's not something that can be changed. But I think what this conference—and what these questions about the Caribbean, and what your work—can do is make us realize that. These things bring the limitations of art history into the foreground. It means that people have to accept, or at least acknowledge, that irreparability. To me, it's powerful to state the impossibility.

WM: I want to share one last little thing. In the 1990s, Kirk Franklin came out with the song "Joy." In the beginning of that song, an organ plays, and then Kirk Franklin invites everybody to sing that first "joy." And in that moment, there is a small break when the music is so sweet that the choir just laughs. You see that moment of laughter, Andrea and Anna? For me that is the moment of hope. It is a moment of decolonial joy. It is a moment of imagining an impossible possibility. And that's nothing to do with optimism. It has to do with fighting. I'm trying to say that I have no optimism for the institution; however, I may have hope.

AC: I believe that is how people feel. They're just not openly honest about it. I think the whole problem with the institution is the lack of truth telling. If we could be honest about reality, then I think we would be in a better place. If we could be honest about history, then art history would probably be a popular class. If we could be truthful about history, I think that we would be more socially engaged and be in a much better place. I think that if you're truthful, there's room for forgiveness. But if you're going to continue the lie, then there's no reason for me to believe anything that comes out of your mouth or anything your institution puts out.

NOTES

1. This conversation was conducted and recorded in advance of a conference, titled "Beyond Boundaries: Seeing Art History from the Caribbean," held at the Clark Art Institute in Williamstown, Massachusetts, October 20–21, 2022. Participants were invited to view the recording, which is available online at https://www.clarkart.edu/Research-Academic/RAP-Events/Clark-Conference-2022/Artist-Conversations, in preparation for one of the sessions.

2. On "coolitude," see Andil Gosine's essay in this volume, "Coolie Créole," p. 42n5.

CHAPTER 4

MICHAEL RICHARDS AND THE POLITICAL WORK OF BLACK ECSTASY

Erica Moiah James

In an email conversation with the artist william córdova (fig. 4.1) shortly before the exhibition *Michael Richards: Are You Down?* opened at the Museum of Contemporary Art North Miami in 2021,[1] I learned that toward the end of his life, Richards, a US-born artist raised in Kingston, Jamaica, created a sculpture called *Every Nigga Is a Star* (fig. 4.2).

The work features a Black man riding what appears to be a meteorite, thunderbolt, or some other celestial object as if it were a bucking bronco. He is dressed in military-style fatigues and boots. His head is covered by an aviator's skullcap, much like the figure in Richards's golden-toned *Tar Baby vs. St. Sebastian* (1999, North Carolina Museum of Art). Both works reference Richards's engagement with the life and legacy of the Tuskegee Airmen, an all-Black World War II aviator unit. Mouth open and animated, the man in *Every Nigga Is a Star* appears to be yelling something at the top of his voice as he descends. I like to think that he's shouting the title of the work.

Because of my ongoing research on the lost film *Every Nigger Is a Star*—a travelogue and musical documentary made in the early 1970s in Jamaica by the actor Calvin Lockhart and featuring now-noted performers such as Big Youth, King Ossie and the Mystic Revelation of Rastafari, Boris Gardiner, Cynthia Schloss, and the playwright Alfred Fagon, among others—a possible link between the sculpture, the film, and its eponymous theme song was compelling. The film premiered on November 13, 1974, at the Carib, Palace, and Tropical Theatres in Kingston, and the evolution of its theme song, written and recorded by Gardiner in 1973 at Ken Khouri's Federal Records studios in Kingston,[2] has extended the film's life into the present through multiple re-recordings by artists from Big Youth to Kendrick Lamar. To learn of this sculpture and, through it, Richards's devotion to Jamaican dancehall music was a revelation. The connection between the film, song, and sculpture embodied in the title of the work was later reinforced by the discovery of a mixtape Richards gave to

Fig. 4.1. Michael Richards (left) and william córdova working on *Tar Baby vs. St. Sebastian* (1999), ArtCenter / South Florida studios, Miami, 1998

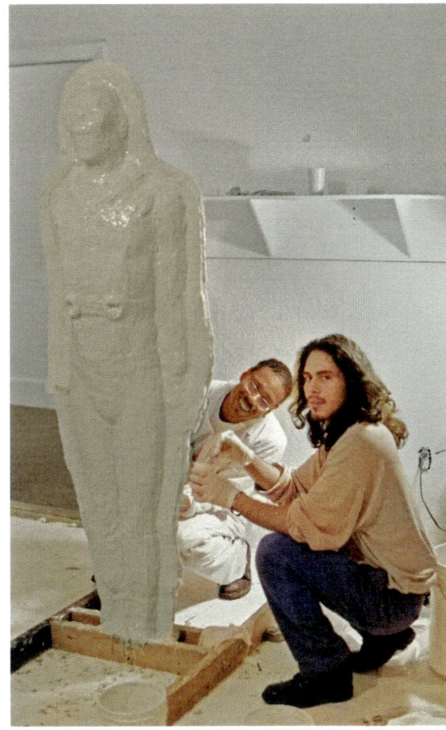

Fig. 4.2. Installation view featuring (from left) Michael Richards's *Tar Baby vs. St. Sebastian* (1999), *Every Nigga Is a Star* (2000), and *Are You Down?* (1999), in the *National Foundation for Advancement in the Arts, Fellowships in the Visual Arts Exhibition*, Corcoran Gallery of Art, Washington, DC, 2000

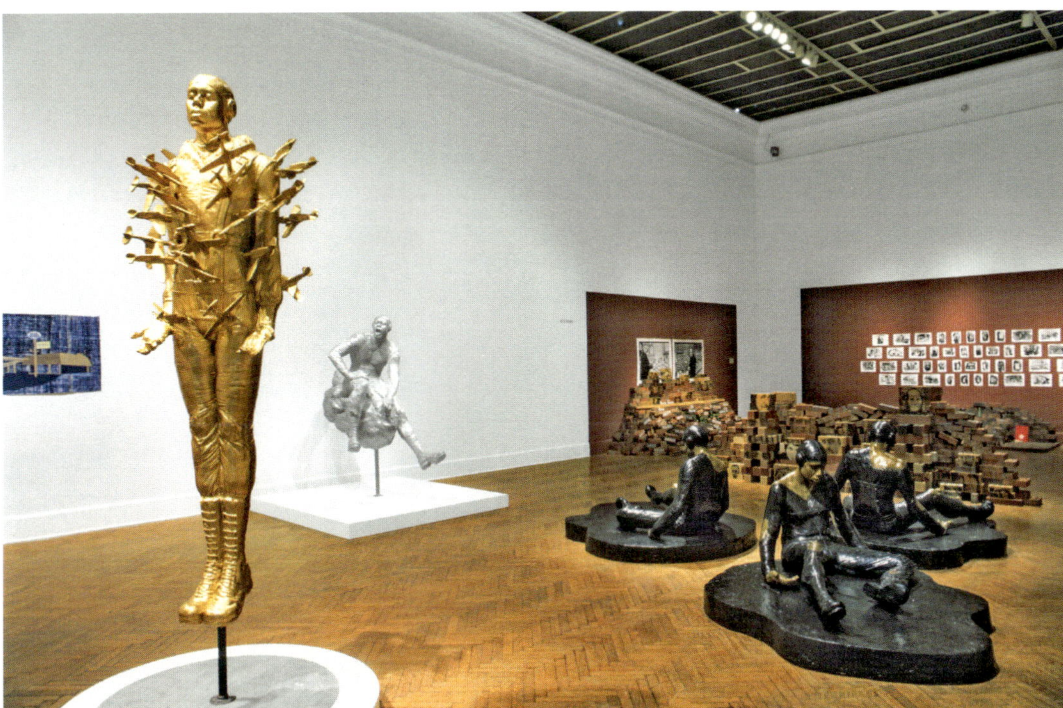

córdova. The mixtape is filled with early (now classic) dancehall tunes such as Capelton's "Tour," Chaka Demus & Pliers's "Murder She Wrote," Shabba Ranks's "Twice My Age" featuring Krystal, and Sister Nancy's "Bam Bam." Like the film, which is lost, the first track on the tape, performed by Super Cat, is now missing without explanation.

The film, its signature song, and subsequent versions of it, from its original R&B / lovers rock[3] recording to its culmination in dancehall,[4] including a version by Super Cat, alongside Richards's sculpture, demonstrate how Black ecstasy—as experienced through art, music, and dance—can be seen as a liberatory and political action within the diaspora. Several scholars have explored notions of Black ecstasy. Jennifer C. Nash is perhaps the best known, through her scholarship on Black female pleasure and pornography.[5] Black feminist theologians building on Nash's seminal work have also attended to the politics of pleasure and the experience of the Black body in ecstasy in both religious and secular contexts.[6] What I am reaching for through my engagement with the concept of Black ecstasy converges with and departs from Nash's work. In this essay, Black ecstasy is autoerotic, nonsexual, public, and often generated or experienced within community spaces. Notions of respectability and propriety are not a consideration. Though it is a form of ecstasy adjacent to what is witnessed and experienced in Caribbean religions such as Vodou, where the body opens for the spirit to enter and move, Black ecstasy as considered here is not about being filled with a spirit as much as it is about entering a spiritual realm that moves beyond the signification of the social and physical limits of flesh. It describes a personal spiritual transcendence that is divinely human. Unlike Christianity, where the ecstatic allows the human to touch a world one cannot see, here body and spirit merge. The Black ecstatic is deeply felt for the time and in the space in which it unfolds. Though individual, it can be infectious, extending beyond the experiential body through witness and affect. I am using affect here as way of relating the experience of ecstasy's production through the visual as akin to "catching the spirit" in church. On its surface this process can be described as seeing someone possessed in a kind of "affective witnessing" where the same unseen spirt witnessed in another then flows into the witness. It is akin to Kevin Quashie's notion of Black aliveness in its capacity to recognize subjectivity in how one "beholds the other" and the "refusal of the specular as a site of Black abjection."[7] Black ecstasy is specular and spectacular, a sublime moment where the body is sovereign and one feels, and is, wholly free.

The song (and one presumes the lost film it accompanied) is both affirmation and claim; it is an aestheticization of the *wheel and come again*[8] that addresses, redresses, awakens, and redeploys the tools of liberatory Blackness through the ecstatic. Richards's sculpture can be seen as a material example of this, *turnt up*.[9] Through a history of the song, I want to explore how this sculpture occupies a multimodal space of the ecstatic where Black people can claim freedom and, through it, life amid day-to-day horror.

The concept of Black ecstasy is central to my rethinking of Caribbean modernism. I am interested in the ways Caribbean modernism is not time-bound but repeatedly rendered and experienced within history and culture, as phenomenology, as methodology, as autohistoriography,[10] and as archival expansion. Modernism, as the literary scholar Jessica Berman proposes, helps us "imagine justice,"[11] and in Caribbean and/or African diasporic contexts often carries a restitutive imperative in its form. Like language and narrative, unbound in the diaspora, it is constantly unfolding, emerging through aesthetic and creative forms—what Dilip Parameshwar Gaonkar, a scholar of rhetoric and global modernism, describes as an "unfinished and unfinishable saga of the modern self and subjectivity."[12] I want to consider how, in and through modernism, one can imagine multimodal Caribbean art forms continually answering the decolonial question posed by Sylvia Wynter that haunts postcolonial creative practices: "How do you [as an artist] deal with the stereotyped view of yourself [cultivated in colonialism] that you yourself have been socialized to accept?"[13] I am keenly interested in thinking through an answer to Wynter's question in the work of various global Caribbean artists such as Richards, Juan Francisco Elso, and Simone Leigh. How does art and how do artists push back against the weight of a colonial definition of itself/themselves to define, affirm, and continually re-create that self, to claim and enact freedom as an ongoing decolonial act toward justice? How did Richards, the actor Calvin Lockhart, reggae artists, and others consciously or unconsciously grapple with this premise through an evocation of the Black ecstatic, which their work embodies, generates, and emanates? How might it render the contours of Caribbean modernism, not as work produced within a fixed time span in the shadow of European modernism but as a phenomenon that exists within and beyond the colonial, a kind of glorious rot that consumes the carcass that held it, regenerates, and leaves all that once entombed it behind?

The Cuban poet and essayist José Lezama Lima, in a discussion of Julián del Casal's poetry and the process of creating Caribbean art under/in colonialism, recognizes all the caveats of creativity that exist under colonial rule and the perceived limits of a colonized artist's use of what are too often deemed "colonial forms."[14] To view language and other forms of creative expression as colonial possessions creates an artificial ideological barrier between language and the colonized. It implies that colonized people have no right to those "other people's things." Lezama Lima's case for Del Casal and Caribbean art is grounded in a complete rejection of what Gaonkar notes is the "false clarity of the Hegelian dyad."[15] It removes the tools of creativity from the possession of the colonizer and rejects critiques of dismissive mimicry leveled at the creative practices of the formerly colonized, disavowing the master/slave dynamic of Western modernism and the valence of any such thing as "the master's tools."

For Lezama Lima, "If we [colonized and formerly colonized people] speak of criticism as creation, not production, then poetry [art, music, etc.] adheres to the theory of knowledge."[16] Here, the "work" of art is critical but its criticality is twofold; it doesn't simply lie in the content of the work, it also exists in the fact of its creation, its form. The thing that will be archived, exhibited, and exist in the world becomes the eternal critique of colonialism. How might the Black ecstatic be seen as one of many signposts for the critical creativity of Caribbean modernism? And how do works of art, like Richards's, embody this?

Let us begin with the Dutch artist Dirk Valkenberg's eighteenth-century painting *Gathering of Enslaved People on One of Jonas Witsen's Plantations in Suriname* (formerly known as *Slave Play on a Sugar Plantation in Suriname*, fig. 4.3). This painting is believed to show a group of enslaved Africans on the Dombi plantation, one of several holdings belonging to Jonas Witsen, a *burgemeester*, or mayor, of Amsterdam. Witsen hired Valkenberg to complete a series of paintings and drawings of his plantations in Suriname. The Africans in the center are performing what is known as the *winti* dance while drummers drum and people gather to watch, talk, drink, cheer the dancers on, or do some other activity. Their bodies are a uniformly dark cocoa brown. Their skins shine in the light. Drawing on the literary and gender theorist Robyn Wiegman's work on the "racial logic of corporeal inscription," the art historian Krista A. Thompson has observed how "the very notion of blackness as locatable on the surface of black skin is an extension, the (il)logical end, of a blinding faith in the deeper epistemological meaning of epidermal shiny surfaces."[17] In the context of the Valkenburg image, this could be read as the commodification of Africans in plantation and slave economies at the time; thus, the painting can be seen as a gross depiction of Witsen's *things*.

But I would like to also think of the painting from the perspective of those represented: shine as a sign of sweat, a sign of ecstatic movement, Quashie's Black aliveness but also Nash's erotic, as witnessed in the remarkable kiss signaling desire and care between the man and woman standing together in the lower right of the painting. These Surinamese Africans are performing for themselves, with themselves. They are aware of, but seem to ignore, the presence and eye of the artist. A long white strip of cloth signals from a pole extended from a cabin. Smoke drifts up from between the structures. Through Valkenberg's eyes, the scene unfolds like a simple party among Witsen's possessions. However, as the anthropologist and historian Richard Price notes in his seminal book *First Time*, not long after this painting was made, and in fact during Valkenberg's time in Suriname, the people represented in this painting burned the plantation to the ground and left, becoming the first known Surinamese Maroons.[18] This fact of history begs the question: What is

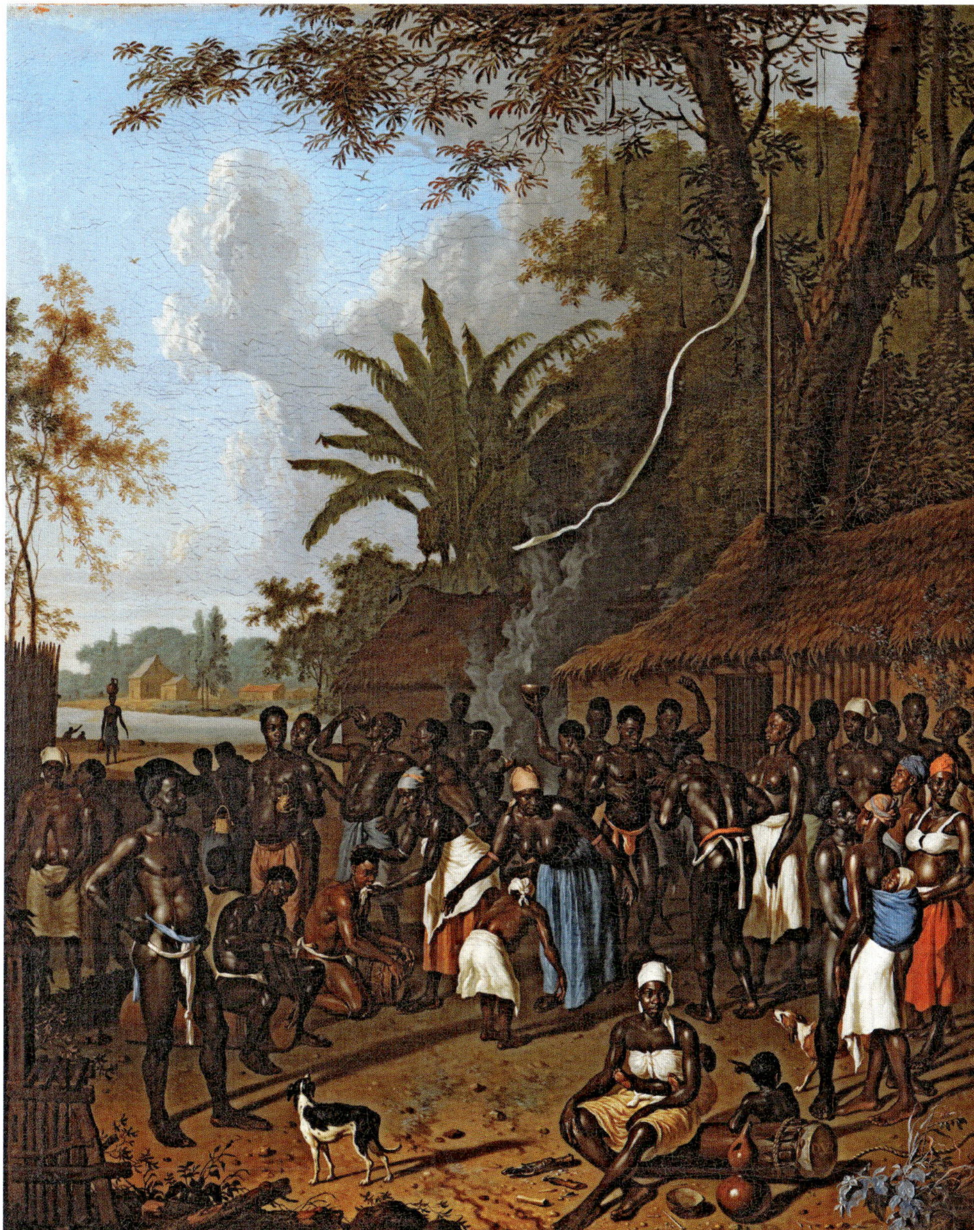

Fig. 4.3. Dirk Valkenburg (Dutch, 1675–1721), *Gathering of Enslaved People on One of Jonas Witsen's Plantations in Suriname*, 1707. Oil on canvas, 22 ¾ × 18 ¼ in. (57.9 × 46.5 cm). Collection of Statens Museum de Kunst, Denmark, KMS376

really going on in this painting? Lezama Lima observed the contrapuntal character of/in the arts of the Americas. Are these Africans organizing amid the white gaze that processed them as commodity? Is this "play" something Valkenberg could represent but was unable to fully see for what it might have been? How might we understand what happened next? How might we see differently ordinary things like movement and dance as discursive and expressive archives of critique, as creation in diaspora, as a way of communicating in colonial gazes and spaces, and as an early archive of critique through creation even in representation?

The political work of the ecstatic Black bodies recorded in this painting precedes and clears passage for African Surinamese self-liberation from slavery. But it is repeatedly signaled and experienced in and through Black diasporic art. One sees it in the extended dance scene in Steve McQueen's *Lovers Rock* (fig. 4.4), where the troubled character Clifton (played by Kedar Williams-Stirling) takes over the living room dance floor, a space cleared and created by specularized, harassed, and over-policed Caribbean immigrants in London and transformed into a place to enact freedom. Clifton sets his body free in an ecstatic dance that builds and flows with the other male characters in the room in a powerful manifestation of Black ecstasy.

One also sees and feels the Black ecstatic when, in episode 5 of the American television series *Lovecraft Country*, Michael K. Williams's character Montrose Freeman stands aloof from the crowd in a dance club (fig. 4.5). His body is maimed from having been beaten up, and his mind is troubled. He is closeted and unable to openly express his desire for his male lover, a drag performer in the club. As the music begins to pulse, he slowly begins to move to the beat, almost subconsciously, as he visually devours the scene around him. At some point, Freeman becomes conscious of his body moving, and as movement takes over his body, one witnesses his burdens gathering in a vortex where the pressure builds until his body releases it all through the ecstasy of the dance. In that moment, he is lifted on high by a bevy of queens and showered in confetti. He shines. He is free.

One also bears witness to ecstasy in Khalil Joseph's short film *Until the Quiet Comes*, which accompanied a studio album by the same title from the American electronic music producer Quiet Lotus in 2013, and featuring Storyboard P. In the film, as Storyboard's dead body reawakens and shimmies with aliveness, he flows through the community into the waiting car of Eshu that will transport him home (fig. 4.6). One feels something similar in the evolution of the song that would go on to inspire Michael Richards's sculpture *Every Nigga Is a Star*.

The first version of the song "Every Nigger Is a Star" to be released, on the eponymous film's 1974–75 soundtrack, was the Boris Gardiner recording.[19] It has a light, ska-style quality greatly influenced by American R&B and the then-rising tide of British lovers rock. With its incendiary declaration and lyrical cadence, it was a hit (unlike the film). Gardiner sings:

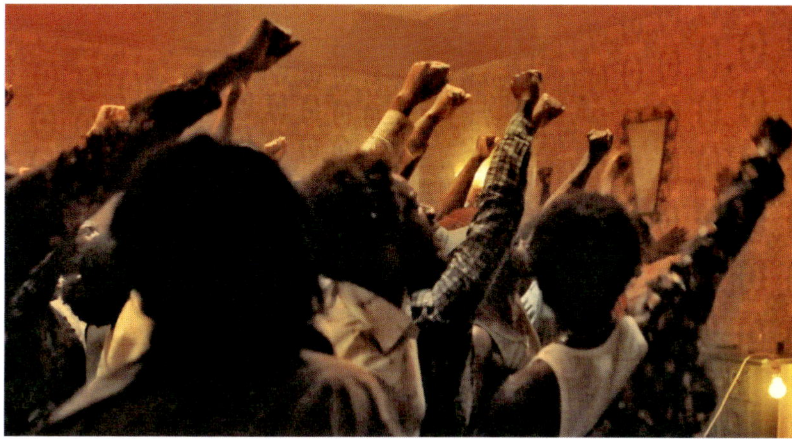

Fig. 4.4. Clifton's dance scene, from *Small Axe: Lovers Rock*, directed by Steve McQueen (British, b. 1969), produced by Amazon MGM Studios, 2020

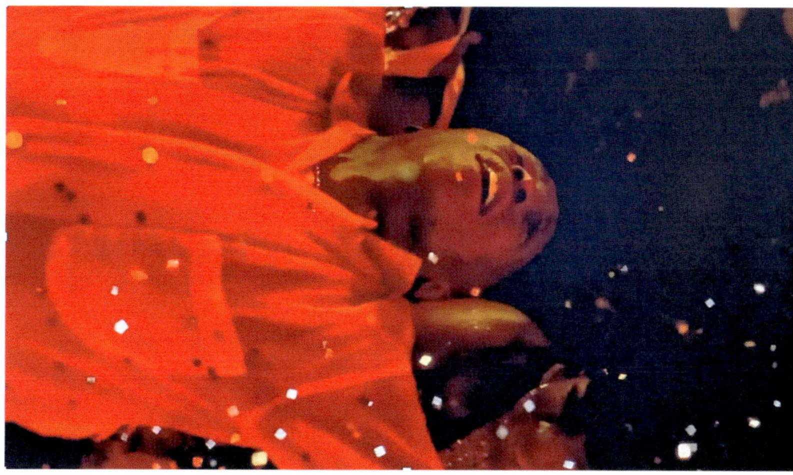

Fig. 4.5. Montrose Freeman's ecstasy / club scene, from *Lovecraft Country*, episode 5, *Strange Case*, directed by Cheryl Dunye (Liberian American, b. 1966), created by Misha Green, produced by Bad Robot, Monkey Paw, and Warner Brothers, 2020

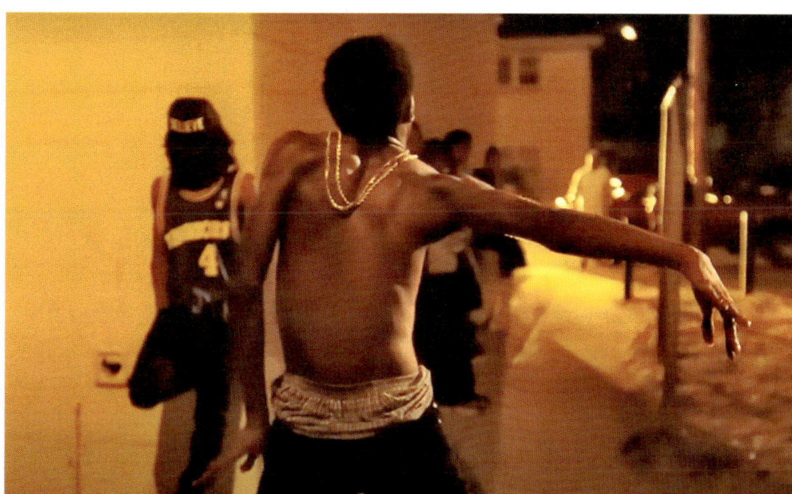

Fig. 4.6. Still from Flying Louts, *Until the Quiet Comes*, featuring Storyboard P, directed by Khalil Joseph (American, b. 1981), produced by Warp Records, 2013

I am not sure anymore just how it happened before
The places that I knew
Were sunny and blue
I can feel it deep inside
This black nigger's pride
I have no fear when I say
And I say it everyday

Every nigger is a star
Every nigger is a star
Who rule the night
But you and I
And every nigger is a star

I have walked the streets alone
Twenty years I have been on my own
To be hated and despised
No one to sympathize
But there is one great thing I know
And I bet you can say I told you so
We got a bright place in the sun
Where there is love for everyone

Every Nigger is a star.[20]

In 1974 and again in 1977, Big Youth, a featured artist in the 1974 film, covered the song, bringing it firmly into the fold of mainstream reggae. His arrangement and lyrics spoke more to the economic and social disenfranchisement of Black people. He opens with four bars of the title before the first verse, adds Bob Marley and the Wailers' I-Threes (Rita Marley, Judy Mowatt, and Marcia Griffiths) as back-up singers, and through them introduces the refrain "poor nigger" to offer a specific emphasis on working-class struggle in the song. Here the word "nigger" is used to embody injured Blackness, or a person who is unfairly oppressed at the hands of others. There is no violence in the deployment of the word, as is often the case in the United States. Instead, the affect is empathy. Big Youth transforms the song into one of hope in which he shares his troubles but affirms a belief in collective liberation that includes him. Big Youth and the I-Threes sing:

I have walked the streets alone
    [I-Threes] Poor Nigger

Twenty years I have been on my own
To be hated and despised
    Poor nigger
No one to sympathize
But there is one great big thing I know
    Poor nigger
And I bet you can say I told you so
We have a bright place in the sun
Where there is love for everyone.[21]

In 1991, Frankie Paul, often described as "the Jamaican Stevie Wonder," remade the song yet again, this time in the style that had emerged to take the world by storm, dancehall reggae. Here Paul directs the song's lyrics to a woman. He takes on the role of "a nigger" who is a star, a star who not only has walked the streets alone in the past but continues to do so, not just because he is an oppressed Black man but also because success has set him apart. He has gained attention. He has risen from poverty. He is being recognized and lauded by his community, is making money, and through it is becoming mobile and migratory and thus free. The lonely lament found in Gardiner's and Big Youth's versions of the song is gone, and there is an understanding that his standing apart, his being independent, has become a necessity, a sign of his freedom but also of his manhood.

The temperature, speed, and gravity of the song rises in each of these reimagined arrangements. The beat quickens, the lyrics gain depth of meaning. The rhythm encourages movement, and the listening body responds with increasing urgency. Paul sings:

Ah baby
I want you to know
I am a star
Eh

I keep walkin' the streets alone
With no port to call my own
And the songs I used to sing
I don't sing them no more
Now to all you massive and cool
Frankie P him just a pass you
Just to sing dem da song (an)to you and you
Dem lyrics we have brand new

Every nigger is a star
Every nigger is a star
From east to the west
Dem say we are da best
Yes, every nigger is a star.[22]

Paul declares his rising status through his appropriated and reworked lyrics. He also extends the song's meaning and power globally—from the east to the west of Jamaica and to the world. Rejecting the word's pejorative use, he sings that in his world every "nigger" (or Black person) is a star everywhere.

Paul also centers the creative power of dub music in his peaceful, musical, and global imaginary, as he name-checks crews that would become central to the rise of dancehall in Jamaica, the Caribbean, and the world:

Jungle (bantam) to Rema dub
Every nigger is a star

Mainland crew are you ready?
Atwell Massive get steady
Jungles Crew stay steady, get ready.

The song resurfaces again just four years later, in 1995, when the don dada Super Cat releases the track. Super Cat—the stage name of William Maragh, a Jamaican *dougla*, or person of African and Indian descent—had by this time risen to the top of the dancehall scene, emerging as one of the preeminent DJs of his generation. By 1995, he had done what many artists seek to do: cross over. He achieved global success working with artists such as Heavy D and the Boyz on the hit "In the Mood for Love"; Biggie Smalls, Mary J. Blige, and Puff Daddy on "Dolly My Baby"; Kriss Kross on a remix of their mega hit "Jump"; and the group Sugar Ray on their hit "Fly," just to name a few.

Maragh's and Richards's lives parallel in notable ways. Maragh was born at home on June 25, 1963, in what was then known as Cockburn Pen, a tough enclave in Kingston (now known as Seivwright Gardens). A little over a month later, on August 2, Michael Richards's Costa Rican mother, Mary, and his Jamaican father, Fred, welcomed him into the world in Brooklyn. In an interview on Jamaican television prior to Maragh's December 2013 return to Jamaica to headline the one-day reggae extravaganza "Sting," performing as Super Cat, the DJ spoke about growing up very poor, walking barefoot to the Majestic School for six months out of the year but doing well in exams.[23] He made it to the fifth grade, then did a bit of schooling up to the eighth grade, and does not appear to have graduated high school. He recalled getting into situations with rivals and the police that required him to sleep in Calvary and May Pen Cemeteries in St. Andrew and the Chinese Cemetery in Kingston, evading the gangsters and police who were looking for him.

Richards moved with his family from Brooklyn to Kingston at the age of five. He and Maragh came of age in Jamaica during the political violence that erupted on the island throughout the 1970s, culminating in the brutal 1980 election that pitted Michael Manley's People's National Party (PNP) against Edward Seaga's Jamaica Labor Party (JLP). Unlike Maragh, Richards graduated high school and, due to his right of birth and family efforts, returned to the United States around 1980 to attend Queens College, later earning a master's in studio art from New York University.

Unlike Richards, Maragh had no obvious path for avoiding the disappointments of post-independence Jamaica. His community was poor. Violence was always close. In his words, he found music because it became a way out, a road to freedom. Maragh gravitated toward reggae music while working with now-legendary sound systems like Soul Imperial, Crystal Blue, and Little John and the Flames discothèque.

As dancehall music expanded to feature stars like Yellow Man, Shabba Ranks, Barrington Levy, and Ninja Man, Maragh, then known as The Wild Apache, debuted in 1982 at the age of eighteen with the song "Mr. Walker" (along with Brok Bak). The lyrics were light and somewhat humorous, a feature of the music at the time. Brok Bak introduces the song, and Maragh, performing as The Wild Apache, sings the verses, with Bak echoing his words:

> De musical is called Mr. Walker.
> Special request to all the lovers in Jamaica originated by de man dem call
> Super Cat and I man Brok Bak, gi dem some lover's rock . . .
>
> Good morning missa walker (a walker) mi love off yu dawta (yu dawta)
> de lickle one weh name Sandra (nuh Sandra!)
> Is a nice chikitita (tita!)
> And she love off de supa
> I am your cool entertainer Brok Bak,
> mi farin partner we come fi tear dung Jamaica
> Well watch ya man . . .
> mi seh good morning missa walker mi divorce yu dawta
> she a get outa order mi send har back to har fada.[24]

In its playfulness, its slow, smoky rhythms, fast chat, and its wide, unapologetic use of Jamaican patois, dancehall distinguished itself from roots or conscious reggae. The song was a hit. Maragh, now known as Super Cat, followed it up in 1985 with the track "Si Boops Deh," a song that generated a subgenre of Boops or lover songs, solidifying his place in the canon of Jamaican dancehall music and Caribbean lingua franca.

While Richards was slowly making a name for himself in the art world, by the 1990s Super Cat's star was also bright, and he was signed to Columbia Records. "Every Nigger Is a Star" appeared on his third album for Columbia, *The Struggle Continues*, released in 1995. In his hands, the song is once again reimagined, fully in the bosom of Rastafari. Rather than the light ghetto opera that was "Mr. Walker," Super Cat's version of Gardiner's 1973 song recalls the music, poetry, and liberation consciousness of the group Count Ossie and the Mystic Revelation of Rastafari, who, on their classic 1972 album *Grounation*, declared:

> The light became morning
> And the morning became day
> Speaking for myself
> I wish the darkness had stayed
> Morning became evening
> The sun is going down
> But equality and justice is nowhere to be found.[25]

For many Jamaicans, independence from Britain did not mean the end of colonialism, and the theoretical postcolonial did not make way for Black freedom. Reggae and dancehall music offered something that could not be found elsewhere. Quintessential modern forms, they answered Wynter's "How" and performed the work of Lezama Lima by criticizing their condition in and through their creative practice and poetics.

Super Cat's version of the Gardiner tune begins with the sound of a thunderclap and the spoken invocation:

> Jah Rastafari
>
> Well me look an' me tell dem seh rude boy
> And me look an' me tell dem
> I and I seh a kingdom that is divided by itself must fall
> All for one and one for all, I and I shall be like a green tree
> That's planted by the bank of Dunn's River falls
>
> A weh me tell dem rude boy
> African people come follow me, hear this.[26]

In this introduction, Super Cat speaks of Jamaica and to Jamaica as an extension of Africa. He positions his address, of what once was and what is to come, to people of the African diaspora before beginning to chat. In his hands, one quickly realizes that the song has become a war cry, one that builds in urgency both lyrically and musically. Like the *Slave Play on Dombi Plantation*, like Clifton's dance, like Montrose being lifted by queens, the song builds toward the ecstatic. It fires the soul in a way that gives permission to mash up the place, where burning a plantation to the ground is not beyond the realm of possibility but rather makes sense. Super Cat chants:

> Well, every nigger is an African and also a star
> And we know where we coming from and know who we are
> Every nigger is an African and also a star
> A no brag we a brag and a no blar we a blar
> Teeth white like a snow, skin black like a tar
> And anytime dem see we a de show we a star
>
> Africans oonu better cut out de war
> United we stand and divided we fall
> Oonu hear me Africans oonu better cut out che war
> United we stand and divided we . . .
> Because deep down in a Africa we fore parents roam
> When we never did have no need fe no scissors nor comb
> When de animals were tamed and we shared de same home
> We use to walk up on silver and cook up on gold
>
> Drink de cow's milk and den we suck de honeycomb
> But that was in the days of beginning and old
> When exploiter they came with religion unknown
> They robbed us our culture an' our kings dem dey dethrone
>
> And they carry us in a Babylon true we strong bone
> But no matter what they do Jah Jah guiding us home
> We a go chase dem crazy bald head out of we town
> A we plant de corn and build de cabin alone
>
> Well, every nigger is an African and also a star
> And we know where we coming from and know who we are.

Super Cat tells an epic story of the Black Atlantic. He later repeats his opening invocations to stop Black-on-Black violence. Calling the names of superheroes, he makes his audience aware that there is no one like He-Man, Superman, or Tarzan to save us. There is instead a need for Black people to see one another as "African children wearing the African scar" of dark skin in the Americas. He continues:

> Let me say, de coming of Jah Jah it is not very far
> He not gon drop out da sky like a falling star
> Naw appear like a soldier from the one James R
> He not gonna come on a jet or in a big fast car
> Him gon come like a thief in the night from afar
> With a fire light, light like a burning cigar
> Hair white like a snow
> Feet like a brown spar
> He not coming with automatic or no SLR
> Hear me now Super, iffy hear me now star
> When Jah Jah come a brimstone, fire, war
> 'im not gonna contribute to the skin color bar
> Neither take the side a da guys who preach war
>
> [Chorus]
>
> Because this is not He-Man an this a not Thundarr
> Neither Superman nor the one Skeletaw [Skeletor]
> This is not Tarzan make believe jungle star
> These are the African children wearing the African scar
>
> Ancient motherland and she so pretty and far
> Millions of children were stolen from her
> Bought into slavery and sol like a car
> Fe cut sugar cane, cotton and quail cigar
>
> Under Jah moon and Jah sun and Jah star
> Hear me now Super you haf fe hear me now star
> A no brag me a brag no blar me a blar
> Them never make no weapon fe go fight no war
>
> But, every nigger is an African and also a star . . .
> Africans oonu better cut out de war
> United we stand and divided we fall.

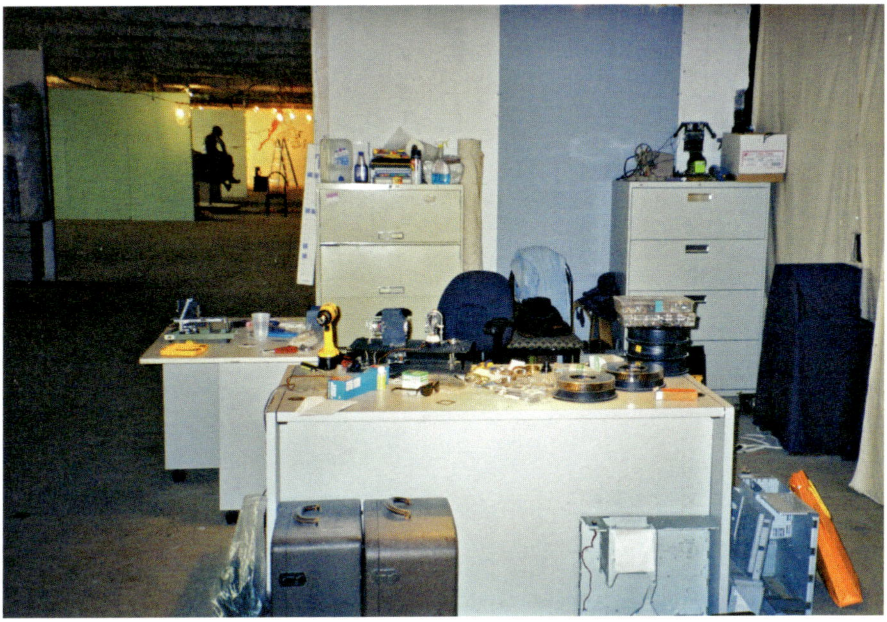

Fig. 4.7. Lower Manhattan Cultural Council World Views Studios, including Hyungsub Shin's studio (foreground) and Michael Richards's studio and sculpture *Every Nigga Is a Star* (2000, upper left), North Tower, World Trade Center, New York, 2001

This is a liberation anthem, a song that embodies the Black ecstatic. It is the cry of Caliban in the playwright Aimé Césaire's postcolonial adaptation of Shakespeare's *The Tempest*, and it is a song that Michael Richards must have felt deeply. For Richards, dance and dancehall music were portals to freedom, and the Super Cat version of the song, which he would have known best, builds to pure ecstasy in the context of the dance. To hear it requires a bodily response; to feel what Montrose feels when he is lifted by those queens; to feel as Clifton does in that living room in London; or as Storyboard P does when he is reborn as Anansi and enters the bowels of Elegba to travel home. It is an ecstasy that opens the doors to Black freedom, carrying those who venture forth all the way to Africa, in spirit if not flesh.

The surface of Richards's sculpture *Every Nigga Is a Star* is the color of aluminum, refined bauxite. It is also the color of ash left in the wake of fire and devastation. Echoing the song's invocation, the appearance of this airman on a thunderbolt can be read as one of many eerily prophetic works in his oeuvre, in which crashing, exploding, or imperiled airplanes are a key motif. The sculpture was with Richards in his studio on the ninety-second floor of the World Trade Center's North Tower (fig. 4.7) on September 11, 2001, when he was killed and the work was destroyed. But beyond its end, part of what we were meant to see in this work are the urgent affirmations and declarations made in Super Cat's "big chune."

Richards's and Super Cat's lives and work intersected and diverged in Jamaica and later New York. Their art mirrored each other's claims to self-worth, self-actualization, self-love, and self-determination amid the waning hope of independence and postcolonial freedom. In the absence of the sculpture, the music gestures toward its content, context, and, more precisely, its consciousness. In claiming this work as global Caribbean contemporary art and an expression of Black ecstasy, I believe that it suggests an alternative to the political disappointments and intimate devastation that too often repeat in Black life to the point of death. The sculpture embodies Richards's faith in the possibility of Black ecstasy to catalyze, recover, reconstitute, and self-author in answer to Wynter's question. As a Caribbean modern form, it renders, lifts, and carries Black people to the freedom of Ginen, even as their bodies remain in the belly of Babylon.

NOTES

1. *Michael Richards: Are You Down?*, curated by Alex Fialho and Melissa Levin, Museum of Contemporary Art North Miami, 2021; North Carolina Museum of Art, 2023; and the Bronx Museum of the Arts, 2023–24. I am deeply grateful to william córdova for sharing his archive with me for this project.

2. The song "Every Nigger Is a Star" was written by Boris Gardiner and originally recorded by the Grammy award–winning singer Billy Paul (1934–2016). Paul's manager refused to allow the song to be released, and Gardiner went on to sing the track to enduring success. Interview with Billy Paul by the author, 2015.

3. Lovers rock is a gentle, melodic form of reggae music influenced by American soul and R&B music covering romantic themes and made popular in the London music scene of the 1970s.

4. Dancehall is a genre of music established in Jamaica that rose in popularity in the 1980s and '90s and expanded quickly into the Jamaican diaspora and the world. It was notable early on for its creative and determined use of Jamaican patois rather than standard English, its reliance on sound systems, and its signature digital beats.

5. Jennifer C. Nash, *The Black Body in Ecstasy: Reading Race, Reading Pornography* (Duke University Press, 2014).

6. See, for example, Joan Morgan, "Why We Get Off: Moving Towards a Black Feminist Politics of Pleasure," *Black Scholar* 45, no. 4 (2015): 36–46.

7. Kevin Quashie, *Black Aliveness, or A Poetics of Being* (Duke University Press, 2021), 3.

8. "Wheel and come again" is a command often heard in dancehall performance in the 1990s. It is a command for the musicians to stop, rewind, and restart the rhythm again. It is also used colloquially to suggest the need for a person to stop where they are going or what they are doing and start again or change directions. There are multiple terms for this action employed by DJs and people outside of music and across the Caribbean diaspora, including "wheel and turn" and "pull up."

9. *Turn up* or *turnt up*: To amplify or expand. To be turnt up means to be lit, excited, or at times drunk or high. An extreme situation.

10. I use the term "autohistoriography" to describe an ongoing decolonial process in which once-colonized people critically question and reengage the authority of colonial archives and histories through literature, art, music, scholarship, and other creative forms to reshape the historical record and the historiographic process from their perspectives.

11. Jessica Berman, *Modernist Commitments: Ethics, Politics, and Transnational Modernism* (Columbia University Press, 2012), 7.

12. Dilip Parameshwar Gaonkar, "Afterword: The Slow Burn of Modernity," in *Behind the Masks of Modernism: Global and Transnational Perspectives*, ed. Andrew Reynolds and Bonnie Roos (University Press of Florida, 2016), 228.

13. Sylvia Wynter, in David A. Scott, "The Re-Enchantment of Humanism: An Interview with Sylvia Wynter," *Small Axe* 8, no. 9 (September 2000): 119–207.

14. José Lezama Lima, "Julián Del Casal," *Small Axe* 23, no. 3 (60) (2019): 131–54.

15. Gaonkar, "Afterword," 229.

16. Lezama Lima, "Julián Del Casal," 131–32.

17. Krista A. Thompson, "The Sound of Light: Reflections on Art History in the Visual Culture of Hip-Hop," *Art Bulletin* 91, no. 4 (2009): 491; and Robyn Wiegman, *American Anatomies: Theorizing Race and Gender* (Duke University Press, 1995), 1.

18. Richard Price, *First Time: The Historical Vision of an Afro-American People* (Johns Hopkins University Press, 1983).

19. All song lyrics hereafter were transcribed by the author except "Mr. Walker," which was transcribed by Kei Miller.

20. Boris Gardiner, "Every Nigger Is a Star," tracks 1 and 9 on *Every Nigger Is a Star*, Leal Records, LP 0010, LP008, 1973.

21. "Every Nigger Is a Star / Poor Nigger," single on Big Youth and the I-Threes, *Every Nigger Is a Star*, Negusa Nagast, NN 12 A, 7" single, 1974.

22. "Every Nigger Is a Star," track 3 on Frankie Paul, *Every Nigger Is a Star*, Leal Records, Greensleeves Records, GREL 165, 1991.

23. "Super Cat Di Don Dadda Returns," Onstage TV, July 9, 2015, https://www.youtube.com/watch?v=TWEa1ZULtMk.

24. "Mr. Walker," single by Brok Bak and The Wild Apache (Super Cat), Techniques Records, 1982.

25. Count Ossie and the Mystic Revelation of Rastafari, "Poem," track 7 on *Grounation*, Ashanti, NTI 301, 1972.

26. Super Cat, "Every Nigger Is a Star," track 11 on *The Struggle Continues*, Columbia Records, 1995. All subsequent lyrics are quoted from the same recording.

PART II
RETHINKING MODERNISM

CHAPTER 5

BEYOND THE ARCHIVES AND VODOU ICONOGRAPHY

LUCE TURNIER, A FEMINIST HAITIAN MODERNIST

Jerry Philogene

In a photograph taken by the well-known Haitian photographer Louis Doret in 1945 at an exhibition opening at the Centre d'Art d'Haïti in Port-au-Prince, eighteen well-dressed individuals pose formally (fig. 5.1).[1] At the center, in the front row, is the artist Luce Turnier, seated between Harold Hilgard Tittmann Jr., then–US Ambassador to Haiti, and DeWitt Peters, the American watercolorist who helped establish and served as the first director of the Centre d'Art. Opened with government support in 1944, the Centre operated as an exhibition space, studio, and school for artists, as well as a meeting space for artists, curators, and collectors from around the world. Among the artists flanking Turnier, Tittmann, and Peters in the photograph are Lucien Price, Antonio Joseph, Rigaud Benoit, Georges (Geo) Remponeau, Maurice Borno, and Tamara Baussan.[2] They variously face Doret's camera or look off to the side. Some appear stiff, frozen in the significance of the moment; others smile or seem distracted. Turnier, legs crossed with hands folded on her lap, stares directly into Doret's camera as if *she* is fully cognizant of the importance of this photograph and her place in this assembly.

Another photograph, taken in October of the same year, places Turnier once again at the center, seated between Centre d'Art board members Emmanuel Lafond and Daniel Lafontant (fig. 5.2) at a meeting of the Comité d'Administration (Board of Directors), which was made up of artists and cofounders of the institution.[3] They are seated around a table. There is a sense that this photograph is also staged to suggest an air of serious purpose, with important matters being discussed. Peters, the white man near the open door, holds a pen in one hand and a cigarette in another, as if waiting to record the proceedings from the meeting. Most of the gazes seem to be directed toward the suited gentleman who has his back to the camera, cigarette in hand. While Turnier is not at the center of the frame, she is made to be the compositional focus thanks to the diagonal axis that runs from the speaker (the suited gentleman), who has the attention of the committee members, to Turnier. Her

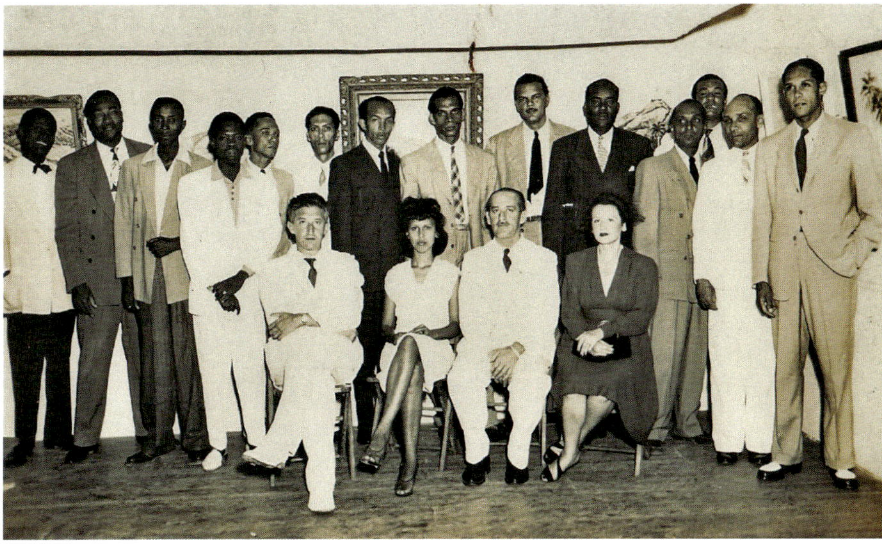

Fig. 5.1. An exhibition opening(?) at the Centre d'Art in Port-au-Prince, Haiti, 1945. Standing, left to right: an unidentified man, Tony (last name unknown, a cabinetmaker and photographer at the Centre d'Art), Rigaud Benoit, Antonio Joseph, Raymond Coupeau, Lucien Price, Georges Remponeau, Jean Chenet, Maurice Borno, Robert Dorsainville, Robert Baussan, an unidentified man (partially obscured), Pierre Pallière, and Max Ewald. Seated, left to right: Harold Hilgard Tittmann Jr., Luce Turnier, DeWitt Peters, and Tamara Baussan. Photo by Louis Doret

relaxed pose and the smile on her face exude a sense of comfort with her position as the lone woman within this circle of men. Compositionally, the frame of the open doorway to the balcony also draws the viewer's eyes to Turnier's central position.

In a later and less formal photograph (fig. 5.3), Turnier dines with the American folk-art critic and dealer Selden Rodman and the American sculptor Jason Seley at Villa Créole, a popular hotel in Haiti.[4] Their proximity and the setting suggest a familiar relationship between the individuals. Rodman, a supporter of the artists and artisans who were associated with the Centre d'Art, was instrumental in promoting their work in New York. Seley helped establish the Centre d'Art's sculpting program.

These three photographs index Turnier's contradictory absence and presence in the historiography of modern Haitian art specifically and in mid-twentieth-century art of the African diaspora more generally. While all three photographs document her physical participation in the Centre d'Art's formative years and her connection to the individuals who were involved in its formation and development, she is minimally present in the institution's written archives and in the canon of Haitian art history defined by the secondary literature.[5] Tellingly, at one point

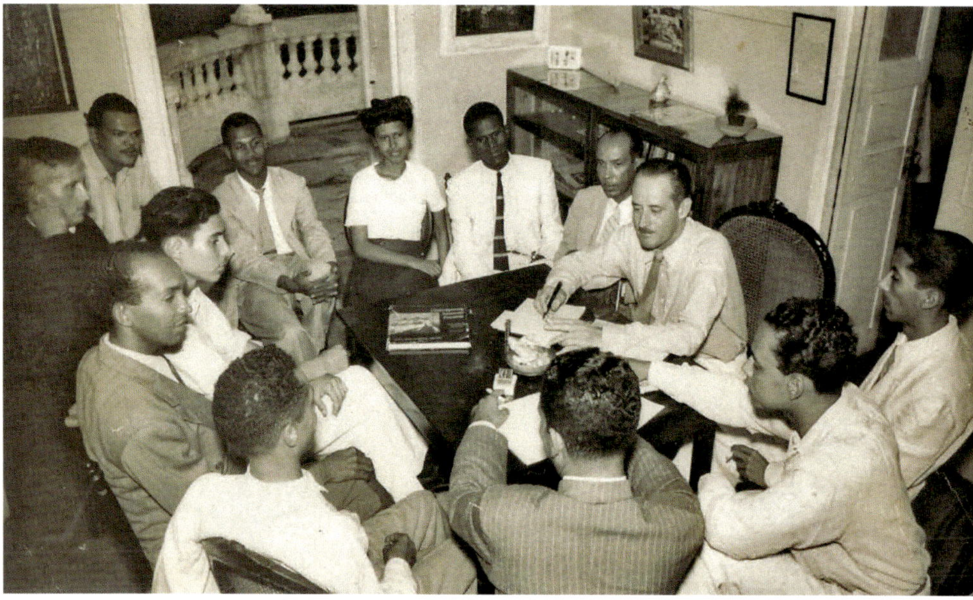

Fig. 5.2. Meeting of the Comité d'Administration, Centre d'Art, Port-au-Prince, Haiti, October 1945. From left to right: Gérald Bloncourt, Geo Remponeau, an unidentified man, an unidentified man, Albert Mangonès, Lucien Price, DeWitt Peters, Raymond Coupeau, Daniel Lafontant, Luce Turnier, Emmanuel Lafond, Maurice Borno, and James Petersen

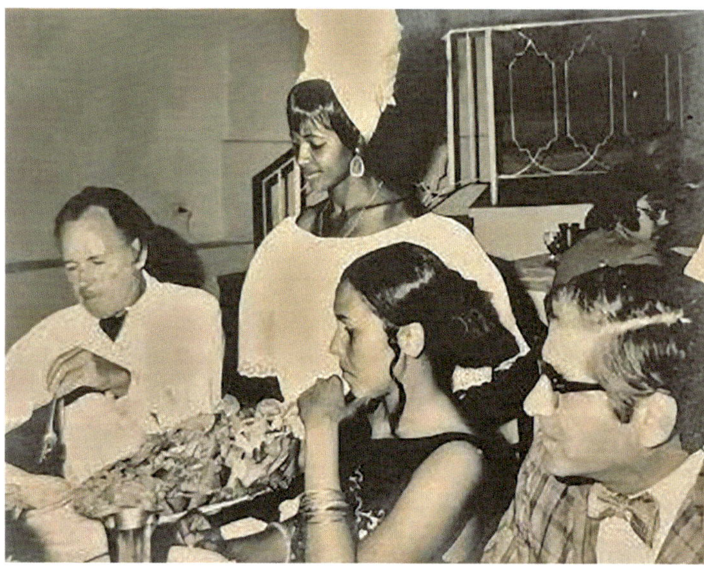

Fig. 5.3. Luce Turnier (seated in foreground) with the American folk art critic and art dealer Selden Rodman (left) and the American sculptor Jason Seley at Villa Créole, date unknown

when the first two photographs appeared on the Centre d'Art's website, the captions listed the names of the members of the Comité d'Administration but not Turnier's, despite her obvious presence in both images. Her visibility in the photographic record contradicts yet compounds her conspicuous invisibility in the prevailing narratives of twentieth-century Haitian art. She exists at the center and at the margin of artistic discourse simultaneously.

While Turnier is mentioned briefly in exhibition catalogues, biographical dictionaries, book chapters, and dissertations, she has never been given significant credit for the formation of Haitian modern art in the ways that others have. The self-taught, or "Kreyòl," artists Hector Hyppolite, Philomé Obin, Rigaud Benoit, André Pierre, and Préfète Duffaut, among others—all men—are extolled as the "fathers of Haitian art."[6] While I am not suggesting that the brilliant and rich Vodou imagery depicted in their work was not central to the creation of modern Haitian art, it is important to note that those were the *only* images promoted by the Centre d'Art. Meanwhile, in most scholarship on Haitian art history, modernist artists such as Turnier, Jacques Gabriel, and Roland Dorcély are relegated to brief mentions as being "important" and "the first to"; they remain understudied, under-exhibited, and sometimes overlooked. Artists like Turnier and her contemporaries Remponeau, Borno, and Albert Mangonès have been underappreciated since they did not create works that affirmed, in the minds of Europeans and Americans, a purportedly dark and dangerous Haiti and its "demonic" religion.

Turnier's marginalization is particularly instructive. I suggest that through these silences, what is being produced is an episteme and expressive cultural tradition dependent on and intensified by biases that include elements of sexism, classism, patriarchy, and paternalism. I am not advocating for the dismissal of the important scholarship that has been done but suggesting, instead, that the primacy of a particular narrative in establishing what is considered Haitian art has hampered consideration of other individuals and styles. As Kaiama L. Glover points out, "It is crucial to examine the ways in which such discursive challenges to a masculine order are marked by the constraining presence of gendered expectations and thus risk flattening, albeit differently, the experience of individual women."[7] An investigation of Turnier's historical erasure demonstrates the importance of locating specific alternative narratives in which Black women factor as importantly as Black men.

My interest in Turnier began over two decades ago when I was researching my dissertation.[8] One chapter focused on the Centre d'Art, and during my research in its archives, I encountered a trove of information about DeWitt Peters; the self-taught artists, mostly men, who worked and studied at the Centre d'Art; and the international artists who had taught there.[9] During the Centre d'Art's early years, its priority appears to have been to promote the work of the Kreyòl artists, whose historical paintings and Vodou iconography rapidly became characteristic of Haitian art.[10] Turnier, Dorcély, and Gabriel, who were seeking new forms and new imagery for self-expression, did not conform to what was coming to be understood, marketed, and written about as Haitian art.

Years of conversations with artists, curators, gallery directors, and art historians based in Haiti, Europe, and North America have revealed that several women artists were active at the Centre d'Art during its formation and development. Nonetheless, little documentation exists about the women who managed the Centre d'Art and the women artists who took classes and taught there, such as the painter and sculptor Marie-José Nadal (later Marie-José Nadal-Gardère) and the painters Rose-Marie Desruisseau and Andrée Malebranche.[11] Why have they not received scholarly attention equivalent to that devoted to their male, self-taught peers, who were more engaged in Vodou iconography and producing scenes of markets and jungles?[12] In some cases they have been overlooked specifically because of their roles as forerunners of the modernist art movement in Haiti—a movement that encompasses the artistic, aesthetic, and representational practices associated with modernism, and also the linguistic and religious elements of Black and African modernist practices that demand a refashioning of the modern self/subject.

What would it mean to study an underrecognized transnational Haitian modernist painter active within the mid- to late twentieth-century arts of the African diaspora? What would it mean to write about a particular formative moment that goes against the well-documented and conventional masculinist narrative of Haitian art history? What might a slight shifting and reformulation of an origin story, or a closer looking into what has been written of that history, bring about? What might be some of the art historical implications of a narrative that not only includes women but also centers them? What is at stake in an inquiry to articulate the artwork of a figure like Luce Turnier—a Black Haitian woman? An exhaustive archival excavation of the life and creative practices of this artist is necessarily beyond the scope of this essay. However, as a point of departure, I propose three foundational texts as theoretical underpinnings that might inform such an undertaking. One poses a way of understanding the problem of Turnier's erasure from the records, and the other two offer methods of intervention.

Michel-Rolph Trouillot's essay on the insurrection that brought about Haitian independence at the end of the eighteenth century, "An Unthinkable History: The Haitian Revolution as a Non-Event," outlines two tropes that he describes as "failures of narration." Both tropes offer a narrative of invisibility that derives from and transcends the historical specificity of the revolution: One, a "formula of erasure," erases the factual event of the Haitian Revolution in written text, while the other, a "formula of banalization," trivializes the event, lessening its effect.[13] Like racism, sexism, and patriarchy, these two formulas also operate simultaneously to delegitimize the artistic production of Black Caribbean women. Either women artists are rendered absent from the origin story of their fields, or their participation is rendered insignificant and eventually neutralized.

The second essay, "In Search of a Discourse and Critique/s That Center the Art of Black Women Artists," by the art historian Freida High W. Tesfagiorgis, introduces the concept of Afrofemcentrism.[14] Tesfagiorgis proposes a Black feminist art history that would be sufficiently epistemologically capacious to allow for transatlantic and transcultural creative practices, as well as a critique of the practice of art historical discourses that have historically placed Black women as the objects of the gaze rather than as creators. Most importantly, Tesfagiorgis emphasizes that "Black feminist art criticism must both utilize aspects of existing paradigms and introduce new ways of thinking about art" that "speak across the boundaries of race, class, gender . . . to be enriched by and to enrich existing knowledge."[15] Thus, for both Tesfagiorgis and Trouillot, in order to resist the basic hierarchal, sexist, and racist assumptions of an art historical canon, it is crucial to question what is written and what is not. Black feminist art historians, such as Tesfagiorgis, Judith Wilson, Leslie King-Hammond, Lowery Stokes Sims, Michele Wallace, and Huey Copeland, along with artists such as Lorraine O'Grady and Adrian Piper, to name a few, have engaged with a kaleidoscope of art historical and interdisciplinary discourses—including social art history, Black cultural theory, and Black feminist theory. Their work transforms the positioning of Black women artists, shifting from objectification, misrepresentation, and omission to a place where "we collectively activate our knowledge and power" to "inscribe new discourses on art wherein we can locate our histories and construct critiques that will appropriately inscribe our lives, production, and interventions in this world."[16] This methodology combats the exclusivity of the art historical canon and ultimately contributes to a more comprehensive art history, reshaping larger art-world practices to include the lives and creative endeavors of Black diasporic women.[17]

Another perspective is offered by the Caribbean feminist anthropologist and artist Gina Athena Ulysse's infinitely generative concept of *rasanblaj*—a deliberate gathering space that "blurs genres, shifting location, time, and space" and offers a deep strategic looking to uncover what is visible to the eye yet made invisible in histories.[18] Such interdisciplinary and multivocal approaches are of significance to art history in general and to Black feminist studies, Haitian studies, and Black modernism specifically. Ulysee describes rasanblaj as "an explicitly decolonial project" and further suggests that "rasanblaj demands that we consider and confront the limited scope of segregated frameworks to explore what remains excluded in this landscape that is scorched yet full of life, riddled with inequities."[19] The brief account of Turnier's career that follows applies the strategies of Tesfagiorgis, Trouillot, and Ulysee to model how shifting our attention can transform the story of Haitian art.

LOCATING LUCE

Luce Turnier was twenty-one when she began studying at the Centre d'Art in 1945.[20] Her struggling, rural middle-class family had relocated from Jacmel to Port-au-Prince in 1937 after a hurricane devastated the southern towns of Jacmel and Jeremie in 1935. Having studied composition and design with Georges (Geo) Remponeau and the African American painter Eldzier Cortor, Turnier received a Rockefeller Foundation grant in 1950 to study at the Art Students League of New York for one year.[21] There, she studied with the painters Morris Kantor, who strongly influenced her attention to Cubism, and Harry Sternberg, whose concentration on the figure can be seen in her fluid portraits. A year later, with gentle prodding from John Marshall, then associate director of the Rockefeller Foundation's Humanities Division, Turnier received a grant from the Institut Français d'Haïti to study at L'Académie de la Grande Chaumière in Paris, where she was exposed to model-drawing workshops, Abstract Expressionism, and other modern art aesthetics.[22] She would stay in Paris until 1955, supporting herself through financial assistance from her family and friends, sales of her work, and additional funds from the Rockefeller Foundation and the French government.

Like other Caribbean, African, and African American writers and artists who departed from the United States to live a permanent or expatriate life in Europe, Turnier subsequently relocated to Paris in 1960, moving between Paris and Haiti and making frequent trips to New York, with a final return to Haiti in 1977.[23] Turnier's Atlantic crossings were central to her modernist artistic formation, a cultural mixing of Haitian Creole formed in the Afrodiasporic communities of Haiti, Paris, and, later, New York. From 1945 to 1990, Turnier had a continuous if under-recognized exhibition record in France, other European countries, the United States, and Haiti. As we know, the dominant history of Western modernism elides or marginalizes artists who have made the political and personal choice to stay in the Caribbean. But in Turnier's case, the marginalization of her body of work stems not only from her geographic location but also from her gender. Writing about Haitian fiction writers, the literary critic Marie José N'Zengou-Tayo notes:

> Haitian women have struggled to make their voices heard. An analysis of their social condition shows that whatever their class, their tremendous contribution to their country and to the economy has never been thoroughly assessed. This social and economic "invisibility" has been reproduced in the field of culture. As writers and artists, they are seen as deviant and marginalized. However, these women have challenged quietly yet decisively male stereotypes concerning them. . . . They have tried to redefine themselves, subverting the dominant male discourse that sought to silence them.[24]

In Turnier's case, her chosen artistic style—working outside of what canonically has been recognized as "Haitian art"—compounded that invisibility. Her adherence to modernist aesthetics constitutes both her challenge to cultural stereotypes and a cause of the silence surrounding her work.

From the mid-1940s through the late '80s, in Haiti, New York, and Paris, Turnier created a body of work that encompasses still life, landscapes, portraits, drawings, and collages. Her work ethic was noted by her contemporaries from the start. In a letter dated November 10, 1949, DeWitt Peters wrote to his friend Anne Kennedy:

> Shortly I am going down for Luce and Maurice's opening. I think they've both gained a lot—perhaps especially Maurice . . . couldn't find a place so I offered her the little house at the end of the garden here and she is installed. I hope you don't mind. . . . She is extremely serious about getting on with her work and plans to go downtown only when she has a class or it is otherwise necessary.[25]

Her still-life paintings, such as *Untitled (Still Life with Coconuts)* (fig. 5.4), capture the floral symbolism of Haiti using the visual language of modernism and attempt, in her use of diagonal, vertical, and horizontal lines, to create a synthesis of balance, rhythm, color, and form. Block-like abstract patterns form the backgrounds for displaying images of coconuts, eggplants, plantains, beets, green onions, and peppers. They highlight Turnier's attention to shape, perspective, and gradations of color and tone upon a painted geometric flatness—all characteristic of modernist aesthetics. Seen at close range and cropped to create abstract patterns, *Still Life with Coconuts* presents a balance between, on the one hand, emphasis on the painted surface rather than an attempt at the illusion of three-dimensionality and, on the other, the use of faceted patches of color to articulate the turn and shape of the fruit.

By contrast, her black-ink line drawings and her limited palette of browns, blues, ambers, and yellows in painted portraits of working- and middle-class Haitian men and women arguably reflect both her attention to figuration and the influence of Abstract Expressionism on Turnier's pictorial aesthetic and abstract mark-making practice.[26] Deceptively simple in its use of brown, ochre, and white tones, her visual language is clearly one of traditional portraiture, where capturing the essence, if not the exact likeness, of the sitter is essential (fig. 5.5).[27]

Turnier was fascinated with figuration. Some of her portraits capture friends and family members in moments of introspection and exploration, while others are character portrayals illustrating the quiet elegance and dignity of individuals whom she would meet in the marketplace or who worked in her home (fig. 5.6). Often sketches for what would later become paintings, the artist's drawings illustrate a

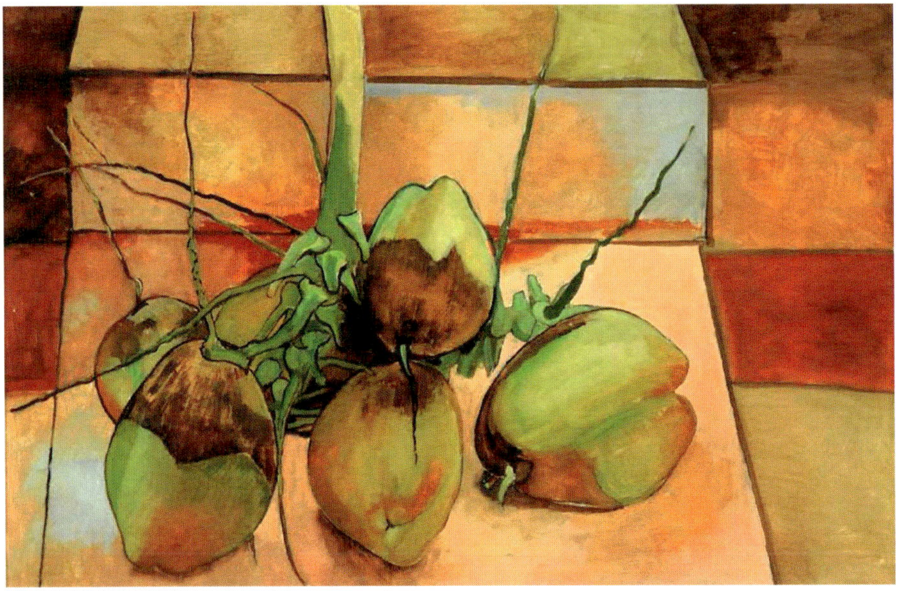

Fig. 5.4. Luce Turnier (Haitian, 1924–1994), *Untitled (Still Life with Coconuts)*, not dated. Oil on Masonite, 31 ½ × 47 ¼ in. (80 × 120 cm). Collection of Jézabel Traube

quiet interiority, a gentle pathos, and a detailed individuality that distinguish them from the quintessential and popular images of market women that we have come to associate with Haitian art specifically and Caribbean art in general. In Turnier's portraits, she immortalized individuals, women in particular, who existed outside the dominant cultures of society. She didn't simply give people back their humanity; she delicately recorded it. In a 1983 interview with the filmmaker Danny Pietrodangelo in Haiti, with *Untitled (Portrait of a Young Boy)* (fig. 5.7) placed on the ground next to her, she states:

> From 1965 to 1972 I was doing more abstract work. Now I am doing people because I enjoy it very much. . . . In Haiti especially. . . . It is not because I am a naturalist . . . but I think people are very graceful. I am very interested in the figure more than anywhere else. I think the landscapes are more beautiful in France, I like and enjoy to do more landscape in France, but I enjoy more to do people here.[28]

In this short documentary, the viewer can sense Turnier's isolation and her deep bitterness at her reception from those she identifies as the bourgeoisie

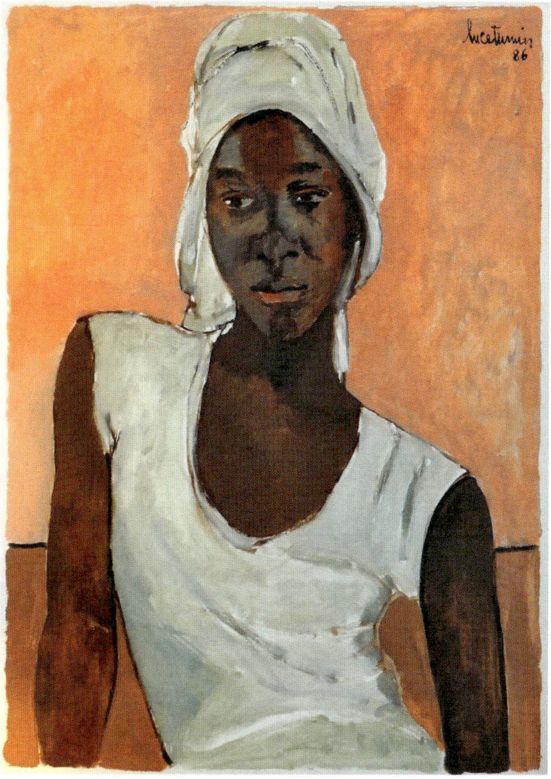

Fig. 5.5. Luce Turnier, *Untitled*, 1986. Oil on Masonite. Collection of John M. Black, Washington, DC

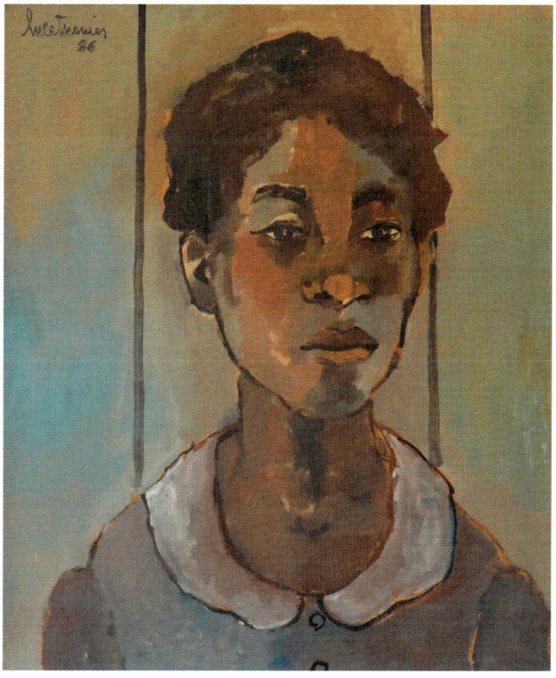

Fig. 5.6. Luce Turnier, *Untitled*, 1986. Oil on Masonite. Collection of John M. Black, Washington, DC

Fig. 5.7. Luce Turnier, *Untitled* (*Portrait of a Young Boy*), c. 1980. Oil on canvas, 47 × 29 in. (199.4 × 73. 7 cm). Private collection

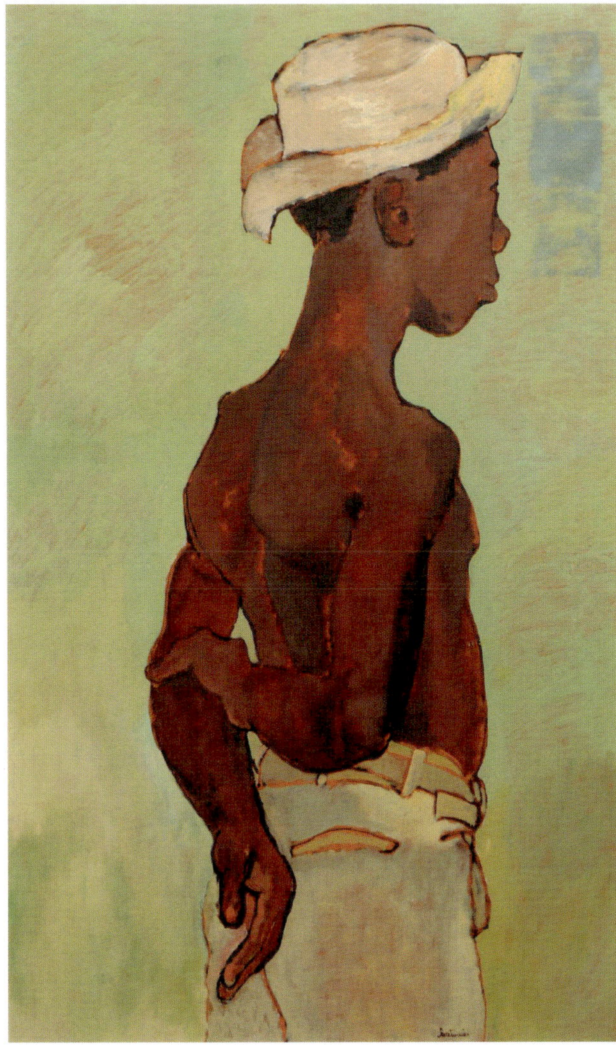

of Haitian society. She notes that modernist artists were widely described as "punks" and "hippies." Despite experiencing this disregard and the lukewarm attention to her work, she reveals her love of working with Haitian models. Vulnerably expressing her marginalization, both as a woman and as a modernist, Turnier conveys the synergy between herself and her models that allowed her to capture their subjectivity, illustrating their personalities and moods and highlighting their individuality in a moment of time. Her brushstrokes blend into strikingly realistic images. The brilliance of Turnier's portraits lies not only in what she was able to capture of their facial features and posture but also in the way her subjects emote.

Celebrating Black subjectivity can be rebellious. While Turnier may neither have been considered a feminist in the conventional sense nor have labeled herself as such, her paintings and drawings of nude and clothed Black women and Black men exhibit a feminist ethos paired with modernist formal practices. These works present the complex nature of racial looking and racial and class representation in ways that defy Haiti's pervasive characterization as "the poorest country in the Western Hemisphere"—a trope produced in and perpetuated by the United States through a visual archive that began in the early twentieth century and has included films, popular culture, plays, and literary texts centered on images of death and decay. Turnier's expressive portraits of rural and working-class Haitian women—market women, female domestic workers, and female tenant farmers—as subjects of beauty, grace, and dignity lend themselves to a reevaluation of the aesthetics of beauty and of the formal and conceptual role of the Black female figure. Rendered with soft brushstrokes and chromatically muted backgrounds, Turnier's canvases vibrate softly with the tranquility and serenity of these women. An attentive examination of her works—particularly her portraits, paying close attention to the sitter's pose, facial expression, gaze, skin tone, and clothing or nudity—can help us consider their power and potential as conceptual provocations in a space that primarily promoted Vodou iconography and the sexualization of the Black female body. Turnier proposes an alternative genealogy, an alternative history of Haitian art, in which a Black woman is placed at the center. Never idealizing or sexually "primitivizing" the Black female or male body, Turnier's portraits, from her pencil-and-black-ink drawings of the 1960s to the limited-palette paintings of the '80s and '90s, redefine the image of working-class Haitians, while her still-life paintings capture the cultural and material forms of Haitian life. Even in a space that has been defined as socially dead, Turnier's work shows how Haiti's people can exude self-possession and claim agency. Moreover, Turnier's assertion that she "enjoy[s] more to do people here" is itself an articulation of a feminist subjectivity.

CONCLUSION

In the foreword to the twentieth anniversary of edition of Trouillot's *Silencing the Past*, Hazel Carby writes:

> We learn how scanty evidence can be repositioned to generate new narratives, how silences can be made to speak for themselves to confront inequalities of power in the production of sources, archives, and narratives. We need to make these silences speak and, in the process, lay claim to the future. For, as Trouillot warns, "While some of us debate what history is or was, others take it into their own hands."[29]

The modest archival record tells us that Turnier exhibited and traveled, but there is very little written about the creative life that she lived in Paris, in Haiti, and in New York or what animated that life, much less a comprehensive analysis of her oeuvre. What if we were to employ what I proposed earlier in this essay: a "strategic looking"—a deep, thoughtful looking that recognizes, acknowledges, and allows for different modalities of seeing (and writing) to better comprehend what is not supposed to be seen? This strategic looking seeks something akin to Tina Campt's notion of phonic substance, which she defines as "the sound inherent to an image; one that defines or creates it, that is neither contingent upon nor necessarily preceding it; not simply a sound played over, behind, or in relation to an image; one that emanates from the image itself."[30] The photographs considered at the beginning of this essay emanate a particular phonic substance that is crucial to disrupting a particular narrative and challenging a particular origin story.[31] They show us that Turnier was there—indexing her presence at the Centre d'Art, at *its* center. By demonstrating her centrality, these photographs also illustrate how visual evidence can inform our comprehension of, and at times challenge, written histories. Furthermore, a repositioning of Turnier's creative oeuvre within what has come to be known and understood as the history of Haitian art is a tectonic shift. It rejects dominant masculinist art historical narratives to reveal the profound and overlooked roles that she and other Haitian women artists at the Centre d'Art had in shaping and advancing diverse Black feminist creative practices and Black modernisms, and it underscores their formative role in the historical understanding of Haitian modern art. Turnier's work compels us to think of art produced by Haitian artists as encompassing an evolving range of aesthetics that refute overdetermined and prescriptive imagery.

NOTES

1. Not pictured in this photo is the artist Andrée Malebranche; she, Turnier, and Tamara Baussan were among the few Haitian women artists teaching at the Centre d'Art during its early years.

2. Tamara Baussan was a Russian-born painter who married Robert Baussan, an architect and owner of the well-known hotel Ibo Lele located in Pétion-Ville. I thank the art historian Gerald Alexis for identifying the individuals in this photograph (see the caption for fig. 5.1) and for many years of guidance and wonderful conversations.

3. The Comité d'Administration consisted of Maurice Borno as president, Georges Remponeau as treasurer, Albert Mangonès as secretary general, Gérald Bloncourt and Raymond Coupeau as assistant secretaries, Raymond Lavelanette as librarian, and Lucien Price, Andre Lafontant, James Petersen, and Philippe Thoby-Marcelin as advisers.

4. This undated photograph belongs to Luce Turnier's archives and was probably taken between 1946 and 1953. The sculptor Jason Seley arrived in Haiti in January 1946 and taught life-modeling classes at the Centre d'Art. Seley was good friends with Albert Mangonès, a leading sculptor and architect, from their undergraduate days at Cornell University. Mangonès was also one of the founding members of the Centre d'Art and created the iconic monumental bronze sculpture *Le Marron Inconnu* (*The Unknown Slave / The Unknown Maroon*), installed opposite the National Palace in Port-au-Prince in 1968. Seley would return to Haiti often from 1946 through 1953, exhibiting and teaching classes at the Centre d'Art.

5. To date, just two in-depth studies have focused on Turnier. Lindsay Twa's essay, "The Rockefeller Foundation and Haitian Artists: Maurice Borno, Jean Chenet, and Luce Turnier," *Journal of Haitian Studies* 26, no. 1 (Spring 2020): 37–72, offers a thorough analysis of the Rockefeller Foundation's support of these three individuals, especially Turnier. Twa relies heavily on written correspondence between John Marhsall and Turnier. Marshall served as assistant director of the Foundation's Humanities Division from 1933 to 1940 and then as associate director from 1940 to 1962. The writer and collector John Hewitt's "The Evolution of Luce Turnier," *Black Art: An International Quarterly* 3, no. 1 (1978): 48–63, details Turnier's initial interest in drawing, her evolution as an artist in Haiti and in Paris, and her determination to perfect her artistic techniques. Hewitt notes that it was one of Turnier's brothers who brought her drawings of medicinal plants to DeWitt Peters, the Centre d'Art's founding director. Turnier had been drawing these medicinal plants since age thirteen, when she was a student at L'École normale in Port-au-Prince. Upon seeing the drawings, Peters enrolled Turnier in the center's art classes. Both Twa's essay and Hewitt's article are essential in the documentation of Twa's oeuvre. However, they do not address her skills and creativity as an artist in any great detail. This essay builds upon their important introductory scholarship.

6. LeGrace Benson, "Kiskeya-Lan Guinee-Eden: The Utopian Vision in Haitian Painting," *Callaloo* 15, no. 3 (July 1, 1992): 726–34.

7. Kaiama L. Glover, "Introduction," in *A Regarded Self: Caribbean Womanhood and the Ethics of Disorderly Being* (Duke University Press, 2021), 21–22.

8. Jerry Philogene, "National Narratives, Caribbean Identities, Diasporic Memories: Haitian and Jamaican Modern Art, 1920–1950" (PhD diss., New York University, 2009).

9. Artists who visited Haiti included William Edouard Scott (in 1931), Aaron Douglas (1938), James Porter (1946), Richmond Barthé (1948), Harlan Jackson (1948–51), Eldzier Cortor (1949–51), and Ellis Wilson (1950–51). Loïs Mailou Jones spent years visiting and living in Haiti after her marriage to the Haitian graphic designer Louis Vergniaud Pierre-Noël in 1953. For a published account of Barthé's Haitian experience and an analysis of his work while in Haiti, see Margaret Rose Vendryes, "Brothers Under the Skin: Richmond Barthé in Haiti," *Journal of Haitian Studies* 10, no. 2 (Summer 2005): 116–34. Barthé would travel regularly to Haiti during the years 1953 to 1969. In 1953, he completed a forty-foot statue of Jean-Jacques Dessalines for the city of Port-au-Prince. For more on Black US artists' engagement with Haiti, see Krista Thompson, "Preoccupied with Haiti: The Dream of Diaspora in African American Art, 1915–1942," *American Art Journal* (Fall 2007): 74–97; Harriet G. Warkel, "Image and Identity: The Art of William E. Scott, John W. Hardrick, and Hale A. Woodruff," in *A Shared Heritage: Art by Four African Americans*, ed. William E. Taylor and Harriet G. Warkel (Indianapolis Museum of Art and Indiana University Press, 1996), 17–76; and Lindsay Jean Twa, *Troubling Island: The Imagining and Imaging of Haiti by African-American Artists, 1915–1940* (PhD diss., University of North Carolina at Chapel Hill, 2006).

10. LeGrace Benson, "Kiskeya-Lan Guinee-Eden: The Utopian Vision in Haitian Painting," *Callaloo* 15, no. 3 (July 1, 1992): 726–34.

11. Recently, Lindsay J. Twa published an essay that includes a thorough discussion of Desruisseau's oeuvre and career. See Lindsay J. Twa, "Meeting Modernism: Rose-Marie Desruisseau, Loïs Jones Piere-Noël, and Haitian Modernist Painting," in *What and When Was Caribbean Modernism?: A 2024 Small Axe Project* (Small Axe, 2024), 78–112, https://smallaxe.net/sites/default/files/inline-images/CM1-ESSAYS%20rev-01.05.2025.pdf.

12. Rose-Marie Desruisseau attended classes and taught at l'Académie des Beaux-Arts, established in Port-au-Prince in 1959 under the directorship of the Italian sculptor Marco Amerigo Montagutelli. Montagutelli cast Mangonès's sculpture *Le Marron Inconnu*. Malebranche taught at the Centre d'Art, as did Turnier. Malebranche was a student of the painter Xavier Amiama (1910–1969), who was originally from the Dominican Republic and settled in Haiti during the mid-1930s.

13. Michel-Rolph Trouillot, "An Unthinkable History: The Haitian Revolution as a Non-Event," in *Silencing the Past: Power and the Production of History* (1995; Beacon, 2015), 70–107, 96.

14. Freida High W. Tesfagiorgis, "In Search of a Discourse and Critique/s That Center the Art of Black Women Artists," in *Black Feminist Cultural Criticism*, ed. Jacqueline Bobo (Blackwell, 2001), 146–72. Tesfagiorgis's faculty web page notes that "she [has] subsequently replaced Afrofemcentrism with Black feminism to expand the ideological and geographical limitations of the former." Tesfagiorgis faculty bio, Department of African American Studies, College of Letters and Science, University of Wisconsin–Madison, accessed August 27, 2025, https://africanamericanstudies.wisc.edu/staff/freida-high-w-tesfagiorgis-emeritus/. Afrofemcentrism's efficacy, for me, does not reside in a geographical specificity; rather, its epistemological capaciousness renders it transformative.

15. Tesfagiorgis, "In Search of a Discourse," 157.

16. Tesfagiorgis, "In Search of a Discourse," 163.

17. See, for example, Judith Wilson, "Hagar's Daughters: Social History, Cultural Heritage, and Afro-U.S. Women's Art," in *Bearing Witness: Contemporary Works by African American Women Artists*, ed. Jontyle Theresa Robinson (Rizzoli, 1996), 95–112; Lorraine O'Grady, "Olympia's Maid: Reclaiming Black Female Subjectivity," *Afterimage* 20 (Summer 1992), http://lorraineogrady.com/wp-content/uploads/2015/11/Lorraine-OGrady_Olympias-Maid-Reclaiming-Black-Female-Subjectivity.pdf; Michele Wallace, "Modernism, Postmodernism, and the Problem of the Visual in Afro-American Culture," in *Out There: Marginalization and Contemporary Cultures*, ed. Russell Ferguson et al. (MIT Press, 1990), 39–50; Adrian Piper, "The Triple Negation of Colored Women Artists" (1990), in *The Feminism and Visual Cultural Reader*, ed. Amelia Jones (Routledge, 2010), 174–86; Lowery Stokes Sims, "African American Women Artists: Into the Twenty-First Century," in *Bearing Witness: Contemporary Works by African American Women Artists*, ed. Jontyle Theresa Robinson (New York: Rizzoli, 1996), 83–94; Huey Copeland, "Making Black Feminist Art Histories," *American Art* 31, no. 2 (Summer 2017): 27–29; and Huey Copeland, "In the Wake of the Negress," in *Modern Women: Women Artists at the Museum of Modern Art*, ed. Cornelia Butler and Alexandra Schwartz (Museum of Modern Art, New York, 2010), 480–97.

18. Gina Athena Ulysse, "Why Rasanblaj, Why Now?: New Salutations to the Four Cardinal Points in Haitian Studies," *Journal of Haitian Studies* 23, no. 2 (2017): 58–80, 70.

19. Ulysse, "Why Rasanblaj, Why Now?," 70.

20. Turnier took composition and design classes from the painter Georges (Geo) Remponeau, oil-painting classes with Tamara Baussan, and design classes with the sculptor Albert Mangonès. The Cuban artists Wifredo Lam, Cundo Bermúdez, Roberto Diago, and Carlos Enríquez also visited Haiti. Enríquez taught and had several exhibitions at the Centre d'Art. He was instrumental in sparking the interest of Maurice Borno and Turnier in the fundamentals of Cubism and Expressionism.

21. Cortor taught at the Centre d'Art from 1949 to 1951.

22. The sculptor Augusta Savage also studied at the Académie during her scholarship years in Paris from 1929 to 1931, as did the African American painter Laura Wheeler Waring, first in 1914 and later in 1924–25.

23. There are conflicting dates as to when Turnier returned to Haiti from Paris (Champigny). The artist and art historian Lindsay Twa writes that Turnier returned in 1972 (Twa, "Rockefeller Foundation and Haitian Artists," 58). However, the art historian Gerald Alexis notes that he first met Turnier in 1977, when she had just returned to Haiti (email exchange with author, January 21, 2024), and in a 1983 interview with Danny Pietrodangelo, Turnier nods in the affirmative when he likewise asserts that she returned to Haiti from France in 1977: *Luce Turnier*, interview footage shot on location in Port-au-Prince, Haiti, 12:18 minutes (Pietrodangelo Production Group [Formerly D&L Communications] and/or Donato [Danny] A. Pietrodangelo, 1983), part 1, 0:05.

24. Marie José N'Zengou-Tayo, "Fanm Se Poto Mitan: Haitian Woman, the Pillar of Society," *Feminist Review* 59, no. 1 (1998): 138, https://journals.sagepub.com/doi/10.1080/014177898339497.

25. John O'Malley Burns, in communication with the author. Anne Kennedy was Burns's grandmother. Burns noted that this would be Peters's house in Turgeau, a neighborhood in Port-au-Prince. Lindsay Twa highlights the emotional and financial support that John Marshall provided Turnier. In their correspondence, he often expressed his pleasure at her accomplishments. See Twa, "Rockefeller Foundation and Haitian Artists," 37–72, 54–55.

26. Gerald Alexis writes that "she was not concerned

by identity issues, nor was she concerned with issues of race or gender. She only wanted to make figurative or abstract works consistent with her aesthetic concerns. If she had more female models, it was because men, less patient, could not remain quiet for long. She did, however, make a few portraits of men." Email exchange with author, January 3, 2024.

27. During her time in Paris, Turnier mainly produced collages created through her presentation of abstract patterns, forms, and color. This paper explores only her paintings and drawings.

28. Luce Turnier, in Pietrodangelo, *Luce Turnier*, 11:00–11:23. Donato Pietrodangelo's essay "A Haitian Original" provides an intimate portrayal of Turnier's life in Haiti at the formation of the Centre d'Art and her artistic philosophy. See Donato Pietrodangelo, "A Haitian Original," *Américas* 37 (September–October, 1985): 39–41. *Américas* was the "official publication of the Organization of American States." It is no longer being published.

29. Hazel Carby, foreword to Trouillot, *Silencing the Past*, 8.

30. Tina Campt, "Black Visuality and the Practice of Refusal," *Women and Performance*, February 25, 2019, https://www.womenandperformance.org/ampersand/29-1/campt#:~:text=phonic%20substance%3A%20the%20sound%20inherent,emanates%20from%20the%20image%20itself.

31. In the context of a discussion about that which is documented (or not) and becomes part of the historical record, it is interesting to note that the second photograph of a meeting of the Comité d'Administration appears to record notes being taken. The author continues to search for these notes.

CHAPTER 6

CARIBBEAN THOUGHT AND HAITIAN ART

THE CATEGORY OF THE MARVELOUS

Anthony Bogues

I want to begin this essay with the conventional Western framing of Haitian art, which typically considers Haitian art as naïve, a so-called primitive or folk art, within the perspective of cultural anthropology.[1] This framing is deployed no matter which of the many schools and genres of Haitian art is under discussion—whether the historical school that emerges in the north, the school of beauty, or the school of Saint-Soleil. By describing all Haitian art production in homogeneous terms under the conceptual category of the primitive, critics and art historians miss the internal dynamics that produce these distinct forms of art and art practices. We need to pay attention to the colonialist origins of this category in order to supplant it with a new, Caribbean view of art from Haiti: the category of the marvelous.

If we returned to early twentieth-century Paris, we would encounter a series of colonial markets featuring African masks and sculptures. These markets were frequented by many local artists. For the purposes of this essay, we will pay attention to two such artists: Pablo Picasso (a Spaniard) and Henri Matisse. It has often been reported that Picasso was captivated by a Vili figure that Matisse showed him, and that Matisse encouraged Picasso to visit the markets.[2] Many of the African "objects" for sale had religious value but, in these markets, they were extracted from their contexts and could be repurposed in whatever way one wanted. Writers and critics have long recognized how both Matisse and Picasso, as well as other artists working in France at the time, engaged with some of these masks and sculptures. Such critics have argued that this kind of adaptation was a form of Africanism, and that this Africanism, described as "primitivism," became a category with which to think about art.[3] However, there was a twist to this story: The critics at the time considered primitivism a form of modernism, "an avant-garde gesture," undermining the French art establishment.[4] More recently, scholars have argued that Picasso's own work is that of expropriation—a sign of colonial extractive artistic practice. In 2017, I was fortunate enough to see the exhibition *Picasso Primitif* at the Musée du quai Branly–Jacques Chirac in Paris, which juxtaposed his work, clearly influenced by African art, and original African artworks from Picasso's own collection, with the African artists now named.[5] The exhibition made clear that one cannot think about certain pieces of Picasso's work without making deep references to African art. Picasso's well-known statement, "I don't know it," when asked about how "Negro art" influenced his work thus becomes troubling.

There are of course two ways to read this moment and Picasso's comment. One reading is overly generous: We could say that for Picasso, all art was simply art, and therefore his quip made it clear that he did not recognize art by any geographic appellation. Or we could read the quip as a form of disavowal, in which Picasso refused to recognize the influence of African art upon his own work. What is critical to grasp for this essay is how quickly primitivism moved, in popular European and US cultural and artistic thought, from being a gesture of the avant-garde—often used to describe the work of artists' collectives like the CoBrA group from Amsterdam, Brussels, and Copenhagen[6]—to becoming a cultural-anthropological description of "backwardness" in Europe's colonies and ex-colonies. This was how the category of primitivism came to be applied to Haitian art.

CATEGORIZATION AND HAITIAN ART

One of the first books on Haitian art, *Renaissance in Haiti: Popular Painters in the Black Republic*, was published in 1948.[7] Written by the American critic Selden Rodman, who also wrote extensively on Mexican art, the book created a stir. Rodman noted that there was an absence of African sculptural forms in Haitian culture. He made this observation by drawing upon the cultural anthropologist Melville Herskovits's book *Life in a Haitian Valley*, published in 1938. However, Herskovits's analyses of the absence of African cultural forms in Haitian culture derived from a series of inaccurate reflections on a specific set of ideas about African sculpture. It ignored, for example, the metal art in Haiti that was being pioneered at that moment—and the rich history of art making in brass, bronze, and iron in Africa over the previous 2,500 years.[8] Rodman suggested that there are two forms of Haitian art, which he called "popular realism" and "religious art." He further noted that both forms belonged to the broader category of the primitive. He considered the work of Hector Hyppolite, perhaps one of the most important Haitian artists in the 1940s. Hyppolite, he wrote, "is unlike any other of the Haitian primitives . . . [in that he] makes no effort to achieve a realistic effect in his pictures; if he ever went in for precise modelling details, he has abandoned it."[9] Rodman continued, "It would be unfair to say that his powers of observation are not good because his intentions so obviously are in the direction of expressionist fantasy."[10]

Rodman's book began a classificatory process that launched the theorization of Haitian art as a form of primitivism.[11] This generalized categorization of

Afro-Caribbean art persisted for some time. (Cuba was an early exception to the undifferentiated theorization of Afro-Caribbean art. Already in the 1930s, there were vigorous attempts to establish what was explicitly called "Afro-Cuban art," a practice rooted in rethinking the place of African cultural forms in Cuba at that time. Here, the remarkable work of Cuban intellectuals like the activist and folklorist Lydia Cabrera was influential.[12]) In the other parts of the region, influenced by the Black Power and anticolonial movements of the 1960s and '70s, scholars began to rethink the monolithic category of Afro-Caribbean art. In Jamaica in the early 1970s, for example, the term "intuitive" emerged to describe artists who did not have formal academic training and whose artworks were previously labeled naïve, folklore, or primitive.[13]

While Rodman laid the foundation for the art historical classification of Haitian art, I want to juxtapose to his approach with those of subsequent artists and scholars, who have posited a different way of seeing Haitian art. Their methodologies move away from some of the formal categories of Western art and attempt to grapple with the practices of Haitian art from the *inside out*. In this regard, we begin from the perspective that the political and the aesthetic are porous in Haitian art. The Algerian-born French scholar Jacques Rancière notes that politics and aesthetics "intervene in the general distribution of ways of doing and making and that these maintain forms and beings of modes of visibility."[14] It is not my view that artistic practices and political practices are homologous. However, I would suggest that the chasm that has opened up between them in our general theoretical formulations about art and politics is tenable in neither Haitian art nor in Afro-Caribbean art more broadly.

One also pays attention to the power of the Western episteme as a way of naming things. Let's take, for example, the idea that Haitian art is a genre of Surrealism. In 1945, André Breton, the founder of Surrealism, visited Haiti and delivered a talk to an audience of over five hundred people. During the talk he noted that the work of Hyppolite and others had taught him things about composition and form, and that Haitian art was *beyond* Surrealism. What happens next in this process of naming demonstrates the power of Western framing, as writers began to describe Haitian art as *Surrealist art*. This association was cemented when Breton brought Hyppolite's works to Paris for the UNESCO international art exhibition in 1947.

This points to how recognizing historical discursive contexts is critical to any understanding of Caribbean art. In the case of Haiti, this discursive context is shaped by how the imperial idea of Haiti becomes located within a colonial episteme that both *represents* and *constructs* Haiti primarily as a site of chaos, of never-ending catastrophic events—from the slave revolution of 1791 to recent earthquakes and political problems.[15] The colonial episteme creates Haiti as a fixed sign marked by a kind of otherness, a place where black magic happens. In dismantling this frame, we begin to understand what the Caribbean thinker Édouard Glissant called Haitian art: a "vocation of refusal."[16] This refusal, in my view, occurs on the terrain of the popular and shapes both the practices and the processes of contestation within the making of Haitian art. The Jamaican-born cultural theorist Stuart Hall makes the point that the "popular should be understood as a tension between what belongs to the central dominant and the elite and the culture and practices of the periphery."[17] In this regard, for example, one might pay attention to the vast body of historical art practices in the work of the Haitian artist Philomé Obin (discussed below).

I want to think through Haitian art on its own terms by grappling both with another current of literature and with different perspectives on Haitian culture in the 1930s and '40s. This line of thought allows us to work alongside Haitian thinkers as we posit new categories. It makes clear that a twentieth-century Haitian intellectual tradition exists, something that the West does not recognize—and, to be truthful, that is often ignored within the Caribbean itself. Our first stop in this exercise is the remarkable 1956 speech made by the Haitian medical doctor and novelist Jacques Stephen Alexis.[18]

THE MARVELOUS

Alexis attended the 1956 Black Writers and Artists Conference in Paris. This was perhaps one of the most important events of twentieth-century Black radical intellectual life and in the history of Black critical thought and culture.[19] Held at the Sorbonne, the conference attracted a plethora of Black writers, all of whom were either cultural or political figures, or in many cases both. Among those in attendance were George Lamming, Frantz Fanon, Léopold Sédar Senghor, Aimé Césaire, Jean Price-Mars, and Richard Wright. Price-Mars was recognized then as one of the world's leading Black intellectuals, and the conference elected him as its chair.

At the conference, Alexis delivered a speech on the "marvelous realism" of Haitian cultural practice. In it, he argued that "negro" art was fundamentally linked to life, and that this link was a form of humanism that "traverses history, mysticism, and naturalism." He then went on to argue that, in Haitian art, this realism "contains order, beauty, logic, and controls sensitivities which presents the real which is an accompaniment of the strange and the fantastic of dreams and half-life of the mysterious . . . the marvelous in Haitian art seems to be looking for type." He then specified that he was deploying the word *type* in the Latin sense of the word *actualis*—"that which acts so actual that all particularized subjects can be found in it."[20] For Alexis, the imagination was critical to all aspects of Haitian culture, and the work of this imagination was to grapple with the real.

In this formulation, Alexis was grappling with the ways in which Haitian art presented itself, how its compositional form engages, then creates, regimes of double representation; it presents and then re-presents itself. In defining Haitian art and culture as subsumed under the category of the marvelous, he was working within a tradition of Caribbean thought that attempts to posit a profound relationship between the marvelous and the conception of the real. This particular understanding of the marvelous is in deep conversation with Caribbean literature, and particularly with the work of Alejo Carpentier, whose novel *The Kingdom of This World* was published in 1949.[21] What is critical about Carpentier's novel for the purposes of this essay is that its main character, an ex-slave named Ti Noel, understands the specific radicality of the late eighteenth-century Haitian Revolution not in terms of the political leadership of Toussaint Louverture or Jean-Jacques Dessalines but instead as the work of the traditional healer and revolutionary François Macandal. Using his understanding of plants and herbs, Macandal developed a strategy of poisoning the planters in the colony of Saint-Domingue. All evidence now points to the fact that his political ambition was the establishment of a Black republic—a goal Haiti achieved in 1804.[22] As the revolution unfolded, Macandal's medical knowledge allowed him to remain on the plantation even after he had lost one of his hands in a slave-work accident. Ironically, he sometimes healed as well as poisoned the planters. Both Macandal's healing and his political practices operated outside the bounds of Western knowledge. Carpentier's novel foregrounds them.

By deploying the term "marvelous realism" in his speech, Alexis posited that at the level of the symbolic order—the imaginary, if you will—Haitian art is the practice of the *real*. Parenthetically, one fascinating aspect of the history of Caribbean and Latin American thought is the way that ideas and words travel. By the 1960s, marvelous realism would become one basis for the emergence of magical realism in Latin American literature through writers like Gabriel García Márquez.

We should also note that the Caribbean conversation around the conception of the marvelous was ongoing. Although Alexis and other Caribbean figures, including the Afro-Cuban artist Wifredo Lam, took up this dialogue in Paris, it was not confined to the colonial metropole. It was already occurring in Haiti and in the French territory of Martinique, where the key figures were Suzanne Césaire and the writer René Ménil.[23] In his essay on the marvelous, published in the journal *Tropiques* in October 1941, Ménil argued for the "marvelous of our absolute Liberty."[24] For Alexis, marvelous realism became the ground of Haitian culture; it was also historically specific to Haiti and the Caribbean, as he argued at the conference against Senghor's idea of a universal Black culture. I would also suggest that Alexis was also obviously attempting to revise the conception of social realism. In other words, while drawing much of his framing perspective from an engagement with Marxism, Alexis was also looking for a distinctive characterization of Haitian art. With all these debates in Paris and the Caribbean by the late 1950s, the marvelous emerges and as an aesthetic frame in Caribbean thought and a category with which to begin thinking about aesthetics and Haitian art.

OTHER HISTORIES

There is another history of Haitian art that we tend to forget and that I wish to briefly explore. Haiti was occupied by the United States between 1915 and 1935. The occupation created a political and historical context that obviously shaped Haitian society. During this period, a 1928 text by Jean Price-Mars titled *So Spoke the Uncle* emerged as influential.[25] It argued that Haiti is an African society and that the enslaved population from different African nations had created cultural practices, including the Afro-Caribbean religion of Vodou, that indigenized them within the Caribbean space.[26] Price-Mars framed these practices as the grounds on which cultural struggles could be waged against the American occupation. The Haitian art historian Michel Philippe Lerebours has noted in various conversations and lectures that Price-Mars's work set the stage for a moment of indigenous cultural revolt.

One of the leading Haitian artists and thinkers in the 1940s, Petion Savain, in the moment of that revolt against the United States, wrote a manifesto about Haitian art and established the journal *La Revue Indigene*. In the journal he made the point that art should engage "the most modern techniques and try to adapt them to the demands of Haitian art."[27] Of course, Vodou itself was central to this indigenous revolt.[28]

Vodou is a system of thought and practice that should be understood not only as a series of religious practices but also as a symbolic order that was born out of the historical catastrophe of the African experience in the French colony of Saint-Domingue. It is rich with a panoply of gods and spirits, or *Lwas*, and alive with a sense of the marvelous. It is not an oral religion, as has been suggested by many; rather, its liturgy is written and kept secret by its priests and priestesses.[29] In Haiti, many artists have drawn from this cosmological resource.[30] At this point I wish to draw your attention to André Pierre's many-layered painting *The Guinean Spirits Returning to Africa After the Haitian Independence War* (fig. 6.1) and briefly touch on some of its motifs. One is the multicolored military attire of the soldiers, who are actually Lwas within the Afro-Caribbean Vodou pantheon. They are on a cloud, which is a reimagining of a slave ship. Notably, the word *Guine* appears in many African Diasporic mythologies. In the African diasporic imaginary, Guine is a placeholder for continental Africa; thus, Pierre's Lwas are returning to Africa after intervening to help Haiti win its independence in 1804. The artist is making it clear that Haitian Independence would not have been achieved without the work of the Lwas. Of course, the Haitian Revolution was a dual struggle—first against racial slavery and then for political independence—both of which opened up distinctive spaces in Haitian art.[31] But it should be noted that Pierre's painting had the Lwas playing a part in the independence struggles, not the revolutionary struggle against colonial/racial slavery. For the artist, achieving independence the key moment in Haitian history.

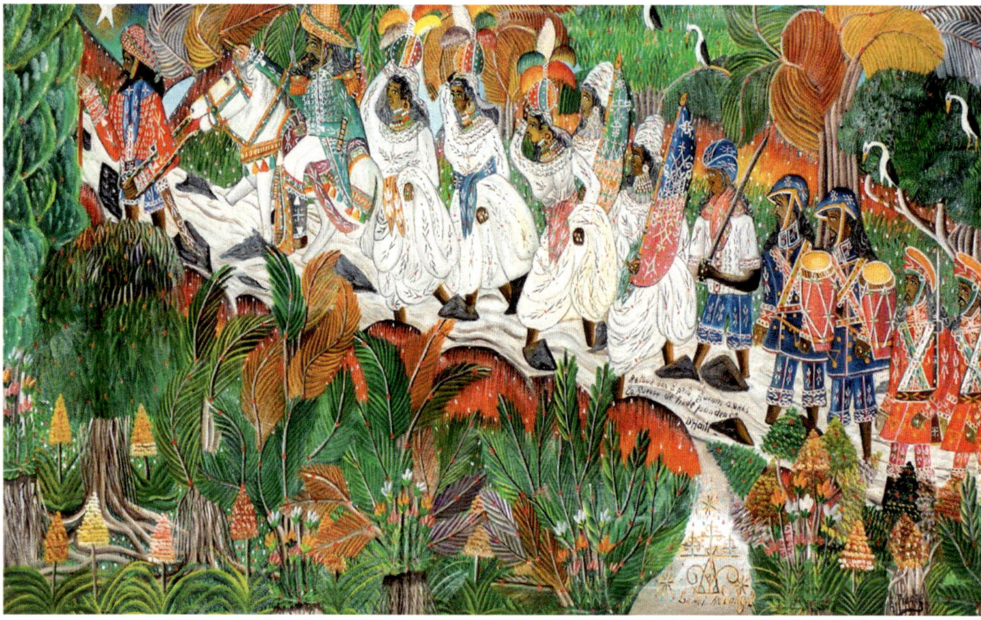

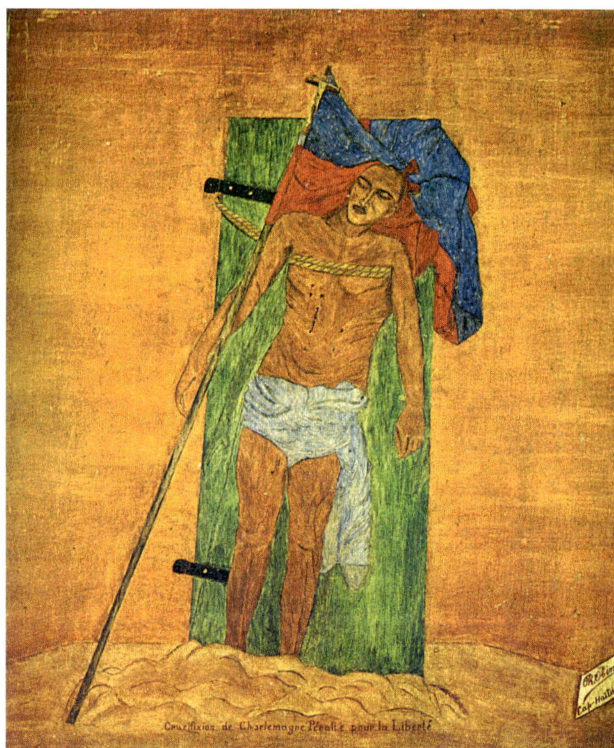

Fig. 6.1. André Pierre (Haitian, 1916–2005), *Retour des Esprits Guinen (The Guinean Spirits Returning to Africa After the Haitian Independence War)*, 1987. 24 × 48 in. (61 × 121.9 cm). John Browning Fulling Collection

Fig. 6.2. Philomé Obin (Haitian, 1892–1986), *Crucifixion de Charlemagne Péralte pour La Liberté (The Crucifixion of Charlemagne Péralte for Freedom)*, 1948. Musée d'art Haïtien du Collège St Pierre, Port-au-Prince

OTHER CATEGORIES

One difficulty in discussions about categorizing Haitian art is that many critics think that it is dominated by Vodou cosmology, so I want to foreground a work that is perhaps one of the most significant in Haitian art history. Recall the American occupation from 1915 to 1935. Many in Haiti resisted, including a group of guerrillas, called Cacos, led by Charlemagne Péralte, who began an armed struggle against the occupation. Péralte was an inspirational leader, so what did the US Marines do? They captured and murdered him. They then took photographs of his corpse and dropped these images from helicopters all over Haiti. One such picture was used by Philomé Obin, who was neither a Vodou practitioner nor a priest—he was Baptist by faith. Obin reinterpreted this photograph as a painting titled *The Crucifixion of Charlemagne Péralte for Freedom* (fig. 6.2). It is a remarkable painting, a seminal piece in Haitian art history. We should note as well that Obin wrote in various letters that he wanted to paint a history of Haiti. Indeed, questions of history emerge forcefully in Haitian art, and if there is a defining aesthetic within the category of marvelous realism, it embodies what one might call "living history."[32] This preoccupation with the historical, both as thematic and aesthetic, leads us to a discussion of a third artist, Edouard Duval-Carrié, with whom I have worked for some time.

Duval-Carrié's mixed-media piece *Memory Without History* (fig. 6.3) comprises six sections stitched together on aluminum panels. The artist tells the story of Haiti as a history of occupation and authoritarian rule and invokes the return of Toussaint Louverture as a kind of savior, riding in on his horse, at lower right, to try to rescue Haiti. In my view, one of the things the artist wants to make clear is that amid the burnished memories of independence are the generals and the elite, seen at lower left, who have driven ordinary Haitians to the wall. Duval-Carrié has juxtaposed memory and history, asking us to recall the events of the revolution, not just its memories. He is asking us to live in history. In other words, for the artist, history becomes a form of critique, not merely the telling of a tale.

In trying to think through this question of history, all three artists attempt to establish a new archive of Haiti, of the idea of Haiti itself. We need to pay attention to how the historical functions in these works, because it is also linked to the issue of politics. The question of politics in Haiti is complex, from the dual revolution to the divisions between a Haitian state, which became authoritarian and separate from the Haitian nation. In this regard, we should note that the late Haitian intellectual Michel-Rolph Trouillot argued that the Haitian state and the nation were launched in different directions.[33] What I want to argue is that within the popular forms of art resides another politics, one that circles around history. Within Haitian art there is, to recall the words of Wilson Harris, a "philosophy of History buried within the arts of the imagination."[34]

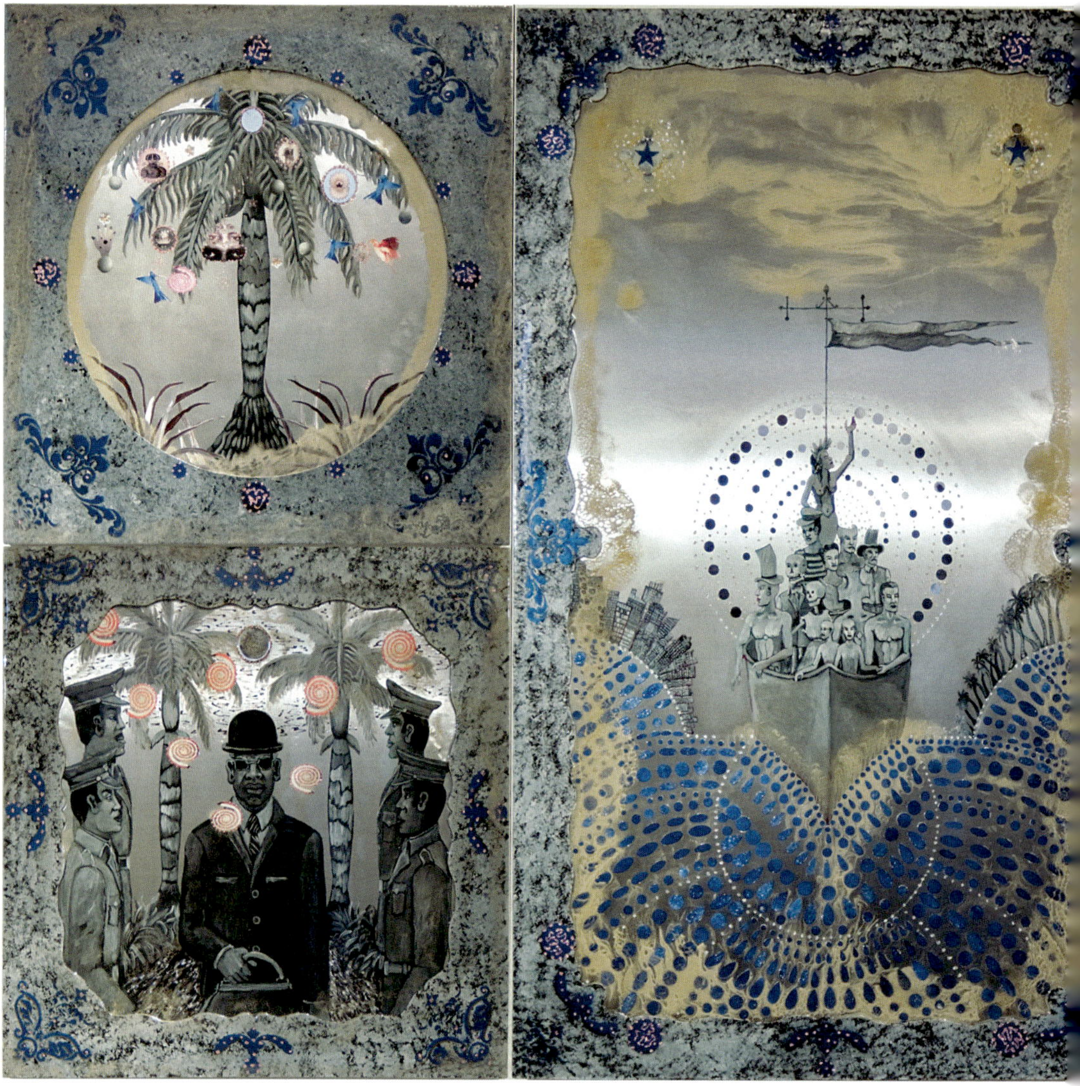

Fig. 6.3. Edouard Duval-Carrié (Haitian American, b. 1954), *Memoire sans Histoire* (*Memory Without History*), 2009. Mixed media on aluminum, 6 panels, overall: 94 × 208 in. (238.8 × 528.3 cm). Collection of Serge and Johanna Coles

I end this essay by saying that the matter of "living history" and its relationship to the marvelous real reframes Haitian art. The aesthetics of marvelous realism in Haitian art reside not beauty, in ways that we may conventionally understand aesthetics, but in the making of the object and in its relationship to the lived experiences of Haiti—in its history and its politics. This kind of aesthetic regime

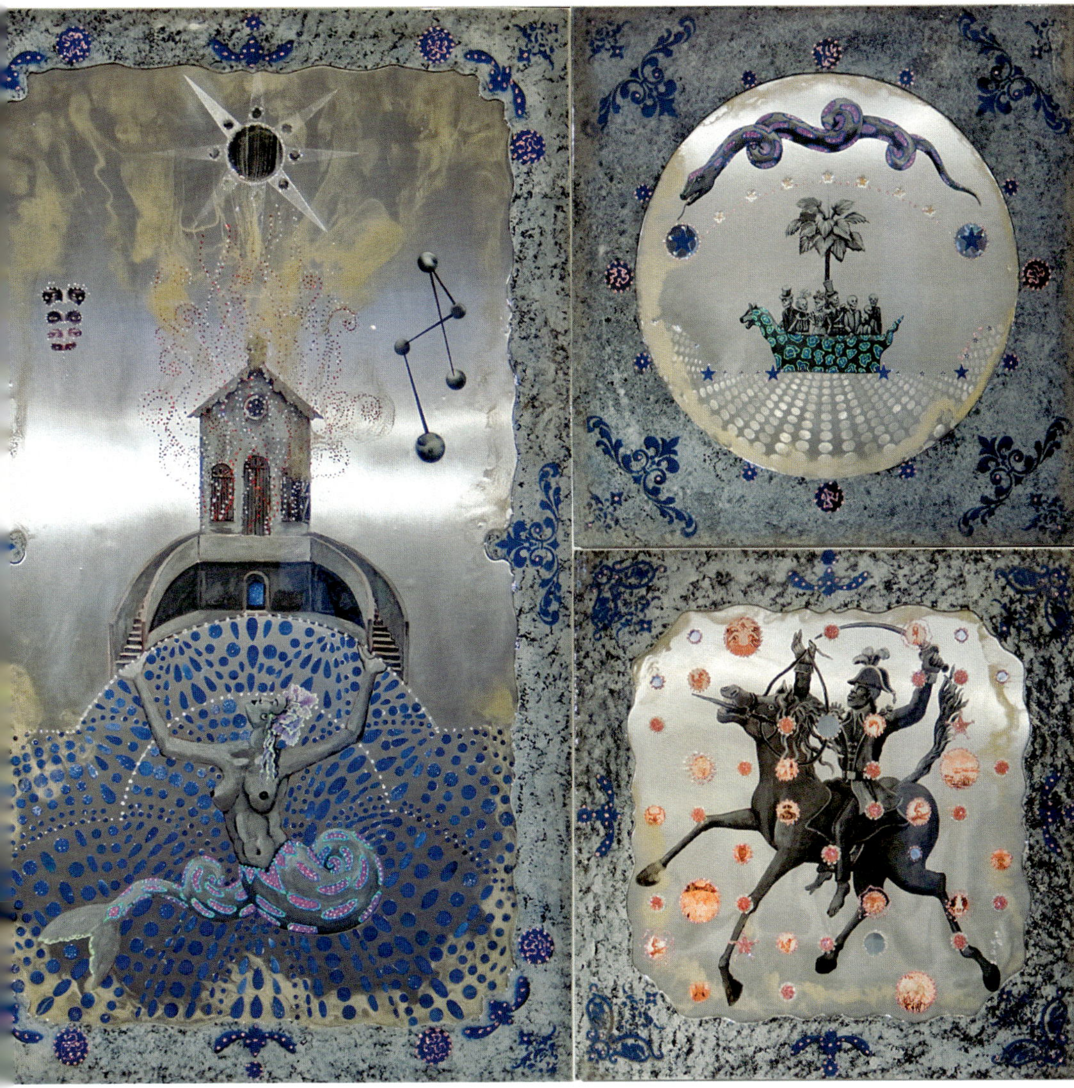

does not negate beauty but locates it elsewhere. Both Haitian and Afro-Caribbean art operate through distinctive grammars that require rethinking conventional histories and categories of art, generating new categories of thought that are produced in the intellectual traditions of the Caribbean.

NOTES

This essay is dedicated to Michel Philippe Lerebours (1933–2025), who was Haiti's leading art historian. He was the founding director of the École Nationale des Arts (ENARTS) and served as curator and director of the Musée d'Art Haïtien du Collège St Pierre, Port-au-Prince, where he oversaw efforts to reconstruct the museum after it was destroyed in the 2010 earthquake. His contributions have deeply shaped my own work in this field.

1. This essay draws from sections of my forthcoming book *Blowing the Abeng: Caribbean Thought and Praxis* (Pluto, 2026) and expands on a paper I presented at the California Institute of the Arts in 2023, which was subsequently published as Anthony Bogues, "The History, Politics, and Aesthetics of Haitian Art: Some Reflections," in *Dominance and Revolution: The Image, the Struggle and the Use of Force*, vol. 2, ed. Amanda Beech and Tabitha Steinberg, *A Document of the Aesthetics and Politics Lecture Series*, California Institute of the Arts (Spring 2023): 56–66, https://issuu.com/calarts/docs/05.23.a_pvol2.issuu3/57.

2. There is, of course, a great deal of literature on how African masks shaped the composition of Picasso's *Les Demoiselles d'Avignon* (1907, Museum of Modern Art, New York).

3. For an early example of scholarship in this vein, see Robert Goldwater, *Primitivism in Modern Art* (Belknap, Harvard University Press, 1938).

4. For a discussion of this, see Simon Gikandi, "Picasso, Africa, and the Schemata of Difference," in *Beautiful Ugly*, ed. Sarah Nuttall (Duke University Press, 2006).

5. Yves Le Fleur, ed., *Picasso Primitif* (Flammarion / Musée du quai Branly–Jacques Chirac
Paris, 2017).

6. The CoBrA Group came to attention with a 1949 exhibition at the Stedelijk Museum in Amsterdam.

7. Selden Rodman, *Renaissance in Haiti: Popular Painters in the Black Republic* (Pellegrini & Cudahy, 1948).

8. Of course, by the late 1940s and early '50s, metalwork artists like Georges Liautaud had emerged as major figures.

9. Rodman, *Renaissance in Haiti*, 68–69.

10. Rodman, *Renaissance in Haiti*, 69.

11. It's important to note that Haitian writers have attempted to revise this category of "the primitive" and present a more complex history of Haitian art. See, for example, Gerald Alexis, *Peintres Haitians* (Éditions Cercle d'Art: 2000); and Michel-Philippe Lerebours's two-volume work, *Haïti et ses peintres de 1804 à 1980: Souffrances et espoirs d'un peuple* (Imprimeur II, 1989).

12. See, for example, her magisterial work, Lydia Cabrera, *El Monte: Notes on the Religion, Superstitions, and Folklore of the Black and Creole People of Cuba* (1954; Duke University Press, 2023). Cabrera took Wifredo Lam to many Afro-Cuban religious ceremonies. These visits transformed his art practice.

13. The categorization of some Haitian art as "self-taught" continues. See, for example, the recent catalogue *Direct from the Eye: The Jonathan Demme Collection of Self-Taught Art* (Material Culture, 2014). For a useful brief study of Caribbean art, see Veerle Poupeye, *Caribbean Art* (1998; W. W. Norton, 2022).

14. Jacques Rancière, *The Politics of Aesthetics: The Distribution of the Sensible*, trans. Gabriel Rockhill (Continuum, 2004), 13.

15. Not only was the European colonial project one of territorial conquest and a political economy of extraction, it was also a project in which colonial power made vigorous attempts to create a "native." At the core of that creation was violence and death, alongside a series of knowledge regimes and "commonsense" configurations in which ideological and political frameworks and imaginaries were created. Underlying these configurations was the colonial episteme, centered on a human classification system in which Blackness signified being nonhuman. The historical processes of racial slavery and colonialism, as Aimé Césaire makes clear, is one that creates for the Black Native a state of "thingification." See his seminal work *Discourse on Colonialism*, trans. Joan Pinkham (Monthly Review Press, 2000).

16. Édouard Glissant, *Caribbean Discourse: Selected Essays*, trans. J. Michael Dash (University of Virginia Press, 1991).

17. Stuart Hall, "Notes on Deconstructing the Popular," in *Cultural Theory and Popular Culture: A Reader*, ed. John Storey (Routledge, 1998), 448.

18. Alexis's most influential novel is *General Sun My Brother* (1955). He was also a radical political figure who was tortured by the Duvalier regime, placed on a boat, and never seen again.

19. For a discussion of this conference, see Bogues, *Blowing the Abeng*.

20. Jacques Stephen Alexis, "Of the Marvelous Realism of the Haitians," in *Présence Africanaine: Cultural Journal of the Negro World* 8–10 (June–November 1956): 249.

21. For a good discussion about the marvelous and Caribbean literature, see Margaret Heady, *Marvelous Journeys: Routes of Identity in the Caribbean Novel* (Peter Lang, 2008).

22. For a discussion of this point, see Anthony Bogues, "The Dual Revolution: Black Freedom and Black Sovereignty" and "The Idea of Haiti: Historical Black Freedom, Post-Colony and Reparative Justice," in *The Road to Democracy in South Africa*, vol. 10, ed. South African Democracy Education Trust (Skottaville, 2023), chapters 1 and 2.

23. For a discussion of Suzanne Césaire's work, see *The Great Camouflage: Writings of Dissent, 1941–1945*, ed. Daniel Maximin, trans. Keith Walker (Wesleyan University Press, 2012).
24. See the full volumes of the journal in *Refusal of the Shadow: Surrealism and the Caribbean Paperback*, ed. and trans. Micheal Richardson and Krzysztof Fijalkowski (Verso, 1996).
25. For an English translation, see Jean Price-Mars, *So Spoke the Uncle*, trans. Magdaline W. Shannon (Three Continents, 1983).
26. This idea of indigenization was then taken up by the theorist Syliva Wynter in the 1960s and became one of her key arguments against the idea of creolization and Caribbean culture.
27. Petion Savain, *La Revue Indigene*, cited in Michel-Philippe Lerebours, "The Indigenist Revolt, Haitian Art, 1927–1944," *Callaloo* 15, no. 3 (Summer 1992): 711–25.
28. In the literary field, some novels reflected the spirit of indigenism. Perhaps the best known of these is Jacques Roumain's *Masters of the Dew* (1944).
29. The author is currently involved in an art project that will display many of the drawings from these books.
30. One of the most recent and remarkable is Shneider Léon Hilaire, who in May 2023 presented his first overseas exhibition, *Rituals and Ceremonies*, at Green Space Miami.
31. For a discussion of the Haitian Revolution as a dual revolution, see Bogues, "Dual Revolution."
32. For a discussion of this idea of living history in Haitian art see, Anthony Bogues, "Making History and the Work of Memory in the Art of Edouard Duval Carrie," in *Decolonizing Refinement: Contemporary Pursuits in the Art of Edouard Duval Carrie*, ed. Paul B. Neill, Michael D. Carrasco, and Lesley A. Wolff (University of Florida Press, 2018).
33. Michel-Rolph Trouillot, *State Against Nation: The Origins and Legacy of Duvalierism* (Monthly Review, 1990).
34. Wilson Harris, *History, Fable and Myth in the Caribbean and Guianas* (Calaloux, 1995), 18.

CHAPTER 7

JOHN DUNKLEY'S PHOTOGRAPHIC EYE

A CLOSE LOOK AT *BANANA PLANTATION*

Nicole Smythe-Johnson

Taking a single painting as its subject, this paper demonstrates how thinking with the work of the Jamaican self-taught painter John Dunkley (1891–1947) asks us to rethink one of art history's most hallowed metanarratives, that of modernism. While in other fields in the humanities, narratives of modernity and their cultural manifestation in modernism have been thoroughly reworked to account for the historically overlooked perspectives and contributions of people of the African diaspora, Paul Gilroy's 1993 book *The Black Atlantic* being among the best-known examples, art history has remained committed to a Eurocentric conception of modernity—and therefore modernism. Despite the body of work on alternate modernisms that has developed—the work of Mari Carmen Ramírez and Luis Pérez-Oramas on Latin American modernism, for example—Europe has remained central. Generally, the story is that modernists visited Europe, often as art students, and returned home to develop their own homegrown, often nativist modernisms to counter the hegemony of European modernism. In short, alternate modernisms remain essentially belated, the outcome of a developed Europe's influence on the backward rest.

The project from which this paper is excerpted proposes a narrative of modernism that does not center Europe but instead recasts modernity from the perspective of the laboring classes of the Americas. Where previous accounts of modernism within the field of art history propose transatlantic travel as the experiential point of departure that manifests itself in formal innovation, this paper proposes travel within the Americas as foundational to the emergence of early hemispheric American modernism. I argue that Dunkley, who produced art as a Black, working-class, colonial subject, provides us with a perspective on modernism's overlooked but nonetheless constitutive underbelly. My focus on South–South exchange, which positions the Caribbean as a fulcrum between North and South America and the disciplinary subfields that address them, is a further shift in perspective that thinking from the Caribbean requires.

Photography is also key to my argument. The quintessential modern (and imperial) technology, it emerged in the early nineteenth century and was deployed throughout the colonies, often as a tool of empire, as Krista Thompson and Ariella Azoulay have argued. It also revolutionized the way that images are produced and seen across the globe. I argue that Dunkley's mixed-media works, and *Banana Plantation* (fig. 7.1), in particular, model an attentiveness to the medium and an understanding of its implications. It is this attentiveness to and criticality of photography that, I argue, nourishes Dunkley's modernist formal innovation.

A basic description of *Banana Plantation*—a burrowed rabbit in a stand of banana trees—might suggest an image from a children's book. The red-eyed white rabbit and depiction of a subterranean world, in particular, bring Lewis Carroll's *Alice's Adventures in Wonderland* (1865) to mind. Yet, the mood of the painting is more menacing than playful. The sky is dark, with a yellow-orange orb that could be the moon or the sun. Four banana trees and two suckers stand out against an eerie darkness, while the foreground is bathed in light, as if illuminated by a camera's flash. On the left is one of Dunkley's recurring motifs, a path that leads into shadowy terra incognita. The path arouses curiosity, but it might be the kind of curiosity that kills the proverbial cat. Like Alice's rabbit hole, it promises adventure, or at least the discovery of parts unknown, but, like Dunkley and millions of other West Indians who sought their fortune as itinerant laborers throughout the circum-Caribbean in the early twentieth century, one follows it at one's own substantial risk.

Dunkley's use of dramatic chiaroscuro and a limited palette recalls the hand-colored photographs popular during the nineteenth and early twentieth centuries, but the painting also does precisely what photography could not do: It sees beyond the surface. It does not see *through* the surface, as in an X-ray. The surface is represented and relevant to the painting's operation. I argue that it is the interaction between the surface *and* its surplus—that which is beyond, not visible but nonetheless present—that is Dunkley's subject in *Banana Plantation*.

Above ground, the focus is on the fecundity of the scene—the heavy bunch of bananas and the bright-white leaves and trunk that frame it, the row of bountiful lettuce-like crops that line the path, and the lush field of gold-flecked, wheat-like crops hinted at on the right. This is in keeping with common representations of the Caribbean at this time, most of which were photographs. Thompson has written about the significance of photography during this period in presenting the Caribbean as potentially profitable for investors and "tamed, safe, and artfully cultivated." The construction of such representations was an effort to quell the post-emancipation fears of "potential travellers and white settlers" who saw "the tropics and the Caribbean as places of wild nature and unruly natives."[1] Born just over two generations after the emancipation proclamation in the British colonies in 1834, and within a generation of the institution of crown colony rule in 1866,[2] Dunkley came

Fig 7.1. John Dunkley (Jamaican, 1891–1947), *Banana Plantation*, c. 1945. Mixed media on plywood, 34 5⁄8 × 23 1⁄4 in. (88 × 59 cm). National Gallery of Jamaica, Kingston

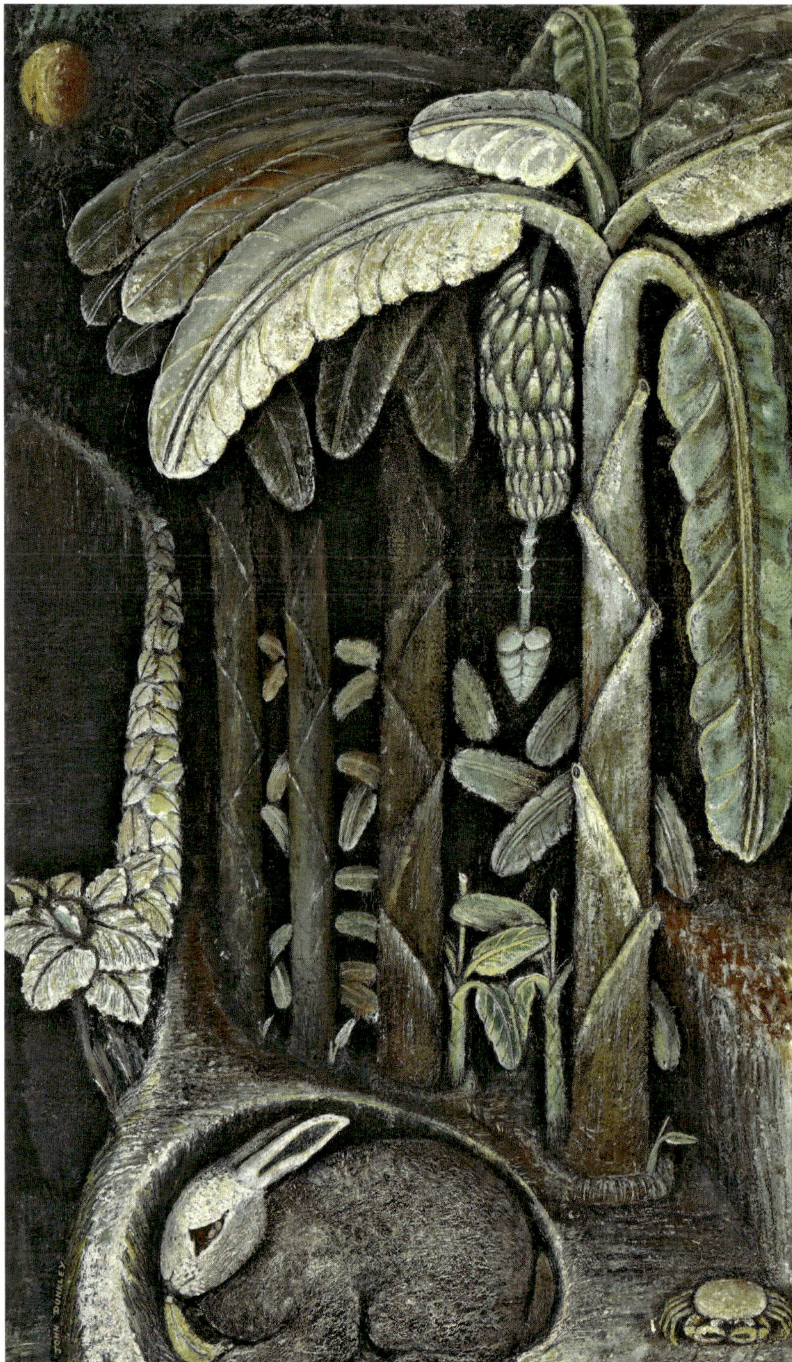

of age in what local elites called "the New Jamaica." Photography was an important tool in presenting this "New Jamaica" as fertile, civilized, and open for business.

And what of the rabbit, the painting's central figure? The best-known reading of this painting is by David Boxer, the Jamaican art historian and founding curator of the National Gallery of Jamaica who was pivotal in the conservation (and articulation) of Dunkley's legacy. Boxer argued, and I agree, that *Banana Plantation* references Dunkley's time "employed by the largest banana plantation in the world," the Chiriquí Land Company, a subsidiary of United Fruit Company on the west coast of Panama. For Boxer, "the rabbit, with its one little banana, as opposed to the rich bunch of eight that hangs on the tree above, is a reflection on Dunkley's own relationship to that plantation, where he worked as a janitor."[3] Boxer's later scholarship also positions Dunkley's depiction of the rabbit (or the hare) within the history of Western and East Asian painting—a symbol of sexual desire, fertility, and the coming of spring—and argues that Dunkley may have been exposed to images of such paintings through books in the library of the Institute of Jamaica (IoJ). According to Boxer, Dunkley's connection to the IoJ, founded in 1879 for the "encouragement of literature, science, and art," was facilitated by Hender Delves Molesworth, the colonial official and English art historian who was director of the IoJ between 1936 and 1938. In this telling, it was Molesworth who placed Dunkley "in intimate contact with cultural activists and other artists," a kind of discovery narrative, as is common in art historical discussions of autodidacts.[4]

I take a different perspective, preferring to privilege Dunkley's wife Cassie Dunkley's account of her husband's influences. She wrote: "One could not teach him for he was self-taught," and "he was never lucky to get any help though good he was and he never asked for any trying to reach his goal without anyone's help."[5] So, if we avoid the temptation to position Molesworth as a central figure and an archival entry point through which we discover John Dunkley's milieu and influences, how else might we perceive the rabbit?

As is often the case with the artist's work, we can take things in a few directions. A popular option has us counter Boxer's turn toward European and Asian visual traditions by reaching for a more culturally indigenous interpretation of the figure of the rabbit.[6] Br'er Rabbit, a figure from folk tales throughout the African diaspora and believed to be of West African origin, seems an obvious choice. A kind of morally ambiguous trickster figure who uses his wits to get out of thorny situations, Br'er Rabbit is often read as representative of the enslaved people of the Caribbean forced to improvise and strategize to guarantee their safety within oppressive conditions. This reading maintains Boxer's assertion that the rabbit is Dunkley himself, while granting the artist more agency, since Br'er Rabbit is best known for manipulating a situation to meet his needs. That is to say, Br'er Rabbit would not have accepted a lone banana he'd been allowed to have. He'd have stolen that banana, insisting on taking something for himself, even in the face of employers who would deny him access to the products of his labor.

I prefer that reading; it is more in keeping with what we know of Dunkley, this producer of trickster artworks that seem to tease and play with their viewers and overflow with sometimes contradictory meanings. To encounter a Dunkley painting is to find oneself wondering things like, "Is it a moon or a Cézanne-esque peach?" as one conference attendee asked when I gave this paper at the "Beyond Boundaries" conference at the Clark Art Institute in 2022. Yet, while there is a resonance with trickster figures like Br'er Rabbit or, more popular in Jamaica, Anansi, this reading does not quite match with what one sees when looking at *Banana Plantation*. Dunkley's rabbit lacks the braggadocio one generally expects from these figures. His hooded eye and tightly confined body read to me as fearful or, at the very least, nervous.

This leads us back to the white rabbit of *Alice's Adventures in Wonderland*, a character that could not be considered indigenous to Jamaica but may well have been known to Dunkley.[7] The creature who, in the first paragraphs of Carroll's book, catches Alice's attention by anxiously hurrying past her, exclaiming, "Oh dear! Oh dear! I shall be too late!" seems to me a better fit. In that story, it is the sight of the rabbit racing by, pausing only to take "a watch out of its waistcoat-pocket" and worry over it, that lures Alice down the rabbit hole. That anxious, overwhelmed figure more closely matches Dunkley's depiction, although his rabbit worries over a banana instead of a clock. Importantly, Dunkley would not have needed Molesworth to shepherd him toward this white rabbit, since references to "Alice in Wonderland" appear in the Kingston *Daily Gleaner*, a publication Dunkley is known to have read regularly, as early as 1899. With this more accessible reference to a white rabbit, other potential readings emerge.

What if we put the top three-quarters of the painting and the lower quarter in conversation with each other? If the upper quarters refer to the processes by which the "New Jamaica" was being produced and marketed, might we think about the lower quarter as gesturing toward its consumption? Put another way, *Banana Plantation* seems to expand the focus beyond what many plantation photographs during this period showed—cultivated, fertile fields ready for harvest. Instead, it foregrounds those who consume the plantation's products, those who never appear in plantation photographs. What photographs of the period almost always do include is workers harvesting or transporting banana bunches, often reproducing the perspective of the plantation owners or their representatives. Dunkley, by contrast, depicts what a worker might see: rows of crops, stretching as far as the eye can see.

Let us think of these things together: the consumption of bananas during this period, rather than their production; the shift in perspective occasioned by considering what a banana laborer sees rather than how they are seen; and Carroll's rabbit's obsession with time, particularly apt in a context where Black plantation workers were routinely accused of being lazy.[8] There is also the rabbit's incitement of an ill-fated and often absurd adventure into parts unknown. Let us also note here the rabbit's whiteness.[9] White like the prospective tourists, settlers, and investors who were the projected audience, the consumers, of the photographs that sought to produce "the New Jamaica." White like the photographers who took those photographs. White like the plantation's overseers, who drove its laborers to do more in less time, often with disastrous consequences and in the face of significant resistance from plantation workers.[10] Might the rabbit represent all that? All those (white) things that the camera shutter, which Azoulay has argued "developed as an imperial technology,"[11] failed to capture?

But if the rabbit represents all these aspects of whiteness, is Dunkley, and his position as plantation laborer, completely absent from *Banana Plantation*? Well, there is that crab. Tucked in the lower-right-hand corner, it's easy to miss. In fact, in an earlier version of this paper, I overlooked it. Where the rabbit is white, the crab is brown. Its hard shell protects its soft insides not only from the attacks that may come in its traverse across land, sea, and swamp, but also from sight. We're not seeing the crab itself, only its shell. This aspect of the crab recalls Thompson's observation:

> Photographs of black people . . . often foregrounded black skin as a signifier, representative of more than a surface: of a host of ever-changing characteristics inherent to black people. In this respect, black people's surface appearances . . . often could not be seen through or beyond. Photography often delimited the ability to see black people as subjects with complex interior lives.[12]

The amphibious crab is also adaptable to different environments, as migrant workers at the literal vanguard of American modernity—cutting into the forests and swamps to build railroads, telegraph lines, and ports and cultivating the cash crops that financed infrastructure and military coups throughout South and Central America and the Caribbean—would likewise have had to be. The crab is also nimble, never hurtling heedlessly toward its target as Carroll's rabbit does, but moving tentatively, thoughtfully, sideways, its intended destination difficult to discern. Might we draw a parallel between this apparent waywardness of the crab, the creature's illegible intentions, and Dunkley's stubborn illegibility within the archive and his refusal to speak to us through any medium besides his challenging, even taunting artwork?

It may seem like a leap to think of Dunkley, a painter and sculptor, in relation to photography rather than to the history of painting or sculpture. However, if we consider the visual landscape that he worked within, the comparison seems quite fitting. It is not likely that Dunkley visited many art museums. There were no dedicated art spaces in Jamaica during Dunkley's lifetime and, even on his travels, there would have been few art spaces a Black, English-speaking migrant laborer would have been welcomed into.[13] Even if we accept Boxer's argument that Dunkley was looking at art books procured from the IoJ library, Dunkley only met Molesworth—his link to the IoJ—in 1937.[14] The following year, in 1938, he exhibited eight paintings at the *All Jamaica Art Exhibition* even as he maintained his barber shop, so he was obviously already painting when Molesworth encountered him.

Photography, on the other hand, was everywhere. The best known of Jamaica's early photographers, a French immigrant named Adolphe Duperly, set up his studio in Kingston in 1840. Though a camera and the materials necessarily to process film would have been a substantial investment and therefore accessible only to elites, photography's products were widely available, especially as postcards and in magazines and newspapers. Giving further credence to the value of thinking about Dunkley's artwork alongside photography from the period is Cassie Dunkley's assertion that photography was pivotal to her husband's artistic formation. She writes, "[Dunkley] got an insight for the art from Clarence Rock, who was the most prominent photographer in Panama."[15]

There has never been serious consideration of Dunkley's practice within the context of the rich history of photography in the English-speaking Caribbean. Though Boxer has referenced specific photographs as source material for certain paintings by Dunkley, he does not consider the way the artist's paintings engage photography conceptually, as a process that is not merely technical but also social. Photography requires, but also brings into being, social relationships between photographer and photographed, viewer and viewed, source, distributor, and intended and actual audiences. These social relationships are what Azoulay has called the "civil contract of photography."[16] She writes:

> Every photograph of others bears the traces of the meeting between the photographed persons and the photographer, neither of whom can, on their own, determine how this meeting will be inscribed in the resulting image. The photograph exceeds any presumption of ownership or monopoly and any attempt at being exhaustive. Even when it seems possible to name correctly in the form of a statement what it shows—this is X—it will always turn out that something else can be read in it, some other event can be reconstructed from it, some other player's presence can be discerned through it, constructing the social relations that allowed its production.[17]

The aesthetics of photography I'm thinking about here, then, are not only how a photograph looks, what it depicts, but also the ways social relations are embedded in the photographic object. The gaze of the photograph's subject, who may be looking at or away from the lens, and the literal and ideological gaze of the photographer, modeled via the framing and composition of the photograph, are all at stake here. The distribution of photographs in print (via popular media like postcards, newspapers, and so on) also degrades the image by, for example, heightening contrast with deeper shadows and brighter highlights. Moreover, the way that photographs are collected, preserved, shared, and deployed leaves traces (rips, fading, the material effects of digitization and reproduction) that change their meaning.

I am here indebted to Thompson's scholarship in her second book, *Shine*, from 2015. Thompson's attention to "literal gaps in translation of the image on screen," "streaks of light within the footage," and "visual noise materialized on the surface of the video" leads to the observation that "the processes of duplication and reduplication [of videotaped dancehall performances] reproduce a type of cultural formation in the African diaspora, one in which the form constantly changes over time and across space, bearing traces of and constituted by these processes of transformation and loss."[18] For Thompson, this and other contemporary lens-based practices in the African diaspora highlight "other ontologies of photography—photographic practices that precede and exceed the material forms conventionally associated with the medium."[19]

Applying this methodological insight to my own scholarship, I am drawn to think about how Dunkley's paintings employ visual (à la Thompson) and conceptual (à la Azoulay) features of the kinds of photographs he would have seen in order to critique those photographs' ways of seeing. In the case of *Banana Plantation*, Dunkley critiques the aesthetic of the "New Jamaica" photographs, which failed to acknowledge the complexity and violence that underwrote the economic model of the "New Jamaica" and its picturesque representation. In the very invocation of the banana plantation, the painting also draws links between seemingly disparate places like Jamaica, Costa Rica, and Colombia, the so-called banana republics being made and broken by foreign-controlled monoculture. In this way, Dunkley's insistence on remaking photographs to include things that were not or could not be photographed prefigures Thompson's analysis of the Jamaican picturesque in her first book, *An Eye for the Tropics*.[20]

Other works by Dunkley, such as *President Roosevelt Gazed at Portland Bight* (fig. 7.2), gesture toward what Christopher Pinney and Nicolas Peterson have called "photography's other histories"—that is, a form of analysis that takes into account "a range of geographic locations and a variety of different media that inform how photography is rethought across cultural contexts and over time."[21] Here we have a depiction of Franklin D. Roosevelt, likely based on a photograph used for the

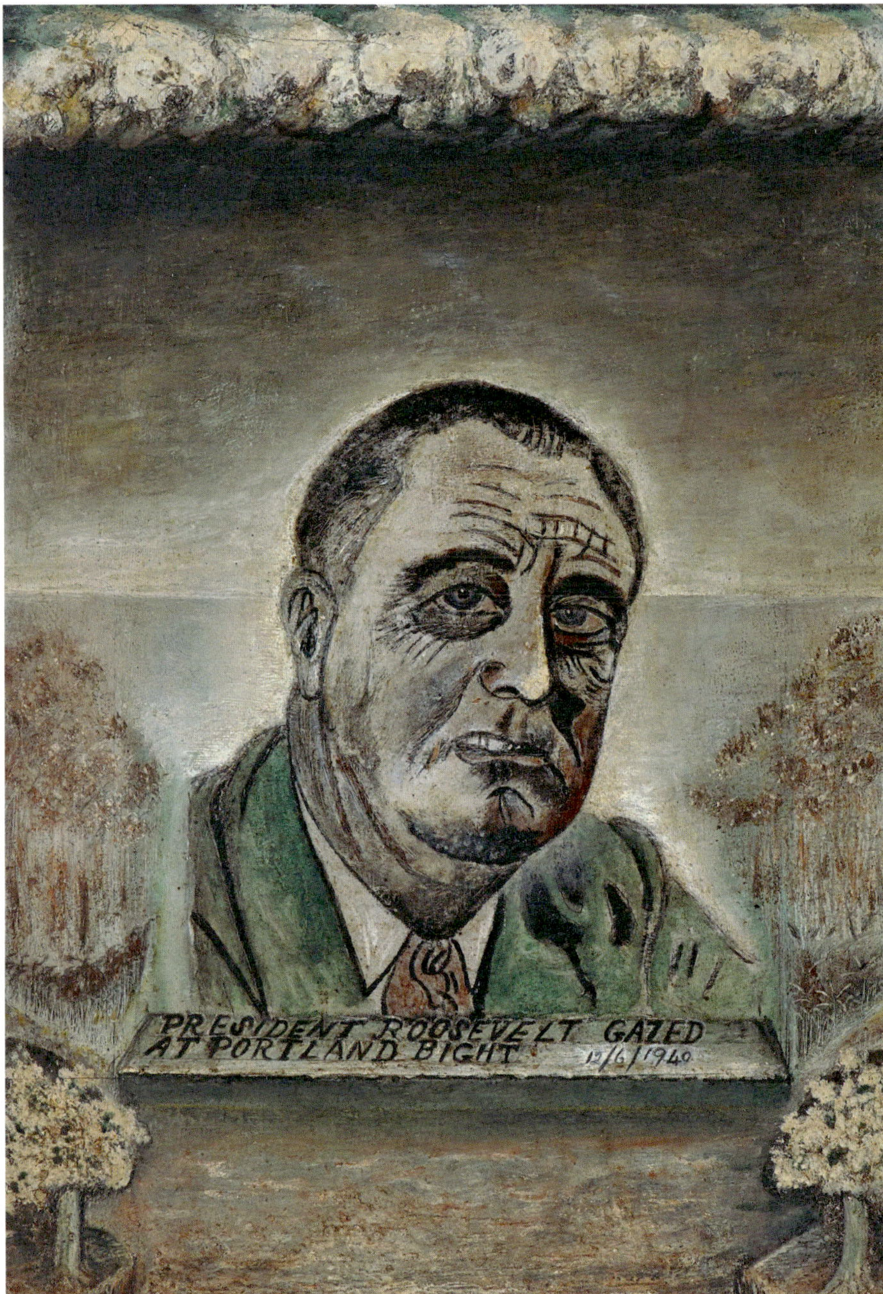

Fig. 7.2. John Dunkley, *President Roosevelt Gazed at Portland Bight*, 1940. Mixed media on plywood, 20¾ × 14½ in. (52.7 × 36.8). Wallace Campbell Collection, Kingston, Jamaica

January 4, 1937, cover of *Life* magazine. That issue included a photo essay that celebrated Roosevelt's first term as president. The essay focused on Roosevelt's handling of the Great Depression, documenting the activities of the National Recovery Administration (NRA) and declaring that after his first one hundred days in office, Roosevelt was as "near Demigod as any president has ever been."[22]

Dunkley's deployment of the photograph in his 1940 painting indicates a very different perspective on Roosevelt. Dunkley darkens the lines around the president's eyes and on his forehead, making for a more foreboding portrait. He changes Roosevelt's mouth, set in a hard line that suggests determination and wherewithal in the photograph, to the kind of mean grimace that might accompany a threat of violence. In the painting, Roosevelt's bust seems to be floating over water, moving inland from the open sea, while dark storm clouds gather overhead. This is not the triumphant depiction of a demigod; rather, it is a warning of impending doom: something evil this way comes.

The painting was made within the context of the 1940 "Destroyers for Bases" deal, which saw the British government displace several small villages on the southeast coast of Jamaica to cede the land to the US government for use as military bases. Dunkley also made an accompanying sculpture, a depiction of a seated Black man with his head resting on his fist, which he called *Sandy Gully* (1941, National Gallery of Jamaica), the name of one of the displaced villages.[23] Giving credence to the idea that Dunkley was invested in challenging *Life*'s American perspective on Roosevelt with his own less flattering one, the *Daily Gleaner*, the premier Jamaican newspaper and in some ways equivalent to *Life*, reports that Dunkley brought the painting to the newspaper's offices in April 1941.[24]

Dunkley's *President Roosevelt* could be thought of as a coordinate in the circum-Caribbean cosmopolitanism that the artist's broader oeuvre maps. According to his wife's account, Dunkley was summoned to Panama by his father but arrived to find his father had died; he then "travelled from Panama to Colon to Costa Rica to Cheriqui Davdd [*sic*] and thence to Camaguey."[25] These likely refer to Colón on the Caribbean coast of Panama, San José de David in Chiriquí on the west coast of Panama, and Camaguey in Cuba, all of which were popular stops on the circum-Caribbean migratory circuit that flourished in the late nineteenth and early twentieth centuries. Throughout this period, the Caribbean coasts of Central and South America, the Caribbean islands, and, later, lands as far away as New York and Canada saw wave after wave of migration of English-speaking Afro-Caribbean people in search of work. To *President Roosevelt* we might add paintings like *Cuban Scenery* (c. 1945, Cassie Dunkley Collection / National Gallery of Jamaica) and *Panama Scenery* (not dated, collection of Michael Campbell), which seem to chart the course of Dunkley's own circum-Caribbean journey. We might also put the less overt *Three Spanish Jars* (not dated, private collection) and *Going to Market* (not dated, private collection)—with its representation of a cactus plant reminiscent of the nopal that appears on the Mexican coat of arms, a notable departure from Dunkley's generally strict visual vocabulary—in the same category. Elsewhere, I discuss these works as Dunkley's rendering of the Black geographies of American modernism.[26]

Lara Putnam's book *Radical Moves* argued for the significance of the circum-Caribbean migratory sphere in understanding the "evolution of the international nation-state system."[27] Putnam focused on the role that migrants played in the rethinking of the purpose of government during the 1920s and '30s. This rethinking laid the groundwork for initiatives like Roosevelt's New Deal, initiatives that, for the first time, depended on the government's ability to determine who was a citizen to be provided for in times of economic distress and who was a foreigner to be ejected in favor of "local" labor. Putnam also notes the role of the circum-Caribbean migratory sphere in fostering Black nationalisms and internationalisms that would go on to shape political life across the Americas and farther afield. The Jamaican political activist Marcus Garvey did, after all, sharpen his skill as a newspaper editor, which he would put to good use in building his United Negro Improvement Association, first in Port Limón, Costa Rica, and then in Colón Panama, before returning to Jamaica in 1912 and continuing to New York in 1916.

Following Dunkley's own crab-walk across the circum-Caribbean migratory sphere requires that we abandon entrenched disciplinary distinctions between US and Latin American history and art history. Only then can we consider Dunkley's critique of the role that photography played in defining the turn-of-the-century American tropics and preparing those places, people, and products for consumption in North America and Europe. To make these arguments, it is necessary to recast Dunkley's context, as I have tried to do here in my reading of *Banana Plantation*, so that we cease to privilege the perspectives and narratives of colonial officials or Jamaican elites and instead seek the outlines of a much-overwritten but still impactful subaltern modernism.

Why subaltern? Why not just another "alternate modernism"? Because I am positing Dunkley's modernism in relation to the dominant narratives of a hemispheric American early modernism. I am pointing out a continuity between the discourse on modernism proper—that is, the Euro-American strain—and Latin American modernism. Both are concerned only with the elite. In fact, if we think about American modernism hemispherically, we find that US and Latin American early modernisms, those of the first half of the twentieth century, share two key features: first, the assertion of a nativist modernism articulated in opposition to European modernisms; and, second, a particular relationship to racial and class-based difference. This relationship is defined by elite artists, those Darby English calls "the voluntary vanguard,"[28] whom I think about in opposition to the different kind of vanguard I referred to earlier—artists who articulate nationalist modernisms through reference to or representations of the cultural production of subaltern populations, generally differentiated by class or race.

I am indebted here to Wanda Corn's groundbreaking study of early American modernism, which traces the role of folk culture in an early nationalist phase of American modernism that sought to distinguish itself from the various European modernisms dominant at the time.[29] Though Corn does not explicitly engage with race, we need only look at Georgia O'Keeffe's citation of Indigenous cultures of the Southwest and various early modernists' engagement with jazz to see these dynamics at play. I am also thinking of the various Latin American modernisms—Mexican muralism, Brazilian anthropophagy, the constructivism of the Escuela del Sur, and Andean *indigenismo*—that saw social elites draw on the cultural production of local Indigenous and Black populations as a way of developing homegrown formal innovation that might compete with European modernism. In this way, subaltern cultural production was always a kind of fuel for the motor of American modernisms, along with a cosmopolitanism that generally emerged from transatlantic travel, a common rite of passage among American elites. It is only when subaltern subjects assume agency and produce art that we call it "outsider"—or "Intuitive," as such artists, including Dunkley, are called in Jamaica.

To perceive Dunkley's modernism, we must make two shifts. First, Dunkley did not look to the subaltern to produce his modernist innovation. He looked instead to his "other," the elite, and drew on an elite form within the context of early twentieth-century Jamaica: photography. Dunkley's paintings employ the very limits of a photograph—the underexposed shadows and overexposed light, the inability to capture color—and level a critique that anticipates a great deal of contemporary scholarship on photography, asking: "How do we visualize what is not, or cannot be seen?" And, further, "How do we contest photographic evidence that does not show the truth?" In other words, "How do we capture what cannot be photographed?" I would argue that Dunkley's paintings anticipate Azoulay's assertion of the camera shutter's role in the third dimension through which imperialism operates, the dividing line "in the body politic (between those who possess and operate such devices [camera shutters] and appropriate and accumulate their product, and those whose countenance, resources, or labor are extracted)."[30]

Second, we must rethink Dunkley's circum-Caribbean travels, a rite of passage among men and women of his time and background, as the nexus of another kind of cosmopolitanism that fed into cultural modernisms, as well as more material strivings toward and challenges to modernity. These travels map the Black geographies of American modernity, which nourished the robust, if overlooked, subaltern modernism of artists like Dunkley.

NOTES

1. Krista A. Thompson, "Object Lesson 21: Castleton Garden 1908," in *Victorian Jamaica*, ed. Tim Barringer and Wayne Modest (Duke University Press, 2018), 115.
2. Crown colony rule saw the British crown assume direct legislative and administrative oversight of the colony, replacing a local assembly composed of the formerly slave-owning plantocracy.
3. David Boxer, "The Life and Art of John Dunkley: Neither Day nor Night," in *Neither Day nor Night*, ed. Diana Nawi (Prestel, 2017), 16–69, 19, 61.
4. Boxer, "Life and Art of John Dunkley," 17.
5. Cassie Dunkley, "Life of John Dunkley," in *Memorial Anniversary Exhibition of the Late John Dunkley, Artist and Sculptor* (Kingston, 1947), n.p.
6. I use the term "indigenous" here with awareness of the complications of this term when discussing the descendants of people who came to the Caribbean via the transatlantic slave trade. My intention is certainly not to overwrite the Taíno, the people whom Christopher Columbus encountered when he arrived in Jamaica in May 1494. Rather, I invoke a term used in Dunkley's own time—in the Haitian *indigéniste* movement—and later reiterated by Sylvia Wynter in her 1970 *Jamaica Journal* article "Jonkonnu in Jamaica: Towards the Interpretation of Folk Dance as Process" to refer to Caribbean folk culture. I regard the tension between the contemporary usage of "indigenous" to refer to aboriginal peoples and this older usage of the word to refer to folk cultures spawned by Afro-descended Caribbean people as ultimately generative, given its restaging of debates around roots and routes. For a more complete discussion, see Amanda T. Perry, "Becoming Indigenous in Haiti, from Dessalines to *Le Revue Indigène*," *Small Axe* 23 (July 2017): 45–61.
7. For those who might argue that my introduction of a character drawn from a book by a British author reinstates Europe as central, I would counter that Dunkley remains the protagonist in this reading. It is also in keeping with Cassie Dunkley's characterization of her husband as a self-made, cosmopolitan man, as well as accounts by the Jamaican scholar and educator Sir Phillip Sherlock (1902–2002) and others who characterize Dunkley as a voracious reader of the newspapers and magazines he kept in his barber shop. Finally, I would invoke Eddie Chambers's observation that "academics and researchers . . . who have studied and presented material on African American artists, have tended to do so in ways that have quarantined or isolated the subjects from the concurrent wider art practice at the time in which the artists studied were working. Time and again we have been denied the opportunity to look at generations of black artists' work in a range of wider contexts. In that regard, the bulk of the alternative art histories that have been served up in the past . . . have ultimately existed as partial black versions of partial white texts." See Eddie Chambers, "The Difficulties of Naming White Things," *Small Axe* 38 (July 2012): 186.
8. For example, the caption of a photograph of a Black man carrying a large bunch of bananas on his back, published in the 1913 book *Panama and the Canal in Picture and Prose*, reads: "One way of carrying bananas: At the docks of the United Fruit Co., mechanical carriers, so perfected as not to bruise the fruit, have replaced the leisurely negro." See Willis J. Abbott, *Panama and the Canal in Picture and in Prose: A Complete Story of Panama, as Well as the History, Purpose and Promise of Its World-Famous Canal* (Syndicate, 1913).
9. Some have suggested that the rabbit is not white, noting that his head is white but his body appears to be gray. I choose to interpret the rabbit's fur as white but cast in shadow, in keeping with Dunkley's penchant for dramatic lighting.
10. The infamous "Banana Massacre" of December 5, 1928, in which the Colombian military opened fire on striking United Fruit Company workers at a train station in Ciénaga, Colombia, is a good example of both worker resistance and the violence such resistance was met with. See Kevin Coleman, "The Photos That We Don't Get to See: Sovereignties, Archives, and the 1928 Massacre of Banana Workers in Colombia," in *Making the Empire Work: Labor and United States Imperialism*, ed. Daniel Bender and Jana Lipman (NYU Press, 2016), 104–33.
11. Ariella Azoulay, *Potential History: Unlearning Imperialism* (Verso, 2019), 30.
12. Krista A. Thompson, *Shine: The Visual Economy of Light in African Diasporic Aesthetic Practice* (Duke University Press, 2015), 17.
13. Although artwork was exhibited at the Institute of Jamaica, there was no space permanently dedicated to the exhibition of art.
14. And further, what he would have been looking at were, in fact, black-and-white photographs of paintings, very different from the paintings themselves.
15. C. Dunkley, "Life of John Dunkley."
16. See Ariella Azoulay, *The Civil Contract of Photography* (Zone, 2008).
17. Azoulay, *Civil Contract*, 12.
18. Thompson, *Shine*, 12.
19. Thompson, *Shine*, 23.
20. Krista A. Thompson, *An Eye for the Tropics: Tourism, Photography, and Framing the Caribbean Picturesque* (Duke University Press, 2006).
21. As discussed in Thompson, *Shine*, 23. See Christopher Pinney and Nicolas Peterson, eds., *Photography's Other Histories* (Duke University Press, 2003).

22. "The Roosevelt Rule (1933–1937): A Pictorial Record," *Life*, January 4, 1937, 28.
23. Boxer, "Life and Art of John Dunkley," 45.
24. "Current Items," *Daily Gleaner* (Kingston), March 15, 1944.
25. C. Dunkley, "Life of John Dunkley."
26. John Dunkley's work is the subject of my dissertation, in which one chapter is dedicated to the relationship between Dunkley's paintings and photography, and another is dedicated to the Black geographies of Dunkley's artwork, particularly his landscape paintings. Nicole Smythe-Johnson, "In Pursuit of a Subaltern Modernism: The Life and Work of John Dunkley" (PhD diss., University of Texas–Austin, 2024).
27. Lara Putnam, *Radical Moves: Caribbean Migrants and the Politics of Race in the Jazz Age* (University of North Carolina Press, 2013), 5.
28. See Darby English, "Modernism's War on Terror," in *Outliers and American Vanguard Art*, ed. Lynne Cooke (University of Chicago Press, 2018), 30–34.
29. Wanda Corn, *The Great American Thing: Modern Art and National Identity, 1915–1935* (University of California Press, 1999).
30. Azoulay, *Unlearning Imperialism*, 31.

PART III
RETHINKING CARIBBEAN ART HISTORIES

CHAPTER 8

RETHINKING CARIBBEAN ART HISTORIES

LESSONS FROM DAVID BOXER'S *JAMAICAN ART, 1922–1982*

Veerle Poupeye

New art histories, as they are produced in a Euro-American context, have an advantage in that they can argue, and position themselves, against already well-established and widely disseminated art historical narratives.[1] There is no such standardized point of reference for the art of the Caribbean. The foundational art historical narratives that have been produced about the region are often quite rudimentary, with limited circulation, while many aspects of its local art histories remain undocumented. Most of these pioneering texts are focused on producing national, and often expressly nationalist, art histories, which limits their scope and hinders their incorporation into broader and interconnected critical and art historical conversations.[2] Furthermore, several have been articulated through an ambivalent critical dialogue with the dominant Western canons, and in challenging their exclusions also reconfirm their significance by claiming a validating relationship with them.

David Boxer's foundational text on Jamaican art history, *Jamaican Art, 1922–1982*, provides an instructive example of these tensions.[3] It positions the story of modern Jamaican art as a fundamental challenge to the cultural impact of colonization, but it is also beholden to the genealogies, hierarchies, points of reference, and labels of conventional art history. As Faye R. Gleisser, talking about the new, decolonial art histories, has recently asserted: "It's really through art history's structural insistence on chronology, comparison, and classification that it reproduces anti-Black and colonial power structures."[4] The conventional methodologies and vocabularies of art history, as a discipline, have indeed been an obstacle to retelling the stories of art effectively, and articulating workable decolonial alternatives is one of the core problems that any new Caribbean art history needs to address.

Jamaican Art, 1922–1982 was first published in 1983 as the catalogue of an exhibition with the same name curated by Boxer, then the director and curator of the National Gallery of Jamaica (NGJ), and its former deputy director, Vera Hyatt, as a joint project of the NGJ and the Smithsonian Institution Traveling Exhibition

Fig. 8.1. Cover of David Boxer, *Jamaican Art, 1922–1982* (Smithsonian Institution Traveling Exhibition Service, 1983), with John Dunkley's *Banana Plantation* (1945)

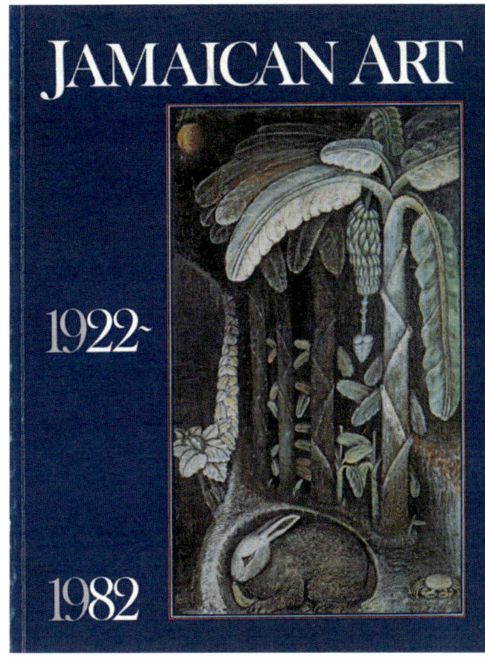

Service (SITES) (fig. 8.1). The exhibition came about after Hyatt migrated to the United States to become a registrar at SITES. *Jamaican Art, 1922–1982* toured to various locations in the United States, Canada, and Haiti between 1983 and 1985, with a final showing at the NGJ in 1986. It consisted of seventy-six paintings and sculptures dating from 1922 to 1982, drawn from the NGJ and private collections. While not the earliest touring exhibition of Jamaican art, *Jamaican Art, 1922–1982* was, and still is, the most ambitious and widely circulated such survey.[5]

Boxer was the first specialist-trained Jamaican art historian, having earned a PhD from Johns Hopkins University, where he wrote his dissertation on the early work of Francis Bacon. He became the NGJ's director and curator in 1975, about one year after that museum opened, and served in that capacity until 1991, when he became chief curator, a position he held until he retired in 2013. Boxer was also an influential contemporary artist who exhibited regularly at the NGJ, and he became one of Jamaica's main art collectors, an art appraiser, and the adviser to a tightly knit circle of fellow collectors, several of whom served on the NGJ board. He was a close friend and protégé of the prominent Jamaican artist Edna Manley and her son, the politician Michael Manley, but he soon also made powerful allies on the other side of Jamaica's highly partisan political landscape.[6] While he was controversial because of the conflicts of interest arising from his combined professional roles, Boxer is widely regarded as the most influential scholar and curator of Jamaican art to date and one of the pioneering art historians in the Caribbean.[7] He died in 2017.

This essay presents a critical, contextualized close reading of the catalogue text of *Jamaican Art, 1922–1982*. Inevitably, this means broaching the professional rivalries and controversies that informed its production and reception, which are an integral part of its story. Such interpersonal dynamics, while common throughout the global art world, tend to be amplified in small, closely knit postcolonial island societies, where they have a more direct impact on artistic hierarchies and narratives. The lack of established competing or corrective accounts of these histories, the limited availability of outlets and audiences for local scholars to share their work, and the high representational stakes intensify the personal aspects of scholarship in a context of historical disempowerment and voicelessness. While this essay provides a close-up and at times unsparingly critical perspective on *Jamaican Art, 1922–1982*, it also acknowledges the pioneering and lasting value of Boxer's work to Jamaica's art histories and those of the Global South. Moreover, it seeks to contribute to the ongoing, broader reevaluation of foundational narratives and of ideas about the arts that challenged the status quo in their own time, reframing these approaches as a crucial point of departure in the articulation of new, decolonial art histories.[8] Beyond the Caribbean, this has, for instance, included the critical responses, in recent decades, to the contradictory ideas, gender dynamics, patronage practices, and personalities that underpinned the concept of the Harlem Renaissance.[9]

The exhibition *Jamaican Art, 1922–1982* was limited to twentieth-century Jamaican art, but Boxer's catalogue essay starts with pre-Columbian art and offers a more comprehensive survey of Jamaican art history. While no more than about ten thousand words long, *Jamaican Art, 1922–1982* represented the culmination of the art historical narrative Boxer had begun articulating, through a sequence of pioneering exhibitions, after he joined the National Gallery of Jamaica in 1975.[10] The narrative also served as the basis for the installation of the NGJ's permanent collection, the modern section of which was first installed in 1983, initially under the title *Jamaican Art, 1922–1982*, after the museum moved to its present location on the Kingston waterfront (fig. 8.2).[11]

In 1998, the essay was republished, with a few minor updates, in the book *Modern Jamaican Art*, to which I contributed a second essay on contemporary Jamaican art. At that time, there was significant debate in the Jamaican art world about the politics of representation within institutional narratives, coming mainly from a younger generation of artists and critics who were challenging the hierarchies of the Jamaican art world and the gatekeeping power of the NGJ. Nonetheless, Boxer did not consider that the original essay might require more substantive revisions or perhaps a different approach altogether.[12] Simply adding a separate essay on recent developments seemed adequate to him.

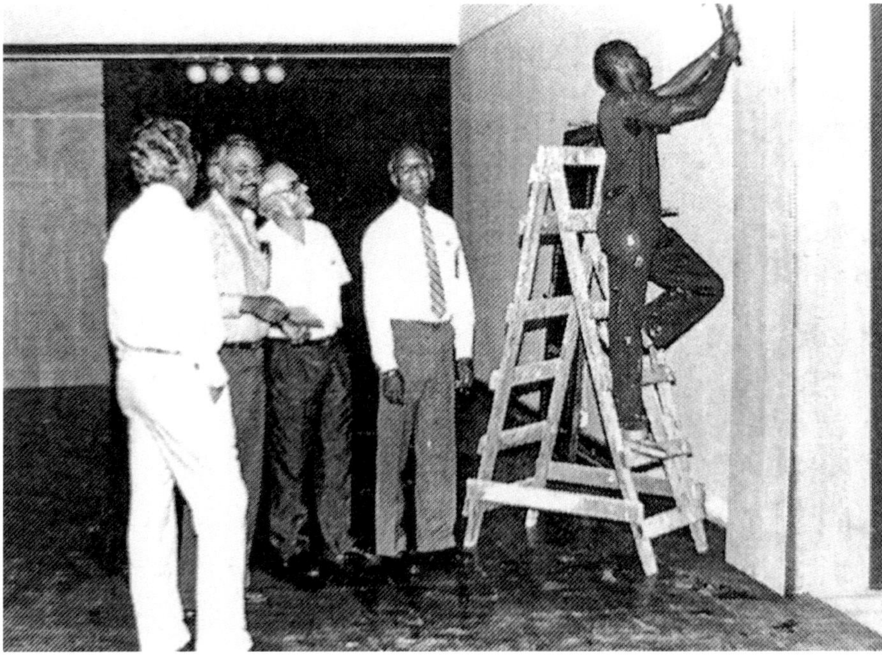

Fig. 8.2. David Boxer (second from left) in the Roy West Building, the new home of the National Gallery of Jamaica, during preparations for the gallery's relocation, Kingston, c. 1983

The manner in which Boxer structured his catalogue essay for *Jamaican Art, 1922–1982* is revealing.[13] After establishing that Jamaican art is, in his view, "the art that has developed as an integral part of the nationalist, anti-colonialist consciousness underlying the cultural and intellectual life of the island since the 1920s" – and that "true Jamaican art" is thus a product of the twentieth century – Boxer moves on to sketching its "prehistory," with the art of the indigenous Taíno and the colonial era.[14] The amount of space dedicated to pre-twentieth-century art in and about Jamaica, much of it colonial, may initially seem contradictory to Boxer's nationalist project. However, as Tony Bennett has argued, this is characteristic of how new nations narrate their histories:

> In so far as they are "imagined communities" – ways of conceiving the occupants of a particular territory as essentially unified by an underlying commonality of tradition and purpose – nations exist through, and represent themselves in the form of, long continuous narratives. . . . This process of stretching the national past so as to stitch it into a history rooted in deep time is particularly evident in the case of new nations

> where, however, it also gives rise to peculiar difficulties. In the case of settler societies which have achieved a newly autonomous post-colonial status, this process has to find some way of negotiating—or leaping over—their only too clearly identifiable and often multiple beginnings.[15]

Boxer's negotiating strategy is twofold: to argue for the crucial absence of African-Jamaican art from before the twentieth century, in spite of an otherwise rich Amerindian and colonial art history, and to insist on the essential Jamaicanness of Edna Manley's early work as the pivotal solution to that problem.

Claiming a deep, locally rooted prehistory for Jamaican art, despite the colonial disruptions, required establishing the art of the Taíno as part of the national art history, even though scholarship on Taíno art in Jamaica was still limited at the time the essay was first written.[16] Boxer singles out four woodcarvings of Taíno *zemís* (or deities), three of which are of undisputed Jamaican origin and presently in the British Museum (fig. 8.3).[17] The fourth one is in the Michael C. Rockefeller Collection at the Metropolitan Museum of Art, New York, where it is attributed to a Taíno maker in what is now the Dominican Republic.[18] That Boxer, who was not a Taíno specialist, opted to attribute this iconic Taíno carving to Jamaica, without providing supporting evidence, illustrates how nationalist agendas, rather than scholarship, may motivate claims of cultural ownership.[19]

Boxer then cursorily mentions the Spanish period (1494–1670). Its main artistic relic, the so-called Seville Carvings (c. 1530), are a group of decorative architectural stone and stucco carvings, recovered in archaeological excavations, that were made to adorn the governor's mansion and other buildings at Jamaica's first, short-lived Spanish capital of Sevilla Nueva, on Jamaica's north coast.[20] The carvings, which are executed in a creolized plateresque style also found in other early Spanish settlements such as Santo Domingo, are of interest as early examples of creolized art in the Caribbean—though Boxer's text makes no such comparisons.

The discussion of the English colonial period, which formally started in 1670 when the island was ceded to England, is divided into three parts. In the first, Boxer discusses the work by major English artists that was commissioned and imported to the island by the plantocracy, especially neoclassical commemorative and funerary sculptures, such as John Bacon's Rodney Memorial (1790) in Jamaica's former capital Spanish Town. In the second, he discusses the work of the itinerant naturalists and topographical artists—most of them Europeans but also a few Americans—who produced landscapes, naturalist depictions of the island's indigenous flora and fauna, and picturesque scenes, often supported by major planters. In this section, Boxer makes special mention of Isaac Mendes Belisario (fig. 8.4), who, he reports, established a painting and printmaking studio in Kingston in 1835 and whose main patron was the Marquis of Sligo, the colonial governor at the time of

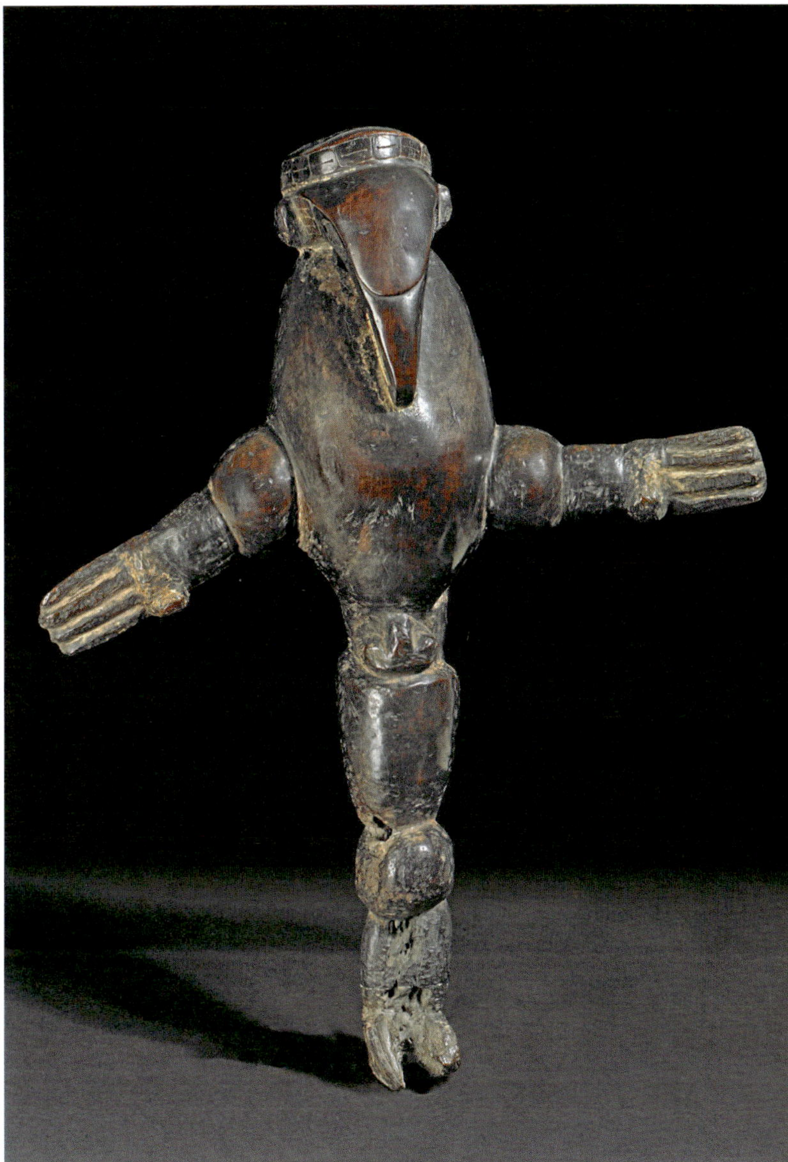

Fig. 8.3. Taíno artist (Jamaica), *zemí* figure (known as *The Birdman*), c. 1029–56. Wood, 34 ¼ × 27 ½ × 8 ⅝ in. (87 × 70 × 22 cm). British Museum, London, Am1977,Q.2

Fig. 8.4. Isaac Mendes Belisario (English, 1795–1849), ***Koo-Koo, or Actor Boy***, from ***Sketches of Character, in Illustration of the Habits, Occupation, and Costume of the Negro Population in the Island of Jamaica***, 1837–38. Lithograph with watercolor, image: 10 × 7 ½ in. (25.4 × 19.1 cm); sheet: 14 ¾ × 10 ¾ in. (35.7 × 27.3 cm). Yale Center for British Art, New Haven, Connecticut, Paul Mellon Collection, Rare Books and Manuscripts, folio A 2011 24

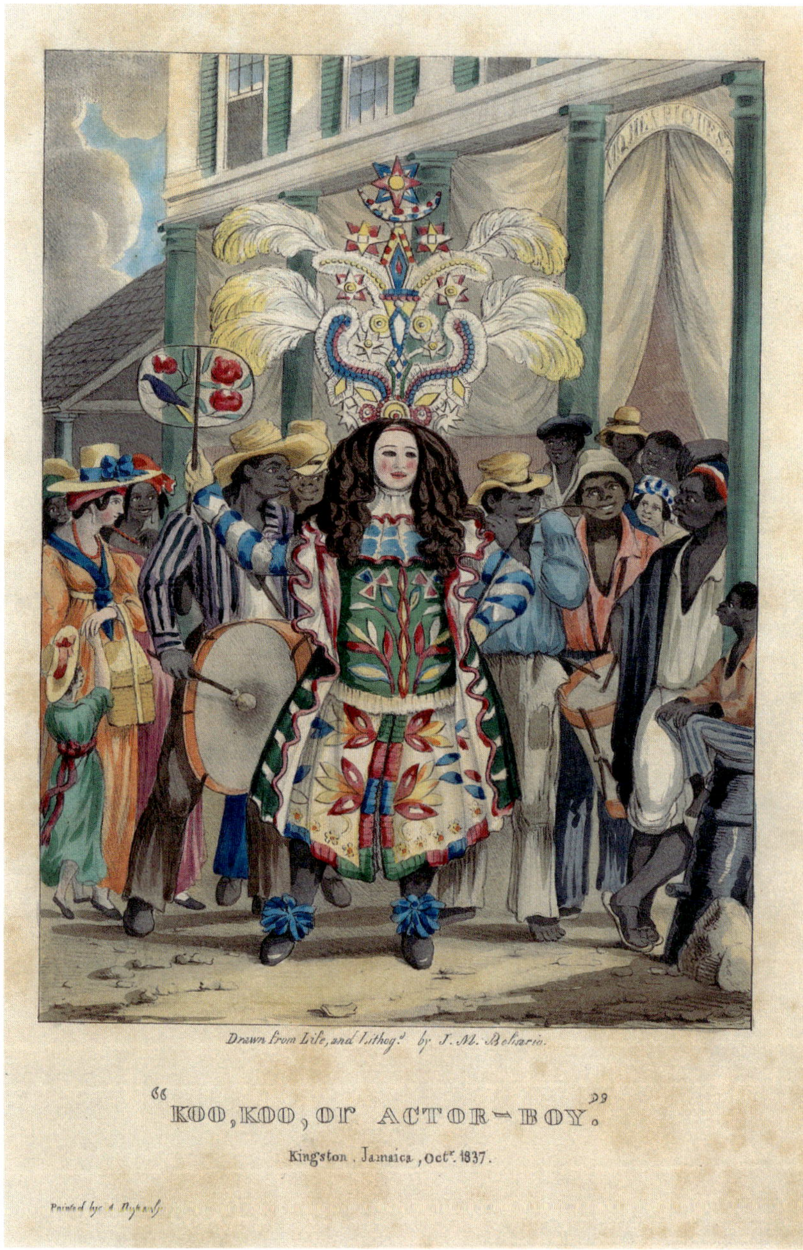

emancipation in Jamaica. Belisario was, in effect, the first *documented* Jamaica-born artist, although this was not yet known when *Jamaican Art, 1922–1982* was written and was still contested when the book was revised for the 1998 edition.[21]

Boxer's discussion of the colonial era concludes with the most controversial assertion in the essay, where he claims, "It is one of the tragedies of slavery that so drastic was the deculturation of the Africans, so harsh were the prohibitions against the manufacture of ritual objects, that with the exception of undecorated ceramic vessels not one object exists as evidence of the continuity of African artistic traditions in Jamaica."[22] This claimed absence, as Krista Thompson observed in her 2004 essay "Black Skin, Blue Eyes," set the stage for what the "true" Jamaican art had to redress in the twentieth century.[23]

The section on the twentieth century in Boxer's text starts with a long discussion of the English-born sculptor and painter Edna Manley's early work, which, he contends, was *the* critical turning point in the "Jamaicanization" of local art production. He even identifies her arrival on the island in 1922 as the starting date of modern Jamaican art. He notes the critical acclaim her work received in England at that time—one of several moments in the essay where he, contradictorily, invokes external validation. He also emphasizes her early influence, in the 1930s, on younger Jamaican artists such as the sculptor Alvin Marriott and the painter Albert Huie, as the earliest stirrings of a national school. The Edna Manley segment concludes with a discussion of the group of carvings she produced between 1935 and 1937—all modernist and depicting assertively Black subjects—which are positioned as the triumphant breakthrough of nationalist Jamaican art, and which coincided with her emergence as a prominent member of the nationalist intelligentsia. Most of this discussion focuses on Manley's best-known sculpture, *Negro Aroused* (fig. 8.5), in the NGJ's permanent collection, as the most iconic artwork of that period.

Manley's artistic and art historical significance is undeniable, but the manner in which Boxer consecrates her as the "Mother of Jamaican Art" (a term he does not use in the essay but that is commonly used in Jamaican art historical accounts) fails to acknowledge the contradictions of her interventions.[24] Manley's groundbreaking sculptures were, despite their nationalist, anticolonial politics, in effect work *about* Black Jamaicans made by an artist who was arguably white, foreign-born, and a member of the late-colonial elite—and who, for all her social and political capital, was regularly challenged as an outsider during her lifetime.[25] In a remarkable, preemptive legitimizing move that also satisfied his personal loyalties to her, Boxer thus positioned Manley as *the* pioneering and defining modern Jamaican artist.

Boxer's discussion of the formative years of the nationalist school continues with a few paragraphs on "the Early Intuitives," three self-taught artists to whom the label *Intuitive* was applied retroactively: the painter John Dunkley (see

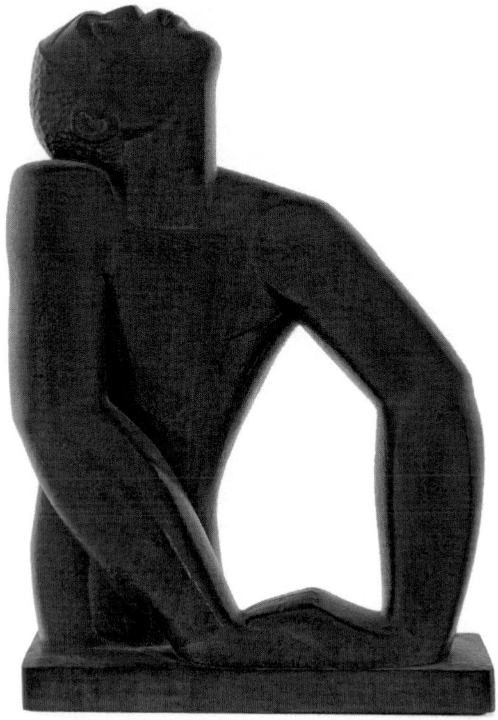

Fig. 8.5. Edna Manley (Jamaican, 1900–1987), *Negro Aroused*, 1935. Mahogany, height: 25 in. (63.5 cm). National Gallery of Jamaica, donated by the David Boxer Collection / Onyx Foundation

p. 132, fig. 7.1, and p. 138, fig. 7.2) and the wood sculptors David Miller Sr. and David Miller Jr., father and son. Boxer had, with the 1979 exhibition *The Intuitive Eye* at the National Gallery of Jamaica, coined this term as an alternative to more obviously problematic descriptors such as *primitive* and *naïve*, and he had started cultivating a selective canon of self-taught, popular artists under the Intuitives label. Rather than characterize these artists as outsiders to the mainstream, Boxer placed them at the center of Jamaica's national art canon. According to his definition, their work was part of a spontaneous, ancestral upwelling of popular artistic genius, uncontaminated by colonialism. However, he also insisted on their artistic individuality and, especially, the visionary quality of their work as the primary reasons for naming them Intuitives.[26]

As with Manley, Boxer had a personal interest in giving the Early Intuitives a central position in his narrative of the national tradition, as he was also the main collector of their work. In *Jamaican Art, 1922–1982*, Boxer presents these artists as personal discoveries of members of the nationalist intelligentsia—the "cognoscenti," as he calls them—who were in search of "native talent."[27] Most of the discussion of the Early Intuitives in this text is devoted to Dunkley, who is categorically labeled as "Jamaica's greatest painter" and whose work featured on the cover of the 1983 SITES catalogue (see fig. 8.1) and the exhibition poster. This prominence reinforced the importance of the Intuitives as the second pillar of Boxer's narrative of Jamaican art (with Manley being the first). Boxer shores up his claims about Dunkley's significance by citing Edmund Barry Gaither of the Museum of the National Center of Afro-American Artists in Boston, who in 1969 had described Dunkley as "a little short of Henri Rousseau [and] the equal of American Primitives such as Grandma Moses and Horace Pippin."[28]

Boxer then continues by describing how the nationalist school developed during the 1940s and '50s. He identifies two subgroups. One, labeled "the Institute Group," includes the young artists who were mentored by Manley at her free art classes at the Institute of Jamaica's Junior Centre during the 1940s, such as Albert Huie, Ralph Campbell, David Pottinger, and Henry Daley. These artists consciously pursued the development of an indigenous iconography based on popular life and the physical environment in Jamaica. The other is presented under the heading "the Independents," artists whose artistic pursuits and politics departed from those of the Institute Group, such as Carl Abrahams and Gloria Escoffery, or who worked outside of Jamaica, such as Ronald Moody and Namba Roy, who lived in England as adults. Boxer's appraisal of the Independents, however, implies that there are significant parallels with the Institute Group, so that they can still be regarded, or recuperated, as part of a Jamaican school.

The third part of Boxer's essay, following his accounts of pre-Columbian and early colonial Jamaican art and developments in the first half of the twentieth century, deals with the decades following independence, namely the 1960s and '70s. Under the heading "Mainstream," Boxer points out that many of the nation's pioneering modern artists were still active (in 1982), and he briefly reviews Manley's later work. He presents the period as one of continuity and change, in which younger artists, who had almost all studied abroad (in Europe, North America, or Latin America), built on but also challenged the legacy of the older generations. He then proceeds to discuss those he regards as the three dominant artists of the 1960s, namely the painters Eugene Hyde, Karl Parboosingh, and Barrington Watson (fig. 8.6), who were more ambitious and adventurous about the formal aspects of their work than their predecessors and insisted on being recognized as professionals.[29]

The discussion starts with Watson's academic landscapes and history and genre paintings on Jamaican themes that, Boxer mischievously states, appeal to "those whose artistic eye had been trained by the museums of Europe [and who] quickly elevated Watson to the role of the Jamaican painter *par excellence*."[30] He thus questioned Watson's legitimacy as a postcolonial Jamaican artist, in implied contrast with Edna Manley and the Intuitives, even though Watson was seen by many,

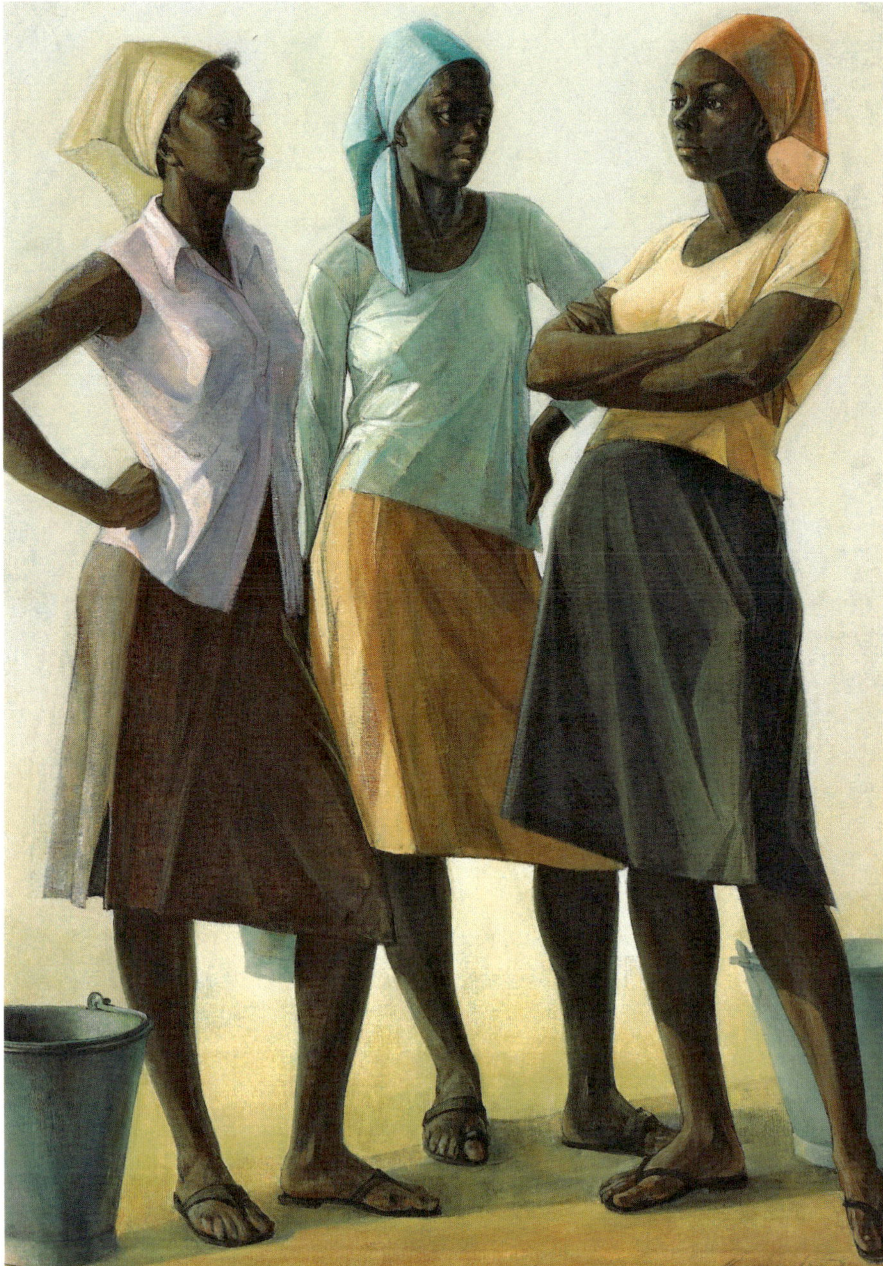

Fig. 8.6. Barrington Watson (Jamaican, 1931–2016), *Conversation*, 1981. Oil on canvas, 55 ½ × 41 ¾ in. (141 × 106 cm). National Gallery of Jamaica, Kingston

and actively positioned himself, as Jamaica's Black "master artist" and one of the defining artists of the independence generation. The subsequent reference to the local commercial popularity of Watson's formal portraits, nudes, and erotica was also subtly disparaging—thinly veiled affronts that reflected the public antagonism between Watson and Boxer, which pertained to the latter's growing control over Jamaica's art historical narratives and artistic hierarchies.

The text then moves to Hyde and Parboosingh, here presented as artists who successfully applied the lessons of expressionism, whether abstract or figurative, to innovative and often provocative Jamaican subject matter. Notably, Boxer writes with great appreciation of Hyde's *Casualties* series of 1978. These works openly criticized the social deterioration under Michael Manley's government in the 1970s, and Boxer's praise shows that was able to transcend partisan loyalties in his artistic appraisals.

The next part of the essay, a subsection of the larger account of the 1960s and '70s, is headlined "Surrealism and Other Influences" and highlights two artists. One is the Australian-born painter Colin Garland, who is credited with pioneering the sort of aestheticized and meticulously executed surrealism that has subsequently been popular in the upper echelons of the Jamaican (and Haitian) art markets. The other is the painter and sculptor Osmond Watson (no relation to Barrington), whose work Boxer describes as a hybrid of Cubism and Surrealism, to which Watson was exposed while studying in London.

The next section, "The Younger Generation Within the Mainstream," discusses younger artists who had emerged in the late 1960s and '70s, most of them after studying abroad. Several were also graduates of the Jamaica School of Art (now part of the Edna Manley College of the Visual and Performing Arts), which had started as an informal, part-time institution in 1950 but introduced full-time diploma programs in 1962. This group includes the sculptors Christopher González and Winston Patrick and the painters Milton George and Hope Brooks. Their formally and conceptually innovative work more decisively departed from the nationalist tradition and announced directions that would become dominant in the 1980s and '90s. Boxer would probably have situated his own work as a painter here, had it been discussed in the essay (one of his paintings was, in fact, included in the exhibition his original text accompanied).

The section on the 1960s and '70s ends with a long and enthusiastic discussion of the "Later Intuitives," starting with Mallica "Kapo" Reynolds, Gaston Tabois, Sidney McLaren, and Everald Brown, who are all flagged as "masters," followed by several younger, lesser-known artists who are discussed in less detail. As with Dunkley, Boxer mentions the support some of these artists had received from high-profile international enthusiasts such as José Gómez-Sicre, a Cuban émigré who was in charge of the art programs of the Organization of American States, and the American promoter of Haitian "primitive" art Selden Rodman, who, Boxer reports, had ranked Kapo "as a painter . . . probably equal to the late Hector Hyppolite of Haiti."[31]

The Later Intuitives are informally divided into realist (Tabois and McLaren) or symbolist (Kapo and Brown). Some attention is paid to the religious background of the "symbolists"—Kapo was a Zion Revivalist while Brown was a religious Rastafarian—and Boxer acknowledges the growing importance of Rastafari in Jamaican culture but stops short of positioning the Intuitives as the bearers of African-derived Jamaican culture. Boxer rounds off the section on the Later Intuitives with his *Intuitive Eye* exhibition of 1979 as the landmark event that led to their naming and recognition as a group—and adds a jab at the "conservative critics" in Jamaica who had, in his view, failed to appreciate their cultural and artistic significance.[32]

Boxer's essay concludes with a short section on "Art Schools, Associations, and Galleries" in Jamaica. The final paragraph somewhat deflates the confident assertions of a shared cultural nationhood that were made at the start of the essay by arguing that the process of national self-discovery is ongoing and full of "contradictions and tensions" but ultimately concerned with forging links with the "wider community of man."[33]

The exhibition for which Boxer wrote this essay was, among other venues, shown at the Wadsworth Atheneum in Hartford, Connecticut; the Museum of the National Center of Afro-American Artists in Boston; the Ontario Gallery of Art; and the Inter-American Development Bank Latin American and Caribbean Art (IDB ArtLAC) Gallery in Washington, DC, where it premiered in June 1983. It was generally well received in North America, where it attracted approximately 117,000 visitors, and was reviewed in major newspapers such as the *Washington Post* and the *New York Times*.[34] These reviews were almost unanimous in their praise of the Intuitives, but several critics expressed reservations about what they saw as the Eurocentricity of the mainstream. John Bentley Mays of the *Globe and Mail* in Toronto wrote: "The most intriguing paintings and sculptures here, however, are not the polished Euro-Jamaican descendants of [Edna Manley's] the *Beadseller*, but the home-spun, punchy pictures of the self-taught Intuitives."[35]

While there was significant local support, the exhibition was also lambasted by some prominent members of the Jamaican art community. Their objections were not overtly about its focus on Edna Manley—who was probably too much of a venerable elder in the local art community to be publicly tackled—but about its foregrounding of the Intuitives, who were represented with twenty-seven out of seventy-six works and thus made up more than a third of the exhibition.[36] Chief among the critics was Barrington Watson, who did not take kindly to the North American critical response and, no doubt, Boxer's dismissive provocations of him in the catalogue essay. And Watson had a point, as the North American response undeniably reflected reductive, primitivist expectations about Black Caribbean art and problematic notions about postcolonial cultural authenticity.

Watson, who rivaled Boxer as a powerful figure in the Jamaican art world, found a willing spokesperson in Andrew Hope (a Polish expatriate whose birth name was Ignacy Eker), who had been the lead art critic of Kingston's *Daily Gleaner* newspaper since the 1960s and who was, no doubt, the "conservative critic" Boxer had alluded to in his essay. A significant proportion of Hope's reviews and columns of the 1980s was dedicated to questioning the NGJ's promotion of the Intuitives, along with Boxer's professional abilities and intentions. The following comment on the 1986 Jamaican presentation of *Jamaican Art, 1922–1982* is typical, and also shows how Hope pointedly refused to use the term *Intuitive*: "The exhibition lacks a guiding intelligence and seems to have been thrown together with the objective of demonstrating that our Primitives are superior to those painters and sculptors who have received formal training and were 'contaminated' by European influences."[37] Legitimate differences of opinion were involved, but the controversy about *Jamaican Art, 1922–82* and the Intuitives ultimately amounted to a struggle for control over the dominant canons, narratives, and power hierarchies of Jamaican art between professional rivals. This erupted at a moment when the local art community was aware of Boxer's political vulnerabilities, since the Manley government had lost the general elections in 1980.

Boxer's original catalogue essay fulfilled several purposes. One was, obviously, to contextualize the exhibition for its viewers. The self-assured, collective voice evident in phrases such as "In Jamaica, when we refer to Jamaican art . . ." suggests that Boxer addressed foreign audiences unfamiliar with the basics of Jamaican culture and history. However, the exhibition was deliberately toured to areas that had large Caribbean-diaspora populations and was also shown in Haiti and Jamaica, so its audiences were not exclusively North American.[38] Addressing these audiences and their interests (including, perhaps, honoring the universalist mandate of the Smithsonian Institution, which co-organized the exhibition) was no doubt a difficult balancing act and may explain some of the contradictions in how Jamaican art is positioned in the essay.

The long-term purpose of the catalogue was, however, something that the NGJ had, up to that point, been unable to do on its own: to publish a well-illustrated, affordable, and widely distributed survey text that placed its emerging narrative on Jamaican art "on the record" and established Boxer as the leading scholar on the subject. As part of the exhibition arrangement, the Smithsonian made available a substantial stock of catalogues for sale and distribution by the NGJ. By the late 1980s, the catalogue was out of print, and the continued demand for a general survey text led to its local republication in 1998 as the coffee-table book *Modern Jamaican Art* (which I coauthored); that volume, in turn, sold out in about two years.

Boxer, a traditionally educated art historian, wrote the history of Jamaican art in the terms he had been trained to use. He gave full reign to his classificatory impulses and structured his story as a set of labeled trends and groups that were incorporated into a larger evolutionary framework that reflects the cultural logic of Jamaica's progression from colony to independent nation-state. While moderated by personal allegiances, interests, and rivalries, his carefully periodized essay reflected a conscious effort at *creating* a national canon and "master narrative" that, ultimately, in the telling final sentence, inserted the "Jamaican school" into the artistic achievements of the "community of man." The same strategy for the consecration of national culture has also characterized the development of the universal-survey museum and its attendant narratives in the metropolitan West.[39] Boxer thus asserted, by implication, that postcolonial Jamaica had an "art history" of its own that, while still emerging, was on par with and related to the grand art histories of the metropolitan West. Limited attention was paid, in the process, to the relationship of this art history to that of the rest of the Caribbean, the African American community, or the broader Global South. The obvious connection between Edna Manley's *Negro Aroused* and Alain Locke's *The New Negro* (1925), for instance, was not made.

Boxer's essay provides a fair amount of cultural and historical contextualization, but the race, gender, and class backgrounds of the artists and, even more so, of their patrons and publics, is virtually absent from the discussion, even though this is an important part of the dynamics that have shaped art production in Jamaica. His narrative about the Intuitives, for instance, pays disproportionate attention to the group's patrons and thus reveals that the Intuitive canon is more unilaterally dependent on patronage than mainstream Jamaican art, but this is not acknowledged or explained. The Intuitives are generally poor Black Jamaicans, many of them of rural origin, while the "cognoscenti" who discovered and supported them are often white expatriates or light-skinned elite Jamaicans. Yet, recognizing these asymmetrical race and class dynamics, and the tensions and conflicts that have at times surrounded these relationships, would have disrupted the projected image of a diverse but essentially harmonious national culture.[40]

Boxer's text toes a difficult line between his efforts to establish the necessary autonomy of postcolonial Jamaican art and simultaneously demonstrate a legitimizing relationship with mainstream Western art history. This is evident in his choice of vocabulary and references, as well as his insistence on a developmental taxonomy that conforms to conventional Western art historical narratives. He goes to great lengths to introduce a few Jamaican terms and concepts, crucially including his own Intuitives. Other than that, however, his descriptive and analytical vocabulary is essentially that of modern Western art history, making liberal use of terms such as Cubism, Symbolism, Surrealism, and Abstract Expressionism. Boxer's discussion of the Intuitives, in particular, relies on references to prestigious endorsements, albeit most of them by Caribbean and African American scholars, that seem designed to counter local objections to their prominence in his essay, mostly by ranking the artists on par, or nearly on par, with internationally recognized self-taught artists.

The self-conscious mannerism of Boxer's text suggests a desire to force it into canonical status at a time when the art history proposed by the NGJ was still preliminary and contested. The essay includes statements such as "historians today date the beginning of the Jamaican Art Movement to the arrival in Jamaica [in 1922] of an especially gifted artist [Edna Manley]," although the only scholar who used that date was Boxer himself. Likewise, labels such as the Institute Group and the Intuitives are presented as if these were well-established in Jamaica, while they were in fact quite new and tentative. This art historical sleight-of-hand proved effective in shaping the critical reception of the exhibition in North America, yet it only added to the controversies in the Jamaican art world.

Written more than forty years ago, *Jamaican Art, 1922–1982* has been a point of departure, and a problem, for most of what has been written on the subject since. For all its troubling politics and contradictions, the catalogue essay was an important decolonial act in its own time, claiming an art history for a place like Jamaica and beginning to develop a new vocabulary to talk about it.[41] The essay, by centering the Intuitives, acknowledged the defining significance of popular culture, although in doing so it unwittingly reproduced the primitivist concepts it sought to critique. And by positioning Edna Manley as a founding figure, the essay also presented a perhaps unintentional challenge to the conventionally masculinist art histories of the metropolitan West.[42]

Important work has already been done to address some of the most obvious omissions, erasures, and contradictions in *Jamaican Art, 1922–1982* and to explore new ways in which the stories of art in Jamaica and beyond can be told. The late Petrine Archer-Straw, for instance, actively brought race, class, and gender into the discussion and opened the narrative to include the diaspora and the transnational dynamics that have helped to shape art in Jamaica.[43] While he never disavowed or substantially revised *Jamaican Art, 1922–1982*, Boxer himself later also opened new perspectives, for instance with his subsequent work on early Jamaican photography, which indirectly acknowledges that modernity entered Jamaican art and visual culture several decades earlier than he had previously asserted.[44] Furthermore, his later curatorial work on Belisario, in the 2008 exhibition *Isaac Mendes Belisario: Art and Emancipation in Jamaica* at the NGJ, actively consecrated this artist as Jamaica's own "old master" and thus paved the way for a longer, "truly Jamaican" art history, even while perpetuating a problematic canonical concept.[45]

There remains, however, no general Jamaican art historical narrative that has substantially challenged or replaced *Jamaican Art, 1922–1982*. Another survey of modern Jamaican art, *Jamaican Art: An Overview, with a Focus on Fifty Artists*, by Petrine Archer-Straw and Kim Robinson, was published in 1990, with an expanded and retitled edition, *Jamaican Art: Then and Now*, in 2011. The text in these books is longer than *Jamaican Art, 1922–1982*, provides more social context, and illustrates a few artists who had not been included in Boxer's survey. It also does not foreground Edna Manley or the Intuitives to the same extent. But, other than that, the narrative it presents does not depart significantly from Boxer's, and he wrote the foreword for both editions.

In the absence of compelling alternatives, and despite some contestations, the histories presented in *Jamaican Art, 1922–1982* and its latter-day spin-offs continue to have a strong hold in Jamaica and are reproduced without much critical reflection. This is reinforced by the local education system, where it still informs syllabi at secondary level. I encountered its effects in my own teaching practice at the Edna Manley College of the Visual and Performing Arts, where I often used the poem "Praise to the Mother of Jamaican Art" (c. 2003) by the Jamaican poet laureate Lorna Goodison:

> She was the nameless woman who created
> images of her children sold away from her.
> She suspended her wood babies from a rope
> round her neck, before she ate she fed them.
> Touched bits of pounded yam and plantains
> to sealed lips, always urged them to sip water.
> She carved them of wormwood, teeth and nails
> her first tools, later she wielded a blunt blade.
> Her spit cleaned faces and limbs; the pitch oil
> of her skin burnished them. When woodworms
> bored into their bellies she warmed castor oil
> they purged. She learned her art by breaking
> hard rockstones. She did not sign her work.[46]

The poem critiques the foundational position granted to Manley and powerfully invokes longer, unacknowledged histories of Jamaican art linked to injustice, loss, resistance, and healing. Invariably, however, some students would assume that the poem was *about* Manley, which illustrates the extent to which the "mother of Jamaican art" epithet is internalized.

Education, in its traditional and still most practiced form, thrives on labels, classifications, and clear developmental narratives. This is certainly the case at the secondary level in Jamaica, where the groundwork for much of the general thinking about art is being laid. The recent critiques of art history that challenge such didacticism are often densely theorized, couched in arcane language, and difficult to translate into a teachable form for use outside the highest levels of academia.

Part of the problem is also that not enough new primary research is being done. There is too much rehashing of established sources, while the archive is woefully incomplete, fragile, and poorly kept; a lot that is of critical value is already lost. This is a troubling reality in a region where historical developments have produced significant and deliberate zones of silence. And this takes me back to the Goodison poem, as it reminds us that the creative arts can play an important role in giving voice to those silences, thus providing us with compelling new tools to retell and reimagine the stories of art in a region where the traditional art historical approaches and methodologies inevitably fail.

Filling the obvious gaps is, however, not enough, and, as the feminist decolonial activist Françoise Vergès has cautioned, the reimagination of the art histories of places such as the Caribbean "cannot simply be a question of adding something to what already exists. It's about profoundly transforming relationships and structures, with ethics as a compass."[47] Important new work to this end is being done in the academy, and the conference at which this paper was originally delivered was a significant example of such scholarship. But this work does not necessarily reach where it is most needed. One largely unrecognized achievement of *Jamaican Art, 1922–1982*, and an important takeaway for the present conversation, was its accessibility as a text written for general audiences, even as it drew on seminal primary scholarship. For the new decolonial art histories to be effective and relevant, they must be informed by a firm commitment to public scholarship and by innovative, effective, and engaging critical pedagogies, with keener attention to how these new art histories can best speak to and for their core audiences.

NOTES

1. Pioneering interventions include Linda Nochlin, "Why Have There Been No Great Women Artists?," *ARTnews*, January 1971; and the wide-ranging project piloted by Henry Louis Gates Jr. and coedited with David Bindman, *The Image of the Black in Western Art*, vols. 1–5 (Harvard University Press, 2010–14).

2. To illustrate this prevailing focus on national art histories, see, for instance, Michel-Philippe Lerebours, *Haiti et Ses Peintre, de 1804 à 1980: Souffrances et espoirs d'un peuple* (Imprimeur II, 1989); Alissandra Cummins, Allison Thompson, and Nick Whittle, *Art in Barbados: What Kind of Mirror Image* (Ian Randle, 1999); David Boxer and Veerle Poupeye, *Modern Jamaican Art* (Ian Randle, 1998); and Chandra van Binnendijk, *Twintig Jaar Beeldende Kunst in Suriname, 1975–1995* (Stichting Surinaams Museum, 1995).

3. David Boxer, *Jamaican Art, 1922–1982* (Smithsonian Institution Traveling Exhibition Service, 1983). Hereafter, the present text will quote from the slightly revised 1998 version of Boxer's essay (also titled "Jamaican Art, 1922–1982") that appears in Boxer and Poupeye, *Modern Jamaican Art*, as that publication is more widely available.

4. Faye R. Gleisser, in Huey Copeland, Sampada Aranke, and Faye R. Gleiser, "Let's Ride: Art History After Black Studies," *Artforum* 62, no. 2 (October 2023), https://www.artforum.com/features/huey-copeland-art-history-after-black-studies-sampada-aranke-faye-raquel-gleisser-512513/.

5. I worked at the NGJ, with some interruptions, from 1984 to 2018, starting part-time in the Education Department in October 1984 and serving as executive director from 2009 to January 2018. While I was not yet in Jamaica when *Jamaican Art, 1922–1982* was written, I have witnessed firsthand, and been part of, most of the debates and contentions that have surrounded the NGJ's politics of representation.

6. Michael Manley served as Jamaica's prime minister from 1972 to 1980 and again from 1989 to 1992. Manley represented the People's National Party. Boxer's main associate in the rival Jamaica Labour Party was Tom Tavares-Finson, who since 2016 has been the president of the Senate as well as the chair of the NGJ board of directors, and who is also an art collector.

7. Boxer's most public critics have been Andrew Hope, in the 1980s, and Annie Paul, in the late '90s and 2000s. See, for instance, Hope's two-part column, "The Crisis in Leadership," *Daily Gleaner* (Kingston), February 21 and 28, 1988; and Annie Paul, "Regarding the South . . . from the South," in *South-South: Interruptions and Encounters*, ed. Tejpal S. Ajji and Jon Soske (Justina M. Barnicke Gallery, 2009).

8. Such reevaluation has been central to my art historical and critical practice. See, for instance, my "Women Artists in the Matalon Collection," in *Gifts for the Nation: The Donations of Aaron and Marjorie Matalon*, ed. David Boxer (National Gallery of Jamaica, 1999); "Intuitive Art as a Canon," *Small Axe* 24 (2007): 73–82; "Between Nation and Market: Art and Society in Twentieth Century Jamaica" (PhD diss., Emory University, 2011); and "Notes on Jamaica's Art Histories #2: African-Derived Sculpture from the Colonial Period," September 20, 2018, https://veerlepoupeye.com/2018/09/20/notes-on-jamaicas-art-histories-2-african-derived-sculpture-from-the-colonial-period/.

9. See, for instance, Richard J. Powell and David A. Bailey, *Rhapsodies in Black: Art of the Harlem Renaissance* (Hayward Gallery, Institute of International Visual Arts / University of California Press, 1997); and Jeffrey C. Stewart, *The New Negro: The Life of Alain Locke* (Oxford University Press, 2018).

10. These exhibitions crucially included *Five Centuries of Art in Jamaica* (1976), *The Formative Years: Art in Jamaica 1922–1940* (1978), and *Intuitive Eye* (1979).

11. In 1985, a historical gallery dedicated to colonial art also opened and, in 1994, several newly recovered Taíno carvings were added, but the narrative presented in the modern and largest part of the exhibition has not changed significantly, save for a few substitutions and updates with more recent work. The modern galleries have been partially closed since the mid-2000s, and their reinstallation is not yet complete.

12. Annie Paul, who had moved to Jamaica from India in the late 1980s, emerged as a vocal critic of David Boxer and the NGJ in that context. See, for instance, her early essays "Pirates or Parrots: A Critical Perspective on the Visual Arts in Jamaica," *Small Axe* 1 (1997): 49–64; and "Legislating Taste: The Curator's Palette," *Small Axe* 4 (September 1998): 65–83. She was a cofounder of *Small Axe*.

13. An earlier version of the analysis presented in this section of this essay appears in Poupeye, "Between Nation and Market," of which a slightly edited excerpt was posted to my blog, *Perspectives*, as "Notes on Jamaica's Art Histories #1: Critiquing the Main Narrative," August 23, 2018, https://veerlepoupeye.com/2018/08/23/notes-on-jamaicas-art-histories-1-critiquing-the-main-narrative/.

14. Boxer, "Jamaican Art, 1922–1982" (1998), 11.

15. Tony Bennett, *The Birth of the Museum* (Routledge, 1995), 148.

16. There was a significant surge in the production and publication of archaeological and historical scholarship on the Taíno in the early 1990s, spurred in part by the debates provoked by the Columbus

Quincentennial. See, for instance, Irving Rouse, *The Taínos: Rise and Decline of the People Who Greeted Columbus* (Yale University Press, 1992); George A. Aarons, "The Jamaica Taíno: The Aboukir Zemis, Symbols of Taíno Philosophy, Mysticism, and Religion," *Jamaica Journal* 25, no. 2 (December 1994): 11–17; and Jacques Kerchache, *L'Art des Sculpteurs Taïnos: Chefs-d'oeuvre des Grandes Antilles Precolombiennes* (Musée du Petit Palais, 1994). More recently, important contributions have been made by Lawrence Waldron, who offers a broader regional perspective in *Pre-Columbian Art of the Caribbean* (University Press of Florida, 2019). Regarding Taíno art from Jamaica, specifically, significant archival and technical research has in recent years been produced by Joanna Ostapkowicz, an archaeologist based at Oxford University. See, for instance, "The Sculptural Legacy of the Jamaican Taíno. Part 1: The Carpenter's Mountain Carvings," *Jamaica Journal* 35, no. 3 (March 2015): 52–60; and "The Sculptural Legacy of the Jamaican Taíno; Part 2: Eighteenth- to Twentieth-Century Discoveries," *Jamaica Journal* 36, nos. 1 and 2 (January 2016): 94–106.

17. The Jamaican government has indicated its intention to demand the restitution of these carvings from the British Museum, but there is, at the time of writing, no update on any further action. See Gareth Harris, "Growing Pressure on the British Museum as Jamaica Is Latest Government Seeking Return of Objects," *Art Newspaper*, August 8, 2019; and Craig Simpson, "British Museum Could Send Tribal Artefacts Back to Jamaica," *Telegraph* (London), March 9, 2024.

18. The entry on this object in the museum's website now places a question mark behind this attribution (https://www.metmuseum.org/art/collection/search/312602). This Taíno carving had been acquired in 1955 by Nelson Rockefeller from Edna Dakeyne of London who had, in turn, acquired it at an estate auction in Ireland (a provenance that offers some grounds for an attribution to the Anglophone Caribbean). It was on loan to the Museum of Primitive Art in New York City from 1956 to 1978 and then bequeathed to the Metropolitan Museum, where it became part of the Michael C. Rockefeller Wing. This wing first opened in 1982, around the time *Jamaican Art, 1922–1982* was being written. The carving has been on public view there most of the time since then, and it has also been included in several major exhibitions, such as *L'Art des Sculpteurs Taïnos* (1994) at the Musée du Petit Palais in Paris and *Arte del Mar* (2019–21) at the Metropolitan Museum itself. In an illustration of its celebrated and iconic nature, it was featured on the cover of the catalogues for both exhibitions. It is unclear when and by whom the Taíno carving was first attributed to the Dominican Republic. The earliest published attribution I have found is Douglas Newton, Julie Jones, and Kate Ezra, *The Pacific Islands, Africa, and the Americas* (Metropolitan Museum of Art, 1987). That attribution appears to have been made on stylistic grounds, in comparison to other Taíno sculptures of secure provenance. Boxer may thus not have been aware of its attribution to the Dominican Republic when he originally wrote *Jamaican Art, 1922–1982*, but he certainly was aware of it for the book's second edition. Other than carbon dating, no other scientific research appears to have been done to confirm its attribution, and no alternative attributions have thus far been offered by any experts on the subject.

19. Traditionally, the Taíno have not played a major role in Jamaica's national imaginary, where identification with the Black and African diaspora is more common—unlike in Puerto Rico and the Dominican Republic, where they have been central to ideas of national identity. A Taíno couple, however, appears on Jamaica's coat of arms, which dates in its original form to 1661. In the early 1980s, then–Prime Minister Edward Seaga launched a competition to replace this colonial-era emblem with a modern design. Certain stakeholders strongly resisted this move and submitted photocopies of the existing design as part of a successful "Save the Coat" campaign, so honoring the foundational role of the Taíno may not be entirely unimportant to Jamaican identities. This occurred around the time Boxer was writing *Jamaican Art, 1922–1982*.

20. There are potential references to the Taíno in the "grotesqueries" in the carvings, and some sources suggest that Taíno artisans from a nearby settlement may have contributed to their execution. See, for instance, "Seville Heritage Park," UNESCO World Heritage Convention, https://whc.unesco.org/en/tentativelists/5431/. This is not referenced in *Jamaican Art, 1922–1982*.

21. Documentary evidence regarding Belisario's birth in Jamaica in 1795 was found, sometime around 1998, by Jackie Ranston, who later authored the comprehensive biography *Belisario: Sketches of Character* (Mill Press, 2008).

22. Boxer, "Jamaican Art, 1922–1982" (1998), 13. The 1998 edition includes a footnote that acknowledges that the Baptist missionary James Phillipo (1843) had recorded the existence of grave-marker carvings in pre-emancipation Jamaica, but this is not signaled in the main text.

23. Krista A. Thompson, "Black Skin, Blue Eyes: Visualizing Blackness in Jamaican Art, 1922–1944," *Small Axe* 8, no. 2 (2004): 1–31.

24. See, for instance, a 1986 article by the American feminist artist and writer Betty Laduke, "Edna Manley:

The Mother of Jamaican Art," *Woman's Art Journal* 7, no. 2 (Autumn 1986–Winter 1987): 36–40, which references Boxer extensively; and a commemorative article in Jamaica's main daily newspaper by Lennox Aldred, "Remembering the Mother of Jamaican Art," *The Gleaner* (Kingston), February 28, 2021.

25. Edna Manley claimed to be of part-African ancestry, but she was widely regarded as white, which is, along with social standing, a much more important factor in how persons are racially positioned in Jamaica. See Wayne Brown, *Edna Manley: The Private Years, 1900–1938* (Andre Deutsch, 1975), 92–94.

26. Boxer defined the Intuitives as follows in his catalogue essay for the NGJ exhibition in which the concept was coined: "These artists paint, or sculpt, intuitively. They are not guided by fashion. Their vision is pure and sincere, untarnished by art theories and philosophies, principles and movements. . . . Their visions (and many are true visionaries), as released through paint or wood, are unmediated expressions of the world around them—and the worlds within. Some of them . . . reveal as well a capacity for reaching into the depths of the subconscious to rekindle century-old traditions, and to pluck out images as elemental and vital as those of their African fathers." David Boxer, *The Intuitive Eye* (National Gallery of Jamaica, 1979), 3. While Boxer acknowledged the importance of Africa to this sort of work, he foregrounded the role of the subconscious, rather than cultural heritage and continuity, in their creative process. This was, probably not coincidentally, consistent with his own surrealist sensibilities as an artist.

27. Boxer, "Jamaican Art, 1922–1982" (1998), 17.

28. Boxer, "Jamaican Art, 1922–1982" (1998), 17. He cited Hans Bhallan and Edmund B. Gaiter, *Thirty Years of Jamaican Art* (Spelman College, 1969).

29. Watson was openly critical of the patronage dynamics that had shaped the nationalist school. For instance, he said in a 1987 interview with the Irish art historian Elizabeth Waugh, "The Edna Manley, the [Junior Center director] Robert Verity, and that lot were doing a really good job in the arts before [but it] had something like a colonial approach to it in a sense. It was [a] sort of 'giving a break to a talented youngster' type of thing. . . . They patronized a lot of the artists and kept them at a certain level, unfortunately or inadvertently, by this kind of patronizing approach." Elizabeth Waugh, "Emergent Art and National Identity in Jamaica, 1920s to the Present" (PhD diss, Queen's University of Belfast, 1987), 137.

30. Boxer, "Jamaican Art, 1922–1982" (1998), 19.

31. Boxer, "Jamaican Art, 1922–1982" (1998), 24. Rodman was less charitable about Kapo's sculptural work, which he scathingly described as "grotesque and inelegant, influenced perhaps by what passes for 'African' in the tourist shops." See Selden Rodman, *The Caribbean* (Hawthorn, 1968), 13.

32. Boxer, "Jamaican Art, 1922–1982" (1998), 25.

33. Boxer, "Jamaican Art, 1922–1982" (1998), 26.

34. As reported in Rosalie Smith-McCrea, *Jamaican Art, 1922–1982 Returns* (National Gallery of Jamaica, 1986), 2. See Benjamin Forgery, "Jamaican Artistry," *Washington Post*, July 14, 1983; and Vivien Raynor, "Works from Jamaica Show an Island Evolution," *New York Times*, August 12, 1984.

35. John Bentley Mays, quoted in Smith-McCrea, *Jamaican Art, 1922–1982 Returns*, 11.

36. Smith-McCrea, *Jamaican Art, 1922–1982 Returns*, 2.

37. Andrew Hope, "Gallery Guide," *Daily Gleaner* (Kingston), March 31, 1986. The NGJ responded to this impasse with symposium "The Crisis in Criticism" on February 2, 1988, which I coordinated, having been recently appointed to head the NGJ Education Department as assistant curator. Hope, who had been a primary target in the symposium papers and discussions, in turn responded with a two-part column under the title "The Crisis in Leadership" (see note 7). The back and forth ended after Hope left the *Daily Gleaner* a year or so later. He briefly wrote for *The Observer*, a new Jamaican newspaper, until ill health and death intervened.

38. Smith-McCrae, *Jamaican Art, 1922–1982 Returns*, 2.

39. See, for instance, Tony Bennett, *The Birth of the Museum* (Routledge, 1995); and Carol Duncan, *Civilizing Rituals: Inside Public Art Museums* (Routledge, 1995).

40. For a discussion of these issues, see Poupeye, "Intuitive Art as a Canon."

41. This contribution was singled out in Petrine Archer-Straw, "Intuitive Lessons: On Naming the Intuitive," in *In Tribute to David Boxer: Twenty Years at the National Gallery of Jamaica 1975–1995*, ed. Leeta Hearne and Veerle Poupeye (National Gallery of Jamaica, 1995), 10–17.

42. While none have received the level of national recognition granted to Edna Manley in Jamaica, women have also played pioneering roles in the modern national movements elsewhere in the Caribbean. See, for instance, Amy Leong Pang and Sybil Atteck in Trinidad, Golde White in Barbados and Guyana, Luce Turnier in Haiti, or Amelia Peláez in Cuba. There is no doubt that these women artists were pioneers who challenged gender stereotypes in their lives and work, but it is also noteworthy that all enjoyed social privilege, while the social backgrounds of their male counterparts was far more diverse. There are many reasons for this, including the fact that art was seen as a socially acceptable pastime, albeit not as a profession, for women of privilege; gendered blind spots also exist in what sort of popular art has been validated in prevailing art historical narratives. It is instructive, for instance, that very few women artists have made it into the Intuitives canon. See Poupeye, "Women Artists in the Matalon Collection," 38–39; and Poupeye, "Intuitive Art as a Canon."

43. See, for instance, Petrine Archer-Straw, ed., *New World Imagery: Contemporary Jamaican Art* (South Bank Centre, 1995), the catalogue of a traveling exhibition Archer-Straw curated, organized by the Hayward Gallery, London, and which subsequently toured the United Kingdom and was also shown in Jamaica.

44. See, for instance, Edouard Lucie-Smith and David Boxer, *Jamaica in Black and White: Photography in Jamaica, c. 1845–c. 1920: The David Boxer Collection* (Macmillan Caribbean, 2013).

45. David Boxer, *Isaac Mendes Belisario: Art and Emancipation in Jamaica* (National Gallery of Jamaica, 2008). The exhibition was the local counterpoint to a 2007 exhibition at the Yale Center for British Art in New Haven, Connecticut, titled *Art and Emancipation in Jamaica: Isaac Mendes Belisario and His Worlds*, which deliberately avoided ascribing "old master" status to Belisario and instead explored the rich contexts of his work. See Tim Barringer, Gillian Forrester, and Barbaro Martinez-Ruiz, eds., *Art and Emancipation in Jamaica: Isaac Mendes Belisario and His Worlds* (Yale Center for British Art / Yale University Press, 2007). The reversal of the title by the NGJ was equally deliberate and refocused the attention on Belisario.

46. The poem is also known as "So Who Was the Mother of Jamaican Art?," which amplifies its critical challenge.

47. As quoted, in English translation, in Jocelyn Valton, "Cultural Extractions in the Caribbean—A Decolonial Counter-Narrative," Mediapart blog, November 25, 2023, https://blogs.mediapart.fr/jocelyn-valton/blog/251123/cultural-extractions-caribbean-decolonial-counter-narrative?fbclid=IwAR0wyJq05XH-j_MSLhL-iZ63y51Bro-cVoP2OBCfb_-Jo65nJD5uGdv3Dm0.

CHAPTER 9
"WHAT LOVELINESS ESCAPES THE SCHOOLS"
CARIFESTA'S EPISTEMOLOGICAL CRITIQUE

Adrienne Rooney

When the influential Barbadian public intellectual and writer George Lamming addressed the nearly ten thousand people gathered at the opening ceremony for the fourth edition of the Caribbean Festival of Arts (Carifesta), he spoke of an ongoing effort by artists to redefine "terms of . . . meaning" and "ways of seeing" within the Caribbean region.[1] The year was 1981, the place, Cave Hill, Barbados—a different Barbados than the one Lamming had grown up in. As a child and young adult in the 1930s and '40s, he learned the island as a place with local cultural practices but as a nonetheless colonial space, a space dictated by the economic, political, and cultural forces of England, where he moved in 1950, as many of his generation from British colonies in the Caribbean had or would.[2] It was also a different Barbados than the one Lamming honored on the occasion of its independence from over three hundred years of British rule in 1966, when he edited a volume of the sovereignty-seeking anglophone Caribbean journal *New World Quarterly* to earmark the juncture and potentialities that independence represented. The special issue opened with a poem by the local poet H. A. Vaughan that began: "Turn sideways now and let them see / What loveliness escapes the schools."[3] It was a poem, Lamming explained upon reading it in his Carifesta '81 address, rebuking educators on the island who recited—even believed—colonial teachings at the expense of Blackness, and in a nation in which roughly 90 percent of the population could claim African ancestry.[4]

By 1980, though, Barbadians were beginning "to accept their African heritage," as the scholar Trevor Marshall recounts—crediting writers such as Vaughn and Edward Kamau Brathwaite, local dramatists, and academics within the African diaspora for the change.[5] They had been methodically attacking "the image of Africa as a continent without history, art[,] culture or civilisation" so central to the colonial plantation imaginary that defined the island—including those once forcibly laboring within it—by its extractive profitability.[6] By 1980, Barbados had even decided to celebrate "the Day of Black Civilisation or Black People's Day"—a decision in part informed, Marshall expects, by then–Minister of Culture Louis Tull's "attendance at the Second Festival of Black Arts and Culture in Nigeria (Festac '77), by Carifesta No. 3 in Cuba," and by the work of Barbadian artists in the mid to late 1970s.[7] This message had not been received by everyone, however, as Barbados was (and is) still often regarded as "Little England" – that is, as the cultural historian Marcia Burrowes explains of the stereotype with colonial roots, the most English of the anglophone Caribbean territories, with its Black population the "'least' Africanised."[8]

As Marshall's 1980 statements affirm, artists and intellectuals had played a key role in reshaping local consciousness by reframing Africa and Blackness in the minds of many Barbadians. This process was still ongoing on the island and in the region more broadly as Lamming addressed the crowd in 1981, and it was central to his speech. His address set the tone for Carifesta that year, perhaps so much so that the journalist Rickey Singh incisively wrote that by its closing day two weeks later, the visitors – which, in addition to other attendees, were estimated to include around two thousand artists from thirty-two Caribbean and Latin American countries and beyond – should have better understood "why young Barbadians today regard as cultural slander the continuing caricature of their vibrant, Euro-creole society as 'Little England.'"[9] Indeed, Singh celebrated, "This 166 square miles sugar cane and tourist island has been transformed into a vast colourful stage for the diverse peoples of the four points of the Caribbean compass to parade their myriad art forms." He continued, "Their cultural expressions underscore a common heritage of slavery, imperial domination and struggle in a Caribbean archipelago perceived by Cuba's famous poet Nicolas Guillen as 'one communal yard.'"[10] Almost as if planned in tandem, a key Barbadian newspaper saluted the festival with a map featuring artists engaged in numerous local cultural traditions (fig. 9.1), jettisoning common representations of the island as engulfed by plantations (fig. 9.2) or sites and scenes for "Western" tourists (fig. 9.3).[11] With Carifesta '81, the map explained, Barbados brought the artists and the audiences (as did other participating locations in the region). It became a stage for cultural forms the colonial gaze denied.

The fourth Carifesta overturned – at least temporarily – the notion of Barbados as "Little England" and, like its three predecessors, presented a highly complex view of Caribbean culture. Both of these acts disavowed ways of knowing Barbados and the Caribbean writ large rooted in colonial epistemology – by which I mean ways of thinking and relating to the world that center "Western" views, deem them universal, and disavow a vast spectrum of ways of knowing and being in colonized societies.[12] In fact, Singh's quote heralds my argument that, as Carifesta evolved during its first decade or so – a revolutionary Caribbean moment (to which we will soon turn) – it enacted multiple epistemological critiques, two of which I discuss here. Most centrally, most simply, and most profoundly, counter to representations of the region as a space of extractive economic production or touristic

Fig. 9.1. Carifesta '81 advertisement in *The Nation* (Barbados) *Sunday Sun*'s Carifesta Supplement, July 19, 1981. The Nation Archive, Barbados

Fig. 9.2. Francis Louis Barrallier (French, 1773–1853), *Trigonometrical Survey of Barbados*, 1825, with markings by the Centre for the Study of the Legacies of British Slavery database, University College, London, denoting plantation estates

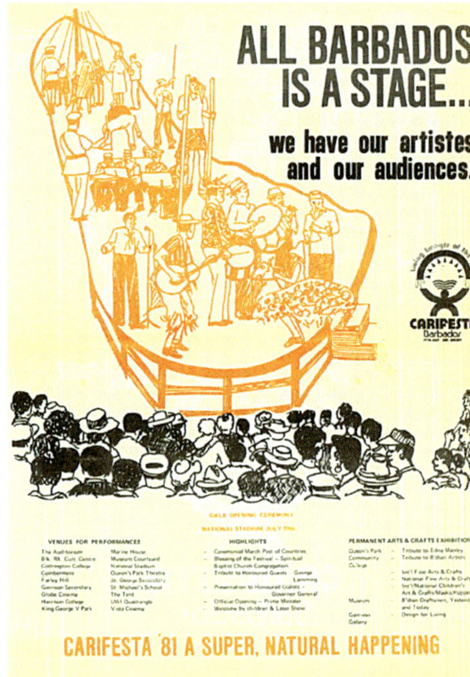

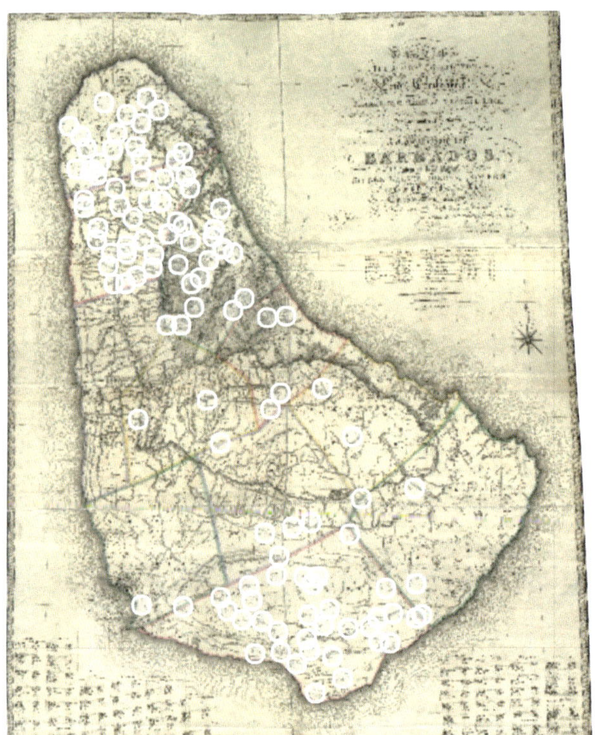

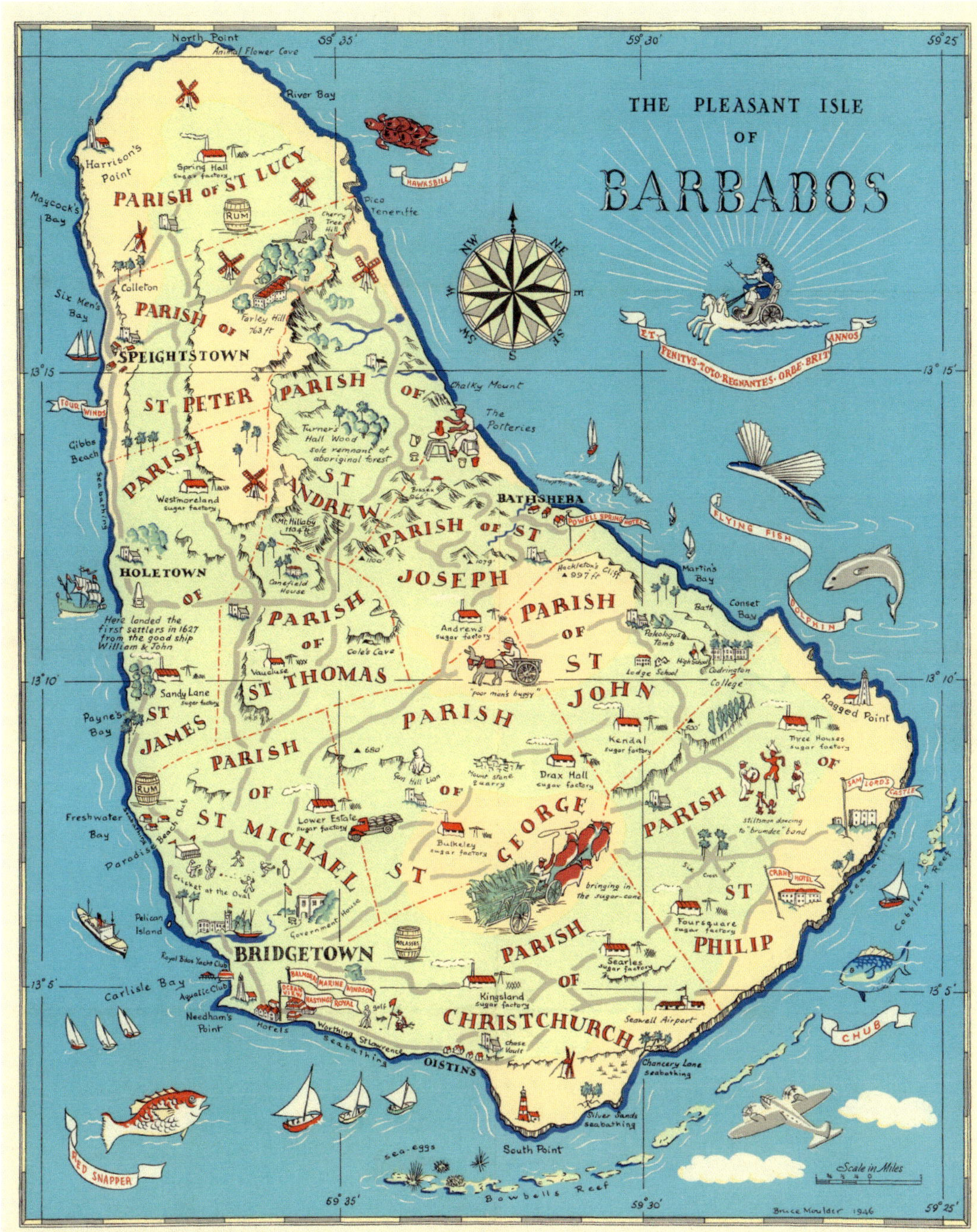

Fig. 9.3. Richard Bruce Moulder (British, 1907–1966), *The Pleasant Isle of Barbados*, 1946. Published by Robert MacLehose & Co. Ltd., Glasgow. David Rumsey Historical Map Collection

pleasure, the festival claimed the Caribbean as a space of vibrant and intertwined cultural production—cultural production rooted in traditions that evolved on, despite, and in relation to the plantation system that recanted their possibility. Moreover, it made palpable the region's cultural and linguistic plurality, which I foreground by turning to the early festivals' regional art exhibitions. These exhibitions started materializing what a regional story of art—here composed of an assembly of national shows, each put together by local cultural administrators, organizers, and/or artists—in all its complexity might look like.

Both critiques hold deep implications for art history, a field entwined with histories of colonialism and anti-Blackness. After all, as the literary and postcolonial scholar Simon Gikandi argues, "The modern idea of art and its judgment was theoretically connected to powerful racial economies."[13] For instance, as European powers grew their projects of colonization, the plantation economy, and chattel slavery, Blackness was used "as the counterpoint to beauty and enlightenment," while Enlightenment philosophers claimed "that the most obvious sign of savagery was the inability of the other to produce high art, or to make aesthetic judgments."[14] Such historically situated and circular logic fueled "the image of Africa as a continent without history, art[,] culture or civilisation" that, according to Marshall, continued to haunt Barbados, which the historian Hilary Beckles has described as the "birthplace of British slave society."[15] It too shaped an enduring Eurocentric art historical canon that posited its universality within colonized spaces.

If well after emancipation and even up to and after independence Barbadians were officially taught to turn their gaze to Europe for the arts, Carifesta called for the opposite as it gathered artists, intellectuals, and residents to help materialize and witness the development of locally rooted and defined criteria for art, aesthetics, music, dance, literature, and more. Homing in on Carifesta's regional visual arts programming, this paper posits that the festivals in fact amassed the (imperfect) makings of an anticolonial story of art, one (like Carifesta as a whole) interrogating the very boundaries of the region and, as I center here, necessarily grounded in plurality.[16] For what emerged was not a singular standard of art or beauty but a multitude of visions, forms, styles, influences, and commitments that, taken together, make plain the fallacy of "Western" aesthetic universality. Such a story of art required (and continues to require) new narratives and pedagogy, and it is no coincidence that a festival of regional culture envisioned for and organized by Caribbean people emerged at a time when dreams of "epistemic sovereignty"—that is, the Caribbean's conceptualization of its "own reality from within"—were top of mind for many.[17] Carifesta even became a site for learning some of what was not yet taught within the hallowed halls of schools—and, as I will elaborate on toward the end of this essay, perhaps even impacted the curriculum in the Anglophone Caribbean.

CARIFESTA'S REVOLUTIONARY ERA

Carifesta is a still semi-recurrent state-sponsored festival, widely known in the Caribbean and its diaspora but largely unrepresented in the field of art history and academic discourse more generally.[18] It emerged during a moment shaped by the Bandung Conference, the Cuban Revolution, attempts to formalize West Indian political unity amid the decline of the British Empire, Pan-Africanism, and Black Power, and it played a multifaceted role in postcolonial worldbuilding. From its start, Carifesta formed a space where artists, intellectuals, and audiences reveled, imagined, and debated among cultural production from the multilingual Caribbean islands, mainland countries touched by the Caribbean Sea, and beyond. After its inauguration in Guyana in 1972, the roving festival migrated to Jamaica, where it was held in 1976, then Cuba, where it was held in 1979, and finally to Barbados, where it took place in 1981 before a decade-long hibernation. Lamming's address set the tone for this final iteration of what I call Carifesta's "revolutionary era," corresponding to a period for the region in which "revolutionary futures were not merely possible but *imminent*; not only imminent, but *possible*," as the theorist David Scott writes.[19] Carifesta is a space of artistic intervention and creative discovery, and at the time its veins pulsed not only with ambitions for sovereignty and decolonizing but also with ethnonationalist tensions, (Cold War) political diplomacy, and the spirit of development (whether inflected by socialism or the Bretton Woods system) and its effort to establish a monetary system for a new world of nation-states, an effort in which culture was a central tool.[20] During this heady, heated moment, artworks, artists, intellectuals, local residents, cultural organizers and administrators, politicians and their special invitees, and countless others (were) gathered together at Carifesta—large-scale, multilingual, multimedia events at once political, politicized, and potentially transformative creatively, culturally, and epistemologically.

"REDEFIN[ING] THE TERMS OF OUR MEANING"

Neither Lamming nor the Caribbean governments supporting the festival anticipated that Carifesta's fourth iteration would be the last until 1992. However, with historical distance, Lamming's speech encapsulates the festival's stakes—and potential—during its first decade. His address paid tribute to six Caribbean cultural figures Carifesta honored that year, many of whom were conceptually integral to the festival's shape or had participated in it: the writer Aimé Césaire of Martinique; the writer, editor, and artist Frank Collymore of Barbados; the poet Nicolás Guillén of Cuba; the visual artist Edna Manley of Jamaica; the dancer Beryl McBurnie of Trinidad and Tobago; and the calypsonian Mighty Sparrow of Grenada and Trinidad and Tobago. Each of them, Lamming stated, had been "an agent of creative upheaval for ruling groups at different times" in the region.[21] In exploring Caribbean realities,

Lamming explained, these groundbreaking, multidisciplinary figures had challenged "established and official ways of seeing." Moving beyond these honorees alone, he continued, "the creative, cultural worker forces us to question . . . to rethink, even to redefine the terms of our meaning."[22]

Centrally, the terms of meaning in the Caribbean imposed by the colonial plantation system, as Lamming states, "den[ied] the human worth of the enormous majority of men and women whose labour made that order possible."[23] Before the audience of thousands—from Barbados, from the region, from the diaspora, and from beyond—he invoked Frantz Fanon's now well-known description of *experiencing* his being through the eyes of a white child, of experiencing, internalizing, and profoundly struggling with being racialized and objectified by the colonial gaze.[24] Lamming invoked Fanon's experience to emphasize the deeply rooted visual, epistemic, psychological force of anti-Blackness that those honored were up against as they disrupted the ruling orders—ruling orders with strong, protracted legacies that continue today. He invoked Fanon to prepare his audience for what he was about to say—in a booming voice that ricocheted across the National Stadium as it rose to a potent crescendo:

> When I say black, it is the name of a profound and unique historical experience, borne by a particular group of men and women whose presence in the world was destined to transform the eyes and ears of the world, and whose ultimate liberation will be the decisive contribution to the liberation of mankind.
>
> It is, precisely, in this connection, that we must perceive the meaning of those we honour today. For each of them has waged a war on that amputation Fanon speaks of: each has battled consistently to heal and restore the rhythm and beauty of that battered black body, which Europe argued, and continues to argue, is ugly, graceless and without history.
>
> For Europe and their successors, the United States, have been trapped in the deceiving habit of seeing themselves, not as a portion of mankind, but as the custodians of all human destiny.[25]

Those receiving tribute that day had sculpted, painted, authored, composed, compiled, improvised, and choreographed interventions that materialized the arduous, ongoing process of redressing colonially derived structures—including art and aesthetic canons—that shaped self-perception, social hierarchies, and cultural standards in the region, and indeed much of the world. As it forged the honorees as founders of a multilingual Caribbean cultural canon with a specific criterion, Lamming's speech also expressed the promise of following their lead: transform the eyes and ears of the world, and in so doing liberate mankind from a self-anointed "Western" custodianship on ways of being in the world. The audience that opening night had now been informed: Over the decade, Carifesta might have gained a reputation for revelry, spectacle, and the political instrumentalization of art, but where Caribbean artists were, there was a potential for disruption, for mind bending, for learning to see and know otherwise.

"NOW WE KNOW DIFFERENTLY"

Like the (ongoing) process of decolonization itself, those who envisioned Carifesta's shape did so with a plurality of hopes for the festival and its possibilities—for the region, for the nation, or for themselves.[26] There is no way to tell a single story of the festival, which has, over its fifty-year lifespan, been experienced by an uncalculated number of people (surely hundreds of thousands, if not more), modulating in form and evolving in tenor with each iteration.[27] The plurality of hope aside, I feel no hesitation in arguing that at its birth, Carifesta fundamentally ruptured one of the most profound tenets of colonial logic, which claimed that the "wider Caribbean" where the plantation reigned was a site for economic extraction—or later tourism—not cultural production.[28] Of course, as Lamming's speech makes clear, artists across media had shattered this logic over the twentieth century; further, his contemporaries argued throughout the 1970s that enslaved individuals had been active cultural producers, devitalizing the idea that those forced to labor on plantations were without culture, a racialized notion further disproven at Carifesta. Carifesta's claim was thus not new, but the pan-Caribbean scale of the claim—facing off with the "world-constituting" colonial enterprise that carved the hemisphere along imperial lines and instilled language divides accordingly yet was ubiquitous—was.[29]

Carifesta assembled and magnified a sprawling, entwined ecosystem of cultural practices that grew out of and in spite of the multilingual colonial plantation system that remade the region. It celebrated them. It brought them together so that people could begin to see kinships with their own eyes, hear and feel them with their own bodies. Describing her time at the inaugural festival in Georgetown, Guyana, the African American, Haiti-based choreographer and dancer Lavinia Williams recalled recognizing shared "dance steps" and "creoles" she encountered and experiencing profound "joy in comparing" them with other participants.[30] Carl Blackman, reporting for Guyana's *Daily Chronicle*, articulated a related sentiment:

> We [in Guyana] have been prattling about the oneness of our history and experiences with those of the rest of the Caribbean, but suddenly we realise what we are talking about. We suddenly are aware that we have more in common with the Cubans, the Brazilians, the Jamaicans, the people from Antigua and Barbados and Surinam and Venezuela than just

pigmentation. Our rhythms are the same, our legends have the same origins and our culture has the same roots.[31]

Further, Blackman realized that people across the region not only shared cultural roots, legends, cosmologies, and rhythms but also the experience of cultural colonization and the devaluation of Afrodiasporic culture: "We were aware that deep in our recent past, we have been made to feel shantos and cumfa and queh queh did not represent culture, but coarseness; that learning African dances was atavistic nonsense and only by plaiting the maypole can we become really 'civilised.'" In gratitude, he wrote, "Now we know differently."[32]

"WHAT ALL GOOD ART SHOULD DO"

Carifesta was a space in which *Blackness* across colonial language boundaries was deeply experienced, delighted in, and seen. However, cultural dynamics in the Caribbean play out within a region shaped by societies living there prior to European colonization, European colonial powers, and those who arrived to the region by force or less-than-free means from West Africa, China, India, Indonesia, and elsewhere to work within systems of enslaved, contract, and indentured labor. At the inaugural Carifesta in Guyana, which like Barbados gained its independence from British rule in 1966, moments celebrating Afrodiasporic kinship took place within the context of a profoundly multiracial country plagued by racial conflict and ethnonationalist politics dividing Afro- and Indo-Guyanese people—a reality, the historian Ramaesh Bhagirat-Rivera makes clear, that Carifesta was entwined with and even fueled.[33] Just as Carifesta was not separate from on-the-ground racialized realities in Guyana, Carifesta was by no means apart from the epistemology I argue it intervened in.

The Guyanese historian and political activist Walter Rodney indirectly anticipated two of the inaugural Carifesta's grave missteps—an under-representation of both Indo-Guyanese *and* Indigenous artists and cultures—in a 1970 interview conducted by the journalist Andrew Salkey, who was at the time actively shaping the first iteration of Carifesta, though he would ultimately boycott it.[34] In their conversation, Rodney discussed racial divisions between Afro- and Indo-Guyanese people, as well as a serious neglect of "the original inhabitants of the country."[35] Ruminating on the enduring impact of colonialism, he noted, "The British or the Dutch or the Spanish or the French owned and, in one way or another, continue to own our minds and our wealth."[36] He argued that it was necessary to expose the Guyanese people to "the true source of the country's present state of exploitation and underdevelopment"—that is, global capitalism. For Rodney—one of the most powerful voices of the Caribbean during the 1970s—embracing socialism held the promise of helping the country eradicate "racism in its most violent forms, a racism which has arisen, historically, through the slave trade, slavery, indenture, class and colonial oppression."[37] He explained how racism had infected local dynamics: The "White World" not only oppressed the "non-White world" but also catalyzed the "forms of division within the non-White world." White, colonial culture became the vector through which people related. He explained, "When I, as an African, in Guyanese society, speak of an Indian, I really am speaking of the European's Indian. I see that Indian through the eyes of the European, and the other way round."[38] The parasitic white eye persisted in local ways of seeing, manifesting what the anthropologist Brackette Williams has called "the ghost of hegemonic dominance" left by the "Anglo-Europeans" who employed race and religion to determine British Guiana's social order.[39] Part of the process of redress was to unlock its grip. As Rodney said to Salkey, people needed to be "made conscious of their own potential, their own dignity, their own power, as people"; to assert their own identities; and, in turn, to "operate on a basis of mutual respect."[40]

Here we turn to Carifesta's second epistemological critique. Given its organizational structure, which calls on each invited nation, territory, overseas department, and so on, to select its contributions within a set of material parameters, the festival is collectively constituted. Thus, while the inaugural Carifesta exhibited ethnonationalist divisions in Guyana, and while each participating location brought its own tensions and biases, the festival also showcased cultural plurality on a regional level, as did the subsequent Carifestas of the long 1970s.[41] Taken as a whole, then, notwithstanding always-present and at times violent politics, the festivals presented the region as a cultural multitude, asserting—albeit neither fully nor perfectly—that those living within the Caribbean could visualize themselves and one another on self-determined terms *despite* that parasitic white world vector.

The festival's sizeable contemporary regional visual art shows, though difficult to learn about in full due to archival gaps, exemplify this well. Assuming the inaugural Carifesta's *International Art Exhibition* (fig. 9.4)—which included over five hundred works sent by over a dozen countries and territories across the region—set the tone for curatorial framing, the overarching themes of Carifesta's regional exhibitions were open-ended. Its organizing committee emphasized the varied languages spoken and "cultural backgrounds" of the exhibiting artists in its statement. With contributions arranged by geographic origin within a single building, the exhibition, they hoped, would "play an important part in the dialogue between cultures and nations that Carifesta embodies."[42] The varied visions, styles, referents, media, and concerns in the resulting exhibition, they wrote, presented "differing manifestations of the artistic imagination" from the region—a region with, the show made clear, inescapably and exquisitely plural forms of art.[43]

The regional art exhibition at the second Carifesta included artwork from thirteen countries. In reviewing the show, the Jamaica-based critic Andrew Hope

Fig. 9.4. Cover of the catalogue for *Carifesta '72 International Art Exhibition*. National Library and Information System Authority, Trinidad and Tobago

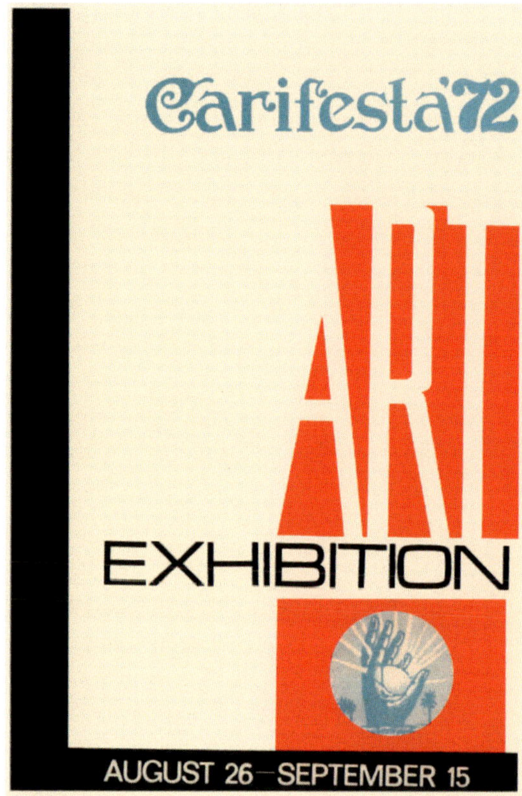

spotlighted a range of works alongside a single image: a reproduction of the Bahamian painter Homer Williams's *Black Madonna* from 1973, a painting that presents, as its present-day title reflects, a *Bahamian Conception of the Black Madonna and Child* (fig. 9.5). However, Hope did not linger on Williams's painting, quickly moving on to other artworks in the heterogenous exhibition. For him, Mexico stole the show with its "sheer daring and technical brilliance" and "up-to-the minute experiments" – seen across a display seeming to dismiss hierarchies of medium and showcasing tapestries, collage and glass work, acrylic sculpture, hard-edged abstraction, and prints.[44] Meanwhile, he declared that Venezuela "firmly holds the banner of Modern Art," with its primarily abstract works by, for instance, Luis Guevara Moreno. Trinidad and Tobago's contributions were, he went on, "surprisingly avant-garde, too," including "an interesting Pop Art work" by the Indo-Trinidadian artist M. P. Alladin "send[ing] up an unnamed African leader." Within Cuba's section, he favored Manuel Mendive, whom he described as "a primitive whose part paintings, part bas reliefs in vivid colours dwell on the subject of slavery." A video by the Jamaica-based Trinidadian filmmaker Franklyn St. Juste confirms that the exhibition included at

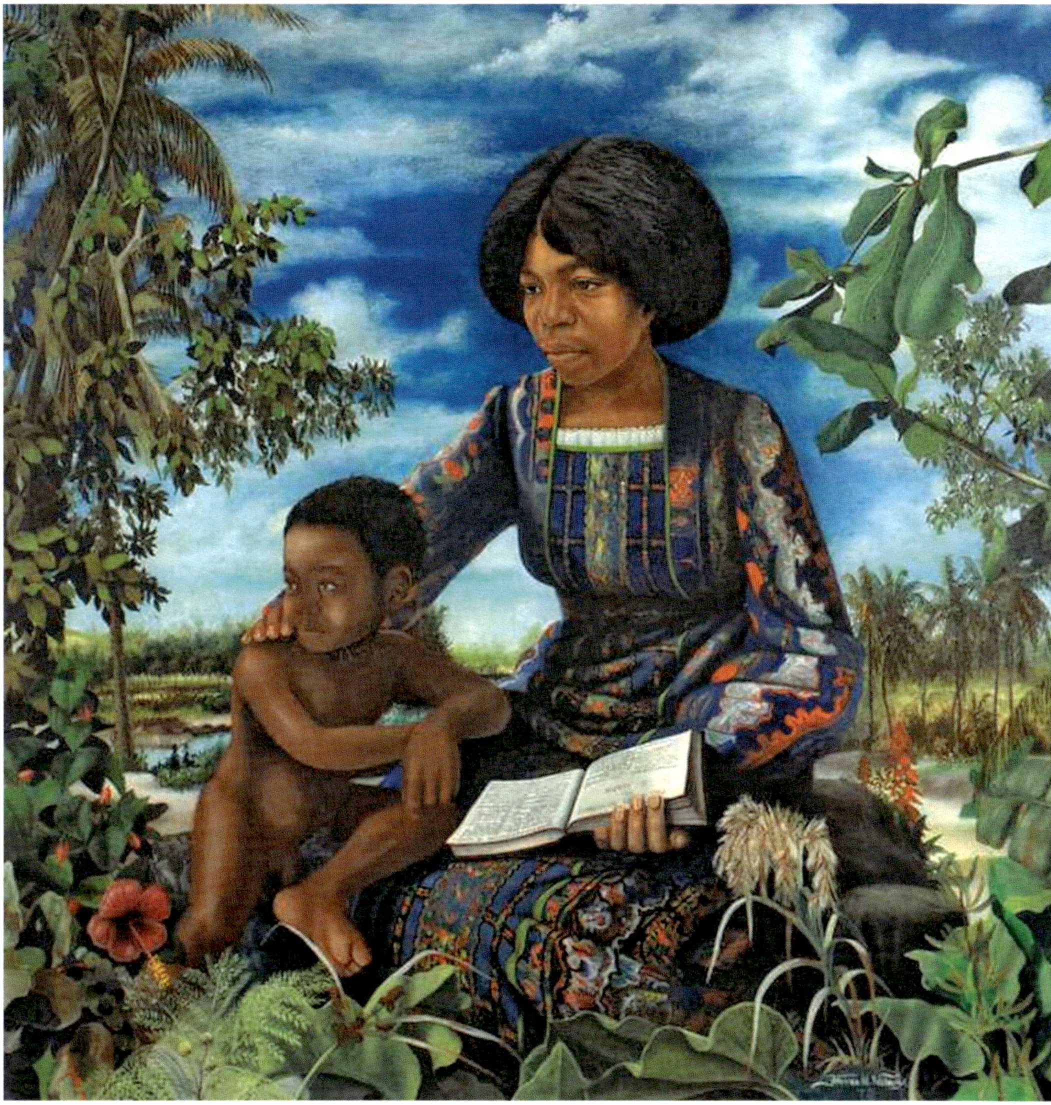

Fig. 9.5. Homer Williams (Bahamian), ***Bahamian Conception of the Black Madonna and Child***, 1973. Oil on canvas, 36 × 36 in. (91.4 × 91.4 cm). National Art Gallery of the Bahamas

Fig. 9.6. Manuel Mendive (Cuban, b. 1944), *El Palenque*, 1976, from the series *Los negros esclavos* (*The Black Slaves*), mid-1970s. Tempera on wood, 40 ½ × 49⅝ in. (103 × 126 cm). Museo Nacional de Bellas Artes de Cuba

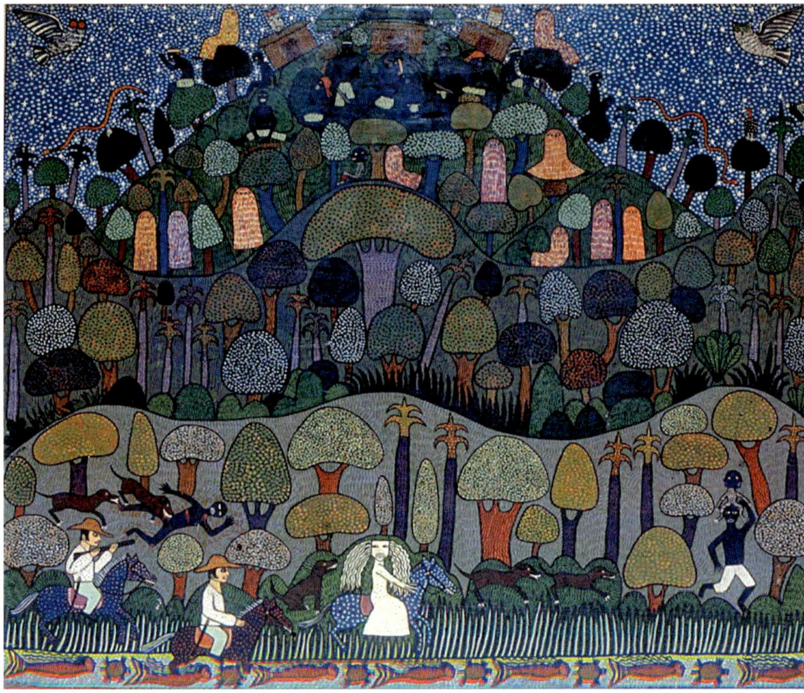

least two works from Mendive's twenty-five painting mid-1970s series *Los negros esclavos* (*The Black Slaves*), including *El Palenque* (fig. 9.6), a painting of a settlement established by Maroons, individuals who fled for freedom from plantation slavery and, like Indigenous individuals had, escaped to the hills.[45]

In his description of Mendive's work, Hope trafficked in a slippery, racialized binary central to "Western" art history produced by that white world eye: primitive versus modern.[46] He did so again and even more strongly in relation to Haiti, for which he had specific expectations: seeing works by so-called "primitive artists." The exhibition, however, forced him beyond his expectations, based in a long-standing, racialized, and paternalistic story of Haitian art.[47] Instead, Hope found himself impressed by Bernard Séjourné and Jacques Gabriel. Séjourné, who described his own work as containing "very strong classical tendencies," had studied at the Academy of Fine Arts in Haiti and at art schools in Jamaica and New York.[48] Gabriel, a figurative painter who studied in New York and exhibited in Paris, moved in circles with the likes of Hervé Télémaque and Édouard Glissant.[49] If "primitive" implied a lifestyle or lineage of teaching beyond "Western" academies, they did not fit the bill.[50] The destructive binary came up again, and again in relation to Haiti, in the Barbadian

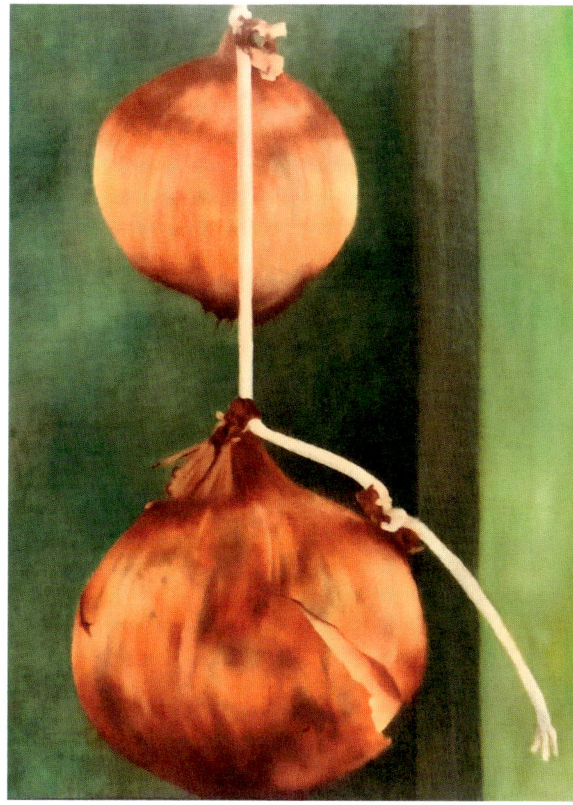

Fig. 9.7. Glenn Fung Loy (Surinamese, b. 1945), *Onion*, c. 1980. Oil on canvas. Location unknown

cultural critic John Wickham's review of the regional art exhibition in Carifesta '81, which he noted offered a fresh opportunity "to see and study Caribbean painting as a whole."[51] Perhaps had Wickham spent more time in the exhibition, say with the painting reproduced alongside his article with a caption reading "A HAITIAN primitive, by Duffaut," he might have moved beyond the wrought label and thought with the work, contemplating its imaginary, bustling seaside city between mountains, a theme that the Haitian painter Préfète Duffaut returned to over and over again.

For Wickham generally made clear that the exhibition was a space for thinking, learning, and being moved, noting that some works even promoted "view[ing] and review[ing]"—part of the process of training the eye to look again and see beyond what it routinely knows. He said as much when musing on the Surinamese artist Glenn Fung Loy's photorealist painting of onions (fig. 9.7). The "delicate oil on canvas treatment of two onions hanging from a ceiling," Wickham wrote, "was enough to persuade you that you have never really seen onions before which, of course, is what all good art should do."[52] Though he elected to remain with Fung Loy's painting, there were plenty of works in Suriname's contribution to think with, such as a batik work by Soeki Irodikromo. A Surinamese artist trained locally and in Rotterdam and, through his practice, engaging his ancestral Javanese mythology and pictorial language, Irodikromo had recently returned from studying the batik technique at the Akademi Seni Rupa Indonesia.[53] Within these wide-ranging exhibitions, works spanning a dynamic spectrum of artistic allegiances and identifications sat side by side—and even rattled expectations pivotal to "Western" epistemology about particular nations and peoples. For Wickham, it was possible to glean "a comprehensive view" and to "emerge with some kind of sense of the Caribbean vision of itself."[54] Several of the works even made epistemological critiques of their own.

GROUNDBREAKING KNOWLEDGE

Carifesta '81 had a panoply of visual arts and "craft" programming, including a two-day Symposium for Visual Artists—a first for Carifesta—proposed by the Barbadian artist Joyce Davis. The symposium reinforced the region's plurality of voices, aesthetics, and imagery, and I will quickly list what I know of the program to emphasize this. Edward Kamau Brathwaite delivered the opening remarks and served as chairperson for the event, at which artists presented "slides, film extracts, recordings and photographs to illustrate various influences which came to bear on regional artists."[55] The Guyanese artist Stephanie Correia presented on "The Art of Guyana's" first peoples; the Martinican artist René Louise presented on "The Plastic Arts in Martinique"; the Cuban art historian Adelaida de Juan presented on "The Cuban Arts of the Revolution"; the Jamaican artist and art historian David Boxer presented on "The Intuitive Painters of Jamaica"; the Surinamese artist Jules Chin A Feong presented on "The Photo-Realist Movement in Caribbean Painting"; the Guadeloupean architect Jack Berthelot presented on "Rural Habitations in the French Antilles"; Joyce Davis presented on "Folk Images in Caribbean Painting"; someone spoke on "The Art of Trinidad Carnival"; and the Surinamese ethnomusicologist Terry Agerkop presented on the "Art, Music, and Motion" of the Saramaka Maroon people in Suriname.[56] The Guyanese artists Philip Moore and Stanley Greaves also addressed the gathering, and the Cuban poet and historian Rafaela Chacón Nardi, the writer Victor Questel reported, "delivered a wide-ranging and very useful survey of the contemporary Arts of the Caribbean."[57]

The symposium loudly expressed regional academic interest in and interpretation of regional artistic forms, a fact surely magnified by Agerkop's address, which included criticism of the exoticizing anthropological gaze of white scholars from Europe and the United States.[58] Equally fundamental, the symposium was also an archival effort, documenting the work and stories of regional artists to share with other artists as well as schoolchildren.[59] Because, to be clear, this was groundbreaking knowledge. So much so that "Davis noted that the material put together for the symposium would serve the Caribbean Examination Council well in the development of its art and culture syllabus"—and it conceivably did.[60]

The Caribbean Examination Council (CXC) was created to fundamentally change the education system in the English-speaking Caribbean, which had, up until that point, been shaped by syllabi and exams designed and scored by British overseas boards.[61] The idea of developing a self-determined educational system had deeper roots in the anglophone Caribbean, but the establishment of the CXC in 1972 gave it an institutional form and thrust.[62] As Barbados's first prime minister, Errol Barrow, put it at the council's inaugural meeting, which took place in 1973 in Barbados (the location of the CXC headquarters): "The time is . . . ripe . . . to Caribbeanize our education."[63] At the same meeting, William Demas, secretary-general of the recently formed Caribbean Community and Common Market—known as CARICOM, one of several coevolving regional integration initiatives, alongside Carifesta and the CXC—expressed that the system on its way out had "glaringly obvious" "ill effects on West Indian education."[64]

In 1979, a frequent contributor to the CXC's magazine wrote, "For the first time Caribbean secondary school students" took exams "prepared by Caribbean people, for Caribbean people and marked and graded by Caribbean people."[65] Among them were new exams in Caribbean history—an exam subject that included (or would very soon include) a section on the arts.[66] The final volume in a textbook series made to prepare students for their new exam subject, titled *Development and Decolonisation* (1981), emphasizes the gravitas of the new pedagogy with particular strength. The book's cover features an acclaimed and symbolic sculpture, *Negro Aroused* (1935; see p. 154, fig. 8.5), by one of the very cultural figures Lamming honored as he opened Carifesta '81: Edna Manley. Officially embraced as a sculpture honoring Black struggle, resolve, and poise (epitomized by its reproduction on Jamaica's stamp for Anti-Apartheid Year in 1978), this choice makes clear that the book was an update for the era: It did things differently than British colonial syllabi. It included theretofore unprecedented material, such as "Social Conditions in the Twentieth Century; Art Forms in the Caribbean; and Religion as a Social Force" (the authors noted that each of these themes "could constitute separate subjects in a discipline other than history").[67] It also expanded coverage of "Regional Co-operation" and covered the non-anglophone Caribbean, "which the British colonial syllabi neglected." Stating a profound, albeit not surprising, truth, the authors wrote in a list of newly added, formerly excluded topics that "Independence Movements and Social Life and Conditions were not parts of the colonial syllabi."[68] *Social life and conditions were not parts of the colonial syllabi.* Schoolchildren would simply not have learned about local art forms from a teacher using the prior exam books without interventions. They were part of the immense loveliness that escaped the schools, to paraphrase Vaughan.

At its start, then, Carifesta not only critiqued the epistemology that disavowed Caribbean art but also became a pedagogical site for seeing and learning about the art of the region. For many, from children to practicing artists, Carifesta was their first (sizable) exposure to Caribbean art, and on a multilingual regional scale—a possibility completely foreclosed by the British colonial syllabi, which neglected not only the arts but also the non-English-speaking Caribbean. And the anglophone Caribbean was not alone in this gaping blind spot. In his symposium address, Agerkop argued for regional academic and artistic exchanges that embraced Suriname—a former Dutch colony that had gained independence less than a decade prior—both generally and, more pointedly, within arts education, underscoring an ache for connection and regional learning beyond the bounds of former British colonies.[69] Sticking to the latter, however, we can turn to an early 1979 interview in which Brathwaite noted that there had been "a movement" since the late 1960s and early 1970s in which "people are themselves discovering their own culture quite naturally," despite its absence from formal education.[70] He cited the inaugural Carifesta as one critical point in manifesting such informal education.[71]

Yet, as noted, formal education was in the process of transforming. The 1979 exams that included Caribbean history also unveiled new tests in other subjects, and more were approved for syllabus and examination development.[72] Among them was arts and craft, and it is highly plausible that Davis or one of her colleagues provided materials from the Symposium for Visual Artists to those fashioning this new program of study—indeed, a symposium participant was among those who ultimately worked to prepare its first syllabus.[73] If Carifesta effected a shift in learning in the informal public realm, it may very well have directly influenced the formal curricula too, though the work to prepare an accessible sourcebook continued.[74]

To be sure, I do not mean to claim that Carifesta *caused* the change to the history syllabus or catalyzed the approval to develop an arts and craft syllabus, even if it coevolved in lockstep with the CXC. But I want to recognize the fact that the festivals assembled unprecedented exhibitions and vast performance programs that, on scales small and large, challenged terms of meaning and "ways of seeing" (within) the Caribbean region, to return to Lamming.[75] Of course the festivals made mistakes to learn from, and certainly not all works challenged the colonial gaze. Yet, I want to sit with the fact that they compiled and amplified thought and creative actions that not only put the region's art on the map for many in the Caribbean but also made *a change to the story of history possible*. An astounding change galvanized by individuals who recognized the "deceiving habit" of "Europe, and their successors the United States . . . of seeing themselves . . . as the custodians of all human destiny"—and *refused*.

Widening our gaze beyond the Caribbean, it is clear through ongoing calls to decolonize curricula and the backlash those calls create that this refusal is as pertinent now as in the era of constitutional decolonization. Carifesta's revolutionary moment resonates today as scholars of all sorts, art historians among them, continue the long-standing project of refusing that "deceiving habit" of Europe and the United States — and often do so by engaging writings by Caribbean theorists who were active in the period discussed in this paper and even participated in these very Carifestas. Yet, today, Carifesta *itself* is largely part of the loveliness that escapes the schools, and with it a capacious story of art in which relations across wide regional kinships and cartographies surfaced, crisscrossing language divides and including forms that both fit within "Western" art history's formal parameters and cause its contested boundaries to buckle and break down.

NOTES

I give profound thanks to Anna Arabindan-Kesson and Wayne Modest for including me in the remarkable gathering at the Clark Art Institute in 2022 that was Beyond Boundaries, as well as for their sage, bighearted feedback on this text. My thanks also go to my generous co-panelist, Veerle Poupeye, to Faith Smith for her energizing response to the work as moderator of the resulting discussion, to fellow participants for insightful conversations at and since the gathering, and to the Clark team for their warmth. For their support for my dissertation, from which this essay emerged, I thank Fabiola López-Durán, Alexander X. Byrd, Nicole Waligora-Davis, and Graham Bader at Rice University, as well as the Wagoner Foreign Study Scholarship and the Brown Foundation. For feedback on an earlier version of the essay, I thank Justine M. Bakker and members of Rice's department of art history. Last but far from least, my enduring gratitude goes to the archivists, librarians, museum workers, and other stewards of cultural memory who made and make this work possible.

1. George Lamming, "Builders of Our Caribbean House" (Carifesta Opening Address, 1981), in *The George Lamming Reader: The Aesthetics of Decolonisation*, ed. Anthony Bogues, Caribbean Reasonings (Ian Randle, 2011), 65. His speech was also printed in the newspaper as "Lamming's Protest Against the Imperialists," *The Nation* (Barbados), July 23, 1981. For the attendance estimates, see newspaper coverage such as Eric Smith, "Burst of Culture," *The Nation*, July 20, 1981.

2. George Lamming and David Scott, "The Sovereignty of the Imagination: An Interview with George Lamming," *Small Axe* 12 (September 2002): 102. For more on this generation of émigrés, see, among others, Anne Walmsley, *The Caribbean Artists Movement, 1966–1972: A Literary and Cultural History* (New Beacon Books, 1992); and Lloyd Braithwaite, *Colonial West Indian Students in Britain* (University of the West Indies Press, 2001).

3. H. A. Vaughan, "Revelation," *New World Quarterly* 3, nos. 1 and 2, Barbados Independence Issue (Dead Season, 1966; Croptime, 1967): 1.

4. Lamming, "Builders of Our Caribbean House," 67. For the demographic estimate, see Trevor G. Marshall, "A Day for Black Civilization," *The Bajan* (Barbados), February 1980; and Marcia P. A. Burrowes, "History and Cultural Identity: Barbadian Space and the Legacy of Empire" (PhD diss., University of Warwick, 2000), 108.

5. Marshall, "Day for Black Civilization."

6. Marshall, "Day for Black Civilization."

7. Marshall, "Day for Black Civilization."

8. Burrowes, "History and Cultural Identity," 91–100.

9. Rickey Singh, "Carifesta: An Explosion in 'One Yard,'" *Caribbean Contact* 9, no. 4 (August 1981): 1.

10. Singh, "Carifesta," 1.

11. I place "Western" in quotation marks to identify the term as a deceptively straightforward historical construct that helps classify and compare societies in an ideological, often highly destructive way. See Stuart Hall, "The West and the Rest: Discourse and Power," in *Formations of Modernity*, ed. Stuart Hall and Bram Gieben, 4th ed., Understanding Modern Societies: An Introduction (Open University Press, 1995), 275–331.

12. Boaventura de Sousa Santos, *The End of the Cognitive Empire: The Coming of Age of Epistemologies of the South* (Duke University Press, 2018). See also Anthony Bogues, "Lloyd Best and the Politics of Epistemic Decolonization," in *Independent Thought and Caribbean Freedom: Essays in Honour of Lloyd Best*, ed. Selwyn D. Ryan (Sir Arthur Lewis Institute of Social and Economic Studies, University of the West Indies, 2003), 145–61.

13. Simon Gikandi, "Race and the Idea of the Aesthetic," *Michigan Quarterly Review* 40, no. 2 (Spring 2001): 325.

14. Gikandi, "Race and the Idea of the Aesthetic," 329, 331.

15. Hilary McDonald Beckles, *The First Black Slave Society: Britain's "Barbarity Time" in Barbados, 1636–1876* (University of the West Indies Press, 2016).

16. The multiplicity of art from the region has been well-acknowledged in subsequent exhibitions of Caribbean art with accompanying catalogues—shows for which Carifesta's regional exhibitions are important precursors, if differently constituted and underacknowledged. As Tatiana Flores and Michelle Stephens write, "Recent exhibitions of Caribbean art have largely embraced the narrative of heterogeneity itself as an organizing principle," citing shows such as *Caribe insular: Exclusión, fragmentación y paraíso* (1998), *Kréyol Factory* (2009), *Who More Sci-Fi Than Us: Contemporary Art from the Caribbean* (2012), and *Caribbean: Crossroads of the World* (2012). Tatiana Flores and Michelle Ann Stephens, "Relational Undercurrents: Toward an Archipelagic Model of Insular Caribbean Art," in *Relational Undercurrents: Contemporary Art of the Caribbean Archipelago*, ed. Tatiana Flores and Michelle Stephens (Museum of Latin American Art / Fresco Books / Duke University Press, 2017), 15, 27n5.

17. Norman Girvan, "New World and Its Critics," in *The Thought of New World: The Quest for Decolonisation*, ed. Brian Meeks and Norman Girvan, Caribbean Reasonings (Ian Randle, 2010), 6, 8.

18. Aaron Kamugisha, "The Promise of Caribbean Intellectual History," *Small Axe* 25, no. 1 (64) (March 2021): 49. In addition to sources cited here, exceptions include Erica Moiah James, "Dreams of

Utopia: Sustaining Art Institutions in the Transnational Caribbean," *Open Arts Journal* 5 (Summer 2016): 9–21; and Jo-Anne Tull "Caribbean Festival Arts: Exploring Praxis for the Future," *Caribbean Quarterly* 63, nos. 2–3 (2017): 291–303.

19. David Scott, *Omens of Adversity: Tragedy, Time, Memory, Justice* (Duke University Press, 2014), 4; and Adrienne A. Rooney, "A Worldbuilding Moment: Aesthetics and Economics in the Caribbean Festival of Arts' (Carifesta) Revolutionary Era, 1966–1981" (PhD diss., Rice University, 2023), https://hdl.handle.net/1911/115260.

20. For this framing of development, see, for instance, Arindam Dutta et al., "Introduction," in *Architecture in Development: Systems and the Emergence of the Global South*, ed. Aggregate (Routledge, 2022).

21. Lamming, "Builders of Our Caribbean House," 64.

22. Lamming, "Builders of Our Caribbean House," 65.

23. Lamming, "Builders of Our Caribbean House," 66.

24. Frantz Fanon, *Black Skin, White Masks*, tr. Charles Lam Markmann (1952, French; 1967, English; Pluto, 1986), 111–12.

25. Lamming, "Builders of Our Caribbean House," 66. For a video recording of Lamming giving his address, see *Carifesta, Barbados Opening 1981: Address by George Lamming* (Banyan Archive, 1981), https://search.alexanderstreet.com/view/work/bibliographic_entity%7Cvideo_work%7C327758.

26. For a primary source concerning the complex dynamics in the formation of Carifesta, see Andrew Salkey, *Georgetown Journal: A Caribbean Writer's Journey from London Via Port of Spain to Georgetown, Guyana 1970* (New Beacon Books, 1972).

27. For a sense of estimated attendances, when available and located, see Keith Nurse, *Reinventing Carifesta: A Strategic Plan*, prepared for CARICOM Taskforce on Carifesta, CARICOM Secretariat, Georgetown, Guyana, 2004 (Caribbean Documentation Unit of the CARICOM Community Secretariat, Georgetown, Guyana), 16.

28. See also Adrienne Rooney, "Carifesta Geographies: Mapping Colonial Afterlives and the Caribbean Festival of Arts' 'Phenomenal Dreaming,' 1966–1976," *British Art Studies* 28 (November 2025): https://doi.org/10.17658/issn.2058-5462/issue-28/arooney; and Adrienne Rooney, "Cartographies of Kinship in the Caribbean Festival of Arts," *The Routledge Companion to African Diaspora Art History*, ed. Eddie Chambers (Routledge, 2025), 307–21. A. J. Seymour, one of Carifesta's originators and organizers, explained that the geography of Carifesta was representative of the "wider Caribbean," a term he learned from George Beckford's then brand-new book *Persistent Poverty: Underdevelopment in Planation Economies of the Third World* (Oxford University Press, 1972). A. J. Seymour, "Mr. Arthur Seymour Addressing the Carifesta Secretariat Seminar," c. 1972, 1, Julian Mayfield Papers, Schomburg Center for Research in Black Culture, Manuscripts, Archives and Rare Books Division, New York Public Library.

29. I borrow the term "world-constituting" from Adom Getachew, *Worldmaking After Empire: The Rise and Fall of Self-Determination* (Princeton University Press, 2019).

30. Lavinia Williams, interview by James Briggs Murray, part 3, November 9, 1983, Lavinia Williams Oral History Collection, Schomburg Center for Research in Black Culture, Moving Image and Recorded Sound Division, New York Public Library.

31. Carl Blackman, "Art for All," *Daily Chronicle* (Guyana), September 3, 1972, in Carifesta '72 newspaper scrapbook, National Archives of Guyana.

32. Blackman, "Art for All."

33. Ramaesh J. Bhagirat-Rivera, "Between Pan-Africanism and a Multiracial Nation: Race, Regionalism, and Guyanese Nation-Building Through the Caribbean Festival of Creative Arts (CARIFESTA), 1972," *Interventions* 20, no. 7 (2018): 1022–36.

34. Frank Pilgrim, "The Five 'Faults' of Carifesta," *Sunday Chronicle*, September 24, 1972, in Carifesta Collection, Digital Library of the Caribbean, http://ufdc.ufl.edu/CA00199628/00001; and letters: Kamau Brathwaite to Andrew Salkey, September 29, 1972; Ismith Khan and Vera Reichler to Andrew Salkey, February 10, 1972; Lynette Dolphin to Patricia Salkey, March 23, 1972, all in the Andrew Salkey Papers, Add MS 89377/10/16 and Add MS 89377/7/7, British Library Archives and Manuscripts, London.

35. Walter Rodney and Andrew Salkey, "Appendix B: Interview with Dr. Walter Rodney," June 4, 1970, in Andrew Salkey, *Georgetown Journal: A Caribbean Writer's Journey from London Via Port of Spain to Georgetown, Guyana, 1970* (New Beacon Books, 1972), 386.

36. Rodney and Salkey, "Appendix B," 383.

37. Rodney and Salkey, "Appendix B," 387.

38. Rodney and Salkey, "Appendix B," 385.

39. Brackette F. Williams, *Stains on My Name, War in My Veins: Guyana and the Politics of Cultural Struggle* (Duke University Press, 1991), 201, 219, 225.

40. Rodney and Salkey, "Appendix B," 387.

41. Bhagirat-Rivera, "Between Pan-Africanism and a Multiracial Nation," 1034; and Rooney, "Worldbuilding Moment."

42. Ron Savory et al., *Carifesta '72 International Art Exhibition* (Carifesta, 1972), 2.

43. Savory et al., *Carifesta '72*, 2.

44. Andrew Hope, "Carifesta '76 Exhibition of Paintings and Sculpture," *Sunday Gleaner* (Kingston), August 1, 1976.

45. Alejandro de la Fuente, *Grupo Antillano: The Art of*

Afro-Cuba / El Arte de Afro-Cuba (University of Pittsburgh Press, 2013), 266. Guadalupe García, *Beyond the Walled City: Colonial Exclusion in Havana* (University of California Press, 2016), 21.

46. For entry points into the term "primitive" within the context of art discourse in Jamaica, see Petrine Archer-Straw, "Intuitive Lessons: On Naming the Primitive," in *In Tribute to David Boxer: Twenty Years at the National Gallery of Jamaica, 1975–1995* (Institute of Jamaica Publication Limited / National Gallery of Jamaica, 1995), 10–17; and Veerle Poupeye, "Intuitive Art as a Canon," *Small Axe* 24 (October 2007): 73–82.

47. Jerry Philogene, "Actes de Transformation: Mixing and Mapping of Haitian Aesthetics," in Flores and Stephens, *Relational Undercurrents*, 191–202.

48. "Haitian Painter at OAS," *Américas* 30, no. 9 (September 1978): 55.

49. "Moi-même," and Silvano Lora, "Jacques: Un celaje fosforecente en la marisma," in *Jacques Gabriel: Une Rétrospective*, Michel Philippe Lerebours and Gesner Armand (Musée d'art Haïtien du Collège Saint-Pierre, 2002), 17–18 and 69–71.

50. Séjourné was in fact associated with the "School of Beauty," the "first mainstream Haitian school to challenge the commercial supremacy of the 'primitives' with some success." Veerle Poupeye, *Caribbean Art*, 2nd ed., World of Art (Thames & Hudson, 2022), 214.

51. John Wickham, "CARIFESTA Visual Arts: Much to See and Think Of," *The Nation: Colour Me Carifesta!*, August 1981, Carifesta folder, Department of Archives, Barbados.

52. Wickham, "CARIFESTA Visual Arts."

53. Gloria Leurs, "Suriname's Beeldende Kunsten," in *De Grote Caraibische Familie: Een Ooggetuigeverslag van het Caraibische Kunstfestival Carifesta IV, Barbados, 19 Juli–3 Augustus 1981*, ed. Thea Doelwijt (Ministerie van Cultuur, Jeugd en Sport in Suriname, 1981), 34–43; and Chandra van Binnendijk, ed., *Soeki Irodikromo: Beeldend Kunstenaar / Visual Artist: Schilderijen Keramiek Batik / Paintings Ceramics Batik, 1965–2005* (Vereniging Herdenking Javaanse Immigratie in Suriname / Association for the Commemoration of Javanese Immigration in Suriname, 2005), 22, 95–99.

54. Wickham, "CARIFESTA Visual Arts." This view emerged despite the "spatial separation" resulting from each country "being allocated its own particular room or space," he explains—though in an unattributed version of this article, Wickham noted that the countries shared exhibition spaces, "with the exception of Barbados which has its own national show going." [John Wickham], "Exhibition of Class," *The Nation: Carifesta Bulletin*, July 31, 1981, 2–3, The Nation Archive, Barbados.

55. "A Symposium for Artists," *The Nation: Carifesta Bulletin*, July 30, 1981, 1, The Nation Archive, Barbados.

56. Alissandra Cummins, Allison Thompson, and Nick Whittle, *Art in Barbados: What Kind of Mirror Image?* (Ian Randle / Barbados Museum & Historical Society, 1999), 174.

57. Questel spells her name Raphaela Chacon, specifying that she is the "wife of Cuban poet, [Roberto] Retamar." Victor Questel, "Two Weeks on 'Mourning Ground': Personal Testimony of a Trinidadian Writer," *Caribbean Contact*, September 1981, 10–11.

58. Terry Agerkop, "Het Carifesta van de Symposia: Caraibische Uitwisseling van Materiaal, Studenten en Wetenschapsmensen," in *De Grote Caraibische Familie*, 58–61.

59. "Symposium for Artists."

60. "Symposium for Artists."

61. Stafford A. Griffith, "The Impact and Influence of CXC on the Regional Education Landscape," *Caribbean Examiner* 11, no. 1 (May 2013): 16–19.

62. Barbara Bailey, "Innovation and Change Strategies: The Case of CXC," *Education in the West Indies: Developments and Perspectives, 1948–1988* (Institute of Social and Economic Research, University of the West Indies, Mona Campus, 1996), 88–99.

63. Errol Barrow, in "Quotes from the Inaugural Meeting of Council: The Right Excellent Errol Barrow, Prime Minister of Barbados," *Caribbean Examiner* 11, no. 1 (May 2013): 12; and Archibald A. Moore, "How It All Began: The Establishment of the Caribbean Examinations Council," *The Integrationist* 1, no. 4 (2003).

64. "Address by Mr. William Demas, Secretary-General of the Commonwealth Caribbean Regional Secretariat at Inaugural Meeting of Caribbean Examinations Council (11th January, 1973, Barbados)" as reproduced in *Caribbean Examiner* 11, no. 1 (May 2013): 10–11.

65. Cleveland Sam, "Celebrating 30 Years of CSEC Examinations: 1979–2009," *Caribbean Examiner* 7, no. 1 (May 2009): 5.

66. Sam, "Celebrating 30 Years." A debate about whether "steel band, calypso, the development of literary works and other indigenous art forms" ("cultural history") could be "legitimately termed history" may have accompanied this change. H. A. Fergus, "Towards the Formulation of an O-Level Syllabus in Caribbean History," *Journal of Curriculum Studies* 9, no. 1 (1977): 64.

67. Robert Greenwood and Shirley Hamber, *Development and Decolonisation*, Caribbean Certificate History 3, 1st ed. (Macmillan Caribbean, 1981), vii.

68. Greenwood and Hamber, *Development and Decolonisation*, vii.

69. Agerkop, "Het Carifesta van de Symposia," 60.
70. Edward Brathwaite and Michael Gilkes, "Barbados Heading for Revival of African Cultural Traditions," *Caribbean Contact*, February 1979, 11.
71. As of 2010, Carifesta remained a rare space for wide publics to view contemporary art from across the region within the region. Anne Walmsley and Stanley Greaves, *Art in the Caribbean: An Introduction* (New Beacon Books, 2010), vii.
72. Sam, "Celebrating 30 Years," 5; and "Four New Subject Panels Approved," *Sunday Gleaner*, October 1, 1978, 4.
73. "Four New Subject Panels Approved." Symposium participant Stanley Greaves, alongside Isaiah Boodhoo and Karl 'Jerry' Craig—all of whom participated in Carifesta in the long 1970s—prepared the first CXC Art and Craft syllabus. Walmsley and Greaves, *Art in the Caribbean*, viii.
74. Walmsley and Greaves, *Art in the Caribbean*, viii. As Petrine Archer wrote, Walmsley and Greaves's *Art in the Caribbean* was "essentially an art history textbook conceived primarily to meet the needs of students sitting Caribbean examinations such as CXC . . . and who were desperate for printed material that could support their studies." "At last," she wrote, they had "a history of art and a visual record at their fingertips." Petrine Archer, "Review: Art in the Caribbean: An Introduction by Anne Walmsley and Stanley Greaves," *Caribbean Quarterly* 57, no. 2 (June 2011), 143.
75. Lamming, "Builders of Our Caribbean House," 65.

PART IV
RETHINKING INSTITUTIONS

CHAPTER 10

THE CARIBBEAN AND US

María Elena Ortiz

What is the role of the diaspora when presenting Caribbean art, especially now that there is significant momentum for contemporary Caribbean art in the United States and Europe? This shift in attention from outside the region has developed in concert with a proliferation of active art organizations and art festivals within the Caribbean. Artist-led spaces, like Fresh Milk (Barbados), Atelier '89 (Aruba), and Beta—Local (Puerto Rico), among others, have generated vehicles for cultural exchange among the islands and throughout the Caribbean diaspora.[1] Iconic, large-scale regional exhibitions, like the Havana Biennial and the Caribbean Festival of Arts (Carifesta), are critical for Caribbean art production. In the diaspora, exhibitions such as the Brooklyn Museum's *Infinite Island: Contemporary Art from the Caribbean* (2007–8); *Who Is More Sci-Fi Than Us? Contemporary Art from the Caribbean* (2012), at the Kunsthal KAdE in Amsterdam; and Independent Curators International's traveling exhibition *En Mas': Carnival and Performance Art of the Caribbean* (2015–18) are early examples of this trend. Since 2013, the number of thematic exhibitions and commercial galleries showing Caribbean artists has accelerated. One could argue that this interest in the Caribbean by US and European institutions is a result of demographic changes. But could it be indicative of something else inherent to the Caribbean experience?

I have been an active participant in this movement, although when I was growing up in Puerto Rico, I never thought my fate would include diasporic movement. My elementary and high school teachers shared stories about Puerto Rican intellectuals in exile, who occasionally returned to the island. Like many others from the Caribbean, I had family outside of the island. I, however, would proclaim, "Yo me quedo en la trinchera, en la isla aquí me quedo" (I will stay in the trenches; on the island I will stay). Espousing nationalistic pride and, with it, national boundaries, I was denying that a migratory experience is fundamental to understanding what it means to be of the region. People stay and others move, generating a constant flow that is part of what defines the Caribbean. We, the Caribbean people, are and have always been the region's most valuable exports. But what does this movement demand for our understanding of Caribbean art history and curatorial practice?

Reconceptualizing the framework of what it means to be Caribbean is also important because it foregrounds Caribbean art history's development in connection with that of other islands, colonial empires, and routes of exchange. If we consider that the diaspora is integral to understanding the Caribbean, then we can establish relationships of cultural exchange that are not focused on extracting knowledge but instead become the networks through which we can both facilitate deeper research into the value of Caribbean art and foster its display. In the recent rise of Caribbean exhibitions in museums in the United States and Europe, this diasporic lens has been used both to negotiate distance and proximity and to reconsider the region in relation to its culturally diverse communities. Transcending insular and nationalistic paradigms, a diasporic perspective might centralize the relationships among multiple localities within the Caribbean and beyond. In this essay, I will reflect on some curatorial strategies that draw on these perspectives in order to build different—and sustainable—institutional frameworks, programming, and exhibitions aimed at "expanding the meaning [of Caribbean art] rather than containing it."[2] As institutions are formed by individual subjectivities, these strategies must almost always be examined from the first-person point of view.[3]

EXHIBITIONS AND INITIATIVES

In 2013, the Miami Art Museum (MAM) reopened as Pérez Art Museum Miami (PAMM) with a new building and location. In the strategic vision of the chief curator, Tobias Ostrander, the Caribbean would be an integral part of PAMM. While MAM had always collected Caribbean art, mainly from Cuba and Haiti, PAMM sought to emphasize Caribbean art within the institution and to include works from other islands and coastal regions. To ensure this took place effectively, the museum expanded its curatorial expertise, hiring curators, including me, who understood the dynamics of the region and its complex history. PAMM also made a collective effort to organize exhibitions of Caribbean art (with accompanying publications) that furthered the understanding of the creative production from the region and its diaspora. My initial mandate was to develop a version of the exhibition *Caribbean: Crossroads of the World*, which was originally curated by Elvis Fuentes and first presented at El Museo del Barrio, the Studio Museum in Harlem, and the Queens Museum, all in New York City, in 2012. Along with my colleague Diana Nawi, we produced a reduced version of this show at PAMM in 2014. This exhibition would become the historical backbone of the museum's curatorial approach toward the Caribbean. With over 150 works and artists from all over the region, *Crossroads of the World* presented a transnational and interconnected approach to Caribbean art histories. It also included artists, such as Ebony G. Patterson and Firelei Báez, who would later have solo exhibitions at PAMM.

Museums are traditionally known for presenting, acquiring, and conserving art. In this sense, curators are responsible for "organizing displays and analyzing or researching their provenance."[4] All of these mechanisms have systematically favored US and European artists, who are still given a higher proportion of museum shows and make up an outsize proportion of museum collections.[5] However, an exhibition like *Crossroads of the World* at PAMM provided important visibility to Caribbean art in a museum setting, cementing its status as a powerful source of cultural production. By undertaking an exhibition that featured artists from all over the Caribbean and by including many artists whose work had never before been shown in a US institution, the curatorial team demonstrated that Caribbean artists must be valued in the same way as other artists in mainstream US museums. This curatorial strategy collectively commits to showing Caribbean art in order to "increase the human capacity for action"[6] within the institution. This presentation was the beginning of a long-term commitment at PAMM.

Several other PAMM exhibitions dealt with Caribbean themes, issues, and artists. These initiatives had a strong impact on the museum while also influencing the programming in other institutions, both locally and nationally. Through this exhibition trajectory, I worked with PAMM to build a compelling case for the establishment of a Caribbean Cultural Institute (CCI), and in 2019 the museum received a Mellon Foundation grant to develop the institute. The aim of the CCI, which I led, was to formalize all of our Caribbean programming on one platform while continuing to support other Caribbean programs and exhibitions.

I used the CCI's curatorial platform to enhance the understanding and appreciation of Caribbean art at PAMM. We wanted to respond to the museum's immediate context in Miami, a city with direct connections to the Caribbean and especially Cuba and Haiti. Since the Cuban Revolution (1953–59), South Florida has become an important destination for diasporic Cubans. Likewise, Haitians have also formed a strong community in Florida, which intensified as people escaped the brutal dictatorship of Jean-Claude Duvalier during the 1970s. Other Caribbean communities have also sought a different life in the Sunshine State. South Florida has strong connections to the Bahamas through the migration of Bahamian laborers to the area from 1880 to 1920.[7] These migratory patterns and connections in the diaspora generate a multifaceted Caribbean identity, like those of people who have moved between the Dominican Republic and the Coasts of Belize, or between Trinidad and Panama City. Many of us, divided by languages, waterways, and islands, and politically divided by colonialism, come to know one another only in the diaspora.

Symbolically, the establishment of the CCI elevated Caribbean art practices and art histories within the museum. Challenging traditional institutional processes, the CCI emerged out of a desire to recalibrate the relationship that museums had with their local diasporic communities. It pushed for a curatorial approach that acknowledged the cultural richness of the Caribbean and sought to make connections across different Caribbean cultures. The CCI did not unilaterally dictate art histories using a traditional, linear approach. Instead, it aimed at revising the place Caribbean content often has within US museums, which is typically characterized by a desire to build on art histories in tune with the needs of a given museum's visitors and the standards of the field.

The CCI was imagined as a curatorial space where Caribbean art would be contextualized within its cultural specificities, as well as connected to international art movements. Another important aspect of its exhibition programming was to create space for new voices that embody Caribbean discourse by providing museum shows to emerging artists and to midcareer artists without established institutional exhibition support in the diaspora. Curatorially, we took risks. We showed young artists, and we presented artists who were not part of the traditional art market. We commissioned new work, and we supported artistic creation without imposing specific outcome-based demands on artists.

INFRASTRUCTURE IN THE CARIBBEAN

Acknowledging the need for institutional infrastructure in the Caribbean, the CCI created a series of programs to generate more equitable relationships among the diaspora and the region. It moved from resource and knowledge extraction to embracing strategies that would also benefit artists and professionals living in the region. The initiative supported a robust education program for different age groups, including art professionals, through the creation of partnerships such as the Tilting Axis program. Conceived with Annalee Davis and Holly Bynoe, Tilting Axis was a gathering of Caribbean professionals in the field that provided a space for intellectual and creative exchange within, and outside, the region. Each gathering occurred in a different city in partnership with a local organization. Prior to the COVID-19 pandemic, Tilting Axis members gathered at Fresh Milk in Barbados, the National Gallery of the Cayman Islands, the Centro Cultural Eduardo León Jimenes (known as Centro León) in the Dominican Republic, and Mémorial ACTe in Guadeloupe, as well as at PAMM itself.

During the first iteration of Tilting Axis, in Barbados in 2015, I met the Trinidadian art historian Marsha Pearce. We started a conversation about the significant number of contemporary Caribbean artists interested in questioning and exploring colonial legacies. We wanted to put these artists in conversation with developments in recent Caribbean literature that reconsidered the region's possibilities through tropes that draw on surrealism, futurism, and science fiction. Writers such as Junot Díaz, Rita Indiana, Nalo Hopkinson, Yoss, and Tobias Buckell, among others, offered additional perspectives through which to understand the Caribbean experience. Pearce and I embarked on an investigation in which we asked artists to reconsider the future of the region beyond the legacies of colonialism. The resulting exhibition, *The Other Side of Now: Foresight in Contemporary Caribbean Art* (2019–20), included the works of Sheena Rose, Angel Otero, Hulda Guzmán, Nyugen Smith, Lavar Munroe, Andrea Chung, Deborah Jack, Alicia Milne, Jamilah Sabur, Deborah Anzinger, Louisa Marajo, Charles Campbell, Manuel Mathieu, and Cristina Tufiño.[8] This project encouraged Caribbean art production through new commissions, and it fostered new dialogues for creative exchange. As I was based in Miami, and Pearce provided her perspective from Trinidad, this collaboration challenged the traditional notion of institutional curating by inviting others outside of the museum to contribute to the discourse and exemplified a collective curatorial dialogue.

Additionally, the CCI sought other partnerships, hosting an annual series of fellowships with artists and scholars from the Caribbean and its diaspora. From the beginning of the pandemic, the CCI partnered with Mémorial ACTe in Guadeloupe to support CCI artist fellow Ronald Cyrille, a Guadeloupean and Dominican painter, sculptor, and performance artist. Mémorial ACTe provided Cyrille with a studio, and the CCI supplied production funds and curatorial engagement. Through an open call in 2021, the CCI selected Monica Sorelle, a Haitian American filmmaker living in Miami, and Eliazar Ortiz, a painter, photographer, and performance and video artist from the Dominican Republic, to become artist fellows. The CCI provided production funds and mentorship to the artists. Sorelle worked in Miami and Ortiz created works in his studio in Santo Domingo. It was important to support artists living in the region, ameliorating the financial constraints that push many art professionals to migrate.

Another important aspect of the CCI's aim was to facilitate research into PAMM's collection. The museum had significant Caribbean holdings, yet they were not regularly exhibited. PAMM needed research on these objects to ensure scholarship was available for museum staff and audiences. The CCI supported a research fellow, Julián Sánchez González, from Columbia University, to begin this work in 2020. Through another open-call process, Jessica Taylor (Barbados) and Erica Moiah James (a Bahamian art historian based in the United States, and a contributor to this volume) were selected as research fellows in 2021. All three research fellows contextualized works through new scholarship that supported their own interests, and their essays were published on the CCI's digital platform. Prior to my departure from PAMM in 2022, I teamed up with the artist Beatriz Santiago Muñoz and the curator Yina Suriel Jiménez to create a series of gatherings in the Dominican Republic and Trinidad centered on exploring higher-education opportunities for artists in the Caribbean. Muñoz and Suriel, who are attempting to create the kinds of infrastructure that would attract professionals to live in the Caribbean, are exploring the possibility of creating a master's program.

SUSTAINABILITY AND COLLECTION BUILDING

Since the 1960s, US museums have, following different trends and with varying success, attempted to provide visibility to artists of color. While these strategies have produced important art exhibitions, these shows have resulted in a limited number of institutional acquisitions. If, however, collecting art institutions are seeking equitable relationships with artists of different backgrounds, collection building to support marginalized artists' work is essential. It is instructive to consider how this dynamic has played out at PAMM, within the very specific regional and economic context in which CCI emerged. Curatorially, the institution made clear efforts to promote Caribbean art, but the US museum fundraising landscape presented challenges, especially when it came to acquisitions. Alongside research, acquiring works for PAMM's permanent collection was central to the CCI's mission, as the collection is the backbone of the museum. Yet, museum acquisitions involve multiple constituencies – including museum directors, curators, and patrons, all with different interests – in the collective work of securing objects of cultural value. Despite PAMM's commitment to prioritize Caribbean art within the institution, this constellation of stakeholders, along with the influence of art market, has limited the success of CCI's acquisitions efforts.

While I continually supported Caribbean artists in the collection by presenting potential acquisitions to museum patrons, this was challenging because the value of Caribbean art in comparison to other contemporary art markets – including Black art – was harder to prioritize. For example, in 2014, the curatorial team selected and presented about five options to PAMM's Young Collectors Council, which was focused on acquiring a work by a Miami-based artist. I presented Juana Valdés's *Colored China Rags 1* (2012) to the group, and although they decided not to acquire Valdés's work, the following year I tried again. By then, however, *Colored China Rags 1* had been privately acquired by Pamela J. Joyner and the Alfred J. Giuffrida Collection. The museum's Fund for Black Art had offered another way to incorporate Black Caribbean artists into PAMM's collection, since Caribbean artists occupy multiple cultural spaces. In the case of Valdés, her work became more appealing when Joyner presented it in the context of Black art, exemplifying the complex dynamics of museum acquisitions when it comes to equitable collecting practices.

On several occasions, it was impossible to acquire works by Caribbean artists, especially when their relatively low art-market value was at odds with the museum-world tendency to prioritize objects perceived as "high value." Many celebrated Caribbean artists are not presented in art fairs or auction houses. This lack of representation affects their art market value, which has a negative effect, even though they have significant cultural currency. For example, when we tried to acquire works by two iconic Caribbean artists, Olga Albizu and John Dunkley, we were unsuccessful. Although both works had been exhibited at PAMM, both attempted purchases reached a dead end. Donations are also impacted by the market: At times, the institution has declined works by established Caribbean artists offered by reputable donors because of the artist's perceived market value, even if the museum had already exhibited their work. Conversely, PAMM was able to acquire, and receive donations of, the work of emerging artists who were making a significant impact in the contemporary world, often because the market for emerging Caribbean art is "hot." Acquiring emerging artists has thus become an important curatorial strategy for expanding PAMM's Caribbean art collection, and we worked with donors and patrons to guarantee their works' acquisition and presentation in the museum. In 2022, for instance, I presented the work of the Dominican artist Bony Ramirez to our Collectors Council group, and while the group did not vote for Ramirez, two group members offered to buy the proposed work for the museum, acknowledging its value.

In an art market known for its systemic inequality, artists whose works are already highly priced are at times considered more valuable for stakeholders, which then makes it difficult for institutions to collect works by artists of color.[9] Even though museum acquisitions add value and highlight the cultural significance of a work, museums often forget their own power in creating value and shaping markets within the art system; instead, they are negatively affected by art market values and their politics. Museums may invest in objects that have the highest dollar value rather than considering how their acquisitions might elevate the cultural relevance of artists who have not yet had an impact in art market terms. Collecting museums can have an important role in reconfiguring art market dynamics, which in turn can draw public and scholarly attention to marginalized art histories.

BEYOND THE NATIONAL

To effectively curate Caribbean art requires strategies that acknowledge its significance in the broader context of the modern and contemporary artworks traded in the mainstream art market or shown in museums. In the diaspora, Caribbean art, when exhibited, has tended to be positioned as *different*, displayed according to a system that has traditionally prioritized other art histories. Curatorial strategies that aim for the equitable presentation, consumption, and acquisition of Caribbean art need to be aware that they operate in tension with this legacy of erasure. Therefore, our curatorial strategies, practices, and initiatives for sharing and presenting these artworks require a particular orientation. One example is the 2024 exhibition that I curated at the Modern Art Museum of Fort Worth, *Surrealism and Us: Caribbean and African Diasporic Artists Since 1940*.[10] The exhibition radically expanded the meaning and significance of surrealism within the broader history of art by foregrounding Caribbean and Black artists and intellectuals. Its title was inspired by the Martinican thinker Suzanne Césaire's essay "1943: Surrealism and Us." In this text, Césaire embraced surrealism as a way to resist Western colonialism. The author made transatlantic connections between Caribbean artists living across the region and Black artists in the United States. Inspired by this Caribbean intellectual, the Fort Worth exhibition asked the question, What if surrealism started in the Caribbean, then emerged in Europe before ending up in the United States? And: What if a group of enslaved people engaging in a Vodou ceremony to create a revolution constituted a surreal act? Here, surrealism is not a traditional Western avant-garde practice but instead a set of strategies that use dreams, the irrational, and the spiritual for emancipation. By employing the term "surrealism" while centering Caribbean and Black art aesthetics, I challenged its traditional Western associations.

Surrealism and Us explored the history of surrealism in the Caribbean and connected this history with the Afrosurreal in the United States. It pointed to how Caribbean and diasporic art histories are rhizomatic, built on migratory flows. Again, this approach challenged a linear construction of art history. This project also showcased a long history of Caribbean thought focused on the contributions of women, challenging the inherent marginalization of female voices. Disrupting the traditional notion that surrealism emerged in France, the exhibition proposed that the human search for emancipatory strategies against Western colonization began in the Caribbean. At the same time, it built a timeline that presented different moments in which Black and Caribbean artists have alluded to this history. Disrupting national boundaries, *Surrealism and Us* attempted—as Ralph Rugoff proposed in a 2006 essay—to "create a context that prompts us to re-imagine and rethink what we already know about art."[11]

CONCLUSION

What is the role of the diaspora when presenting Caribbean art? In the diaspora, we can continue to create new contexts and scholarship to highlight our art histories and practices, forging transnational connections from which to reconsider what it means to be Caribbean. This might mean forming alternative curatorial strategies that will be in tension with the traditional processes of art museums and other cultural institutions. These strategies, however, present an opportunity to forge new collaborations that move institutions away from an emphasis on the sole curatorial voice to engage a plurality of voices. Institutions have the capacity to engage with and expand on traditionally marginalized art histories by committing to long-term plans that include exhibitions, publications, programming, education, and – vitally – collecting that add to and build on the cultural identity of the museum.

I will never forget the summer opening of *The Other Side of Now* in Miami. It was during PAMM's low season, at a time when the museum typically did not plan celebratory meals to coincide with summer openings. As the day approached, I was contacted about the festivities for the show and, after consulting with the rest of the team, decided to host an opening dinner after all. As the invitation list grew, and more people flew in from the Caribbean, we found a sponsor and organized what the people wanted: a party. It became my summer *quinceañera* celebration. At the opening, I saw joy in our audiences and patrons, and this celebratory moment encapsulated the need for new art initiatives that can add to the art historical record. I learned not to doubt that all cultural production has value for audiences of all kinds – not only for those who experience the joy of seeing themselves represented, but also for those who experience the wonder of discovery as they learn about other cultures and their local communities' connections to them. Therefore, presenting these Caribbean art histories should not be relegated to specific contexts (after all, Caribbean, Black, and other people of color are everywhere), or to meet institutional diversity quotas. Instead, they should emerge from genuine curatorial curiosity and a commitment to expanding the art historical canon.

NOTES

1. In the insular Caribbean, artist-led spaces have been a driving force in the production and presentation of contemporary Caribbean art. There is a need for the historization of these practices. There is a need for local museums or national galleries to dedicate efforts in conserving, preserving, and contextualizing these histories.
2. Robert Storr, "Show and Tell," in *Questions of Practice: What Makes a Great Exhibition?*, ed. Paula Marincola (Pew Center for Arts and Heritage, 2006), 31.
3. John Searle, "What Is an Institution?," in *Institutional Critique and After*, ed. John C. Welchman (JRP|Ringier, 2006), 50.
4. Jens Hoffmann, "The Curatorialization of Institutional Critique," in Welchman, *Institutional Critique and After*, 323.
5. Hakim Bishara, "Artists in 18 Major US Museums Are 85% White and 87% Male, Study Says," *Hyperallergic*, June 3, 2019, https://hyperallergic.com/501999/artists-in-18-major-us-museums-are-85-white-and-87-male-study-says/.
6. John Searle, "Review of *What Is an Institution?*," in Welchman, *Institutional Critique and After*, 35.
7. Howard Johnson, "Bahamian Labor Migration to Florida in the Late Nineteenth and Early Twentieth Centuries," *International Migration Review* 22, no. 1 (Spring 1988): 84–103.
8. María Elena Ortiz and Marsha Pearce, eds., *The Other Side of Now: Foresight in Contemporary Caribbean Art* (Pérez Art Museum Miami, 2019).
9. Margaret Carrigan, "How the Art Industry Is Grappling with Its Systemic Race Inequality," *Art Newspaper*, July 10, 2020, https://www.theartnewspaper.com/2020/07/10/how-the-art-industry-is-grappling-with-its-systemic-race-inequality.
10. María Elena Ortiz, ed., *Surrealism and Us: Caribbean and African Diasporic Artists Since 1940* (Modern Art Museum of Fort Worth / Delmonico, 2024).
11. Ralph Rugoff, "You Talking to Me? On Curating Group Shows that Give You a Chance to Join the Group," in Marincola, *Questions of Practice*, 51.

CHAPTER 11

THE ARCHIPELAGIC METHOD

A MODEL AND POETIC TOOL FOR COMPLEXIFYING THE HISTORY OF LATINX ART AND PHOTOGRAPHY

Aldeide Delgado

In the 2021 essay "What Does Archipelagic Thought Offer Toward the Understanding of Latinx Identity?," I ventured into a critical engagement with art history and Caribbean theory by exploring the intersection of archipelagic thinking and Latinx art.[1] Departing from the state of things as described by the author Arlene Dávila in the critically acclaimed book *Latinx Art: Artists, Markets, and Politics* (2020),[2] I noted the scarcity, within most US academic art history programs, of novel, border-crossing methodologies that disrupt the imperial/colonial politics of knowledge production. Latinx art has been neglected from the canon of art history in Latin America and the United States, but the case of Latinx photography takes this omission further: Latinx photography has been disregarded as a discipline in the art world and in the historiography of photography in Latin America and the United States. According to the art historian Elizabeth Ferrer, speaking shortly after the publication of her book *Latinx Photography in the United States: A Visual History* in 2021:

> Photography by Latinx artists has been essentially excluded from the documented history of photography. There has been no book on the subject before this one, no comprehensive museum exhibition, and little discussion of these photographers in scholarly discourse or within the photo community at large. Their omission from the historical record—from books, college courses, major museum collections—has limited our understanding of the full scope of the history of American photography, in the same way that the absence of photography by Indigenous people, by African Americans, and by members of other marginalized groups has resulted in an incomplete history.[3]

Ferrer's *Latinx Photography in the United States* can be understood as part of a group of studies that challenge the continental history of photography and the lack

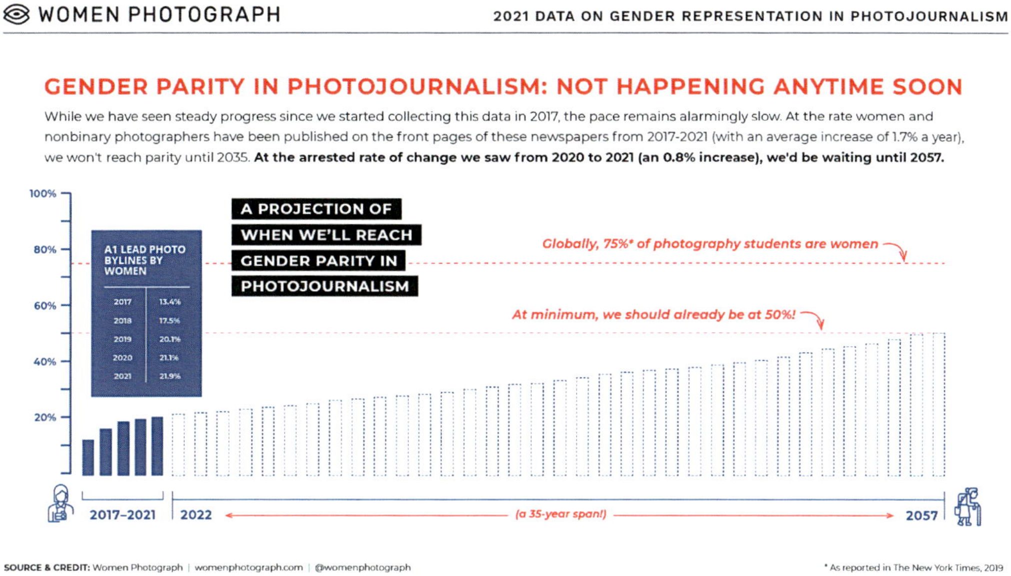

Fig. 11.1. ***2021 Data on Gender Representation in Photojournalism***, **Women Photograph, 2021**

of intersectional narratives in the art world. The statistics are revelatory. World Press Photo, a global platform connecting photojournalists and documentary photographers since 1955, reports that of more than five thousand worldwide photographers who applied to its competitions between 2015 and 2018, approximately 80 percent identified as male. Among these applicants, more than half are identified as Caucasian/White, 1 percent as Black, and only 0.2 percent as Black women.[4] Women Photograph, a nonprofit organization that publishes annual data on the representation of women and nonbinary photographers in the photojournalism industry, notes that in 2021 only 21.9 percent of front-page photographs in leading newspapers such as *The New York Times*, *The Washington Post*, or *The Guardian* were made by women photographers (fig. 11.1), with an average increase of only 1.7 percent per year between 2017 and 2021.[5] In addition, the "Fast Forward Report 2022: Equality, Diversity, and Inclusion," published by the University for the Creative Arts' research project Fast Forward: Women in Photography, establishes:

> There are often blockades to photographic and feminist education that prevent black and brown women, those from less privileged socioeconomic backgrounds, and those who are neurodiverse or have a disability

from accessing valuable skills and knowledge to help pursue a career in photography. . . . Reading lists, artist references in lectures, and artists who are taught within mainstream higher education are too often dominated by white, heteronormative, able-bodied men.[6]

In moving forward, I introduce "continental history of photography" as a conceptual framework to identify the prevailing understanding of photography's history within academia, which operates from the geographically centered perspective of Europe and the United States and often assumes that these regions' stories are universal. This approach finds one of its most successful exponents in Beaumont Newhall's 1937 book *The History of Photography: From 1839 to the Present*. Focused on Germany, France, Great Britain, and the United States, Newhall's historiographical narrative (emphasizing the aesthetic paradigm of images) served as a reference for the subsequent "universal histories" of the medium.[7]

The continental history of photography describes a collective hallucination[8] that validates the grand narratives of newness, progress, and universality that nurtured the imaginary of the modern/colonial world. On the one hand, this discursive framework embraces the invention of the camera (attributed to experiments conducted in the 1820s by the French inventor Joseph Nicéphore Niépce) and its innovative technological development to produce, at each turn, more "transparent" images fully charged with details and sharpness. On the other hand, this discourse emphasizes the explorer's method[9]—that is, belief that photography is a praxis to look at the world in search of knowledge and truth. In this context, it is worth noting the work of the art historian and researcher José A. Navarrete, who unveils in his book *Fotografiando en América Latina: Ensayos de Crítica Histórica* (2017) the labor of traveling photographers in registering natural and urban spaces and classifying archetypes and professions for the symbolic consumption of the cultural Other: among them, the French photographer Désiré Charnay, who was working in Mexico in 1857–58; the Portuguese photographer José Christiano Júnior in Brazil in 1865; and the German photographer Emilio Herbruguer Wheling in Guatemala in 1865–70.[10]

The photographs that fill private and public Western collections represent this hallucination almost exclusively, which means that our view of the world thus far has been mediated through the lens of masculinity and whiteness. How do we remap these imperial/colonial politics of knowledge production? What follows is my proposal on the potential of the archipelagic method: first, as a model for complexifying the history of Latinx art and photography[11]—that is, a model to challenge the idea of "Latinidad"[12] and the continental history of photography—drawing on the Caribbean intellectual tradition; and second, as a poetic tool to foment an international network of women's photography organizations where sisterhood, solidarity, and cooperation are core values. Recognizing the epistemological turn that since the sixties has permeated the historiography of photography — influenced as it is by postmodernist, feminist, and decolonial theories — my contribution resides in foregrounding archipelagic thinking as crucial to debates on the history of photography. The archipelagic framework helps us to recognize the forms of oppression that narratives of Latinidad produce while centralizing relationality and infinitude in the study of artistic practices from racialized voices in the United States.

In proposing an archipelagic method, I consider the archipelago less as a constellation of islands or as a trope addressed by curatorial projects and more, following the definition proposed by Michelle Stephens and Yolanda Martínez-San Miguel, as a provocative "analytical framework to interrogate epistemologies, ways of thinking, and methodologies informed implicitly or explicitly by continental paradigms and perspectives."[13] For the Martinican intellectual Édouard Glissant, the "great" narratives of the world, which aim at unification, totalization, and reducing complexity, describe a continental consciousness. In contrast, the archipelagic method foregrounds the "abyss-consciousness" — an acknowledgment of the historical suffering arising from the unknown, as projected by "the abyss of the belly of the slave boat," "the abyss of the depths of the sea," and "the abyss of an eternal land-sea ahead." The abyss-consciousness grants a political condition where the unknown becomes knowledge transmitted across generations among those who have experienced the abyss.[14]

This approach is particularly helpful to shed light on the work of the street photographer and studio portraitist Moira Pernambuco, who has lived in the United States since age ten. Pernambuco finds inspiration for her creative practice in her multiracial heritage as an Amerindian (Wapishana) Guyanese photographer of African descent. From 1995 to 1998, she developed one of her most acclaimed documentary series, titled *A Tribute to the Ancestors of the Middle Passage* (figs. 11.2, 11.3). It consists of black-and-white portraits of participants in an annual ceremony on the shores of the Atlantic Ocean on Coney Island in New York. Dressed in white as a symbol of healing, purification, and spirituality, the participants bring flowers and pray to the Orishas to honor the lives lost during the transatlantic slave trade. This artwork, which depicted the ocean as a place of memory and trauma, marked the first time Pernambuco specifically addressed her multiracial identity as a person, in part, of African descent. The titles of the photographs in the series reinforce the idea of the abyss or a shared legacy between the subjects and herself.[15]

There is a poetic relation between the abyss (of the Middle Passage as a traumatic experience) in Glissant's writing and the colonial wound that the Argentinian philosopher and semiotician Walter Mignolo describes as hidden under the narrative of modernity. In his essay "La colonialidad a lo largo y a lo ancho: El hemisferio occidental en el horizonte colonial de la modernidad," Mignolo draws

Fig. 11.2. Moira Pernambuco (Guyanese, b. 1969), *Save a Space for Me*, 1998, from the series *A Tribute to the Ancestors of the Middle Passage*. Gelatin silver print, 13¾ × 10¾ in. (35.1 × 27.5 cm), Yale University Art Gallery, New Haven, Connecticut, Leonard C. Hanna, Jr., Class of 1913, Fund, 2000.31.1

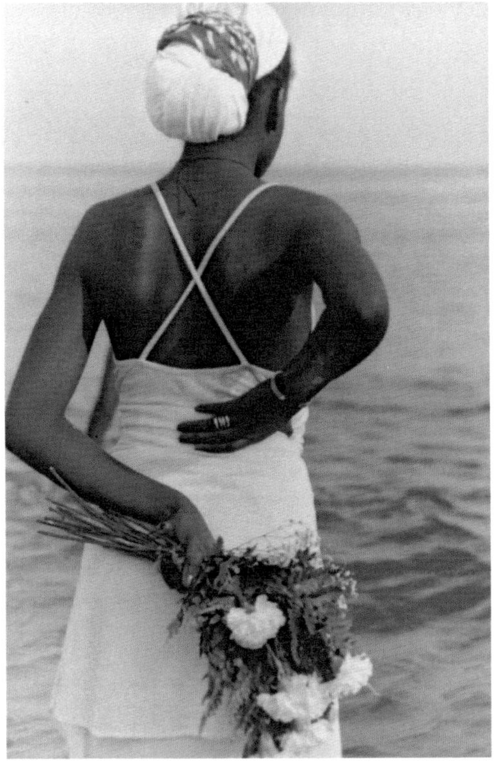

Fig. 11.3. Moira Pernambuco, *From One World to Another I*, 1998, from the series *A Tribute to the Ancestors of the Middle Passage*. Gelatin silver print, 23¾ × 19¾ in. (60.3 × 50.2 cm), Yale University Art Gallery, New Haven, Connecticut, Leonard C. Hanna, Jr., Class of 1913, Fund, 2000.31.2

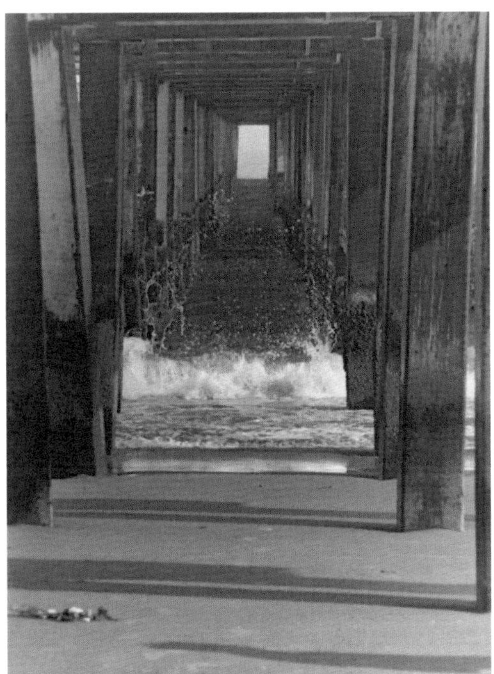

upon the concept of the "imaginary" that Glissant articulated. The imaginary, in this context, refers to "the symbolic world through which a community (racial, national, imperial, sexual, etc.) defines itself."[16] Expanding on this concept, Mignolo describes the imaginary of the modern/colonial world as the result of a lengthy process of constructing the idea of Western civilization through the dual colonization of time and space.[17] The imaginary of the modern/colonial world emerged within the exercise of the coloniality of power, the coloniality of knowledge, the coloniality of being, and the coloniality of gender; that is, following Mignolo's thesis, "the complex articulation of forces, of voices heard or silenced, of memories compact or fractured, of histories told from only one side that suppress other memories, and of histories that were and are told from the double consciousness that generates the colonial difference."[18]

According to the anthropologist and researcher Arturo Escobar, one of the main disciplinary contributions of the modernity/coloniality group associated with Mignolo[19] is its deviation from considering "Latin America" as an object of study and instead seeing it as an epistemic framework with an intellectual tradition.[20] So, the imaginary of the modern/colonial world must be understood from a geo-historical and critical Latin American perspective. However, I will take this statement further by emphasizing that debates on the imaginary of the modern/colonial world should commence from the critical and geo-historical perspective of the Caribbean specifically, because it was in this region that European colonialism began to unfold.[21] As the philosopher Nelson Maldonado-Torres expressed, it is important to *decontinentalize* the Americas by focusing on the archipelago of the Caribbean, its historical transcendence, and its philosophical, creative, and artistic production.[22] This consideration is crucial, as the Caribbean is frequently excluded from discourses on the history of Latinx art and photography.

The question of why art history, a discipline often defined by its relationship with shifting terrains of theoretical critique and analysis, has been slow to engage with Caribbean writers and thinkers, taking seriously their multidisciplinary, multi-theoretical, and multilingual voices,[23] resonates with the ethos of Linda Nochlin's famous essay "Why Have There Been No Great Women Artists?"[24] or Maurice Berger's "Are Art Museums Racist?"[25] Both authors questioned the role of the discipline of art history—its academies, museums, galleries, and systems of patronage—in perpetuating a Western imaginary. Nochlin's essay, originally published in *ArtNews* in 1971, deconstructed "the myth of the artistic genius" by revealing the societal and institutional barriers that historically deprived women of achieving artistic excellence. Berger's landmark essay, published in 1990 in *Art in America*, specifically addressed the conditions of institutional racism in the United States. But a response to the question of why has art history been too slow to expand its canons can also be found in Maura Reilly's interview with Nochlin in the book *Curatorial Activism:*

Towards an Ethics of Curating, where Nochlin observes that the field of art "is an hegemony that privileges white male creativity to the exclusion of all Other artists. . . . This white Western male viewpoint, may—and does—prove to be inadequate not merely on moral and ethical grounds, or because it is elitist, but on purely intellectual ones."[26] The archipelagic method presents the failure of academic art history to render visible marginalized voices and ways of thinking and complexify our understanding of the world-system. Its instrumentalization demonstrates art history's conceptual inaccuracies and exposes its meta-historical fallacies.

To engage with Caribbean writers and thinkers such as Glissant and the Saint Lucian writer Derek Walcott is not arbitrary when considering the history of Latinx art and photography. As the scholars Tatiana Flores and Michelle Stephens have noted:

> An exclusively insular narrative makes sense partly because of the distinction between island and continent but also because it brings to the fore issues arising from the colonial legacy—such as sovereignty, migration, sustainability, and, of course, race and ethnicity—that are relevant to the [Latin American] region as a whole but that simply cannot be overlooked when dealing with the Caribbean.[27]

Likewise, recent critical approaches to the continental history of photography have contended that the inauguration of photography is related to the fateful landing in the "New World" of Christopher Columbus in 1492 and the logic of European colonialism. As Ariella Azoulay argued in her 2018 book *Potential History: Unlearning Imperialism*:

> Suggesting that the origins of photography go back to 1492 is an attempt to undermine the imperial temporality that was imposed at that time, enabling people to believe, experience, and describe interconnected things as if they were separate, each defined by newness. To put it another way, for photography to emerge as a new technology in the late 1830s, the centrality of the imperial rights on which photography was predicated had to be ignored, denied, or sublimated, or in any case pushed into the background and not perceived as constitutive of its operation as a technology. Foregrounding these rights requires a simultaneous exercise—unlearning the accepted origins of photography and those of the "new world," their familiar spatial and temporal connotations, which even today are still closely associated with modernity and "the era of discoveries," and attending instead to the configuration of imperial violence and its manifestation in . . . the right to destroy

> existing worlds, the right to manufacture a new world in their place, the rights over others whose worlds are destroyed together with the rights they enjoyed in their communities and the right to declare what is new and consequently what is obsolete.[28]

The complicity of photography within the imperial project is revealed in the work of the photo-based artist Stacey Tyrell, born in Canada to parents from Nevis of Scottish descent. Tyrell's visual practice explores identity, race, and heritage as it relates to the specificity of the Caribbean and its diaspora. In the series *Pour La Victoire* (2015–18), she researched the Eurocentric constructs of white and Black femininity by embodying the allegorical personifications of major powers involved in the slave trade, including Spain, England, France, Portugal, and the Netherlands. Inspired by other remarkable artists, such as Cindy Sherman and Nikki S. Lee, Tyrell transforms her Black skin tone and physical features through (self-)portraits of historical women characters, such as *Columbia (United States)*, *Hispania (Spain)*, and *Britannia (England)* (fig. 11.4). These images expose a canon that idealizes white women—and by extension the imperial motherland—as pure, civilized, and glorious. In contrast, Tyrell argues, a sexualized (and racialized) woman would not be deserving of respect (fig. 11.5).[29] Her work also facilitates an interrogation of the Caribbean beyond nation-state divisions. For example, seen together, her photographs from *Pour La Victoire* visualize the notion of serial colonialism—as when Columbus's 1493 sighting of the island of Nevis led to its subsequent colonization by the Spanish, the Dutch, and ultimately the British. (I'll revisit the term "serial colonialism" later.)

One of the main references for analyzing the intersection of archipelagic thought and Latin American Art is the 2017–18 exhibition *Relational Undercurrents: Contemporary Art from the Caribbean Archipelago* at the Museum of Latin American Art, Long Beach, California.[30] Curated by Tatiana Flores, the exhibition remapped the exclusionary continental concept of Latin America—as a place "south of the border" that includes the Spanish Americas and Brazil—by centering the artistic production of the insular Caribbean and favoring an island-to-island perspective over a mainland-to-island approach.[31] In the words of Flores and Stephens, "The archipelagic shapes our view of the Caribbean as less a bounded or fragmented cultural area and more a geomaterial and geohistorical assemblage of sea spaces and islands."[32]

Relational Undercurrents inaugurated archipelagic thought as a valid conceptual frame through which to complicate the definitions of Latin America.[33] It also highlighted the less-visible connections between Caribbean islands, their diaspora enclaves, and other island systems in the world. Following Flores and Stephens's narrative, through archipelagic thinking, "diaspora locations become not privileged metropolitan mainland cities but their own types of linked nodes in an insular network."[34]

Fig. 11.4. Stacey Tyrell (Canadian, b. 1978), *Britannia (England)*, 2015, from the series *Pour La Victoire*. Archival pigment print, 40 × 30 in. (101.6 × 76.2 cm). Collection of the artist

Fig. 11.5. Stacey Tyrell, *Mistress and Slave*, 2018, from the series *Untitled*. Archival pigment print, 30 × 40 in. (76.2 × 101.6 cm). Collection of the artist

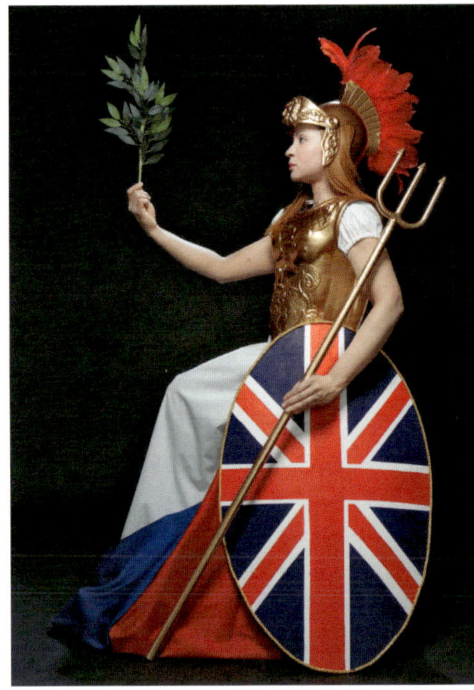

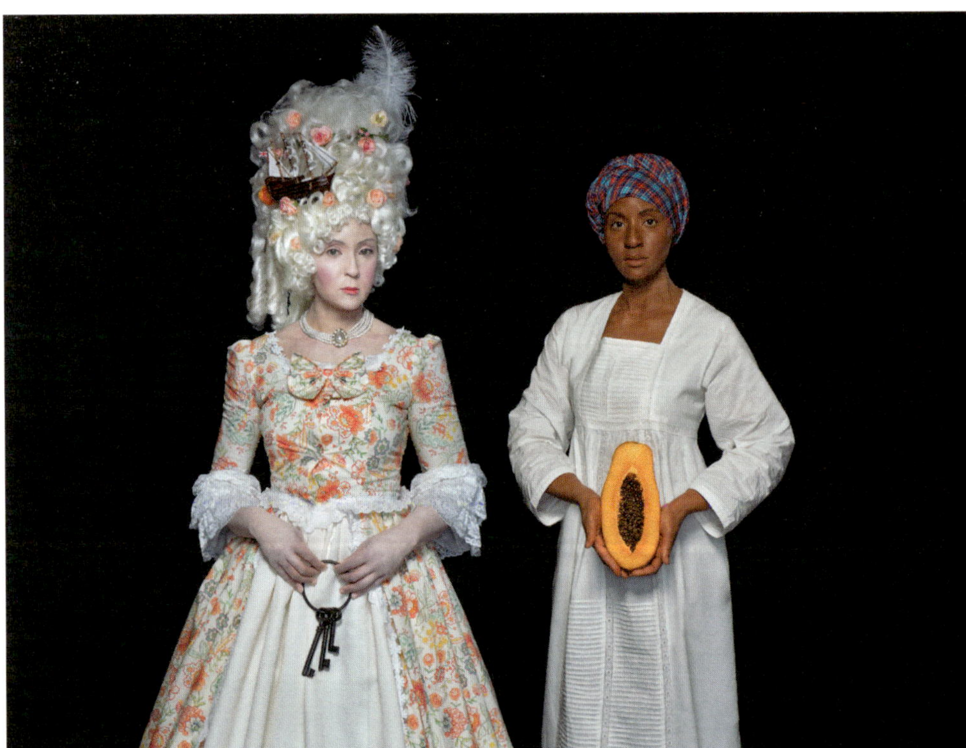

The archipelagic method proves to be a useful tool to emphasize relationality and demonstrate the infinite layers of Latinidad—notions that are not coincidental but rather integral to the theory. The former refers to Glissant's conceptualization of relationality as a means to unveil the "entangled historical, material, and affective connections that would otherwise be obscured by dominant, truncated, and ahistorical narratives."[35] The latter refers to the apprehension of the island's fractal infinitude, meaning "moving away from the explorer's method and toward the anti-explorer's method, which involves looking at the supposedly known world and attesting to its final unknowability."[36] Extrapolating from this idea to the context of the history of Latinx art and photography, we must consider the impossibility of measuring identity as fixed and monolithic: As you examine the cultural compositions of Latinx more closely, other mixing processes appear multiplied to infinity. For example, in the installation *Terrestrial Bodies* (2019), the Cuban visual artist Juana Valdés displays the ancestral timeline of her mother going back eight generations to reflect her multiethnic identity at the crossroads between Africa, Asia, and the Americas (fig. 11.6). As we approach any national identifiers within the postcolonial world, whether Congolese or Indonesian, Nigerian of Chinese, we will encounter the same contingent and overlapping character of identity stemming from these regions' unique processes of creolization.

The archipelagic method also allows us to question which regions are included in the notion of Latinidad and which are not. In the book *Queer Latinidad: Identity Practices, Discursive Spaces*, the author Juana María Rodríguez asks:

> If Dominicanas are Latinas, are Haitianas? Geographically they share the same island, el mismo Caribe. And what can we say about those multilingual islands that defy easy classification: Aruba, Curaçao, Trinidad, are they part of el mundo Latino? Even when we think of South and Central America, do we forget the English- and Creole-speaking countries of Guyana, Surinam [*sic*], and Belize, or the polylingual regions of Nicaragua, Costa Rica, and Panamá? How do we categorize the huge Portuguese-speaking anomaly of Brazil? If we decide that Spanish or at least a shared linguistic "Latin" heritage is the common thread that unites us, it is a precarious thread indeed. Clearly there are other official and unofficial languages spoken in Latin/o America and the Caribbean: Quechua, Aymara, Guaraní, French, Hindi, Creole, Lucumi, Papiamento, and English, to name a few. These languages remind us of the Indigenous past before successions of European colonizers, African enslavement afterwards, and centuries of transnational migration.[37]

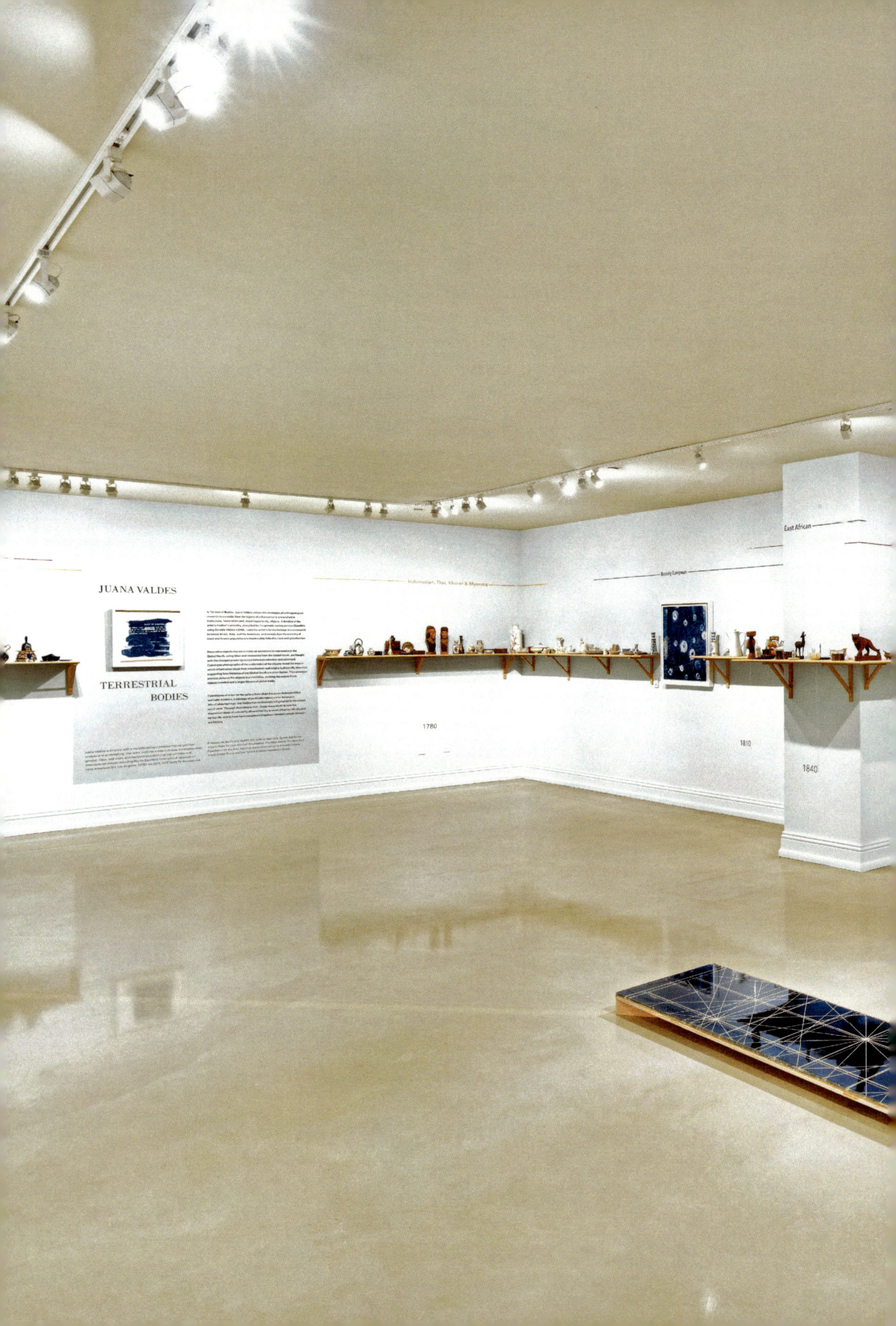
JUANA VALDES
TERRESTRIAL
BODIES
East African
1780
1810
1840

Fig. 11.6. Installation view, *Juana Valdés: Terrestrial Bodies*, Cuban Legacy Gallery, MDC Special Collections, Freedom Tower, Miami, 2019–20

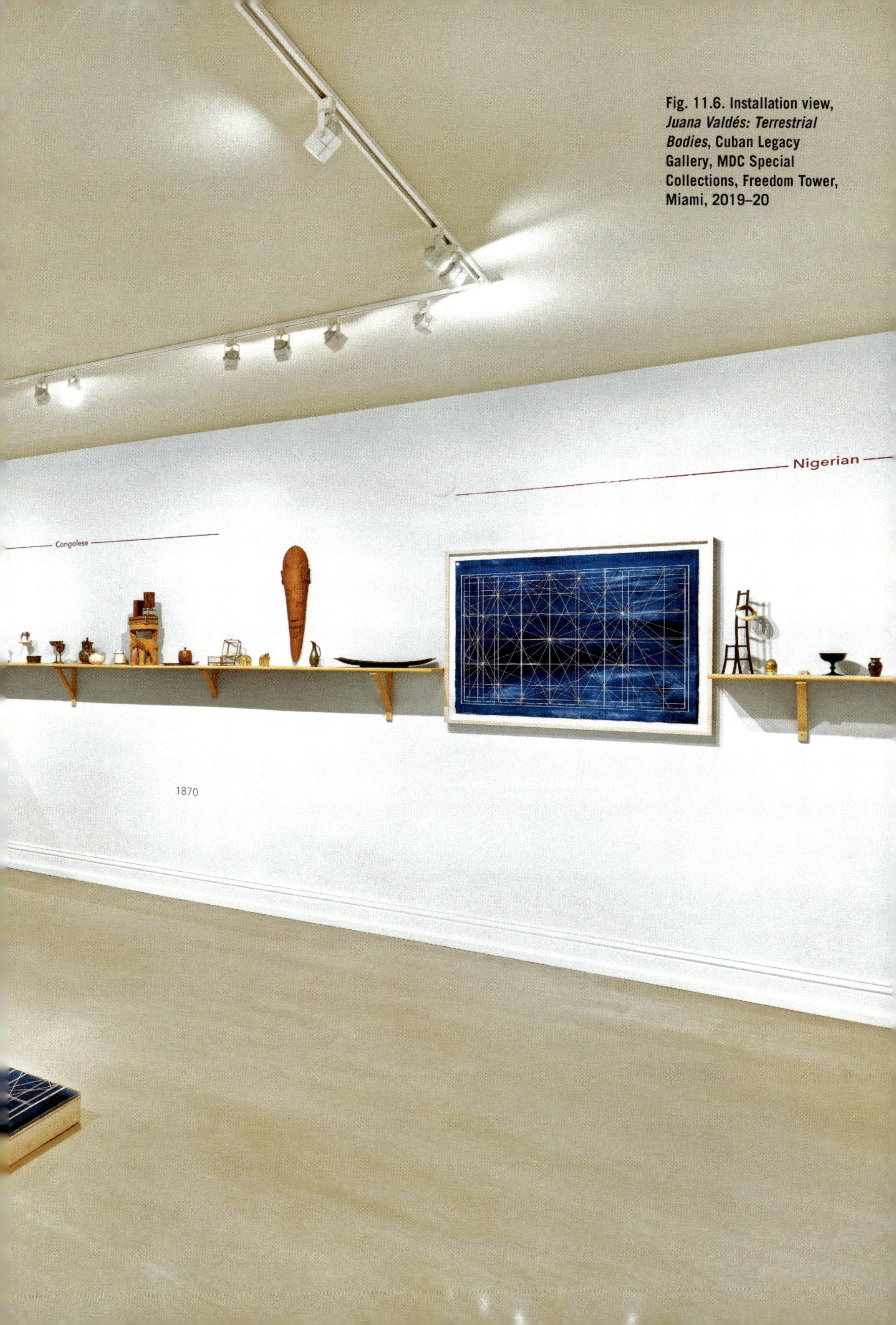

And, she continues, when we think on Latinidad, it is important to consider the impact of serial colonialism. "Brazil was under Dutch rule before being conquered by the Portuguese. Jamaica was a Spanish territory before becoming a British colony. The Philippines and Puerto Rico were Spanish colonies before they became US territories. And, of course, vast segments of the continental United States were previously claimed by the French, the Spanish, and México."[38] Yolanda Martínez–San Miguel corroborated the notion of serial colonialism with the term "extended colonialism," which denotes the coexistence of more than one colonial system (Spanish and French in Martinique, Spanish and English in Puerto Rico, among many other islands in the Caribbean) spanning from the sixteenth century to the present.[39]

The archipelagic method recognizes the complexities of mixed heritages, multilingualism, and transnational migration by denaturalizing geographic discourse and suggesting new spatial configurations that respond to a metaphoric understanding of interrelated islands. This notion does not position itself in analogy with the ideological narratives of national creole or mestizaje. Rather, it engages with the process of detaching from preestablished categories of identity to construct other systems of relations conditioned by an attitude of dissent toward the nation-state.

The archipelagic method considers the distinctive racial and cultural diversity present in Latin America and the Caribbean as a result of the concurrent transplantation of populations from Europe, Asia, and Africa within the modern/colonial project, resulting, for example, in the presence of large Jewish, Arab, Muslim, Buddhist, Chinese, Japanese, Italian, German, and Slavic communities that can also be of any skin color and should not be considered as homogeneous entities. In this regard, I would like to highlight the work of the visual artist Muriel Hasbun, who examines identity and family legacy through an intergenerational, transnational, and transcultural lens.

Born to a Salvadoran-Palestinian-Christian father and a French-Polish-Jewish mother in El Salvador, Hasbun moved to the United States in the 1980s. In the photograph *All the Saints (Izalco Volcano, Amen)* (fig. 11.7), from the mid-1990s, she presents the most active volcano in Central America, located in El Salvador, emitting a Greek Orthodox prayer written by her great grandfather in Arabic calligraphy. According to Hasbun, she created "this photograph to resist institutional prejudice and cultural erasure against Palestinians in El Salvador and to mark [their] presence in the Salvadoran landscape."[40] She also references the traumatic event of La Matanza in 1932—the killing of about thirty thousand mostly Indigenous people by order of the dictator Maximiliano Hernández Martínez, using the volcano's eruption as a backdrop to cover the genocide.

If, so far, I have presented the potential of the archipelagic method as a model to complexify the history of Latinx art and photography, I want to briefly

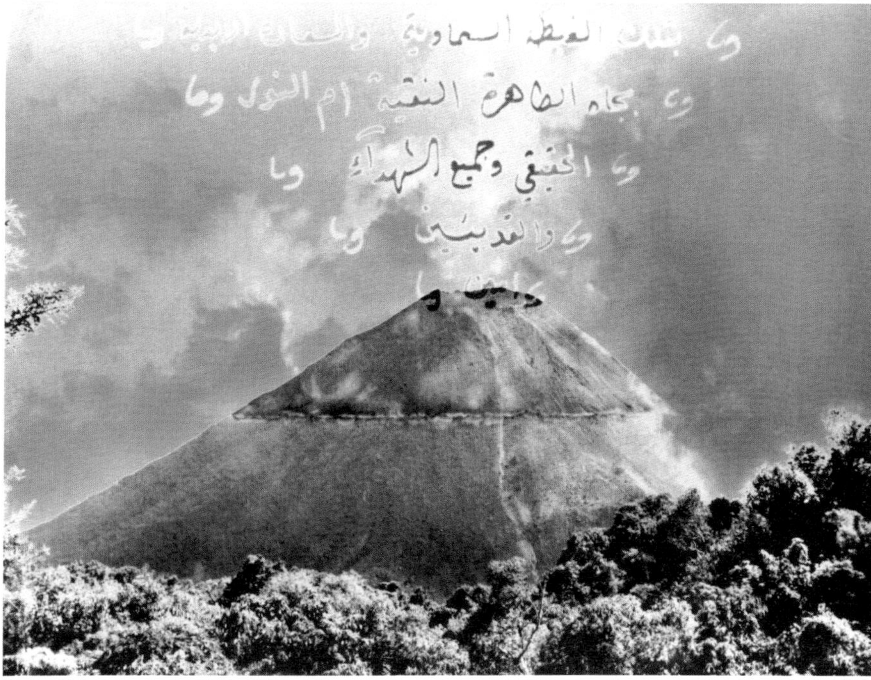

Fig. 11.7. Muriel Hasbun (Salvadoran, b. 1961), *Todos los santos (Volcán de Izalco, amén)* (*All the Saints [Izalco Volcano, Amen]*), 1995–96, printed 1996. Gelatin silver print, 15 7/8 × 19 3/4 in. (40.3 × 50.3 cm). Whitney Museum of American Art, New York, purchase, with funds from the Photography Committee, 2022.212

turn now to the potential of the archipelagic method as a poetic tool to foment an international network of women's photography organizations (or, as I call it, "feminist archipelagos"), taking as a case study the 2021 photobook *Becoming Sisters: Women Photography Collectives and Organizations* (fig. 11.8). For Glissant, through archipelagic thinking we see the world metaphorically as a collection of islands connected to one another, engaging through exchange, fluids, mobility, and border crossings. This imaginary allows us to decentralize single and linear narratives of continental photography history by embracing multiplicity and connections with other people, places, and species who share similar struggles and experiences.

In 2018, I founded the Miami-based Women Photographers International Archive (WOPHA) in response to the lack of dedicated spaces for preserving, documenting, and promoting women photographers' work. I have employed the archipelagic method to problematize the archive as a modern/colonial institution itself

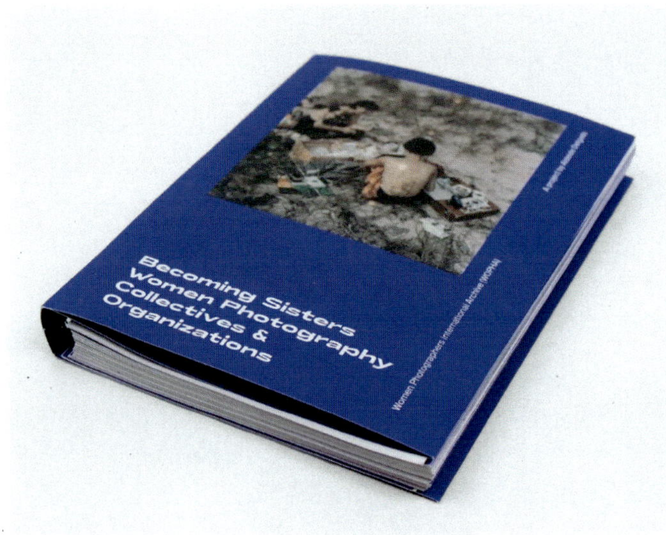

Fig. 11.8. Cover of Aldeide Delgado, ***Becoming Sisters: Women Photography Collectives and Organizations*** (Women Photographers International Archive, 2021)

Fig. 11.9. Teresita Fernández (American, b. 1968), *Island Universe 2*, 2023. Charcoal. 77 ½ × 303 × 3 in. (197.1 × 769.6 × 7.6 cm)

while questioning its systems of operation, categorization, and knowledge production. From this perspective, WOPHA's geopolitical location is crucial, positioned in Miami, a border space at the crossroads of the Americas. The organization defines the archive as meeting place and embraces photography as a collaborative tool for connecting and creating community. With a strong focus on historical research, WOPHA's current projects document the diverse artistic production of Latin American and Latinx communities, including photographers from Mexico, Central and South America, the Caribbean, and artists of Latin American descent living and working in the United States.

Becoming Sisters: Women Photography Collectives and Organizations (published in tandem with the 2021 WOPHA Congress[41]) serves as a registry and collective manifesto of 138 international women and nonbinary photographers, collectives, and organizations reframing the history of continental photography. In the main essay, spread across five sections of the book, I argue that women photographers have created communities based on tenets of solidarity and networking as a fundamental strategy to highlight women's contributions to the photographic arts. To prove this thesis, the essay references the collaborative photo-performance *El Picnic* (1989) by the artists Nereida García-Ferraz (Cuba), Laura González-Flores (Mexico), and Eugenia Vargas-Pereira (Chile); the Ovular feminist photography workshops held in Oregon from 1979 to 1983; *Polareyes*, the London journal by and about Black women working in photography, founded in 1987; and the Feminine Division of the Photography Club in Cuba (1947–1962). Simultaneously, forty collectives and organizations, grouped as eight island systems within an archipelagic network, were featured and

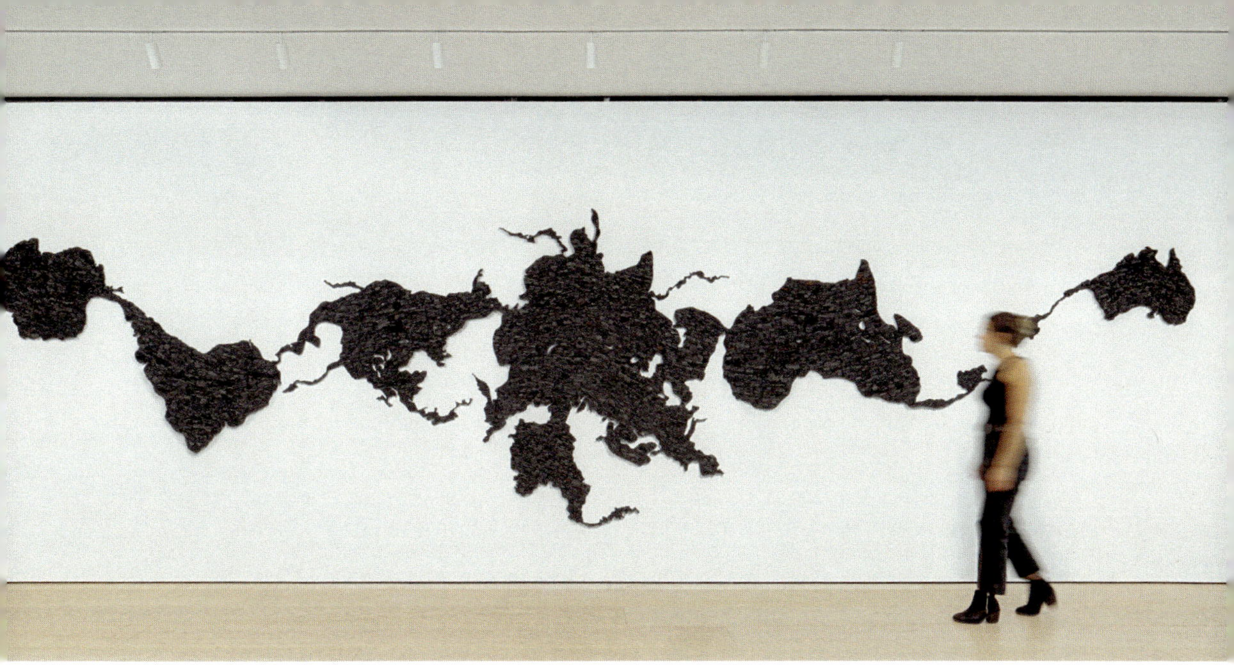

further activated through online and in-person meetings during the pandemic lockdown, the 2021 WOPHA Congress, and post-Congress programs.

Instead of highlighting contemporary women photographers as singular creative subjects, *Becoming Sisters* centers, from an archipelagic perspective, collaborative practices in photography—and by doing so, encourages new scholarship on the shared experiences of women photographers. The WOPHA Congress was an international gathering defined by the social interactions of sisterhood and solidarity. It marked a paradigm shift as we displaced the discussion from the realm of the camera and the right to see others' worlds and instead focused on relationality and the collaborative nature of the photographic act.

As a way of concluding what remains an ongoing research project, the cultural and political implications of the question "Why has art history been slow to engage with Caribbean writers and thinkers?" continue to resonate. Does the appropriation/assimilation of Caribbean intellectual thought by mainstream institutions reveal structural change? What is the geo-historical location of this Caribbean thinking? What role have Caribbean and diaspora cultural institutions played in preserving and providing access to the region's theoretical lineages? How can we work toward creating an archipelagic network among Caribbean art historians? As we are invited to imagine new cartographies of knowledge (as suggested by the artist Teresita Fernández's powerful 2019 piece *Island Universe*, fig. 11.9), the archipelagic method facilitates more nuanced, interconnected, and situated narratives to complexify our understandings of art histories and the world.

NOTES

1. See Aldeide Delgado, "What Does Archipelagic Thought Offer Toward the Understanding of Latinx Identity?," *Latin American and Latinx Visual Culture* 3, no. 2 (April 1, 2021): 72–78, https://doi.org/10.1525/lavc.2021.3.2.72.

2. Arlene Dávila, *Latinx Art: Artists, Markets, and Politics* (Duke University Press, 2020).

3. Elizabeth Ferrer, "Latinx Photography in the United States: The Search for a Fuller History," posted by Women Photographers International Archive, November 18, 2021, video, 1:30:11, https://www.youtube.com/watch?v=UIMYnq-WhS8&t=3865s. Elizabeth Ferrer, *Latinx Photography in the United States: A Visual History* (University of Washington Press, 2021).

4. Adrian Hadland and Camilla Barnett, *The State of News Photography 2018: Photojournalists' Attitudes Toward Work Practices, Technology and Life in the Digital Age* (World Press Photo, 2018), https://www.worldpressphoto.org/getmedia/4f811d9d-ebc7-4b0b-a417-f119f6c49a15/the_state_of_news_photography_2018.pdf, cited in Savannah Dodd and Andrew Jackson, "The Impact of the White, Male Gaze," *Trigger*, FOMU, June 3, 2020, https://www.fomu.be/trigger/articles/the-impact-of-the-white-male-gaze.

5. "2021 Data on Gender Representation in Photojournalism," *Women Photograph*, 2021, https://www.womenphotograph.com/data.

6. Elizabeth Ransom, Anna Fox, and Maria Kapajeva, "Fast Forward Report 2022: Equality, Diversity and Inclusion," Fast Forward: Women in Photography website, accessed July 29, 2023, https://fastforward.photography/our-projects/fast-forward-report-2022-equality-diversity-and-inclusion/.

7. See José Antonio Navarrete, "Adiós, Mr. Newhall," in *Fotografiando en América Latina: Ensayos de crítica histórica* (CdF Ediciones, 2017), 31–40.

8. In this context, a hallucination refers to the nonperception of something that is present. See Brian Russell Roberts and Michelle Ann Stephens, *Archipelagic American Studies* (Duke University Press, 2017), 9–10.

9. The explorer "sallies forth with confidence that if the world is as yet unknown, then it at least may be surveyed and hence known via [photography]." See Roberts and Stephens, *Archipelagic American Studies*, 20.

10. See José Antonio Navarrete, "Del tipo al arquetipo: Fotografía y tipos nacionales en América Latina durante la segunda mitad del siglo XIX y comienzos del XX," in Navarrete, *Fotografiando en América Latina*, 65–76.

11. By referring to "the history of Latinx art and photography," I emphasize my approach to thinking across these two fields, the history of Latinx art and the history of photography, through an archipelagic lens.

12. Latinidad is a racial category and a cultural and historical identity validated by technologies of production of "truth," such as photography. It emerged, in the second half of the nineteenth century, as an ideological construction forged by intellectuals and officials in France amid imperial tensions with the Anglo-Saxon world (principally England and Germany). At that time, Spain had fallen behind in the modern imperial enterprise, and France sought to articulate a political project and collective identity that could justify its "civilizing mission" in the Global South. On one front, Latinidad positioned France advantageously in relation to other Latin-European powers with interests in the Americas, such as Italy, Spain, and Portugal. On another, it functioned as a discursive counterweight to US expansionist influence in the hemisphere. In South America and the Spanish-speaking Caribbean, white and mestizo Creole elites appropriated the framework of Latinidad to construct postcolonial identities at a moment when France served as a dominant intellectual reference for cultural, political, and development aspirations. See Walter Mignolo, *La idea de América Latina: La herida colonial y la opción decolonial* (Editorial Gedisa, S.A., 2005), 81–95.

13. See Michelle Stephens and Yolanda Martínez-San Miguel, *Contemporary Archipelagic Thinking: Towards New Comparative Methodologies and Disciplinary Formations* (Rowman & Littlefield, 2020), 6.

14. See Édouard Glissant, "The Open Boat," in *Poetics of Relation*, trans. Betsy Wing (University of Michigan Press, 1997), 5–9.

15. See Aldeide Delgado, "Moira Pernambuco," AWARE: Archives of Women Artists, Research, and Exhibitions website, accessed September 10, 2023, https://awarewomenartists.com/en/artiste/moira-pernambuco/; and Daniell Cornell and Cheryl Finley, *Imaging African Art: Documentation and Transformation*, exh. cat. (Yale University Art Gallery, 2000), 24–25.

16. Walter D. Mignolo, "La colonialidad a lo largo y a lo ancho: El hemisferio occidental en el horizonte colonial de la modernidad," in *La colonialidad del saber: Eurocentrismo y ciencias sociales; Perspectivas latinoamericanas*, ed. Edgardo Lander (CLACSO, Consejo Latinoamericano de Ciencias Sociales, 2000), 34.

17. The colonization of time was made possible through the simultaneous invention of the Middle Ages and conceptualization of the Renaissance. The colonization of space was achieved through the conquest of the "New World" and the commercial control of the Atlantic, which marked the origins of modernity and its hidden side: coloniality. See Walter D. Mignolo, "La colonialidad: La cara oculta de la modernidad," in *Modernologías: Artistas*

contemporáneos investigan la modernidad y el modernismo, ed. Sabine Breitwieser (Museu d'Art Contemporani de Barcelona, 2009), 41.

18. Mignolo, "La colonialidad a lo largo y a lo ancho," 39. In Mignolo's text, the term "double consciousness" characterizes the imaginary of the modern/colonial world emerging within racialized communities inside and outside the margins of empires.

19. The modernity/coloniality group consists of interconnected transdisciplinary researchers in Latin America, the United States, and other parts of the world. While it is primarily associated with scholars like Enrique Dussel, Aníbal Quijano, and Walter Mignolo, it also includes several other notable members, such as Nelson Maldonado-Torres, Arturo Escobar, María Lugones, Edgardo Lander, Santiago Castro Gómez, Oscar Guardiola, Eduardo Restrepo, Catherine Walsh, Zulma Palermo, Jorge Sanjinés, Freya Schiwy, Fernando Coronil, and Ana Margarita Cervantes-Rodríguez, among others. Arturo Escobar, "Worlds and Knowledge Otherwise: The Latin American Modernity/Coloniality Research Program," *Cultural Studies* 21, no. 2–3 (March/May 2007): 203, accessed July 27, 2023, https://doi.org/10.1080/09502380601162506.

20. Escobar, "Worlds and Knowledge Otherwise."

21. See Nelson Maldonado-Torres, "El Caribe, La Colonialidad, y El Giro Decolonial," *Latin American Research Review* 55, no. 3 (2020): 560–73, https://doi.org/10.25222/larr.1005.

22. Maldonado-Torres, "El Caribe, La Colonialidad."

23. This question was proposed by the scholars Anna Arabindan-Kesson and Wayne Modest as a starting point for the two-day conference titled "Beyond Boundaries: Seeing Art History from the Caribbean" at the Clark Art Institute in 2022. This essay is a revised version of the paper presented during the "Caribbean as Critique" session of the conference.

24. Linda Nochlin, "From 1971: Why Have There Been No Great Women Artists?," *ArtNews*, May 30, 2015, https://www.artnews.com/art-news/retrospective/why-have-there-been-no-great-women-artists-4201.

25. Maurice Berger, "From the Archives: Are Art Museums Racist?," *Art in America*, March 31, 2020, https://www.artnews.com/art-in-america/features/maurice-berger-are-art-museums-racist-1202682524.

26. Linda Nochlin, in Maura Reilly, *Curatorial Activism Towards An Ethics of Curating* (Thames & Hudson, 2018), 21. See also "Common Ground | Curatorial Activism," *Brooklyn Rail*, September 21, 2020, video, 2:14:40, https://www.youtube.com/watch?v=AYwF6OC7euk.

27. See Tatiana Flores and Michelle Stephens, "Contemporary Art of the Hispanophone Caribbean Islands in an Archipelagic Framework," *Small Axe* 20, no. 3 (51) (November 2016): 85.

28. Ariella Azoulay, "Unlearning the Origins of Photography," Verso Books website, September 7, 2018, https://www.versobooks.com/blogs/4013-unlearning-the-origins-of-photography.

29. See the interview of Stacey Tyrell by Clare Samuel published on Lensculture under the title "Bluid and Sweat," referenced in Aldeide Delgado, "Deconstructing Whiteness Through Studio Portrait Photography," Feminist Photography Network project website, *Identity, Connection, Place*, accessed March 8, 2023, https://www.fpnexhibit.com/aldeide-delgado.

30. See Tatiana Flores and Michelle Ann Stephens, *Relational Undercurrents: Contemporary Art from the Caribbean Archipelago* (Museum of Latin American Art, Long Beach | SF Design / Fresco, 2017).

31. Flores and Stephens, *Relational Undercurrents*, 135.

32. Flores and Stephens, "Contemporary Art," 87.

33. Other exhibitions, such as *Poetics of Relation* (2015) at Pérez Art Museum Miami (PAMM), and essays, such as *Queer Chinese Feminist Archipelagos* (unpublished) by Alpesh Kantilal Patel, assumed an archipelagic perspective; however, these were not framed in the context of discussion about Latin America.

34. Flores and Stephens, "Contemporary Art," 87.

35. See Yomaira C. Figueroa, "A Case for Relation: Mapping Afro-Latinx Caribbean and Equatoguinean Poetics," *Small Axe* 24, no. 1 (61) (March 2020): 26.

36. See Roberts and Stephens, *Archipelagic American Studies*, 23–24.

37. Juana María Rodríguez, *Queer Latinidad: Identity Practices, Discursive Spaces* (New York University Press, 2003), 13–14.

38. Rodríguez, *Queer Latinidad*, 14.

39. Yolanda Martínez–San Miguel, "Colonialismo y decolonialidad archipielágica en el Caribe," *Tabula Rasa*, no. 29 (July–December 2018): 40, http://www.revistatabularasa.org/numero-29/03-martinez.pdf.

40. Claudia Pretelin, "Between Memories: An Interview with Muriel Hasbun," Instruments of Memory: Conversations with Women in the Arts website, October 12, 2021, https://instrumentsofmemory.com/2021/10/12/between-memories-an-interview-with-muriel-hasbun/.

41. The inaugural WOPHA Congress, "Women, Photography, and Feminisms" (November 17–20, 2021), was hosted by the Women Photographers International Archive at the Pérez Art Museum Miami and presented seminal and emerging research, addressing both national and international discussions regarding women and feminism in the history of photography.

CHAPTER 12
OTHER ART WORLDS ARE POSSIBLE
INTRODUCING THE KIBII FOUNDATION, A CONVERSATION WITH MARCEL PINAS

Anna Arabindan-Kesson and Wayne Modest

Anna Arabindan-Kesson and Wayne Modest: Marcel, thanks for agreeing to be part of this project. Perhaps we could start by setting the context. You are an artist and the founder of the Kibii Foundation in Moengo, Suriname. So, Moengo, where is it? And what were the conditions that led to this project?

Marcel Pinas: Moengo is a town in the district of Marowijne. In its early years, the town experienced a huge boom. From the nineteenth century onward, the city was an important trade center. During World War II, Moengo became the epicenter of bauxite extraction in Suriname. In 1943, the United States extracted 60 percent of its required bauxite from Suriname. Shortly thereafter, the company that extracted the bauxite, Alcoa, moved its operations north to the United States. This affected employment and led to an economic decline. A few decades later, the area deteriorated even further because of what is known as the Interior War, which took place from 1986 to 1992 in Moengo and surroundings. This war disrupted the community, leading to social problems that are still felt today. In 2015, the sister company of Alcoa, Suralco (the Suriname Aluminum Company), also left. This led to a decimation of the area's economy and a complete end to the employment that the bauxite industry had offered the community.

AA-K and WM: This is quite a difficult and tragic story, even though it's not unfamiliar. It feels like you are telling the story of many Caribbean and Central and South American states – in fact, of many formerly colonial states, where specific companies that were part of colonialism's extractive economy would leave when their extraction was no longer lucrative, for example because of the loss of cheap labor.

So, you saw a role for art to intervene in this tragic situation, to help the community. Can you tell us a little bit about this? This is your Kibii Foundation.

MP: Yes, this postindustrial city needed a sustainable alternative to the decimated bauxite industry. At the same time, the city needs to solve the societal problems created by the domestic war. The Kibii Foundation was established with the purpose of addressing these economic and social problems through arts and culture. Sustainability is important to the foundation, as are participatory projects done together with the community, with a focus on cultural education for young people from the area. These projects make social themes topics of conversation among young people. In addition, participation in the arts and culture provides support for self-development, so individuals can fashion better selves. This means more confidence in their own artistic talents as young people and growth in their appreciation for their own culture and community. To do this, the Kibii Foundation is committed to a set of objectives, which we achieve through the various projects:

> investment in children and young people;
>
> the use of arts and culture for innovation in Moengo and its surroundings;
>
> the use of the enterprising abilities of artists;
>
> inducing an economic and social impulse;
>
> positioning Moengo as a cultural capital of Suriname; and
>
> giving the past a future through the Kibii Wi Koni Maroon Research Center.

AA-K and WM: Marcel, this is amazing. What kinds of projects do you do? Could you give us a few examples?

MP: It may be hard to choose. Since our establishment in 2009, we have initiated many projects. For example, the Tembe Art Studio is a workplace where children take weekly classes in dance, visual art, and musical expression. The classes are taught by local and international artists. We also have an International Residence Program, and every year we welcome national and international artists who contribute to the expansion of the Art Park Moengo. This is done in collaboration with the local community. We also established the Contemporary Art Museum, Moengo, which has two locations, CAMM I and CAMM II. CAMM I is focused on my nationally renowned body of work. In CAMM II, there are temporary exhibitions of national and international artists. And there are many others. There is the Research Center

Kibii Wi Koni, where we want to study and create an archive of the past, present, and future of the culture of the Maroons and present this knowledge to the widest audience possible. We also have the Train the Trainers guide program to facilitate young talent, and the Free Theater, where we organize free dance and theater performances for the community. And we have our restaurant, Masanga, which offers employment possibilities for eight women from the community. The restaurant also trains young people as catering staff and stimulates local production by working with local products. And the Afaka Guesthouse offers accommodation to artists-in-residence, staff, and tourists. At the same time, it offers employment possibilities to the local community.

Together this wide array of offerings, embedded in the community's values, serves the community's social, intellectual, and, importantly, economic development.

AA-K and WM: Can you say a little bit about how this model of art practice, of the kind of art ecology that so directly serves the interest of the community, emerged?

MP: Most of the Kibii Foundation's activities are based on the needs of the community of Moengo. For example, the Masanga restaurant was needed because my aunty used to cook for me and three other artists at her home. As our art practice expanded, preparing meals for twenty-five or more visitors was impossible for her at home, thus the need was there to start the restaurant. The Masanga guesthouse emerged because the Kibii Foundation started to accommodate trainers, first in houses owned by Suralco. When we could not use these accommodations anymore, we started the guesthouse. The restaurant and the guesthouse are run by local people, with whom the Kibii Foundation serves the community.

AA-K and WM: We have heard about the Moengo Festival. Can you say a little more about this?

MP: Yes. Every year, the Kibii Foundation organizes the Moengo Festival in collaboration with the community and with national and international artists and curators. As part of our commitment to education, young people are actively engaged in the production of the festival. Also, they are offered a stage in the side programming. The theme of the festival switches annually between four disciplines: dance, theater, music, and visual art. With the organization of this festival, the Kibii Foundation wants to induce an impulse in Moengo. At the same time, we strive to achieve a positive view of art (in all its forms) among the Surinamese population. The foundation does this by making various art forms accessible for a large and diverse audience during the festival. With the national and international character of the festival, the Kibii Foundation wants to position Moengo as a cultural capital of Suriname.

AA-K and WM: Marcel, perhaps you can say something about what, in your opinion, has been the main effect of the festival, and of the foundation itself.

MP: The projects now make visible contributions in the field of employment, local entrepreneurship, and cultural tourism from Paramaribo and elsewhere. The Moengo Festival in particular makes an important contribution to the long-term vision of the Kibii Foundation and the realization of its objectives. The earlier editions have taught us that the festival brings an enormous economic and social impact. Eight thousand people visited the closing weekend of the Moengo Festival of Visual Art in 2018, and the community made very active contributions to that success. The Moengo Festival is now a strong concept in Suriname and is also becoming increasingly known in the Netherlands, Belgium, French Guiana, and Brazil. During the last two editions, the cultural tourism around the Moengo Festival became strongly noticeable. The Kibii Foundation owes that to the multicultural organization of the festival.

Less visible but just as important are the long-term effects among young people in the areas of independence, self-development, consciousness of their own artistic talent, and knowledge about their own culture. The Kibii Foundation has seen many youngsters who participated at the festival grow as actors, photographers, musicians, or dancers.

Over the last few years, the Kibii Foundation has received many invitations from international organizations such as the Vrije Universiteit in Brussels, the Musée du quai Branly–Jacques Chirac in Paris, the University of the West Indies in Trinidad, the University of Chicago, Small Axe Projects (for an exhibition in Miami), and Unearte (the national university of the arts) in Venezuela. These organizations consider the projects of the Kibii Foundation to be a great source of inspiration for how art can matter and how the arts can be mobilized to different ends in the service of communities. It is the belief of the Kibii Foundation that sharing experiences and knowledge strengthens every organization. We therefore work hard on building a large, international, and sustainable network.

CHAPTER 13

TRANSFORMATIVE JUSTICE

AN INTERVIEW WITH patricia kaersenhout

Anna Arabindan-Kesson and Wayne Modest

Wayne Modest: Anna and I are interested in rethinking art histories. We are especially focused on rethinking art histories from what one could call a pluriversal perspective, or a perspective that is located within and from the Caribbean. As I tell people, I don't work *on* the Caribbean, I work *from* the Caribbean. I work from the intellectual space that is the Caribbean. The Caribbean demands of us that we think otherwise around some of the concepts that we've come to know. I'm always confounded by the way in which the Caribbean pushes us to think disciplines differently. It is with that framework in mind that we wanted to have this conversation with you, as an artist working with questions that animate our own critical thinking. Those questions are around coloniality, decoloniality, modernity, Blackness, Black modernity, and imagining more equitable and more just planetary futures. We want to have a conversation about everything. And a part of that is to have a little joy together as we think together of undoing and unlearning and relearning histories and disciplines that we've come to know.

Anna Arabindan-Kesson: Wayne's point about working *from* the Caribbean versus working *on* the Caribbean is crucial to the way we've been conceiving what this conversation and, more broadly, what the "Beyond Boundaries" conference can ask us to think through.[1] At the moment, we're facing increasing and urgent calls across academia, museums, and, more broadly, society, for rethinking and for reckoning. Some would describe this moment in terms of growing calls for decolonization. We want to ask you to reflect with us. What role do you see for artists in this moment of reckoning and rethinking? And what role do you see for yourself in your own practice as an artist in this moment?

patricia kaersenhout: I'm thinking a lot recently about what kind of position my work can take in these very violent and complex times. I think it's important that we keep in mind that art institutions and the art world in general are, at their core, capitalist and racist systems. As an artist, I try to navigate a system that I know is highly exclusive. It excludes people, or artists, or certain artists. How can I navigate within that? On the one hand, I am moving around in this contemporaneity. But I do not consider myself a contemporary artist. I am more of an artist who works from a decolonial perspective. I'm working also from ancestrality, which is a very important aspect in my work. Therefore, a lot of the things that I do within these institutions are based on disrupting the space. It already starts when I move with my Black body in these white spaces. That itself is a disruption. I use that disruption within my performances to create moments of discomfort. I think those moments of discomfort are an important starting point for a different conversation.

In the Netherlands, it's still very difficult for people to talk about racism—to really examine the racist structures within their institutions. Even though Dutch institutions are trying to be more inclusive, you hardly see them question their own power structures. They maintain the same power structures, but they want Black people and other people of color to do all the emotional labor to help them become more inclusive, to become more diverse. The whole story is probably similar in the States. I've said many times that the only way those institutions can change is if they make real sacrifices. Transformation comes with pain. It's not an easy path. Everybody wants to maintain their positions. They are not willing to experience the pain of making a sacrifice in order to transform.

This is what I often do with my work. I create moments of transformative justice. That's connected with my ancestrality. I feel that I need to make things right or just for my ancestors, who were involuntarily displaced. I need to use my work to create a form of justice and to disrupt spaces—but always with the thought of bringing people together. It's not only disrupting. It's also looking for ways to connect those different groups and make them have different conversations about painful topics. I think that is an important task that artists can take up in their work. At the same time, the work is protecting you as an artist. You are not literally doing all this emotional labor. The work is sort of protecting you, personally, from doing the work.

WM: I'm very interested in your use of the words "transformative justice" and your work that creates these moments of transformation. In that sense, you are suggesting, then, that a rethought art institution or artistic practice is a project in justice. Is that what you're suggesting? That this can be a project in fashioning more just societies and just futures?

pk: Yes, exactly.

WM: But how would you respond to the critique, which is very common in the Netherlands now, that when artwork does this it is not good art but "only identity politics"?

pk: I haven't figured out the cause of identity politics. Because yes, on the one hand I can see that problems may arise if we speak from identity politics. But on the other hand, I'm also thinking to myself, What is the paradigm through which identity politics are being judged? Because not everybody has the luxury of choice about whether or not to engage with identity politics. For some people it is a form of survival. I haven't figured that one out yet. It's a very difficult threat to balance. I cannot answer that question. I don't know yet.

WM: I must tell you that I am very comfortable with the identity politics that emerged out of Black feminist thought. I'm very comfortable with that kind of politics being urgent and important. [*Laughs*]

pk: I totally agree. But I can also see why certain people problematize things.

AA-K: I was thinking that the point you made about the artwork protecting the artist from emotional labor seems like a key way of navigating this question of identity politics. Particularly in the case of Black diaspora artists working outside of the Western framework, the artwork almost becomes an instantiation of the artist. I love the way you're thinking about the artwork doing that work and being a kind of barrier. It pulls up art historians who are thinking about how art and authorship and agency work. I think that's a powerful point.

I'm also interested in this question of transformation and transformative justice. I wanted to ask you to talk a little bit more about that process of transformation. One of the things I love about your work is how tactile and material it is. It's performance, but it requires an embodied response from viewers. I've noticed this tendency in other artists' work, too. In this moment, there seems to be . . . I don't know if we can call it a turn, but an interest in what the materiality of an artwork does to create embodied responses in an audience. I wonder if you could talk about how you think about process and materiality in this form of transformation.

pk: Thank you; this is a wonderful question. I work with different materials because the material I use is not merely an artistic device. It also comments on the themes of the work. For example, I recently worked with glass, which is quite a new material for me. Glass is a very mysterious material because it's not really solid, but at the same time it's also not fluid when it's cooled down. It's a very complex material. Glass stood for me as a symbol of opacity and transparency. As the poet Édouard Glissant wrote, Black people have their "right to opacity."[2] That caught my interest. Then I worked further on this and decided that if Black people have the right to opacity, then white people, who are the colonizers who created so much violence and destruction, do not have that right to be opaque. They should be completely transparent.

I took a couple of generals from the Dutch colonial army who are still seen as heroes and had them produced in glass. Then I had the heads exploded. The explosion was filmed in very slow motion, so it almost became like a magical sight, all this glass slowly floating through the air. It almost became like stars, or as if there was something happening in the universe, while they were exploding. While the audiences were looking at these explosions, they were protected by flowers and plants made of glass. Those flowers and plants are very important within the Caribbean tradition because they protected runaway slaves. While the audience is looking at this violence, at these explosions, they are protected by flowers. While everybody is watching, you hear a text from Shakespeare: "What a piece of work is a man, how noble in reason, how infinite in faculties, in form and moving how express and admirable; in action how like an angel, in apprehension how like a god: the beauty of the world, the paragon of animals—and yet, to me, what is this quintessence of dust? Man delights not me."[3] It's Hamlet. It's a very existential text about what it means to be a human being. I like to connect those different realities. These stories come together to create this new story. That's a form of transformation already. I am transforming the meaning of a very old text by Shakespeare. I am transforming the meaning of glass in relation to coloniality and spiritually. It's also about protection—and protecting one another.

There was an art historian who called it a work of iconoclasm. Yes, but not in the European definition of iconoclasm, because that's a practice of total destruction. What I am doing is not destruction. I am transforming something. While I'm transforming it, negative energy is released so that a new and positive and healing energy can emerge. Healing is also a very important aspect in my work.

WM: I see a relationship between destruction and transformation, as you've described it, and the idea of the abolition of institutions. Abolition is a kind of destruction, but also a way of thinking anew about what the institution can be. Before we go into this, I want to invite you to think about another material that you use: salt. Salt appears in the work of the Trinidadian author Earl Lovelace and in Rastafarian cosmology. Salt references return, about flight—or, actually, it prohibits return. This idea comes back in Toni Morrison's work, I think in *Song of Solomon* [1997]. Perhaps you could tell us a little bit more about why you've chosen to work with salt. For example, many people do not know that salt was a part of the colonial economy of the Netherlands. Why salt?

pk: I came across this Caribbean legend in which enslaved people refrained from eating salt, thinking they would become lighter and they could fly back to Africa. For me, this story was also a metaphor for the power of imagination while being held captive—the idea that you can always think yourself free. That is what a lot of enslaved people did. Many people forget that enslaved people used their imaginations to survive harsh circumstances. In my artwork *The Soul of Salt* [2016/24], I had around eight thousand kilos of salt placed in different locations. For me, it's always important to look at the locality where my artwork will be installed. Where is the salt placed? And what is the local history of that place? When I was showing the work in Palermo, it was at the time we faced a huge humanitarian crisis concerning refugees from sub-Saharan countries who were drowning—literally drowning—in the Mediterranean. I had salt from the Mediterranean and placed it in a palazzo. I contacted a local refugee center and invited local refugee girls to sing the song "Many Thousand Gone" during the opening performance. There was a Winti priest—for those who don't know, Winti is an Indigenous religion from Suriname—who blessed the salt mountain. After the mountain was blessed, people could take a little bit of the salt home and dissolve it in water as a symbol of the pain of the past.

It was a very magical moment in Palermo. Italy had rejected a ship with a couple hundred refugees at its border. When we did the performance, the ship was entering Spain, where the refugees were allowed to disembark. I'm a very spiritual person, and I really believe that while we were doing this performance, there was a direct relation—ancestral relationship—between what we were doing and what was happening just a couple hundred kilometers away.

Two years ago, I did the same installation, but with salt from the salt plains of Bonaire. As you might know, Bonaire is a part of the Dutch Caribbean. There is a kind of neocolonialism taking place there. It was at its worst during the pandemic, because the Dutch government refused to help the people of Bonaire. They were given money, but the conditions under which they received that money, which they needed to survive, were ridiculous. The Dutch can move freely and can live in Bonaire; they receive financial aid while the local people are living in poverty. It's horrible. I arranged the salt mountain from the salt plains of Bonaire in the Bonnefanten Museum in Maastricht, the Netherlands. I invited the Dutch Bonairean Society to come to the museum and to give an opening performance. I always make sure that audiences that come to the museum can participate in helping activists. In this project, I made handkerchiefs printed with text. The audiences could buy the handkerchiefs, and the proceeds went to Bonaire to help activists I knew there. This is a way of connecting different people and different histories. Even though some of the art audiences might be complicit, consciously or subconsciously, [in injustice enacted by the Dutch government,] somehow, by buying those handkerchiefs, they become connected with the activists in Bonaire. Again, it's a form of transformative justice.

AA-K: Your point about the difference between iconoclasm and transformation, particularly in the ways those terms are used in art histories, is a way of pulling up what becomes de rigueur in art history. "Iconoclasm" is often a sexy term. It's used to talk about tearing things down. I think you're right, though. It doesn't often take us to the next step, which is to reimagine. It has also become a term used in the current calls for tearing statues down. But what I think is often missed in those conversations is the history of these moments of calling for decolonization, and the ways *that* work is tied to reimagining. I'm wondering if what you're doing here in making us aware of our history—in illuminating the limits of what some of this deconstruction can do—is connected to how you're thinking from the Caribbean. In other words, is this form of transformation—which is both a form of deconstruction but also one of renewal—something that you think of as emerging from your position in relation to the Caribbean?

pk: Yes, I think so. The Caribbean itself is such a beautifully hybrid, complex, multilayered group of islands. It's also still a beautiful mystery. It's important that this so-called destruction—of course, it's not really destruction, but a transformation—is also an act of healing. I really believe that. I spoke to activists from the #RhodesMustFall movement [in South Africa], and I said to them, "Instead of tearing Cecil Rhodes down, wouldn't it be interesting if everybody got tools to transform that sculpture together and release its negative energy?" While you are doing that act of transforming together, it's also an act of healing.

In that context, I can speak of my own Caribbean background. I'm very reluctant to speak of "the Caribbean," because the Caribbean has so many different layers, and so many different local histories. I can only speak from my own Surinamese background, where healing is always connected to being with the ancestors. When somebody dies, there is a whole process of being together, mourning together, grieving together, and supporting each other so that, after a period of time, you can continue with your life after loss. There are very beautiful rituals within Surinamese culture. Healing is almost always an intrinsic part of daily life.

I must say that, for me, the realization of being part of a Caribbean history came quite late, in 2009. I was introduced to the Wakaman group with Remy Jungerman, Charl Landvreugd, Marcel Pinas, Iris Kensmil, and Kurt Nahar. We were Surinamese artists in the Netherlands and in Suriname, connected and working together. That was the first moment when we decided to turn our back to the Netherlands. Suriname has a very particular position in South America, because it's the only country in South America where people still speak Dutch. A lot of Dutch culture is still experienced in society and in daily life. We decided to turn our back to the Netherlands and face the Caribbean and say to each other, "We are more Caribbean artists than Dutch Surinamese artists." For me, this was a whole different way of looking at my own work and my own position as an artist. That said, I cannot deny the fact that I was brought up within a Western European culture. That aspect of my upbringing also influences my thinking.

The shift to face the Caribbean came from the realization that the Caribbean was a bridge that covered the colonial gap. Being a child of double migration is a complex position. My parents are descendants of enslaved people who then migrated to the Netherlands. I was born in the Netherlands. It's very complex being Dutch Surinamese in the Netherlands. There is always what I call the colonial gap. You do not really belong there, but you also do not really belong here. The Caribbean was, for me, the bridge. The realization of being Caribbean became the bridge between those two worlds.

WM: Thank you, patricia. I came to the Netherlands in 2010, right after your realization about the Caribbean. I was coming from the British colonial context and trying to find what was Caribbean about the Caribbean. What are its specificities? What are its differences? I was looking at the Caribbean intellectual tradition and wondering which Dutch intellectual I could think about as part of what could be described as the canonical thinkers. I recently worked on a special section for the journal *Small Axe* about Anton de Kom and just participated in a special section looking at the works of Hermine and Otto Huiswoud.[4] The idea is to bring the Dutch Caribbean intellectual tradition into dialogue with all the ongoing work from and about the Spanish, French, and English Caribbean.

I still want to go back to this idea of deconstruction. I don't come from the art museum field. I come from what we call the field of ethnographic or world cultures museums. An amazing decolonial activist, Sumaya Kassim, wrote a striking article recently; it was titled "The Museum Will Not Be Decolonized."[5] That article lodged a critique of the museum institution and its inability to shift. How and what might we do? What, for you, is the next step that institutions need to take? By institution, I mean the museum but also the field of art history. What would you say is necessary right now for us to make this step after a long history of conversation around decoloniality? Where do we go next?

pk: I have very radical thoughts about that. [*Laughs*] I think that museums should literally be torn down. I really think that. The sites where they stood should be spiritually cleansed and healed. From there, we can start a completely different conversation about whether we really need those institutions in our societies. Can we build something new together, something based on total equality and love? Let's not forget love. The proper democratic way. Not the way the West made democracy—or maybe I should refer to "assemblies." I think that's a more accurate word. Of course, that's not going to happen. [*All laugh*]

WM: Exactly. [*Laughs*] Until then, what do we do?

pk: I keep on saying that the power structures within the museum should be seriously questioned and changed. As long as those power structures are not acknowledged, then you can do whatever you want to do. You can make wonderful exhibitions and have amazing conversations, but if those systems of oppression and power structures are still maintained within that museum, then it's not really going to change.

AA-K: I think this is wonderful. Unfortunately, it's not going to happen, but I also wish it would. I feel like one of the reasons that we have museums is because of the discipline of art history. What you're talking about is a completely different way of approaching art. I'm wondering, then, how should we be writing as art historians? How would you tell us to write differently? Or in a way that would allow this different kind of accessibility or engagement?

WM: Or even love.

AA-K: Yeah, approaching it with love and joy.

pk: I think that the importance of love, joy, and celebration is often overlooked. I'm not an art historian. I'm not a scientist. I'm a person who works from my heart and my feelings and my intuition. But I think it's important to always question yourself and what you write and never see what you write as the absolute truth—to understand that it's always open for critique or new interpretations or doubts, even. I read a lot of texts from art historians. I'm always amazed by the lack of doubt. Western art history is so self-assured. Writers are so confident about their own ideas of what the world should be, what art should be, the aesthetics of art, and how art should look. I wish that there was a little bit more insecurity and vulnerability—particularly vulnerability. I really miss vulnerability in a lot of texts that I'm reading. It would be interesting to change that.

I also think that it's okay to write a text and at the same time question yourself or admit that you do not know everything—that you question things or that you doubt things. I'm really talking about Western European art history as I know it. It has so many blind spots. What do you do about your blind spots as writer or as an art historian? How can you open your mind and properly do research on your own blind spots? That's very difficult because your blind spot is probably about what your blind spots are, if you know what I mean. [*Laughs*]

WM: Your work also gives us a lot of clues. I like the idea of vulnerability. I had been working, some time ago, with the idea that every piece of writing is a piece of writing shame. This is from an article that I read a while ago on affect theory and the speculative or the doubtful.[6] In your work, and your own description earlier of art history's link with a colonial genealogy, I appreciate this stubborn insistence that one attend to the question of the spiritual. I think that the work of emotion and the spiritual is important.

There's something else that I see in your work. You name it "ancestrality." In your work *Guess Who's Coming to Dinner Too?* [2017/23], I see ancestrality in terms of honoring generations of feminist practice. How do you, as an artist, relate to that kind of generational thinking? Or generational honoring? Or even an ethical citational practice, one of care?

pk: Thank you for that beautiful question, Wayne. I come from a tradition where the elders are always honored. People who are from your preceding generations will at a certain point become elders. In the West, people only become older. There is a difference between becoming older and becoming an elder. To me, it's important to honor the elders. I consider a lot of the women at the table in *Guess Who's Coming to Dinner Too?* as my elders. They are not literally my elders, but they are elders who did something for the world and from whom I gained knowledge. Because of what they did, they brought me further, they helped me. From what I could read about them, I felt the need to honor them. A lot of these women are also literally erased by the colonizer. Their bodies are literally destroyed. If you read the stories about many of the women, such a perversion of violence has been imposed upon their bodies. That was, for me, also an important reason to honor them at the table. When I did the research for the project, I was often in shock. We tend to forget the many acts of violence that have been imposed on the Black female body—of course, also on the Black male body, but we tend to forget the Black female body, even today. I wanted to bring that to attention. It felt very important to show a long history of Black female liberation struggle.

The table is a citation but also a comment on the famous work by Judy Chicago, *The Dinner Party* [1979], now permanently exhibited at the Brooklyn Museum in New York. Predominantly, white women got a seat at her table. She had a couple of Black women and women of color at the table. I think there are three in total. Every woman at the table is represented by a plate, and on that plate there is a visualization of their vulva. It's celebrating female sexuality, except for the Black woman, Sojourner Truth, which is interesting—as if Black women do not have sexuality or it is difficult to talk about their sexuality. It was very complex for me, so I thought, "Okay, I need to change something here, I need to give a comment that comes from a Black aesthetics." My piece is commenting on Chicago's table, but it's also moving away from it, because otherwise the discussion will always compare *Guess Who's Coming to Diner Too?* to *The Dinner Party*.

Four museums decided to buy the table jointly. It has become a completely different story with its own Black history, a Black female history, with its own Black aesthetics. The table is still active. It's not a static installation. Every time the table gets exhibited, the museums need to do their work to approach different communities and invite them into the museum and to work on the table to do the embroidery on the table runners. This is a way of creating a communal body but also of forcing the museum to connect itself with different communities that it would normally never connect with. That was one of the conditions I included. I wrote a fifty-page protocol about how to activate the table. The table can only be exhibited if it's activated. Otherwise, they are not allowed to exhibit it.

WM: From a museum's perspective, that's a nightmare. Thank you! [*Laughs*]

pk: I know! [*Laughs*]

AA-K: It's a disruption.

pk: Earlier you asked, "What can museums do to transform?" Well, this is my modest contribution to help them transform a little bit. They need to do their homework before they can exhibit the table. To date, they've been doing it.

AA-K: I love how this work also disrupts the art historical idea of influence and referentiality, which is always about the genealogy of style or being able to connect an artist to an Old Master. As you say, Wayne, this is a different kind of citation that creates a relationship. It also goes back to what you were saying at the beginning about disruption and transformation and how, through this embodied response, audiences can come into community in new ways. It's beautiful.

pk: I started this whole project in one the poorest areas of the Netherlands. A lot of women, particularly from North African countries, lived there in complete isolation. The project became a way to connect those women with women who lived in a domestic violence shelter, as well as with more privileged women. I feel like it's important that women come together and listen to each other's stories. In the Netherlands, as you know Wayne, we have a very separate society. "Apartheid" is a Dutch word. There are not many communities that connect with one another and know about each other's lives. I wanted to connect these different women, because once you are connected and once you get to know each other's stories, it creates understanding and, hopefully, empathy. When you can create understanding and empathy, hopefully something can change within society.

For a long time, my position as an artist connected me to the center of the city—where predominantly white, rich, privileged people live—and to the marginalized part of Amsterdam. It allowed me to be in-between, connecting these two worlds with each other. Sometimes it was literally connecting and bringing these groups together. But sometimes I did it with money. I knew how to get funding or subsidies from the center and made sure that part of the money went to marginalized people. That position has changed a little bit, because I'm now partially living in France. When you're busy with transformation, it is inevitable that you yourself also transform! [*Laughs*]

WM: You've taken us through a lot: not only your engagement with materiality and what materiality helps us to understand, but also the practices of togetherness that you've described as an important part of how you want to inaugurate a different kind of world. You demand that our institutions change in ways that open up horizons of justice—what you call "transformational justice." There is a certain idea of abolition as justice in your work. When we invited you to the Clark conference in 2022, you said to us it might not be possible to come because one must care for the planet. But you didn't have to travel to be a part of it. We wanted to open that space [by organizing this prerecorded conversation].

What is the one thing that you want us to take with us as we try to rethink and reckon with the troublesome space that art history and art institutions are in right now? What would you want to leave with us with?

pk: Within the context of colonialism and relationality, I think it's important that we start to realize that everything is connected. You cannot talk about art and not be busy with climate justice. You cannot talk about race and not be busy with gender and climate and poverty. Everything is connected. This is maybe a hopeful change, because as more and more people start to realize that everything is connected, more and more people will start to realize that the problems we have are a direct consequence of the project of colonial modernity. Everything is connected.

AA-K: Thank you so much, patricia, that was beautiful.

WM: In a Rastafarian way, I want to leave, patricia, by reiterating your call to love. So, "blessed love." Thank you.

NOTES

1. This conversation was conducted and recorded in advance of a conference, titled "Beyond Boundaries: Seeing Art History from the Caribbean," held at the Clark Art Institute in Williamstown, Massachusetts, October 20–21, 2022. Participants were invited to view the recording, which is available online at https://www.clarkart.edu/Research-Academic/RAP-Events/Clark-Conference-2022/Artist-Conversations, in preparation for one of the sessions.

2. For more on Glissant's notion of the right to opacity, see Édouard Glissant, *Caribbean Discourse: Selected Essays* (University of Virginia Press, 1989). See also Édouard Glissant, *Poetics of Relation* (University of Michigan Press, 2024).

3. William Shakespeare, *A Midsummer Night's Dream*, ed. Barbara Mowat et al. (Folger Shakespeare Library, n.d.), accessed September 4, 2025, https://www.folger.edu/explore/shakespeares-works/a-midsummer-nights-dream/.

4. Wayne Modest and Susan Legêne, "Other Radicals: Anton de Kom and the Caribbean Intellectual Tradition," *Small Axe* 27, no. 1 (2023): 52–58; and Wayne Modest, "Introduction: Public Secrets and the Archives of Black Internationalism," *Small Axe* 28, no. 3 (2024): 83–86.

5. Sumaya Kassim, "The Museum Will Not Be Decolonized," *Media Diversified*, November 11, 2017, https://mediadiversified.org/2017/11/15/the-museum-will-not-be-decolonised/.

6. Elspeth Probyn, "Writing Shame," in *The Affect Theory Reader*, ed. Gregory J. Seigworth and Melissa Gregg (Duke University Press, 2010), 71–92.

CHAPTER 14

ATLANTIC TRANSFORMERZ AND ARTS INFRASTRUCTURE

AN INTERVIEW WITH CHARL LANDVREUGD

Wayne Modest

Wayne Modest: Charl, as you are well aware, the last few years have seen growing challenges to art infrastructures from diverse quarters, whether it is activists pushing for decolonization or the demands for ethnographic museums to address their colonial pasts and answer questions of ownership and restitution or about the diversity of their collections. Across Europe and North America, students are demanding different curricula, especially a different kind of art survey course in their introductory years. It is within this shifting terrain that we want to consider how thinking *from* and *with* the Caribbean may push us to imagine other kinds of futures for the art world. But before we go there, I wondered if we could invite you to say something about your own practice as an artist, as a curator, and as a team member in museum senior management. What would you say is the current state of art history and the art world more generally?

Charl Landvreugd: [*Laughs*] This is such a big set of questions, and there is so much to say. So, in addition to my art practice, I now work at the Stedelijk Museum, in Amsterdam, as head of research and curatorial practice. In fact, this takes up most of my time. For an institution like the Stedelijk, one of the largest museums of modern and contemporary art and design in the Netherlands, we can think about the collection in two parts. The first part, let us say, is addressed to the long twentieth century; the second is more contemporary. Well, *contemporary* may not be the right word. Perhaps it's more precise to say the part of the collection acquired since 2000 or 2001; perhaps we can even use 9/11 as the dividing line. Why do I propose this? Because I believe that, from a curatorial standpoint, this long twentieth century requires a different kind of work, or a very different way of thinking, as compared to what is happening today. If we look at the high modernist period, let's say the 1950s, '60s, and '70s, for example, there is so much discourse already produced around this period. So much has already been said.

Sometimes I even wonder what else is there to say, or whether it is useful to keep on adding more to this history.

Today, artists create work—and approach their work—differently. It comes from a different place than this older, romantic idea we had about the artist as individual genius. I reckon that today the artist is more like a social genius, someone who is more capable or more willing to be engaged in what is going on in a society. This requires a different view, or understanding of, art production. If we look at the todayness of art—I don't want to use the word "contemporary," because I'm not sure it's the right word—then we need to create or rethink the parameters of art, of good art, and of what art does. Where does art start and end? Where does social practice start and end?

Of course, these kinds of questions were also being asked in the twentieth century. But there is, I would say, something different now, especially as this kind of work is also being done by a lot of Black and Brown artists—work that comes from a social positioning, perhaps a social awareness. What we are seeing in the Netherlands is that this kind of practice has grown significantly, especially around questions of ethics and aesthetics. Of course, the question of ethics has long animated artists. However, today, at least in the Netherlands, because it is being done by Black and Brown people, I see this as a change. And because these artists are raising these questions, this change can be seen as a problem. So, going back to my first point: By making an (artificial) divide between, let's say, the long twentieth century and now, we can start thinking through or creating new theoretical frameworks to understand what we are looking at today. They draw on strong modernist paradigms, but you could call them deviant. Perhaps this isn't the right word to use, but it is the word that comes to me right now.

WM: Well, I am fine with the word "deviant." Can I ask you, though, are you suggesting we forget this "long twentieth century"? I am not sure about this.

CL: Not forget it.

WM: Okay, if not forget, I want to push back or push further this idea about the period being over-theorized. While I understand this suggestion, I still want to ask about how the Caribbean fits within this. Does it feature in this theorization? Or are you saying that there is no greater analytical yield that we can gain by retraining our lenses on that period from the perspective of the Caribbean?

CL: This is a difficult question. And this brings me basically back to my education, to my studies at Columbia University with Kelly Jones and David Scott, which has informed my thinking about this. First, I want to say a few things about the

Caribbean. My focus is often on the Caribbean from a European perspective. So, the Caribbean in the European. Second, when we look at the Caribbean, we need to acknowledge that it comprises very different spaces. In a sense, it's akin to Europe, with many different languages and many different cultures. Anyway, the argument is often made—which I agree with—that the Caribbean is like a blueprint for the world we live in today. It is a blueprint for a changing Europe, even for a Black European identity. We have spoken about this before.[1] I take the hybridity of the region as a jumping-off point. But it is much more than that; it is like a mixture of mixtures. For me, the Caribbean is a model to think with. It is a model for thinking about art created from a different space, from another "original" that isn't just a derivative of what we already know.

WM: Okay. I will come back to this later, as I like this idea of another "original" or, I would say, another "originary." But I am also interested in role of the institution. You work with just such an institution, which staged two shows recently that were about or engaged with the Caribbean: *Surinamese School: Painting from Paramaribo to Amsterdam* [2020–21] and *Felix de Rooy: Apocalypse* [2023].[2] Both of these shows dealt with the nineteenth and twentieth centuries, a period you suggest has been overtheorized. Both were about the Caribbean. So, what was it that you were trying to do with these shows?

CL: Well, if we are talking about changes in the art scene and in how artists work today, the institution's desired outcome of the *Surinamese School* exhibition was not just the show itself, but also the acquisitions we made as a result of it. It was a prominent part of our collection and display agenda, yes, but also our publication agenda. What we intended to do—and this is the director's vision—is a big show every year with an artist who has been excluded or whose work was never recorded or collected by the art establishment. So, we did the show with Remy Jungerman, then we did Felix de Rooy, and then Ellen Gallagher. And we will continue this. So, when I came in, it was important to see how we can acknowledge the colonial and migrant-worker histories of the Netherlands. For an institution like the Stedelijk, it is important to acknowledge these dynamics as part of Dutch identity formation. The acknowledgement of all these groups of people as part of the Netherlands is important to me. So I advocated for it. But this acknowledgement has consequences for how we work. To give an example: We made several acquisitions from the *Surinamese School* exhibition, as well as from Felix de Rooy. And not just his work but also that of the artists he pointed us to. The strategy here, as I see it, is to build anchors into our twentieth-century collections, so that, after us, when works by other artists from a similar position or place are bought, there is a lineage for how their works are seen, a relation to others.

WM: This makes sense. It is framing their work in a longer history, in larger concerns. It's a kind of historically contingent way of collecting, creating a genealogy that is currently not there.

CL: Yes, what interests me is the need to locate work within a genealogy of collecting. The problem with the Felix de Rooy exhibition, for example, was that there is not enough knowledge in the Netherlands about his work, not enough scholarship, but also not enough knowledge within the museum.

WM: But if I remember correctly, Willem Sandberg, a previous and well-known director of the Stedelijk from 1945 to 1963, had already collected art from the Caribbean, right?

CL: Already in the 1950s.

WM: From the Dutch Caribbean islands and from Suriname, right?

CL: Dutch Caribbean and Haiti, yes. But when we look at the visual language that interested Sandberg, we could describe this as a more narrowly modernist one, the modernist canon. Well, if you look at the visual language of Felix de Rooy, or other artists like him, there is no precedent for that in our collection.

WM: Okay. Are you suggesting that Sandberg was trying to basically conscript the Caribbean into modernism, or a specific idea about modernism?[3]

CL: Exactly. When you look more specifically at Remy Jungerman, for example, you see what I am saying. He can be more easily located within a frame of modernism, even a frame of European modernism, right? Felix de Rooy, on the other hand, I would say, is more specifically a Caribbean modernist. It's a different kind of modernism. To make this happen, to help frame it properly, I asked the Belgian Jamaican art historian and curator Veerle Poupeye to write an essay that frames De Rooy's work within a broader Caribbean tradition.[4]

WM: Okay. But when I read the text in Felix's show, it felt to me that you were trying to locate Felix's work within a narrative of "global art history." Am I correct?

CL: I'm not sure about that. I was trying to avoid forcing him into a kind of global art history. But this is the first time we recognized him and his work in the Stedelijk Museum.

WM: Okay. Say more.

CL: I was trying to avoid exceptionalism and a self-congratulatory mode of speaking about his work. What I liked about the exhibition with Felix is that when you visited his house, it contained a collection of his own works but also what we would call ethnographic works, things that he had acquired. This became the basis for the show. It was not a solo show about his work in any conventional sense. It was an expression of his world, of the genius of the person as a whole—and here I do not mean the genius artist. I didn't feel it to be a classical retrospective: "Oh, let's look at all the great paintings that Felix made." It was, instead, "Let's look at Felix as a phenomenon, as someone who did all these different things: made films, collaborated with many artists." And collaboration was an important part of his practice. Even if the people who came understood it as a retrospective exhibition, it wasn't that; it was an exhibition about a phenomenon.

WM: Right. Working in the kind of museum that I do, I can appreciate your use of the concept of Felix's worlds. Reflecting on the exhibition with this in mind, I can see what you mean: his making worlds, or his practice of or as world making.

CL: And that was the only way to go about it, because we lack the kinds of scholarship needed to understand why certain works are important. And what I am arguing is that this may be a broader concern if we are to address the works of artists like Felix in our museums.

WM: And why do you think this is needed? What kind of scholarship is needed to understand Felix's work, to understand other artists like Felix?

CL: If we made this exhibition in the Caribbean, there would be a context within which to understand the work, a scholarly tradition within which we can embed the work. As I mentioned earlier, I felt that I needed to get some of that scholarship into what we do; thus, the article from Veerle Poupeye, which explored Felix's visual art, his films, his theater. This, for me, was important. There are a lot of younger Black and Brown artists, artists of color, in the Netherlands who see Félix as their . . . how would they say it? What's the word I'm looking for?

WM: Hero? A mentor?

CL: Yeah. He's like the original gangster. He's the guy. He was one of the first to open galleries, to have big shows, to talk about Blackness. He did that. He broke ground so that what is happening today can happen, whether in theater or in art.

And, still, modern and contemporary art institutions had not acknowledged his work. So we needed to do this.

WM: This is an important point for the publication where this conversation will appear. Because we are interested in asking: What might attending to Félix and his work do for rethinking art history? And we could go further to ask the same of Remy Jungerman, or Iris Kensmil. Ellen Gallagher has been included in your vision. Is she Caribbean or American?

CL: She's American.

WM: And the exhibition, the *Surinamese School*? What would you say that such an exhibition asks of us in terms of rethinking art history?

CL: I'm not sure I understand the question.

WM: In your answers you have tried to make an important distinction between Remy and Felix. One, according to you, is more explicitly a Caribbean modernist, while the other is working within a European modernist model, even if from and addressing Caribbean themes. Right? But by training your eyes on these two artists, or the artists in the *Surinamese School* exhibition, what do you think is being said through these artists, through their works, that we wouldn't have gotten from elsewhere? What I am trying to say is, What does being positioned from the Caribbean allow or not allow in the rethinking of the canon of (Dutch) art history? And, of course, the answer could be that it allows nothing.

CL: I'm not sure if . . .

WM: Is it for you only about showing the works of artists who have not been recognized?

CL: No, it's not only about that. In fact, this raises an important issue. Our director, Rein Wolfs, has been here for three, three and a half years. In two and a half years he will be retiring. He's leaving in 2027, because he will be at a pensionable age. Rein is serious about what he wants to do with the museum and, especially, about diversifying the collections. Two and a half years is not a lot of time to make the changes we would like to. So we are pushing this agenda. At the same time, however, we are noticing a kind of "diversity fatigue" in the art world.

WM: Yes, I can understand what you mean. So what is your strategy?

CL: To be honest, we expected the diversity fatigue to come. I have to say this "diversity wave" lasted longer than I thought it would. So I'm quite happy with what it has already allowed. But for us this is not a fad, a fashion, and we are trying to secure positions, to change the system within the time frame that is available.

WM: You're saying, therefore, that the strategy is to consciously include artists whose works have not been shown or collected before and anchor them in the system. Is that correct?

CL: What we are trying to do is make sure that, in the available time frame, there is an established history of showing and collecting the works of "diverse" artists for the future museum, and to embed this work into future art histories. I feel the need to create a situation that makes it logical to continue working with, and collecting the works of, Black and Brown artists in the future, because they are already part of the system. Within the curatorial practice framework, I'm not interested in giving a show to an artist simply because they're Black. That's not the game. That's boring. How do you, as much as possible, reshape the system so that it stays changed? People say, "Yeah, open doors." I'm not here to open doors. I am here to make sure that the door stays open. So, yes, the Caribbean is here. I am ready to move on and think about Morocco and about Turkey. My goal is to make sure that all the major migrant groups in the Netherlands that have not found proper representation in the modern and contemporary art museum are, in a way, anchored in that system, so that when this group of curators leave, there's a logical continuation of that process. It is Rein Wolf's policy to spend 50 percent of our acquisitions budget on artists with non-Western backgrounds, artists marginalized by traditional art histories and the art system. This includes other marginalized groups beyond the Caribbean, including women. The year before last, we succeeded when more than 55 percent of the works we acquired were by women artists. This year, it was 48 percent. Establishing such a quota is not just symbolic; it helps to shift the way curators think about their acquisitions and exhibitions.

WM: In principle, what you are describing is a form of infrastructural decolonization. This is not simply about diversity. It is about the infrastructural change that needs to happen so that things become systemic. Yes?

CL: And that's the work. That's what I'm trying to do. So, why am I telling you this? We need strategy. With every exhibition that we make in house, I ask the curator, "With whom do you want to talk about this exhibition?" And then we talk to these people. This brings in other perspectives. Collecting is part also part of this strategy.

WM: I have experienced this. Vincent van Velsen invited me to be in conversation with him about the exhibition the museum did on the work of Ellen Gallagher.

CL: Yeah, this is part of the strategy. We provide the kinds of context needed through publications. It is about a particular kind of commitment to shifting how we work, about including external voices in what we do, about anchoring diversity in our work. Doing this helps to shift the mechanism of the museum and how it works.

WM: In a way, this is one of the questions that we were going to ask—about the growing conversation around the diversity or decolonization of art (historical) perspectives and the role that the Caribbean can play in such discussions. You have already answered this in part. Is what you're saying that your concern is not so much with the Caribbean?

CL: This is part of our conversation published in *Small Axe* some time ago.[5] Then, I said that I wanted the museum to be Caribbean, right? I wanted it to be Surinamese. Let me put it differently. When I was studying in the United States, I remember thinking that everybody was kind of obsessed with African art, yet nobody talked about the art from people of African descent who live in Europe. It was Okwui Enwezor, when I spoke to him about it, who said that this was something that I was to address, not others. I guess he was saying that I had to fix it. So, for me, one question is, Where does the Caribbean stop, and where does Caribbeanness in Europe begin? What is the relationship between Caribbeanness and Europeanness? I hope this question makes sense. When you look at a country like the Netherlands, there are a lot of Black Caribbean people but also a lot of Black people from across the African continent. All have different interests, different ways of seeing the world, different sensibilities. And together they produce a kind of "Africanness." Of course, we can see this as a community, though it's not singular; it has many internal differences. But, as I said earlier, I think the Caribbean can provide a kind of template to Europe for how to live together with difference. But where, then, does this Caribbean begin or end? Is it in the geographic space of the region, or is it also in Europe? For me, a lot of Caribbean things, Caribbean ways of seeing, Caribbean ways of living, Caribbean ways of expressing oneself, are intricately part of Dutch culture today. Do we call this Caribbean? Do we want to call it European? What is it? This remains a tricky question.

WM: Okay. Perhaps we can turn a little to your work as an artist and the relationship between your artistic practice and your curatorial work. Perhaps this can help us find answers to this tricky question. And, drawing on your presentation at the "Beyond Boundaries" conference, I want to talk more about your *Atlantic Transformerz* series.[6] But let's start more generally and speak about your art practice and its relation to you as a dancer. What is the relationship between your work as an artist and your work in the art institution?

CL: Early in my career, I had no relationship with the art institution.

WM: So how did you think about the (art) institution, or institutions more generally, in relation to your creative practice?

CL: When I was an undergraduate, I had a tutor who was Japanese. I remember him saying that the artwork is not that important; it is only a snapshot. It's a Polaroid of your thinking at that moment. And he made me understand very early on that the actual artwork is the lifelong commitment to a set of questions, to a practice, to an idea. This is how I see the works that I have made to date. Similarly, the medium isn't that important for me. Sometimes it can be photography, sometimes it can be writing, sometimes it can be an interview, because it's a continuation of a thought or an exploration of an idea. I approach it from many angles, through many materials. So, I was never in a hurry to be part of an institution, or to have my work shown in an institution or bought by an institution. I was interested in my questions. For me, then, at the end of the day, it's not about the individual works. It's about, if you have a fifty-year-long practice, what it does as a whole. What does it produce in the world?

WM: And when you started to do that, what were some of the questions, the ideas that animated your practice?

CL: There were many. I remember talking to friend as an undergraduate at Goldsmiths, University of London, about what position to take in the landscape. I thought about the Black queer artist position but thought it may have been too exploitative of myself and my own identity. The other big issue that I came to in those years was the question of Blackness, and especially Blackness within the Netherlands, within Europe. I was really looking at what it means to be Black Dutch. For me, this question could be understood in many ways; I was just trying to figure it out. In school, I was making these very pristine, highly polished plaster forms. At the group critique, my peers basically said that they looked like fetishes. I didn't get it, because they were abstract geometric forms. "How can they look like fetishes?" I asked. This happened twice; I was really upset. So, in an act of rebellion, I started making everything black. I was like, "You want fetishes, you're going to get fetishes." That was a turning point, in my first year, when I started making everything black. Everything. And at that moment, I started asking questions about what this blackness/Blackness meant in all its different forms: as a material, as a color, as a construct, and so on.

WM: You said that this was tied to what you felt, at the time, to be an inability to engage with or to understand what Blackness meant within the Dutch or European context, right?

CL: Yes. But, for me, at the time, it wasn't just a sociological question. It was a question of material. What is this black material that I connected to personhood? It was also a way for me to understand that so many different shades of black exist. And when you come to understand this, then you can connect it to the expectation of Blackness by non-Black people; they sometime see Blackness as a monolithic thing. This would have far-reaching effects on me. When I was writing my dissertation, I remember one paragraph taking me a month to write because it was so difficult. The difficulty was in accepting that there were forms of Blackness that were not seen or not accepted as Black.

WM: Can you say a little bit more about this?

CL: I'm talking about where I wrote that I am a European Black person. This meant that who I am is constituted through many of the same cultural references, the same mechanisms, as my white counterparts.

WM: Okay. And what do you mean this to say?

CL: First, because Blackness is never taken to mean European. But also I am convinced that being Black in a European context means something—it is different. I know that many American colleagues would disagree with me; some of them have accused me of acting white. For me, this has nothing to do with acting white; for me, it is a Blackness that is being misunderstood.

WM: So, for you, there is a specific struggle of being Black and European?

CL: Yes. There is often a particular idea of what Blackness ought to be, which is not what I see here in Europe.

WM: But is that the same for people of Somali descent, or Eritrean or Ethiopian descent, living in the Netherlands? Or is this something that is more oriented toward the Caribbean? Some would say that it is the Caribbean notion of Blackness, which sometimes aligns more with certain discourses on Blackness, that dominates what Blackness is in the Netherlands.

CL: There is the Caribbean Blackness that I am talking about. And perhaps I can't even speak of Caribbean Blackness. I can speak about Surinamese Blackness. And there is American Blackness. But when you come to a country like the Netherlands, where the population is presumed to be white, all Blacknesses are reduced to the same thing. Right? But they're definitely not the same.

WM: But how does that get articulated within the art world and within the art institution?

CL: For me, being in the institution, in the Stedelijk Museum, it's clear that the system doesn't acknowledge these different Blacknesses. They only acknowledge Blackness in relationship to, let's say, colonial discourses, or through a discourse of subjugation, for example. Blackness, in this sense, is often reduced to negative ideas. The system is not capable of discerning the different kinds of Blackness apart from the logic of, let's say, colonialism and slavery. Vincent van Velsen wrote a very good piece recently about a similar issue in *Metropolis M*. Specifically, he wrote about these differences that our colleagues in the field don't see because they're like, "Oh, it's a Black artist." No, it's not just a Black artist. I am not denying a shared framework or conditionality of Blackness. I am asking us to really think about Black artists having specific backgrounds and bringing specific sensibilities to the table.

WM: Okay, but isn't this always the case? Couldn't we also ask who is a white artist? Or is this not the same for thinking about gender—as not limited, singular? What is the difference?

CL: Yes, it's a systemic question. This is not simply a subjective question to be dismissed. This is a systemic question. Who does the system exclude? And who has the right to being individual rather than being representative of a category? However, Blackness, which is my concern, is taken as a category that covers difference, while whiteness has individuality.

WM: OK, now I understand. Now, I want to take this back to the work you presented at the conference, and which we have spoken about previously: *Atlantic Transformerz*. Can you tell me a little about that work, about its genealogy?

CL: Well, I can speak to you about the genealogy of the work because I have recently been going back to my practice and trying to understand what I'm doing, especially in relation to the institutional setting that I am now in. I have described this as a kind of arts governance—though I am not sure this is the right term. But being involved in the museum and on the boards of different arts institutions, it is the term that I use.

WM: You mean *raad van toezicht* in Dutch? That is, supervisory boards, in English?

CL: Yes, supervisory boards. And through these mechanisms, through these positions, I am able to change the structure of these institutions – or at least influence certain parts of the structures of these institutions – to be decolonial without it being overly present; the institutions may not even be aware of it. The change sneaks up on you. I have been thinking that maybe arts governance could even be seen as an artistic practice, as part of my art practice. Recently, I have concluded that all of my work is *Atlantic Transformerz*. So, basically, from the first work that I made until the last decision that I make at the Stedelijk Museum, it's all about that transforming. It's all about constantly transforming systems. In my dissertation, I called it "action curating." I consider action curating as a derivative of action research, where the research doesn't only change the researcher but also changes the environment. So, as a curatorial strategy, it changes me, but it also changes the environment, the museum. This is how, then, the visual and intellectual writing practice turned into a curatorial or governance practice. For me it's part of the same project, aimed at the same question about what it means to be European, or what it means to be Dutch. And, of course, what role art making or curating plays in this.

WM: I'm very interested in this. It sounds as if everything goes back to your tutor from your bachelor's degree who said that it's not just about the work you make but about the commitments in your life. Are you saying that *Transformerz*, to transform, is your life commitment?

CL: That's the commitment, yes.

WM: And *Transformerz*: Let's go back to this work and what it means.

CL: [*Singing*] Transformers: robots in disguise. We were, like, fourteen. What was it, 1985, 1986? We were like this . . . hip-hop had just landed in Europe. We were making tags with spray cans. And we were trying to breakdance, to rap, with this group of inner city kids in Rotterdam. We were called Transformers. And then we would get that Transformers mask for the character of Optimus Prime. And the robot voice. The Transformers mask entered my practice when I read an article at Goldsmiths about Blackness. I cannot reproduce the exact essay, but the essence of it was that Black people – Black women specifically – gave so much to the world, with so much compassion. And I linked that idea, that idea of what Blackness has done for the world, what Blackness *does* for the world, to Optimus Prime, who is a robot but who gives himself to trying to save the world. These ideas merged. So, this Optimus Prime mask, this Optimus Prime head, is almost like a Christ figure, self-sacrificing for the world. Okay, so you read the theory, and then you connect it to things from your own life. Let's say to your own history. And this is how the visual language emerges.

WM: And since then, that work has transformed. How?

CL: Later, beginning in 2010, I created the *Atlantic Transformerz* series of photographs in Amsterdam, in New York, in Moengo,[7] and in Dakar. In Amsterdam, in New York, and in Moengo, I painted the guys I photographed black. And then, when I came to Dakar, I was like, "You're not going to paint African guys Black." This is again how, through material, knowledge comes to you. That's why I said Black European, Black American. But, for me, there was no such thing as Black African. To me it was African.

WM: Right. But doesn't this deny the fact that white or Asian people are also African? Aren't there white Africans?

CL: Yes, of course, but white people are not my concern. I stopped painting the guys black because I understood it was not necessary; we were now in Africa. And, for me, it came full circle. That's when I stopped being Black, if that makes sense.

WM: You mean when you were in Dakar? I'm not sure I understand. What do you mean?

CL: After I made the series in Dakar, I let go of the . . . I don't know if I let go of Blackness, but I tried to let go of the Blackness that was forced upon me, so to speak.

WM: Is this what you meant in our earlier interview when you said that Blackness becomes self-evident?

CL: It is. Blackness for me was self-evident in the world.

NOTES

1. Wayne Modest, "On the Self-Evidence of Blackness: An Interview with Charl Landvreugd," *Small Axe* 18, no. 3 (2014): 123–36.
2. See the related online publications that accompanied each exhibition: *Surinamese School: Painting from Paramaribo to Amsterdam*, Stedelijk Studies reader, 2020, https://stedelijkstudies.com/exhibition-surinamese-school/; and *Felix de Rooy: Apocalypse*, Stedelijk Studies reader, 2023, https://stedelijkstudies.com/exhibition-felix-de-rooy-apocalypse/.
3. David Scott, *Conscripts of Modernity: The Tragedy of Colonial Enlightenment* (Duke University Press, 2004).
4. Veerle Poupeye, "Situating Felix de Rooy," in *Felix de Rooy: Apocalypse*, April 21, 2023, https://stedelijkstudies.com/situating-felix-de-rooy/.
5. Modest, "On the Self-Evidence of Blackness."
6. This conversation was conducted and recorded following a conference, titled "Beyond Boundaries: Seeing Art History from the Caribbean," held at the Clark Art Institute in Williamstown, Massachusetts, October 20–21, 2022. Charl Landvreugd gave an artist's talk on October 21 during a session titled "Caribbean as Critique," where he spoke about his *Atlantic Transformerz* series.
7. Moengo is a town in Suriname. See also the interview with Marcel Pinas in this volume, where the town and its cultural initiatives are explored in more detail.

PART V
CODA

CHAPTER 15

REORIENTATIONS

Faith Smith

As we gathered in Williamstown, Massachusetts, in fall 2022 for the conference at the Clark Art Institute that would result in this volume of essays, two art exhibitions in town (*Frantz Zéphirin: Selected Works*, curated by Tomm El-Saieh for the Williams College Art Museum, and *Tomm El-Saieh: Imaginary City*, at the Clark) provided context for our reflections on the implications of "beyond" in thinking about Caribbean genealogies of art history. If each exhibition reflected the complex range of historical, spiritual, artistic, and other traditions that we have come to expect from Haitian artists, it is also the case that El-Saieh's abstract visions of urban space in Haiti would be less immediately recognizable as "Haitian art" than Zéphirin's metaphysical exploration of the entanglement of *Lwas*, animals, and humans. Both exhibitions offered an invitation to challenge something apparently settled; something that has made us comfortable; a negotiation, narration, or disposition that we draw on, and that in turn shapes what we see. How has Zéphirin's work (fig. 15.1) come to fulfill an expectation about the "sacred," for example, that we as viewers bring to "Haitian art," an expectation that Jerry Philogene's essay in this volume explicitly asks us to rethink? Does El-Saieh gesture toward this expectation in his curation of the Zéphirin exhibition but away from it in his own abstractions (fig. 15.2), exhibited at the Clark, or does my question assume some incommensurability that is not, in fact, the case? In the essays convened here, we are being asked to reorient our expectations regarding the circulation and reception of artists connected in some way to particular time periods, "schools," or styles of Caribbean art, with implications for how we might begin to re-narrate "national" or competing projects of sovereignty in the region. How might an orientation toward the unexpected—going "beyond"—shape what we see when we return to what is supposedly conventional, or fixed? In what follows, I make my way with these questions through a series of national, aesthetic, or other signs.

Barbados. It is a space into and around which the region's artists, writers, and politicians rethought performance, art, and Caribbean identities. Adrienne

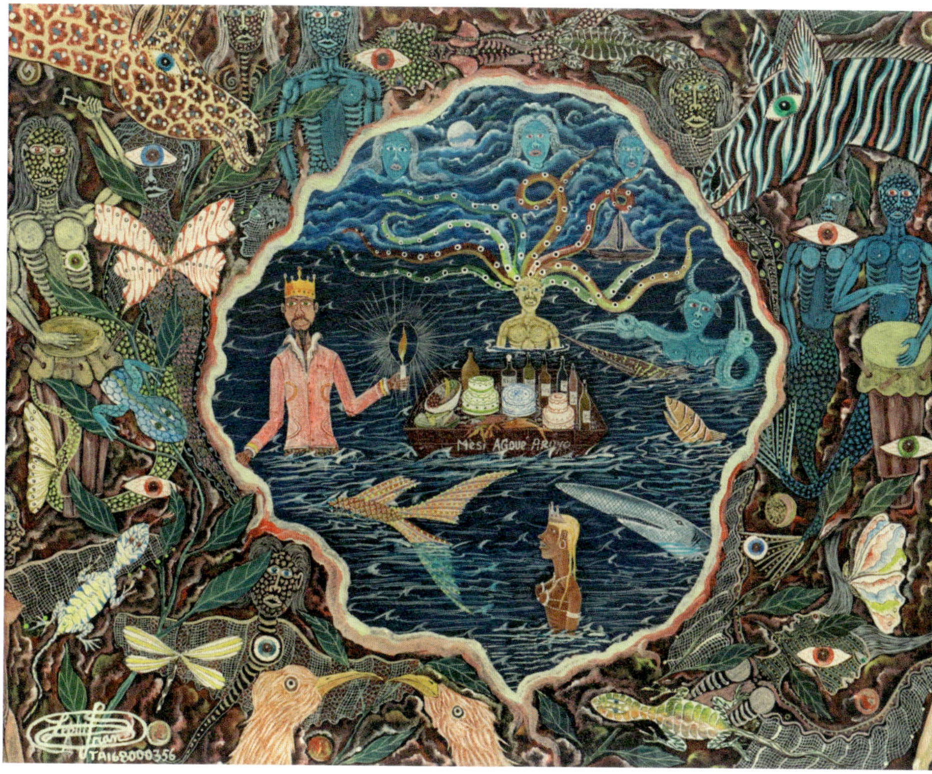

Fig. 15.1. Frantz Zephirin (Haitian, b. 1968), *La Descente d'Agoue chez les Esprits de la Mer (Agwé)*, 2001. Acrylic on canvas, 20 × 24 in. (50.8 × 61 cm). Courtesy of Central Fine, Miami Beach

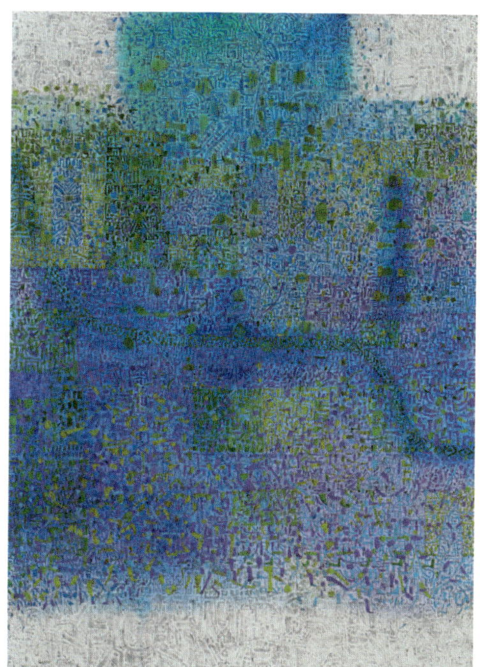

Fig. 15.2. Tomm El-Saieh (Haitian, b. 1984, lives and works in Miami), *Canapé Vert*, 2021. Acrylic on canvas, 84 × 60 in. (213.4 × 152.4 cm). Courtesy of the artist, Luhring Augustine, New York, and Central Fine, Miami Beach

Rooney's essay in this volume highlights Carifesta '81, hosted by Barbados, in which participants encountered one another in formal and informal settings around the country, whether painting (Mexican-inspired) street murals or on the dais, where the Barbadian-born Caribbean and postcolonial novelist and critic George Lamming joined others as part of a thrilling gathering that Rooney calls "a cultural multitude" celebrating artists from Trinidad, Martinique, Cuba, and elsewhere. In Rooney's original presentation, we were invited to consider how the event in Barbados was influenced by, or influenced, other cultural festivals: São Paulo 1951, Festac '77 in Nigeria, Carifesta '79 in Cuba, and the Bienal de La Habana 1984. Thus the Guayabera shirts, Nehru suits, and Kariba jackets in the photographs shown to us of Lamming and other Carifesta '81 participants reflect something other than the twilight of radical political possibility with which these sartorial choices have come to be identified, what with the subsequent rise of neoliberalism, the defeat of the Grenada Revolution, and so on. Instead of a site for or source of exhaustion or nostalgia, then, Rooney's discussion of the festival renders Barbados a site of regional and linguistic entanglement that remains available for our rejuvenating projects.[1]

Modernism. Writing of Jamaica and Haiti, respectively, Veerle Poupeye and Jerry Philogene nudge us to dislodge prevailing accounts of Caribbean modernisms, using the careers of two Caribbean women artists in divergent ways. Poupeye traces the impact of David Boxer's collecting and curatorial practices on how we have come to see or not see aspects of Jamaican art history (and notes the migration of Vera Hyatt to North America as a serendipitous key to Boxer's influence, leading as it did to the international traveling exhibition and foundational catalogue *Jamaican Art, 1922–1982*). In particular, Poupeye focuses on Boxer's consecration of the painter and sculptor Edna Manley as a towering figure in the narration of this history, displacing other artists and currents. While Manley is hyper-visible, Philogene in turn shows us that the artist Luce Turnier is barely detectable in accounts of Haitian modernism, even as she is photographed literally sitting at the table among her fellow Haitian modernists. How does Turnier's centrality in these images visualize the complexities of presence? As Philogene suggests, gender, class, and color are interwoven in opaque ways to explain both Turnier's place at the table and her displacement in matters of access to all the privileges of training, power, practice, and posterity.

Maroon. In the invitation to consider the Caribbean as a region central to Western modernity but also pivotal to how empire expanded in other places in the world, I find myself disoriented as the essays and interviews in this volume speak about encounters the authors themselves came to find orienting as they traveled. In her interview, the artist Andrea Chung describes her time in Mauritius as "passing as Mauritian." Anna Arabindan-Kesson, the coeditor of this volume, has referred in conversation to her time in Jamaica's Maroon country in terms of a "sense of recognition" of Sri Lankan orientations. Here, a Jamaican American artist based in San Diego rescripts Mauritius for me, and a Sri Lankan Australian based in New Jersey makes Jamaica's Maroon spaces cartographically legible in a different way. Chung and Arabindan-Kesson usefully unmoor concepts of familiarity, "recognition," and belonging that I realize I bring to the sign "Maroons," a constituency that I invoke more often than not as *past* and *passed* — part of the temporality of eighteenth-century insurrections and treaties rather than of ongoing time in the present, whether this contemporaneity is within or exceeds the bounds of nation-time.

Marcel Pinas's contribution to the volume invokes (though indirectly) the violent events of November 1986, and he demonstrates that Maroon time and Maroon persecution by the state has never ended. It is ongoing. What would it mean to place such events at the center rather than at the margins of our narration of Caribbean histories of the 1980s and '90s? What do the region's converging timelines look like, particularly when we rehearse (and mourn) the end of radical projects of sovereignty? Which state? Which sovereign power? Working far from the capital, Paramaribo, Pinas and his community make a claim on sovereignty that is not coincident with nation-time or nationalism, as we might otherwise understand it. He reminds us of what happens when we go beyond the nation's glorification-by-marginalization of Maroon communities and shows us how his community claims the right to imagine from a space they theorize as their center.

Dutch. When they are in conflict with a national entity that is no longer ruled by the Netherlands, where is the "Dutch" for Pinas and his community? Speaking from within the space of the Netherlands (that is to say, "metropolitan" or "continental" or "hexagonal" space, as the French would put it, rather than in its more comprehensive imperial geographical dimensions), Charl Landvreugd and Wayne Modest, in their conversation published here, problematize Black identities: If there are African American and Black British identities in North American and British contexts, and even a space for *European* Blackness, what does the Dutch lexicon permit? Terms that would translate into English as "of migrant background," "of cultural background," and "of diverse background" seem to fill a void created by the fact there is no Dutch word for "race," even as such terms would be understood to bypass German migrants to the Netherlands.

This makes me think about the presence of "Dutch" as a sign in the (non-Dutch) Caribbean — or rather its absence for me, as someone socialized in the English-speaking Caribbean and living in another space, North America, in which the global hegemony of English is taken for granted. For me, *Dutch* is already an experience that can be lopped off, forgotten, done without in relation to the delineation of the Caribbean. When I have diversified Caribbean experiences — often patronizingly, as my colleagues in non-English-speaking territories have pointed out — it has been to name Spanish and French and Haitian identities and lineages, but not Dutch or

Fig. 15.3. Tessa Mars (Haitian, b. 1985), ***A Vision of Peace, Harmony and Good Intelligence II***, 2020. Acrylic on canvas, 74 3⁄4 × 51 1⁄8 in. (190 × 130 cm)

Fig. 15.4. Tessa Mars, ***A Vision of Peace, Harmony and Good Intelligence***, 2020. Acrylic on canvas, 74 3⁄4 × 74 3⁄4 in. (190 × 190 cm)

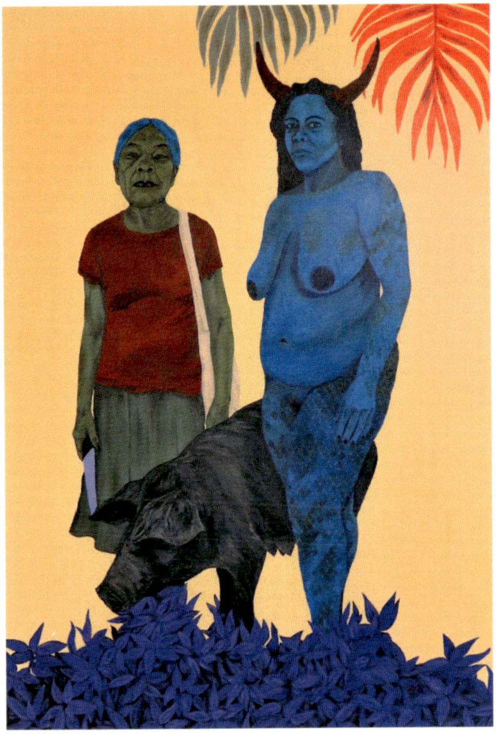

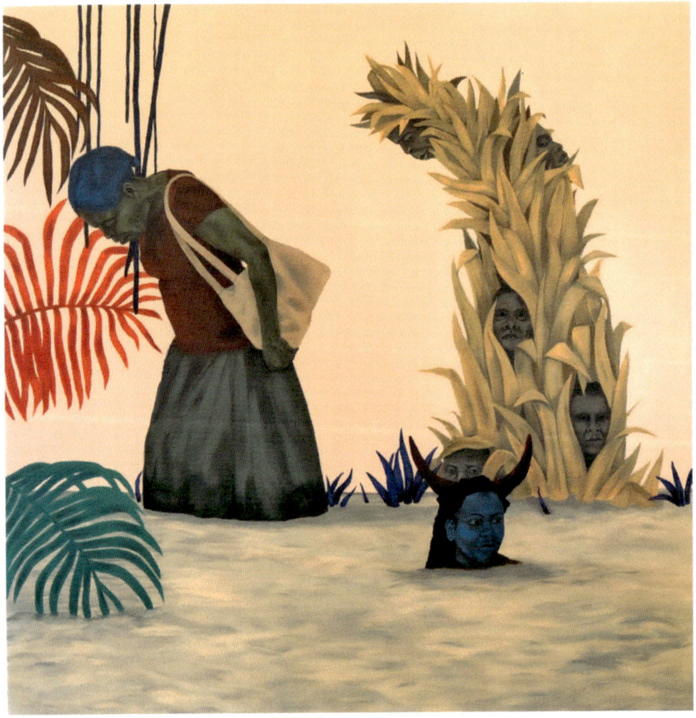

Danish ones. The marvel of this gathering of essays is the extent to which they name and even center worldviews shaped in the Netherlands, St. Maarten, Suriname, and Bonaire (through patricia kaersenhout's conversation about salt).

I will end with the Haitian painter Tessa Mars's images of Caribbean Indigenous people side-by-side with those who work on the land now, in the present (figs. 15.3, 15.4)—canvases that take for granted Vodou's full participation in material and symbolic modes of life, and that pay homage to but also sidestep revolutionary icons. This is a collapsing of time and space that exceeds the realist logic of nation and narrative. Mars did not contribute to this volume, but during an artist's talk at the original convening from which these essays evolved, she invoked a lullaby alluding to a "Dutchman" cutting down a tree. I found this deeply, deeply resonant. It made me place Dutch intervention in (or rather *restore* it to) its foundational historical role, alongside that of the Portuguese, in the play for land and humans and capital that would move north from Brazil through to Curaçao, Barbados, and so on, as sugar and slaveholding became the norm in the region. How did "Dutch" and "Danish" escape our histories of our regional Caribbean identities, when their forts were some of the oldest on the Atlantic slave coasts? A Dutchman cutting down a tree in a Haitian nursery rhyme names Dutch violence and skills as a fever dream for Haitians and others in the region. It reminds us that the British learned from and then erased Dutch settler-colonial management from the Caribbean origin story—an erasure that also permits the Netherlands to script itself as neutral or benevolent. What lessons might the British have learned from the Dutch about withdrawing from the taint of enslavement to remake themselves as liberal and benevolent? *Dutch* haunts nursery rhymes across the region, reminding us of the imbrication of our histories and identities.

NOTES

1. In her presentation for the conference, not included in this volume, Yanique Hume discussed the Cuban artist Leandro Soto and the way that, during his almost decade-long residence in Barbados, he imbued the space of the estate with African Caribbean sacred practice and the spirit of the Cuban novelist Alejo Carpentier. In so doing, he demonstrated the openness of Barbados (often thought of as not merely anglophone but quintessentially so) to the cultural complexity of the region, along the lines of Rooney's discussion, and also made space for a willingness to embrace rather than merely critique the late twentieth-century estate's transformation into a site for tourist entertainment.

CONTRIBUTORS

Anna Arabindan-Kesson holds the position of associate professor of Black diasporic art, with a joint appointment in the Departments of African American Studies and Art and Archaeology at Princeton University. Her work emphasizes histories of race, empire, medicine, and migration from the eighteenth century to the present. She practiced as a registered nurse before completing her PhD in African American studies and art history at Yale University. She is the author of *Black Bodies, White Gold: Art, Cotton, and Commerce in the Atlantic World* (2021) and *Empires States of Mind* (forthcoming). Arabindan-Kesson is the director of Art Hx, a platform for exploring art's intersections with medicine, and sits on the boards of local and international arts organizations.

Anthony Bogues is a scholar, writer, and curator. He is the Asa Messer Professor of Humanities and Africana studies at Brown University, where he is the inaugural director of the Simmons Center for the Study of Slavery and Justice. He is the author and editor of eleven books.

Andrea Chung lives and works in San Diego. Her work was the subject of solo exhibitions at the Museum of Contemporary Art San Diego, the Manetti Shrem Museum, the Art Gallery of Ontario, Canada, and a mid-career survey titled *Between Too Late and Too Early* at the Museum of Contemporary Art North Miami in 2024–25. She has participated in residencies including the Vermont Studio Center, McColl Center for Visual Arts, Headlands Center for the Arts, and Skowhegan School of Painting and Sculpture. Her work is included in collections such as the Museum of Contemporary Art San Diego, Rhode Island School of Design Museum, Minneapolis Institute of Art, Davis Museum at Wesley College, the Addison Museum of American Art, and the J. Paul Getty Museum.

Petrina Dacres is head of the Art History Department at the Edna Manley College of the Visual and Performing Arts in Kingston, Jamaica. Her research focuses on Caribbean art, African diaspora art, cultural studies, public sculpture and memorials, and memory studies. She is an independent curator and founding member of Tide Rising Art Projects, an initiative created to support and promote contemporary Caribbean art and film. Dacres has organized exhibitions at the International Studio and Curatorial Program, where she was the 2022 Jane Farver Curatorial Resident, the Clemente Soto Vélez Cultural & Educational Center, New York; the National Museum, Jamaica, Kingston; and National Gallery of Jamaica, Kingston, among others.

Aldeide Delgado, the founder and director of Women Photographers International Archive (WOPHA), is a prolific art historian and curator. She explores critical themes in the history of photography and abstraction, particularly within Latin American, Caribbean, and Latinx contexts, from feminist and decolonial perspectives. Delgado's pioneering work led to the conceptualization and realization of the inaugural WOPHA Congress, "Photography, and Feminisms" (November 17–20, 2021). She recently authored the photobook *Becoming Sisters: Women Photography Collectives and Organizations*.

Andil Gosine is author of *Nature's Wild: Love, Sex, and the Caribbean* (2021) and is professor of environmental and urban change at York University, where his focus is on visual and performance arts. In 2014, he introduced the field Visual Arts After Indenture, which led to the presentation of several exhibitions, including *everything slackens in a wreck* at the Ford Foundation Gallery, New York, as well as audiovisual media, performances, conferences, and several publications, including special issues of *Small Axe*, *Wasafiri*, and *Asian Diasporic Visual Arts of the Americas*.

Erica Moiah James is an art historian, curator, and associate professor at the University of Miami. Her research centers on indigenous, modern, and contemporary art of the Caribbean, Americas, and African Diaspora. Select publications include "Decolonizing Time: Nineteenth Century Haitian Portraiture and the Critique of Anachronism in Caribbean Art," *NKA* (2019); *La Luz de Cosas / The Light of Things* (2023), on the work of the Cuban artist Juan Francisco Elso; "Prismatic Blackness: Art, Being and Aesthetics in the Global Caribbean," in *Image of the Black in Latin American and Caribbean Art*, ed. David Bindman et al. (2024); and *After Caliban: Caribbean Art in a Global Imaginary* (2025).

patricia kaersenhout was born in the Netherlands to Surinamese parents. She describes "an artistic journey in which we investigate our Surinamese background in relation to our upbringing in Western Europe . . . and raises questions about African diasporic movements in relationship to feminism, gender and sexuality, racism, and the history of slavery. With many of our projects we try to empower (young) men and women of color, supporting marginalized groups in their struggles against exclusionary and oppressive structures. By revealing forgotten and suppressed histories, our work is committed to reclaiming dignity, while fostering transformative justice. We are the first black woman to have made a monument in the Netherlands honoring our enslaved ancestors."

Charl Landvreugd is an artist, curator, and educator who serves as head of research and curatorial practice at the Stedelijk Museum in Amsterdam. He holds a PhD in curating contemporary art from the Royal College of Art in London and has held various fellowships, including at BAK Utrecht, the Van Abbemuseum, and the Research Center for Material Culture. His writing has been published in leading art journals and magazines such as *Open Arts*, *Small Axe*, *ARC Magazine*, *Uprising Art*, and *Metropolis M*. Landvreugd is a member of the Akademie van Kunsten and the author of *Dutch Afro Becomings: Hybrid Being in Black Art and Culture* (2026).

Wayne Modest is a cultural studies, museum, and heritage scholar and curator. He is director of content at Wereldmuseum (Amsterdam, Leiden, Rotterdam, Nijmegen) and professor of material culture and critical heritage studies at Vrije Universiteit Amsterdam. His work is guided by a commitment to collaborative practices in research, teaching, and curation. He has coedited numerous publications, such as *Matters of Belonging* (with Nick Thomas et al., 2020) and *Spaces of Care: Confronting Colonial Afterlives in European Ethnographic Museums* (with Claudia Augusta, 2023). More recent books include *Museum Temporalities: Time, History and the Future of the Ethnographic Museum* (with Peter Pels, 2025) and *Museums in Focus: Decolonizing the Museum: Art, Activism and the Question of Race in Curation* (with Chiara de Cesari and Marta Pagliuca Pelacani, 2026).

María Elena Ortiz is a curator and writer who has organized international exhibitions, programs, and publications. At the Modern Art Museum of Fort Worth, Ortiz curated *Jammie Holmes: Make the Revolution Irresistible* (2023), *Surrealism and Us: Caribbean and African Diasporic Artists Since 1940* (2024), and *Feeling Color: Aubrey Williams and Frank Bowling* (2025). Ortiz co-curated, with Susana Temkin and Rodrigo Moura, *Flow States: LA TRIENAL 2024* at El Museo del Barrio in New York. In 2023, with Marina Reyes Franco, she co-curated *Puerto Rico NegrX* at Museo de Arte Contemporáneo de Puerto Rico. At the Pérez Art Museum Miami, she founded the Caribbean Cultural Institute, a curatorial platform centered in Caribbean art. She was born and raised in Puerto Rico.

Jerry Philogene is associate professor and director of the Black Studies Program at Middlebury College. She specializes in interdisciplinary American cultural history, art history, and visual arts of the Caribbean and the African diaspora with an emphasis on the Francophone Caribbean. Her publications have appeared in edited collections, peer-reviewed journals, and exhibition catalogues. As an independent curator, she co-organized *Myrlande Constant: The Work of Radiance* (with Katherine Smith 2023) and curated *Living in Brilliant Suspension (Viv pandye nan briyans): Didier William* (2025). Philogene's forthcoming books include *The Socially Dead and Improbable Citizen: Visualizing Haitian Humanity and Visual Aesthetics* and a monograph on the Haitian modernist painter Luce Turnier.

Marcel Pinas was born in Suriname, where he trained at the Nola Hatterman Art Institute before studying at the Edna Manley College for the Visual and Performing Arts in Jamaica. He has held residencies at the Vermont Studio Center and the Rijksacademie in Amsterdam. The theme *Kibri A Kulturu* (preserve the culture) is his driving force and source of inspiration. With his art, Pinas aims to create a lasting record of the Maroons and to foster worldwide awareness and appreciation for the unique traditional communities in Suriname and the serious threats they face today. He established the Kibii Foundation, which includes an art park and cultural center where the youth from his hometown are trained and motivated to build a future based upon the strength of their own culture.

Veerle Poupeye is a Belgian Jamaican art historian, curator, and critic specializing in art from the Caribbean. Her past professional associations include the National Gallery of Jamaica, where she served first as a curator and then, from 2009 to 2018, as executive director, and the Edna Manley College of the Visual and Performing Arts, Kingston, where she lectured until 2022. Her recent publications include *Caribbean Art*, of which the second revised and expanded edition was published in 2022 in the *World of Art* series by Thames and Hudson.

Adrienne Rooney is a postdoctoral fellow in the Frederick Douglass Institute and Department of Black Studies at the University of Rochester. She is working on her first book project, based on her dissertation, "A Worldbuilding Moment: Aesthetics and Economics in the Caribbean Festival of Arts' (Carifesta) Revolutionary Era, 1966–1981." She has shared her work through published criticism and scholarship and presentations at the annual conferences of the Caribbean Studies Association and College Art Association, talks at the Paul Mellon Centre, the Tate, Oxford University, and the international symposium "The Inaugural Caribbean Festival of Arts as Prism: Twentieth-Century Festivals in the Multilingual Caribbean" (2022), which she co-organized. She received her PhD in art history from Rice University.

Faith Smith chairs the Department of African and African American Studies at Brandeis University. Her work on the later nineteenth and early twentieth centuries includes *Creole Recitations: John Jacob Thomas and Colonial Formation in the Late Nineteenth-Century Caribbean* (2002) and *Strolling in the Ruins: The Caribbean's Non-sovereign Modern in the Early Twentieth Century* (2023). She is the editor of *Sex and the Citizen: Interrogating the Caribbean* (2011). Smith is working on "DreadKin," a project on fiction and visual culture in our contemporary moment.

Nicole Smythe-Johnson is a writer and independent curator from Kingston, Jamaica. She is currently a doctoral candidate in the Department of Art and Art History at the University of Texas, Austin. Most recently, she curated *If we are here . . .* at the Visual Art Center at UT Austin (2023–24). She was also on the curatorial team of the 2022 Kingston Biennial and *John Dunkley: Neither Day Nor Night* (2017–18), which traveled to the Pérez Art Museum Miami, the Folk Art Museum in New York, and the National Gallery of Jamaica in Kingston.

CLARK STUDIES IN THE VISUAL ARTS

The Two Art Histories: The Museum and the University (2002)
Edited by Charles W. Haxthausen
With essays by Dawn Ades, Andreas Beyer, Richard R. Brettell, Stephen Deuchar, Sybille Ebert-Schifferer, Ivan Gaskell, Eckhard Gillen, Richard Kendall, John House, Patricia Mainardi, Griselda Pollock, Mark Rosenthal, Barbara Maria Stafford, Gary Tinterow, William H. Truettner, and Michael F. Zimmermann, and an afterword by Richard Brilliant

Art History, Aesthetics, Visual Studies (2002)
Edited by Michael Ann Holly and Keith Moxey
With essays by David Carrier, Philip Fisher, Hal Foster, Ivan Gaskell, Jonathan Gilmore, Thomas DaCosta Kaufmann, Michael Kelly, Karen Lang, Stephen Melville, Kobena Mercer, Nicholas Mirzoeff, W. J. T. Mitchell, Griselda Pollock, Irene J. Winter, and Janet Wolff

The Art Historian: National Traditions and Institutional Practices (2003)
Edited by Michael F. Zimmermann
With essays by Mieke Bal, Stephen Bann, Horst Bredekamp, H. Perry Chapman, Georges Didi-Huberman, Eric Fernie, Françoise Forster-Hahn, Carlo Ginzburg, Charles W. Haxthausen, Karen Michels, Willibald Sauerländer, Alain Schnapp, and Michael F. Zimmermann

Anthropologies of Art (2005)
Edited by Mariët Westermann
With essays by Hans Belting, Janet Catherine Berlo, Suzanne Preston Blier, Steve Bourget, Sarah Brett-Smith, Shelly Errington, David Freedberg, Anna Grimshaw, Jonathan Hay, Howard Morphy, Ikem Stanley Okoye, Francesco Pellizzi, and Ruth B. Phillips

The Lure of the Object (2006)
Edited by Stephen Melville
With essays by Emily Apter, George Baker, Malcolm Baker, John Brewer, Martha Buskirk, Margaret Iversen, Ewa Lajer-Burcharth, Karen Lang, Mark A. Meadow, Helen Molesworth, Marcia Pointon, Christian Scheidemann, Edward J. Sullivan, and Martha Ward

Compression vs. Expression: Containing and Explaining the World's Art (2006)
Edited by John Onians
With essays by Cao Yiqiang, Wilfried van Damme, Rita Eder, James Elkins, Arlene K. Fleming, Derek Gillman, Jyotindra Jain, Cecilia F. Klein, Yves Le Fur, Dominic Marner, Anitra Nettleton,John Onians, Edmund P. Pillsbury, Michael Rinehart, David Summers, and Georges S. Zouain

Asian Art History in the Twenty-First Century (2007)
Edited by Vishakha N. Desai
With essays by Frederick M. Asher, Melissa Chiu, John Clark, Gao Shiming, Yukio Lippit, Saloni Mathur and Kavita Singh, Kaja M. McGowan, Rana Mitter, Alexandra Munroe, Jerome Silbergeld, Nancy S. Steinhardt, Akira Takagishi, and Gennifer Weisenfeld

Architecture Between Spectacle and Use (2008)
Edited by Anthony Vidler
With essays by Mario Carpo, Beatriz Colomina, Mark Dorrian, Kurt W. Forster, Hal Foster, Sarah Williams Goldhagen, Michael Hays, Mark Jarzombek, Felicity D. Scott, Terry Smith, Anthony Vidler, and Mark Wigley

The Meaning of Photography (2008)
Edited by Robin Kelsey and Black Stimson
With essays by Geoffrey Batchen, François Brunet, Mary Ann Doane, José Luis Falconi, Robin Kelsey, Douglas R. Nickel, Blake Stimson, John Tagg, and additional contributions by Lars Kiel Bertelsen, Anne McCauley, Jorge Ribalta, John Roberts, Eric Rosenberg, Eric C. Shiner, and Bernd Stiegler
Photo essays by Sharon Harper, Lilla LoCurto and Bill Outcault, Fiona Tan, and Akram Zaatari

What Is Research in the Visual Arts? Obsession, Archive, Encounter (2008)
Edited by Michael Ann Holly and Marquard Smith
With essays by Ernst van Alphen, Mieke Bal, Marc Gotlieb, Serge Guilbaut, Michael Ann Holly, Akira Mizuta Lippit, W. J. T. Mitchell, Joanne Morra, Sina Najafi, Alexander Nemerov, Celeste Olalquiaga, Alex Potts, and Reva Wolf

The Migrant's Time: Rethinking Art History and Diaspora (2011)
Edited by Saloni Mathur
With essays by Stanley Abe, Esra Akcan, Iftikhar Dadi, Jennifer González, Ranajit Guha, May Joseph, Miwon Kwon, Kobena Mercer, W. J. T. Mitchell, Aamir R. Mufti, Nikos Papastergiadis, Richard J. Powell, Edward W. Said, and Nora A. Taylor

Fictions of Art History (2013)
Edited by Mark Ledbury
With essays by Paul Barolsky, Thomas Crow, Gloria Kury, Mark Ledbury, Ralph Lieberman, Maria H. Loh, Alexander Nemerov, Joanna Scott, Cole Swensen, Marianna Torgovnick, Caroline Vout, and Marina Warner

Art History in the Wake of the Global Turn (2014)
Edited by Jill H. Casid and Aruna D'Souza
With essays by Esra Akcan, Jill H. Casid, Parul Dave-Mukherji, Aruna D'Souza, Talinn Grigor, Ranjana Khanna, Kobena Mercer, Nicholas Mirzoeff, Steven Nelson, Todd Porterfield, Raqs Media Collective, Kishwar Rizvi, David J. Roxburgh, and Alessandra Russo

Art History and Emergency (2016)
Edited by David Breslin and Darby English
With essays by Thomas Crow, Kajri Jain, Molly Nesbit, Caroline Arscott, Anatoli Mikhailov, Mary Miller, Howard Singerman, Patrick D. Flores, Manuel J. Borja-Villel, Our Literal Speed, and Theaster Gates

Ecologies, Agents, Terrains (2018)
Edited by Christopher P. Heuer and Rebecca Zorach
With essays by Maggie Cao, Jeffrey Jerome Cohen, Matthew Coolidge, Vittoria Di Palma, Robert Felfe, Chelsea Mikael Frazier, Ghana ThinkTank, Christopher P. Heuer, Jessica L. Horton, Sarah Kanouse, Sonya S. Lee, Dylan T. Miner, James Nisbet, Verity Platt, Aurora Tang, Julian Yates, and Rebecca Zorach

The Expanded Field of Conservation (2023)
Edited by Caroline Fowler and Alexander Nagel
With essays by Jennifer Bajorek, Fernando Dominguez Rubio, Sven Dupré, Noémie Etienne, Annika Finne, Caroline Fowler, Yukio Lippit, Murad Khan Mumtaz, Brian Michael Murphy, Alva Noë, Iwataro Oka, Kavita Singh, and Gabriela Siracusano Zorach

Breaking the Silence (2025)
Edited by Caroline Fowler
With essays by Mieke Bal, Stephen Bann, Dore Bowen, David Carrier, Mark A. Cheetham, Elena Ciletti, Mary-Dailey Desmarais, Darby English, Caroline Fowler, Marc Gottlieb, Hanneke Grootenboer, Christopher P. Heuer, Elliot Krasnopoler, Mark Ledbury, Alexander Nemerov, James Nisbet, Glenn Peers, James Pilgrim, Mary Roberts, Michael S. Roth, Nathan Stobaugh, Kari Weil, Janet Wolff, and Oliver Wunsch

PHOTOGRAPHY CREDITS

Every effort has been made to credit photographers and image sources, and permission to reproduce images is provided courtesy of the owners listed in the figure captions. Please notify the Clark Art Institute of any errors or omissions so that corrections can be made in any subsequent edition. Additional photography credits are as follows:

Gosine, Coolie Créole: Photo by Sebastian Back, 2022 (figs. 1.1, 1.2); courtesy of Ford Foundation Gallery, photo by Sebastian Back (fig. 1.3).

Dacres, *Who Disappeared the Tallawahsaurus*: The Visual Afterlife of Caribbean Heroic History: © 2026 Artists Rights Society (ARS), New York / DACS, London, courtesy of Hew Locke, P·P·O·W, New York, and Hales Gallery, London, photo by Charles Robinson (fig. 2.1); image courtesy of *The Gleaner* (Kingston) (fig. 2.2); photo by Petrina Dacres (figs. 2.3, 2.7, 2.14, 2.15); photo courtesy of the estate of Barrington Watson (fig. 2.4); image courtesy of Renee Cox (fig. 2.5); image courtesy of the estate of Michael Thompson (fig. 2.6, 2.8, 2.9); photo by Omar Dean Kennedy (fig. 2.10); image courtesy of Camille Chedda (fig. 2.11); image courtesy of Phillip Thomas (fig. 2.12); image courtesy of Omari Ra (fig. 2.13).

James, Michael Richards and the Political Work of Black Ecstasy: Photo by Nina Ferre Cohen, courtesy of william córdova and Nina Ferre Cohen (fig. 4.1); COR0005.1-RG: Corcoran Gallery of Art registrar's office records, series 9, box 73, folder 14, Special Collections Research Center, George Washington University Libraries, Washington, DC, courtesy of the Corcoran Gallery of Art Archive (fig. 4.2); screen capture by the author (figs. 4.4–4.6); photo by Hyungsub Shin, courtesy of Hyungsub Shin (fig. 4.7).

Philogene, Beyond the Archives and Vodou Iconography: Luce Turnier, a Feminist Haitian Modernist: Courtesy of Jézabel Traube and Leonora Carpi de Resmini and Permanent Collection of the Centre d'Art, Haïti (fig. 5.1); courtesy of Jézabel Traube and Leonora Carpi de Resmini (figs. 5.2, 5.3); courtesy of Jeězabel Traube and Leonora Carpi de Resmini (fig. 5.4); courtesy of John M. Black, Washington, DC (figs. 5.5, 5.6); courtesy of the Centre d'Art, Haïti (fig. 5.7).

Bogues, Caribbean Thought and Haitian Art: The Category of the Marvelous: Image courtesy of Edouard Duval-Carrié (fig. 6.3).

Smythe-Johnson, John Dunkley's Photographic Eye: A Close Look at Banana Plantation: Collection National Gallery of Jamaica (cover, fig. 7.1).

Poupeye, Rethinking Caribbean Art Histories: Lessons from David Boxer's Jamaican Art, 1922–1982: Courtesy of the Institute of Black Imagination, the Holder Collection (fig. 8.1); collection of the National Gallery of Jamaica (figs. 8.2, 8.5); © The Trustees of the British Museum, all rights reserved (fig. 8.3); collection of the National Gallery of Jamaica, image courtesy of Orange Park Trust / Legacy of Barrington Watson (fig. 8.6).

Rooney, "What loveliness escapes the schools": Carifesta's Epistemological Critique: Courtesy of The Nation Publishing Co. Ltd. (fig. 9.1); David Rumsey Map Collection, David Rumsey Map Center, Stanford Libraries (fig. 9.3).

Delgado, The Archipelagic Method: A Model and Poetic Tool for Complexifying the History of Latinx Art and Photography: © Women Photograph (fig. 11.1); courtesy of Moira Pernambuco, © Moira Pernambuco (figs. 11.2, 11.3); © Stacey Tyrell (figs. 11.4, 11.5); courtesy of Juana Valdés (fig. 11.6); courtesy of Muriel Hasbun and RoFa Projects, © Muriel Hasbun (fig. 11.7); © Teresita Fernández, courtesy of the artist and Lehmann Maupin, New York, Seoul, and London, photo by Dan Bradica (fig. 11.9).

Smith, Reorientations: Courtesy of Central Fine, Miami Beach, photo by Madeline Ruckle (fig. 15.1); © Tomm El-Saieh, courtesy of Tomm El-Saieh, Luhring Augustine, New York, and Central Fine, Miami Beach, photo by Farzad Owrang (fig. 15.2); © Tessa Mars (fig. 15.3); © Tessa Mars, photo by Fujimura Takeshi (fig. 15.4).

This publication was conceived by the Research and Academic Program at the Clark Art Institute. A conference, titled "Beyond Boundaries: Seeing Art History from the Caribbean," was held October 20–21, 2022, at the Clark. For information on programs and publications at the Clark, visit www.clarkart.edu.

Produced by the Publications Department of the Clark Art Institute, 225 South Street, Williamstown, Massachusetts 01267

Anne Roecklein, *managing editor*
Kevin Bicknell, *editor*
Annie Jun, *assistant editor*
David Murphy, *rights and image use editor*
Liz Lewis, *publications and exhibitions research assistant*

Copyedited and proofread by Brian Sholis and Kristin Swan

Design and layout by Roy Brooks, Fold Four, Inc.

Printed by Puritan Capital

Distributed by Yale University Press, New Haven and London
www.yalebooks.com/art

Authorized Representative in the EU:
Easy Access System Europe
Mustamäe tee 50
10621 Tallinn, Estonia
gpsr.requests@easproject.com

Printed and bound in the United States
10 9 8 7 6 5 4 3 2 1

Cover: John Dunkley, *Banana Plantation*, c. 1945 (detail, fig. 7.1)
Title page: Edouard Duval-Carrié, *Memoire sans Histoire* (*Memory Without History*), 2009 (detail, fig. 6.1)
Pages 24–25: Stacey Tyrell, *Mistress and Slave*, 2018, from the series *Untitled* (detail, fig. 11.5)

Library of Congress Control Number: 2026930118

ISBN: 978-1-935998-70-9 (Clark Art Institute)
ISBN: 978-0-300-27997-9 (Yale University Press)